In the Dominions of Debt

A volume in the series

Cornell Studies in Political Economy

EDITED BY PETER J. KATZENSTEIN

A full list of titles in the series appears at the end of the book

In the Dominions of Debt

HISTORICAL PERSPECTIVES ON DEPENDENT DEVELOPMENT

HERMAN M. SCHWARTZ

CORNELL UNIVERSITY PRESS

Ithaca and London

First published 1989 by Cornell University Press.

International Standard Book Number 0-8014-2270-1
Library of Congress Catalog Card Number 88-43289
Printed in the United States of America
Librarians: Library of Congress cataloging information
appears on the last page of the book.

The paper in this book is acid-free and meets the guidelines for
permanence and durability of the Committee on Production Guidelines
for Book Longevity of the Council on Library Resources.

Contents

v

Acknowledgments

"The experience, the experience. Haven't you learned?" Profane
didn't have to think long. "No," he said, "off-hand I'd say I haven't
learned a goddamn thing."

Thomas Pynchon, *V*

All books are tests of emotional as much as of intellectual endurance.
Pride of placement in the acknowledgment of such debt is thus due to
those who saw me through emotionally to the end: Eve Schwartz (who
passed her own endurance test during the many revisions); Beth Var-
coe, Jeremiah Reilly, Syzygy, especially Ruth Haas, Laura Goering,
Morris Dye, Mike Miller, and Steve Van Holde, the unusually caring
graduate student population in Government at Cornell University,
especially Dan Wirls and Helene Silverberg, my family, and three
cats.

Intellectually, Benedict Anderson, Susan Buck-Morss, Peter Katzenstein, and Richard Rosecrance were all helpful in their own ways,
as were Steve Jackson and my colleagues at the New School for Social
Research, Richard Bensel, Elizabeth Sanders, Thomas Vietorisz, and
Aristide Zolberg. In the Antipodes, I owe a variety of debts: in Australia, Virginia Cooke, Rita Gebart, Peter Jackson, Bette O'Brien,
Randal Stewart, Fran Walsh, and Alan Wells; in New Zealand, Bie
Baker, David Bedggood, and John Miller. All made my stay more
pleasant and productive than it might otherwise have been, providing
support, opening their houses, and sharing what they could. A pecu-
liar but definite debt is owed the many people who picked me up
while I was hitch-hiking and tolerated my impolite inquisition on
matters otherwise hidden from the scholarly researcher. The International Relations Department of the Australian National University
graciously hosted me in Australia. A variety of faculty—indeed, the

cream of Australian social science—tolerated my erratic visits and wild ideas while guiding me to material I might otherwise have overlooked. I also owe enormous thanks to a host of archivists and librarians, especially at the Archive of Business and Labour of the Australian National University and at the National Library of Australia. Roger Haydon guided the manuscript through Cornell University Press's labyrinths, and Teresa Johnson helped render my turbid prose transparent. Finally, unlike Profane, I did learn something from my students at the New School, who helped me bounce some of the ideas in this book around.

Funding for this project came from a New York State Higher Education Corporation Lehman Fellowship and from a Cornell University Sage Fellowship.

HERMAN M. SCHWARTZ

Bridgeport, Connecticut

Abbreviations

AAC	Australian Agricultural Company
AA CRS	Australian Archives Commonwealth Record Series no.
ABL	Archive of Business and Labor, Research School of Social Studies, Australian National University Manuscript no.
AEHR	*Australian Economic History Review*
AEHR*	*Business History and Archives* (in 1966 changes to AEHR)
AIBR	*Australasian Insurance and Banking Record*
AIPA	Australian Industries Protection Act
AJPH	*Australian Journal of Politics and History*
ANA	Australian Natives Association
APR	*Australasian Pastoralists Review*
ASOF	Australian Ship Owners Federation
ASP	Anti-Socialist Party
BHP	Broken Hill Proprietary Company
CAR	*Commonwealth Arbitration Reports*
CLP	Commonwealth Liberal Party
CWPD	*Commonwealth of Australia Parliamentary Debates*
CWPP	*Commonwealth of Australia Parliamentary Papers*
FTP	Free Trade Party
GPO	Government Printer's Office
HSANZ	*Historical Studies, Australia and New Zealand*
IBRD	International Bank for Reconstruction and Development
LPP	Liberal Protectionist Party
MHR	Member of the House of Representatives
MLA	Member of the Legislative Assembly
ML MS	Mitchell Library (Sydney) Manuscript no.
NLA MS	National Library of Australia Manuscript no.
NSW	New South Wales
NSWEF	New South Wales Employers Federation
NSWPD	*New South Wales Parliamentary Debates*
NSWPP	*New South Wales Parliamentary Papers*
NSWSR	*New South Wales Statistical Register*

Abbreviations

NSW V&P	*New South Wales Votes & Proceedings of the Legislative Assembly*
OECD	Organization for Economic Cooperation and Development
OYBCWA	*Official Yearbook of the Commonwealth of Australia*
OYBNSW	*Official Yearbook of New South Wales*
Qld	Queensland
QSU	Queensland Shearers Union
SA	South Australia
Tas	Tasmania
VEF	Victorian Employers Federation
VEU	Victorian Employers Union
Vic	Victoria
VSR	*Victoria Statistical Register*
WA	Western Australia

PART ONE

THEORY

Introduction

> There are no general laws of social formations, but only a set of
> scientific concepts that make it possible to formulate laws for particu-
> lar formations.
>
> Samir Amin, *Unequal Development.*

Analysts with a variety of ideological bents often treat the newly
industrializing countries (NICs) of Asia—South Korea, Taiwan, Singapore, and Hong Kong—as novel phenomena in the international
system.[1] Their rapid export-driven economic growth seems unlike
the historical trajectory of any other countries. Some analysts cite this
rapid industrial growth to dismiss Dependency theory for its pessimistic portrayal of the international system. Typical is this recent review
of literature on the NICs:

> The postwar expansion of trade, lending, and foreign investment has
> provided a context within which the NICs have achieved rapid industrial-
> ization. "Dependence," however, appears to be a result of particular na-
> tional strategies rather than a characteristic of the international system
> per se. Static portrayals of a hierarchic international structure cannot
> account for the upward movement that the NICs represent; nor can they
> account for the differing strategies that states have adopted to manage
> interdependence.[2]

1. See A. Amsden, "Taiwan's Economic History: A Case of Etatisme and a Challenge
to Dependency Theory," *Modern China* 5:3 (1979), for an institutional view; C. Barone,
"Dependency, Marxist Theory, and Salvaging the Idea of Capitalism in South Korea,"
Review of Radical Political Economy 15 (Spring 1983), for a Marxist view; B. Balassa, *The
NICs in the World Economy* (New York: Pergamon, 1981), for a neoclassical view; T.
Gold, *State and Society in the Taiwan Miracle* (Armonk N.Y.: M. E. Sharpe, 1986), for a
"dependency" view.
2. S. Haggard, "The Newly Industrializing Countries in the International System,"
World Politics 38 (January 1986), 368. Here Haggard uses "dependence" where I would

The author cautions those who urge all less developed countries (LDCs) to emulate the Asian NICs that the latter's success represents a "unique conjunction of domestic and international factors." This comment reinforces the sense that the Asian NICs are something new, a phenomenon at odds with the widely accepted, if pessimistic, view of the world economy that Dependency theory articulates.

Most analysts suggest three factors account for and help maintain the Asian NICs' rapid economic growth.[3] First, their highly directive states have nurtured internationally competitive industries by tightly controlling access to credit and foreign exchange while disciplining labour.[4] Second, they have depended on vast transfers of capital from the very economies to which they later exported. These capital transfers underlie what is popularly known as the "debt crisis." In 1982, just five NICs owed 37.5 percent of all long term nonconcessional foreign debt.[5] In the Asian NICs, state-dominated banking systems channeled this borrowed money into return-oriented investment, financing construction of highly efficient industries. In turn, these industries generated the exports needed to service debt. Third, the whole process has depended on creditor economies' ability and willingness to absorb those exports.

But none of this is new. In the 1890s, too, there was a debt crisis, involving a group of countries that had borrowed to create highly efficient agricultural economies capable of astounding levels of growth and export expansion. (See Table 1.) These countries were the formal and informal British Dominions: Argentina, Australia, Canada, Chile, New Zealand, South Africa, and Uruguay. They re-

use "dependency"; throughout, I use "dependency," following the differentiation proposed by J. Caporaso in his introduction to a special issue on Dependency, *International Organization* 32 (Winter 1978): "dependence [is] external reliance on other actors and dependency [is] the process of incorporation of Less Developed Countries (LDCs) into the global capitalist system and the 'structural distortions' resulting therefrom."

3. To simplify citation, this characterization is largely drawn from the efforts at synthetic analyses in F. Deyo, ed., *The Political Economy of the New Asian Industrialism* (Ithaca: Cornell University Press, 1987). However, interested readers should also see the articles cited in note 1. The similarity between analysts' descriptions and the pioneering descriptive work of A. Gerschenkron on late industrialization is worth note; see *Economic Backwardness in Historical Perspective* (Cambridge: Harvard University Press, 1966).

4. I use the spelling "labour" to indicate workers, and the spelling "labor" to indicate the various political parties in Australia representing worker interests. These are the spellings used in Australia and are adopted to avoid confusion.

5. In 1982, Brazil, Hong Kong, Mexico, Korea, and Singapore owed $161.5 billion of $430.8 billion total nonconcessional debt. Adding in the other countries the World Bank calls NICs—Algeria, Argentina, Chile, and Yugoslavia—raises the NIC share to 53 percent. Taiwan is the only net creditor among the NICs. Calculated from OECD, *External Debt of Developing Countries* (Paris, 1984).

Table 1. Dominion and NIC debt in historical perspective (as percentage of GDP)

Country	1890s		1938		1985	
	Foreign Debt	Debt Service	Foreign Debt	Debt Service	Foreign Debt	Debt Service
Argentina	102%	5.0%	99.2%	1.4%*	79.9%	9.7%
Australia	139	7.5	98.7[+]	4.1[+]	30.3**	5.5**
Brazil	56*	3.3*	48.6	—	51.3	4.9
Chile	—	—	144	—	142.2	14.5
Mexico	—	—	92.2	—	58.3	8.6
New Zealand	115	5.1	164.0[+]	6.0[+]	60.0	—
S. Korea	—	—	—	—	57.7	8.5
Uruguay	(69)	(3.8)	—	—	83.2	10.3

*Public debt or debt service only.
[+]1931.
**FY 1985/86.
Numbers in parentheses are estimates.
SOURCES: 1890s: OYBCWA 1915; *Statistics of the Dominion of New Zealand*, 1914; *New Zealand Official Yearbook*, 1950; I. Stone, "British Direct and Portfolio Investment in Latin America before 1914," *Journal of Economic History* 37:3 (September 1977); A. Ludwig, *Handbook of Brazilian Historical Statistics* (Boston: G. K. Hall, 1985).

1938: C. Lewis, *Debtor and Creditor Countries 1938, 1944* (Washington: Brookings Institution, 1945), pp. 77, 85–86; United Nations, *Public Debt of Member Nations* (New York, 1948); Butlin, *Australian Domestic Product; New Zealand Official Yearbook*, 1950; *International Historical Statistics, Americas and Australasia*.

1985: IBRD: *World Debt Tables 1986/87* (Baltimore, 1986); Reserve Bank of Australia *Bulletin*, December 1986, p. S102; Reserve Bank of New Zealand *Bulletin* 49:7 (1986), p. 331, and 49:12 (1986), p. 555.

ceived nearly half of British capital exports, and provided Britain with a substantial portion of its food and raw material imports. Like today's NICs, these countries also confounded the economic heterodoxy of the day, relying on free trade and export-oriented strategies rather than the protectionist strategies European countries used to create modern economies.[6] Although their states did not possess all the attributes of what Chalmers Johnson calls the NICs' "capitalist developmental states," the Dominion states were highly interventionist compared to their European state contemporaries. Late-nineteenth-century observers even referred to the Antipodean political economies as "state socialism."

6. On European protection see D. Senghaas, *The European Experience: A Historical Critique of Development Theory* (Dover, N.H.: Berg, 1985). On Australia as a "free trade" area before Federation, see D. Denoon, *Settler Capitalism* (Oxford: Oxford University Press, 1983), chap. 2, and G. Patterson, *The Tariff in the Australian Colonies, 1856–1900* (Melbourne: F.W. Cheshire, 1968). "Protection" in the Antipodes is discussed in more detail below. For one of the few historically rooted discussions of the current debt crisis, see A. Fishlow, "Lessons from the Past: Capital Markets during the 19th Century and the Interwar Period," *International Organization* 39 (Summer 1985).

Two aspects of the Dominion experience underscore the familiarity of the NIC experience and emphasize the caution with which we should treat any dismissal of Dependency theory. First, the Latin Dominions, despite rapid growth rates, high levels of gross domestic product, and extremely competitive exports, were unable to sustain GDP growth and competitiveness after their nineteenth-century spurt—the very experiences which, indeed, gave rise to Dependency theory. Second, the formal Dominions of Australia and New Zealand have had similar difficulties in the twentieth century, especially persistent high levels of multinational penetration and external indebtedness, that led indigenous scholars to adapt Dependency models to their own countries' experience. These difficulties are currently spurring intense internal debates over Australia's place in the "new international division of labor" and a far-reaching restructuring of New Zealand's political economy.

Nonetheless, the various permutations of Dependency theory—world systems, unequal development or underdevelopment, dependencista, and imperialism—face a critical problem if they are to remain persuasive: they must accommodate their core claims about structural constraints on national economies with the very obvious evidence of economic development and growth in certain peripheral countries. Critics typically have used the development of both the Latin and the Asian NICs as evidence of the inutility of Dependency theory and the utility of either diffusionist or heteroclite models.[7] In response to the industrialization of the Latin NICs, Dependency writers generated a new wave of Dependency theory focusing on the internal politics of the "triple alliance" of state, multinational, and national capital.

In this book, I argue that Dependency theory and its sister theories are salvageable on terms that preserve their core claims; understanding the Dominions' experience in the 1890s is crucial not just for such a reconstruction but also for understanding the NICs today. The experience of the nineteenth-century Dominions suggests three things. First, while one or more of the NICs may be able to sustain

7. See S. Pollard, *Peaceful Conquest: the Industrialization of Europe* (New York: Oxford University Press, 1984), or C. Trebilcock, *Industrialization of the Continental Powers*, (New York: Longman, 1981), for examples of diffusionist economic history. See Senghaas, *European Experience*, for an implicit critique. See Haggard, "Newly Industrializing Countries in the International System," or "Pathways from the Periphery" (Ph.D. dissertation, University of California, Berkeley, 1983), for a heteroclite "model." By "heteroclite," I mean the use of an eclectic combination of medium-range theories to explain various facets of NIC development without any overarching vision of the process of development.

4

growth and development over the long term as Australia did, most are not likely to be as successful. Second, the ability of any NIC to sustain growth, to be the "Australia" of its cadre, depends critically on its internal politics. Finally, Australia's continued dependency suggests that there are limits on even the most successful of the NICs.

Demonstrating the continuing validity of Dependency theory requires three steps. The first step, beginning in Chapter 1, is a modest reconstruction of Dependency and sister theories that elucidates their common core claims.[8] My reconstruction reveals two distinct "lines" within Dependency theory. The first line derives from recognition that the decisive difference between developed and underdeveloped societies lies in the qualitative differences of their social relations of production. The second line derives from recognition of on-going primitive accumulation in the relations between or among core and dependent capitals. Describing these different sets of social relations permits clarification and disaggregation of the meaning of "dependency" and of "underdevelopment."

Chapter 2, the second step, sets forth a model of the foreign debt–financed dependent development that is typical of the Dominions. This model reveals that the contradictions inherent in indebted development lead inevitably to political and economic crises; it also shows why the dependency and development outcomes of these crises vary from society to society. Within limits, classes in indebted Dominion developers can form political coalitions capable of changing the social relations underlying both dependency and development or underdevelopment. Variation in coalition formation creates variation in outcome.

The third step, in Chapters 3 through 7, is to apply the concepts from Chapter 1 and the model laid out in Chapter 2 in case studies of Australia, New Zealand, Argentina, and South Korea. Each of these countries experienced the crises predicted by the model. Specific outcomes differed, for in each case different political coalitions triumphed. In these case studies, Australia may appear to receive a disproportionate amount of attention, taking up two chapters where the others occupy one shorter chapter each. In traditional academic practice, usually either equal attention is given to all the cases or one

8. Naturally, conflating a variety of perspectives and proposing to reconstruct them along similar lines does some violence to the subtleties of each. My first justification for doing so is the essential similarity of these theories, not just in their problematics but also in the way they approach dependent, underdeveloped, imperialized, and other societies. This similarity is the focus of the analysis below. The second justification is that of necessity—without remedial action the entire body of work is likely to be unnecessarily put aside.

5

case is studied in depth while the other examples are used to frame the primary case. But I have preserved the spirit of the law. Chapter 3, the first chapter on Australia, fulfills the first traditional usage, providing a case study of Australia's debt crisis that contrasts with the equally detailed cases on the difficulties of New Zealand (Chapter 5) and Argentina (Chapter 6). Studied as a group, Australia, New Zealand and Argentina in the period 1880–1900 reveal the essential similarities of the Dominion countries as a group of indebted developers and their potential relevance for understanding the NICs of the 1970s and 1980s. The second chapter on Australia fulfills the second traditional usage. Only in Australia did the events of 1880–1900 create a situation in which it was possible for a national bourgeoisie (in the specific sense I define in Chapter 2) to emerge and to decrease Australia's dependency profoundly. This Australian divergence merits its own separate chapter. Remarks at the ends of the other cases and in the conclusion provide a comparative context for understanding this divergence. In Chapter 7, South Korea provides a contemporary test case of the Dominion model and of my reconstructed Dependency theory. This choice, too, calls for some justification—why South Korea and not Taiwan? Unlike the choice of Australia, which has both intellectual and practical merit, the choice of South Korea is more of a judgment call. Despite its pariah status, Taiwan is currently the most successful of the Asian NICs. It is a net creditor because it chose not to borrow abroad to finance export-quality (and export-quantity) heavy industrial goods during the late 1970s. Instead, its strategy was to leap from a low-technology light industry, revolving around textiles, shoes, and simple assembly of imported electronic components, to a high-technology light industry revolving around locally developed computer hardware and software. South Korea's debt-financed and multinationally aided leap into heavy industry seems the more viable long-term strategy, if only because it generates less opposition from the developed countries than does the Taiwanese approach.

THE EXISTING LITERATURE ON THE DOMINIONS

Although this book primarily investigates dependent development, it also has a second purpose. Very few comprehensive comparative studies of the nineteenth-century Dominions exist. Aside from Louis Hartz's collection, now twenty-five years old and, in any case, a study of differences not of similarities, the existing literature is largely composed of ideographic or paired studies, typically comparing Australia and Argentina. Furthermore, most Dependency analysts typically assimilate Australia and New Zealand with the core; but this is problematic.[9] More recent and on firmer ground than Hartz is Donald Denoon's monograph, which argues that nineteenth-century Dominions constitute a distinct type. Denoon charts political, cultural, economic and social parallels from the beginning of colonization to World War I in the histories of Argentina, Australia, Chile, New Zealand, South Africa, and Uruguay. All started as imperial outposts protecting more economically important colonies, then expanded into "empty lands" by eliminating native populations. All experienced fantastic growth exporting raw materials to Britain while importing vast quantities of capital and manufactures. All organized production in a geographically extensive but capital intensive fashion using wage labour, not coerced or "plantation" labour. And all experienced crises in the 1890s in "which the internal workings of the societies were made unusually manifest."[10] Denoon's work makes mine possible, for his findings allow organized examination of the cases according to what Adam Przeworski and Henry Teune call a most-similar-systems analysis.[11] The study thus can focus on essential similarities and so remedy some of the failings of earlier studies. John Fogarty, for example, has justly criticized Denoon for not properly defining his objects of study in terms of the same "overall cause."[12] By providing a structural anal-

9. L. Hartz, ed., *Foundation of New Societies* (New Haven: Yale University Press, 1962). Typical paired studies are T. Moran, "The 'Development' of Argentina and Australia," *Comparative Politics* 38 (1970); A. Smithies, "Argentina and Australia," *American Economic Review* 55 (1965); B. Dyster, "Argentine and Australian Development Compared," *Past and Present* no. 84 (1979); J. McCarty, "Australia as a Region of Recent Settlement," *Australian Economic History Review* 13 (September 1973). D. C. M. Platt and G. Di Tella have been particularly active in editing comparative work. See their *Australia, Argentina, and Canada* (New York: St. Martin's, 1985). Interesting but ultimately misleading is P. Ehrensaft and W. Armstrong, "Dominion Capitalism: A First Statement," *Australia–New Zealand Journal of Sociology* 14 (October 1978). The best study is Tim Duncan and John Fogarty, *Australia and Argentina: On Parallel Paths?* (Melbourne: Melbourne University Press, 1985). For a critique of this literature, see my "Foreign Creditors and the Politics of Development in Australia and Argentina, 1880–1910," forthcoming; and Chapter 1 of my "Foreign Debt and Dependent Development in the Dominions, 1890–1914," (Ph.D. dissertation, Cornell University, 1986).

10. Denoon, *Settler Capitalism*, p. 15.

11. A. Przeworski and H. Teune, *Logic of Comparative Social Inquiry* (New York: Wiley, 1970). Aside from space considerations, the desire to conduct a most-similar-systems analysis rules out using Canada and South Africa, the former because of the influence of the United States, and the latter because of the question of race. Uruguay is excluded because of a dearth of available source material. Chile is not clearly a dominion in my terms because of the presence of a peasantry formed of the indigenous population.

12. J. Fogarty, "The Comparative Method and the Nineteenth Century Regions of Recent Settlement," *HSANZ* (Historical Studies, Australia and New Zealand) 19 (April

ysis of Dominion political economy, this study will enable comparisons not just among the historically and juridically defined nineteenth-century Dominions but also among similar and dissimilar contemporary societies. Comparative works on the Dominions also tend to take contemporary political units as the appropriate unit of analysis—their other major failing. As Fogarty points out, economic regions are the true area for comparison. Thus the Argentine pampas, not Argentina per se, is the "Dominion" area. This failing is harder to remedy, but by approaching Australian Federation, New Zealand's nonparticipation and "separate peace," and the peculiarities of Argentine federalism in terms of the structural features by which I characterize Dominions, I hope at least to make a start.

These countries were and are extraordinarily important economically and so deserve further consideration. With a population just 5 percent of the Peoples' Republic of China, Australia, Canada and New Zealand alone had a combined gross national product almost double that of China in 1983. Australia alone received more direct foreign investment (DFI) between 1970 and 1983 than did West Germany, Japan, or Italy. In 1984 the stock of U.S. DFI in Australia exceeded U.S. DFI in Mexico, France, or Japan, and rivaled investment in Brazil, a country with ten times Australia's population. Then, as now, publicists' misplaced fixation on getting one billion Chinese to add an inch to their shirttails obscures the fact that for much of the late nineteenth-century Britain's largest export market was consistently Australia, as Canada has been for the United States since World War II.[13]

1981), 413. "Overall cause" is Marc Bloch's terminology, taken from "Towards a Comparative History of European Societies," in F. Lane and J. Riemersma, eds., *Enterprise and Secular Change* (Homewood, Ill.: R.D. Irwin, 1953).

13. IBRD, *World Development Report 1985* (London: Oxford University Press, 1985), pp. 154–158; United States Department of Commerce, *Survey of Current Business*, August 1986, p. 48; United Nations Center on Transnational Corporations, *Trends and Issues in Foreign Direct Investment and Related Flows* (New York, 1985), 91. Canada alone hosts 22 percent of U.S. DFI. Six Dominions—Argentina, Australia, Canada, Chile, New Zealand, and Uruguay—supplied these shares of selected world commodity exports in 1983: wheat, 40 percent; meat, 25+ percent; wool, 62 percent; butter, 10.5+ percent; coal/coke, 11.8 percent; iron, 34.6 percent; aluminum, 10.1 percent; copper, 15 percent; lead, 30.1 percent. United Nations Commission on Trade and Development, *Handbook of International Trade and Development Statistics*, (New York, 1983), pp. 208–220.

CHAPTER ONE

Dependency and Underdevelopment

The earliest versions of Dependency theory emerged in reaction to positivist modernization theories, such as Walt Rostow's *Stages of Economic Growth*.[1] These neoclassically oriented theories assumed an ontogenetic similarity among all nations. All the "Third World" need do to become like the "First World" was to divest itself of traditional vestiges and accrete the trappings of modernity. No barriers stood in the way of this accretion, and each aspect of modernity was inextricably tied to the others.

Raul Prebisch and others at the United Nation's Economic Commission for Latin America (ECLA) argued against this view. Where Rostow and others saw developmental similarity, they saw a world divided into two dissimilar sorts of countries: a developed, autonomous core and an underdeveloped, dependent periphery. The core produced and exported manufactured products, the periphery, primary products; the periphery exported far more of its total production than the core. Because of these two structural imbalances, the periphery could not expect to take off into self-sustaining growth. Despite its supposed comparative advantage in primary production, Prebisch argued, the periphery would stagnate because different demand elasticities for manufactured and for primary products caused consistently declining terms of trade for peripheral primary product exports. In the Marxist tradition, Paul Baran made a parallel "supply side" argument.[2] He argued that monopoly control of world trade and of man-

1. W. Rostow, *Stages of Economic Growth*, (Cambridge: Cambridge University Press, 1960). For quick surveys of the Dependency literature see G. Palma, "Dependency: Formal Theory of Underdevelopment or Methodology for Analysis of Concrete Situations of Underdevelopment," *World Development* 6 (August 1978); and R. Chilcote, *Theories of Development and Underdevelopment* (Boulder, Col.: Westview Press, 1984).
2. P. Baran, *Political Economy of Growth* (New York: Monthly Review Press, 1957).

9

ufacturing in the periphery redistributed surplus from periphery to core, producing growth in the core and stagnation in the periphery.

These earliest versions of Dependency theory evidenced a curious ambivalence about politics. Clearly what mattered was not the internal politics of peripheral countries but rather what they exported. If, somehow, large landowners, or latifundistas, could produce transistor radios, or state trade companies replaced the foreign monopolies exporting them, then peripheral countries would not face declining terms of trade or lose surplus from trade. But both ECLA and the more Marxist scholars saw the concentration on production of primary products as a consequence of *external* desires, power and influences—imperialism. Practically, therefore, ECLA scholars advocated political support for a progressive national bourgeoisie through policies of import substitution and decreases in foreign penetration of the economy and foreign control of overseas trade.

"EXTERNAL FORCES" ARGUMENTS AND UNDERDEVELOPMENT

This ambivalence about politics gave birth to two different streams of Dependency theory. One seems to argue the importance of external factors, the other the importance of internal factors.[3] In one of the first analyses arguing that external forces in one form or another irremediably shaped internal class and productive structures of peripheral countries, Andre Gunder Frank posited a highly segmented hierarchy of interlocking metropoli and satellites.[4] Metropolitan capital distorted satellites' development, pushing growth and investment in unwanted directions, disrupting social relations, and transferring surplus value out of the satellite. Once satellites were locked into this hierarchy, vertical movement was impossible for them. Rather, as the core's needs changed, world markets either abandoned satellites or pressed them into new orbits. But Frank's critics quickly pointed out evidence of satellites' vertical movement and of domestically generated policies contrary to the interests of the core nations, as well as the costs and difficulties of Frank's autarkic policy prescriptions.

3. These terms are taken from Chilcote, *Theories of Development and Underdevelopment*, p. 130. Neither is wholly precise, as virtually no one argued that solely internal or external factors caused the effects being observed, but they do provide a handy shorthand.

4. See A. Frank, "The Development of Underdevelopment," *Monthly Review* 18 (September 1966), and *Capitalism and Underdevelopment in Latin America* (New York: Monthly Review Press, 1967).

In response to these criticisms, Immanuel Wallerstein generated a new model in the same line Frank had pursued.[5] In Wallerstein's "world system," a country's hierarchical position determined internal class structure and state strength but allowed more maneuvering room than in Frank's model. Between periphery and core was the semiperiphery, a collection of countries whose relatively greater state strength had permitted a degree of industrialization. As with Frank's market-driven change, this development occurred "by invitation" of the core, but semiperipheral countries with relatively strong states could also undertake "mercantilist semi-withdrawal" to improve their relative position. However, Wallerstein's response to Frank's critics contained the same theoretical flaws. Wallerstein and world systems theorists never formulated any distinct criteria to distinguish the semiperiphery from the periphery. Descriptions were always relative—"trades with the core like a periphery; trades with the periphery like the core"—or functional—"needed for global stability." This did not explain to what ends semiperipheral state power was put. Next, Aristide Zolberg showed that although Wallerstein's theoretical premises excluded interstate politics as a determining variable, he consistently resorted to it in his historical explications, as, for example, in cases of war-enforced mercantilist semiwithdrawal. Finally, as Robert Brenner argued, it was impossible to tell whether it was internal class struggles that determined a country's position in the world system, or the reverse, as Wallerstein argued, that world markets drove political and social change in the periphery and semiperiphery.[6]

Despite these weaknesses, the usefulness of the external forces line was in its theoretical appreciation of how forces external to what became peripheralized areas and countries created social relations inside them that made development extraordinarily difficult. This appreciation anchored the emphasis of the external forces line on the persistence, if not inevitability, of hierarchy in the international system. Dieter Senghaas reflected this emphasis when he argued that "peripheralization [is] the norm, and successful development [is] the exception"; it is what led Samir Amin to talk about "peripheral capital-

---

5. See I. Wallerstein, "Rise and Future Demise of the Capitalist World Economy: Concepts for Comparative Analysis," *Comparative Studies in Society and History* 16 (September 1974), and *Modern World-System*, vols. 1 and 2 (New York: Academic Press, 1976 and 1980).

6. A. Zolberg, "Origins of the Modern World System: A Missing Link?" *World Politics* 33 (January 1981); R. Brenner, "Origins of Capitalist Development," *New Left Review* no. 104 (July 1977).

ism" as a distinct mode of production.[7] Underdevelopment is understood not simply as a relative backwardness but as a set of social relations that blocked modernization. The apparent hierarchy of world economic zones did not reflect a developmental "bell curve" whose origins lay a perpetual *relative* poverty—"the poor will always be with us." Rather, hierarchy reflected a "kinked" curve whose discontinuity lay between areas with social relations conducive to development and those with social relations antagonistic to development. This approach directly attacked the diffusionist assertion that homogeneous economies inevitably emerged out of temporarily unequal situations. From the diffusionist point of view, any innovation creates a relative backwardness. But nothing blocks the spread of innovations; non-innovators can catch up. Modernization theorists thus fetishized the power of modern objects, believing that the simple accumulation of machines and other modern technologies in and of itself would be sufficient to create "development," no matter what social relations happened to be present in the recipient society. The simple insertion of modern hardware into any society was capable of changing that society into a modern society. Delays might occur, but only because of the persistence of "traditional" (i.e. "irrational") social practices that hindered the spread or efficient use of modern technologies.

The "external forces" line argued against the diffusionst assumptions and instead defined development in terms of the kinds of social relations that encouraged the spread of labour-saving devices and productive processes to all branches of industry and agriculture. Consequently, rather than being more or less neutral instruments of change, modern technologies outside the context of capitalist social relations were actually deleterious. Introduction of modern technologies or goods by politically more powerful societies changed social relations in the periphery in such a way that those social relations blocked modernization.[8] The "traditional" social relations condemned

7. D. Senghaas, *The European Experience; A Historical Critique of Development Theory* (Dover, N.H.: Berg, 1985), p. 16; S. Amin, *Accumulation on a World Scale* (New York: Monthly Review Press, 1974). Senghaas uses "peripheralization" as I use "underdevelopment" here.

8. Development is "the *utilization* of machines and technicians in any branch [of production] *whatsoever*." A. Emmanuel, "Myths of Development vs. Myths of Underdevelopment," *New Left Review* no. 85 (May 1974), p. 65, "Productivity of labor is the only relevant magnitude for measuring development." A. Emmanuel, *Unequal Exchange* (New York: Monthly Review Press, 1972), p. 373. Emphases in original. The best examples of the "external forces" approach are S. Amin, *Accumulation on a World Scale*, and Amin, *Unequal Development* (New York: Monthly Review Press, 1976). The first elaborates a model of "peripheral capitalism" whose key feature is oversupply of la-

by modernization theory were products of contact with modern society, not autochthonous residues.

The external forces line argued that contact with capitalist societies distorted social relations of production within an existing precapitalist economy in a process Senghaas calls "displacement competition."[9] Because of the core society's high level of economic efficiency, its sales of imported goods and use of the political coercion of poll and kindred taxes displaced indigenous craftworkers and cultivators from their traditional occupations; later, commercial monoculture agriculture aggravated this displacement. The resulting oversupply of displaced labour in the periphery caused massive underemployment and unemployment, pushing down wages through the mechanisms described by Arthur Lewis and Samir Amin. This absolute oversupply of labour, willing to work at subsistence wages, then makes it economically irrational for capitalists to invest in labour saving devices in either agriculture or manufacturing.[10] Underdevelopment comprises the aggregate effect of the labour surplus and low wages on agriculture, manufacturing, and the integration of the local economy's markets.

Commercialized agriculture in the context of an oversupply of labour led to a pattern of concentrated landholding that intensified the forces against laboursaving investment. Landlords have no interest in the intensification of production through laboursaving investments, for they extract surplus from direct producers—peasants, sharecroppers, debt peons—in the form of rent and interest. They are thus shielded from market forces by the relatively fixed form in which they

---

bour; the second, where not repetitive of the first, is a typology of the reactions of different social formations to the creation of labour oversupply. See also Senghaas, *European Experience*, pp. 14–26, 37–45, and, of course, Emmanuel, *Unequal Exchange*. See W. A. Lewis, "Economic Development with Unlimited Supplies of Labour," *Manchester School Journal* 22 (May 1954), for the *locus classicus* of arguments suggesting that labour surpluses might block development. Though Lewis agrees that productivity-increasing investment is deterred by labour surpluses, he does not see these as blocking the inevitable spread of capitalism or capitalist wage relations in such a way that the labour surplus disappears.

9. Senghaas, *European Experience*, p. 15.

10. J. Furnival, *Colonial Policy and Practice* (Cambridge: Cambridge University Press, 1948), provides an exemplary description of the displacement process in British Burma and Dutch Indonesia. Threshold levels of mechanization exist for certain industries, so some mechanization will always occur. The question is, What kind and quality of mechanization? Studies of Taiwan's machine tool industry show that machine tool manufacturers produce low-quality, cheap machines so as to be able to compete against low-wage labour. See A. Amsden, "The Division of Labor is Limited by the Type of Market: The Case of the Taiwanese Machine Tool Industry," *World Development* 5 (March 1977); and M. Fransman, "International Competitiveness, Technical Change, and the State: The Machine Tool Industry in Taiwan and Japan," *World Development* 14:12 (December 1986).

receive income. A decline in prices for whatever their renters produce does not affect their claims. Though their tenants might react to declining prices by trying to become more productive, the oversupply of potential renters makes such increases unlikely. The renter over-supply means landlords can skim off any productivity increases as rent, depriving tenants of the surplus they need to invest in further productivity increases. Landlords, in the meantime, continue to invest in land—in more claims to surplus in the form of rent—rather than in improvements that increase productivity. Investment in land posi-tions landlords to continue skimming off the benefits of any produc-tivity increase. This investment in land sterilizes the extra surplus that tenants' increased productivity has yielded, blocking reinvestment and further increases in productivity.[11] This is not a vestige of "tradi-tional" practices; rather, it is economically rational behavior on the part of these landlords. In contrast, owner-operators of all sizes who are entrepreneurs receiving their income as profit, faced with declin-ing profits, might very well react by trying to lower the cost of labour inputs. But they also try to increase productivity, shift to higher–value-added products, or intensify production, so as to increase or maintain their profits.

The same is true in manufacturing. A large pool of surplus workers willing to accept very low wages raises the threshold at which produc-tivity-increasing investment by manufacturers makes economic sense. Instead, cyclical increases in demand are met by hiring additional hands, and decreases by firing. Without uniform pressure by all workers to push up wages, introduction of laboursaving machinery in one discrete sector actually tends to worsen the situation, raising the investment threshold by enlarging the pool of underemployed and unemployed workers in other sectors.[12] Increasing mechanization in isolated sectors only displaces workers whom other sectors cannot absorb; it only furthers underdevelopment. Finally, for both man-ufacturing and agriculture, low wages imply a narrow local market

11. See Amin, *Accumulation on a World Scale*, chap. 2, part 2, for an elucidation of the *sterilization* phenomenon.

12. Such wage pressures were also present in early industrial Europe. England, and what became Germany, avoided surplus worker problems by virtue of massive out-migration to what became, appropriately enough, the Dominions. From 1830 to 1930, roughly 55 million people emigrated from Europe, 19 million of them from Britain. At times, 40 percent of the natural increase in European population migrated; see F. Thistlethwaite, "Migration from Europe in the 19th and 20th Centuries," *International Congress of Historical Sciences* (1960), pp. 36, 38, 40.

and the absence of multiplier and accelerator effects from forward and backward linkages.[13]

The social relations consequent to dispossession from land and displacement competition thus maintain underdevelopment in the absence of any forces to remedy the situation. Contrary to modernization theory, simply increasing the amount of machinery will not help, for it was contact with modernity that created the social relations blocking modernization. This focus on the social relations affecting development is the theoretical core of the external forces argument about the inevitability of underdevelopment. The external forces line also sees underdevelopment as a persistent phenomenon because the "competence differentials" that create displacement widen with time. As underdeveloped societies lag further behind developed ones, their uncompetitiveness increases, making it harder for them to shrink the pool of surplus labour. Active state intervention to close local markets to world market signals is thus only a first, remedial step, for productivity in the whole society must be brought to core levels to prevent later regression when the society re-enters world markets. To stand still only makes future underdevelopment likely, as development in the core creates continuing displacement pressure. Unlike the diffusionist view, that the difference between developed and "less developed" countries is simple and relative, the difference between developed and underdeveloped countries is *qualitative*. Thus, the larger game is not relative movement in the rank-ordering of nations but a struggle to change domestic social relations so as to be able to participate in relative advancement. Wallerstein's and Senghaas's prescriptions draw directly from this view. For both, continued contact with the world market and the unmediated investment signals it sends to rational entrepreneurs only results in continuation of unequal exchange and lack of investment in higher–value-added processes or capital goods. For both, the state must change the signals that the market sends local capitalists. For Wallerstein the state must do "mercantilist semi-withdrawal" and order or create incentives for modernizing investment. Senghaas prescribes protection, land reform, and agricultural modernization as prerequisite to setting a floor on wages,

---

13. See Amin, *Accumulation on a World Scale*, pp. 223–237, 261–298, for the most coherent explanation of the absent multiplier mechanism; the explanation benefits from a familiarity with the rest of the book. Much of Senghaas's argument revolves around the question of integrating domestic markets; see Senghaas, *European Experience*, chap. 2 and chap. 7, especially pp. 214–226.

thus creatings incentives for laboursaving investment.[14] Arghiri Emmanuel's *Unequal Exchange* presents the most extreme version of this view: development hinges on fights between capital and labour over the socially necessary wage. Capital's nationality is irrelevant to development; development occurs only to the degree that wage gains force capital to innovate and invest in laboursaving devices, and to the degree that higher wages make investment possible by reducing unequal exchange. Thus, while this line has been characterized as looking too much at external forces and desires, it really focuses on relations between direct producers and those individuals and organizations with various claims to surplus inside the society.

Precisely because this line focuses on relations between capital and labour in the context of world market pressures, it has been most vulnerable to critiques attacking its fundamental assumptions about causality in those relations. Thus from one side, Brenner attacks Wallerstein's argument that development (or underdevelopment) is market-driven and that external markets structure internal class formation; from the other, Zolberg attacks Wallerstein's exclusion of war and interstate politics as decisive spurs to development.

"INTERNAL FORCES" ARGUMENTS AND DEPENDENCY

In contrast to what we call the "external forces" line, a line that seemed to emphasize internal politics emerged. Where the external forces line focused on the *quality* of investment, the internal forces line focused on *control* of investment and accumulation. For this group, of which Fernando Cardoso and Enzo Faletto are the best example, the metropolis or metropolitan markets did not mechanically condition peripheral economies:[15] external desires, pressures, and interventions were insufficiently to explain political and economic outcomes in the periphery. Instead, the key question was how ex-

14. Senghaas, *European Experience*, pp. 46–56, 214–226. Wallerstein, *Modern World System*, chap. 7.

15. F. Cardoso and E. Faletto, *Dependency and Development in Latin America* (Berkeley: University of California Press, 1979; original, 1969; cited hereafter as Cardoso and Faletto, DDLA), especially p. xvi. See also the voluminous literature on Bureaucratic Authoritarianism, which in large part takes its methodological cues from DDLA. For a critique that discusses significant changes between the original 1969 version and the expanded 1979 English translation, see R. Packenham, "*Plus ca change. . .*: The English Edition of Cardoso and Faletto's *Dependencia y Desarrollo en America Latina*," *Latin American Research Review* 17 (1982).

ternal political and economic interests were internalized in peripheral class structures and politics, the process that constituted dependency for this line. But because internalization was in part a *political* phenomenon, dependency allowed a space within which peripheries could change themselves: political organization, will, and gambles all could push structurally dependent societies down alternative development paths. Although this group defined "development" by reference to "normal" capitalist development, and talked about "distorted development" as the outcome of dependency, it did not seem to have a notion of "peripheral capitalism" as Amin did.[16]

Despite this emphasis on the political nature and opportunities of dependency, Cardoso and Faletto's definition of dependency was peculiarly nonpolitical and economistic: an economic system is "dependent when the accumulation and expansion of capital cannot find its essential dynamic component inside the system."[17] Their descriptions of the three major situations of dependency were also peculiarly economistic. Early in *Dependency and Development in Latin America*, they laid out two major situations of dependency emerging from countries' individual historical experiences with imperialism: local bourgeoisie economies, in which the starting point for accumulation was internal and a local bourgeoisie controlled the economy, and enclave (or "comprador") economies, in which the starting point for accumulation was external; foreign capital operated without much contact with the surrounding society. In both, value was appropriated locally but realized externally. Either situation could lead to the third, current, situation, in which capital has external origins in multinational companies (MNCs), but value is appropriated and realized internally.[18]

Most works in the internal forces line analyze the third situation, MNC economies; among the earliest and best known analyses in En-

16. See for example, Cardoso and Faletto, DDLA, pp. 18–21; 22.

17. Cardoso and Faletto, DDLA, p. xx. See also T. dos Santos' similar definition: "By dependenc[y] we mean a situation in which the economy of certain countries is conditioned by the development and expansion of another economy to which the former is subjected. The relation of interdependence between two or more economies, and between these and world trade, assumes the form of dependenc[y] when some countries (the dominant ones) can expand and can be self-sustaining, while other countries (the dependent ones) can do this only as a reflection of that expansion, which can have either a positive or negative effect on their immediate development." Dos Santos, "Structure of Dependence," *American Economic Review* 60 (May 1970), 231.

18. Cardoso and Faletto, DDLA, pp. xviii–xx. T. dos Santos also sets out these same three situations in "Structure of Dependence." The "local bourgeoisie" situation parallels the "informal empire" or "imperialism of Free Trade" argument made by J. Gallagher and R. Robinson, "Imperialism of free trade," *Economic History Review* 6:1, 2nd series (1953).

glish was Peter Evans's *Dependent Development*.[19] For Evans, a triple alliance of state, multinational, and local capital permitted development, albeit of a dependent sort, to occur because the alliance allowed the dependent country "to capture some control over [its] own surplus."[20] The crucial problem facing the state in would-be dependent developers was to control the behavior of multinational companies, that is, to modify the effects of global markets. But unlike the external forces line, the market effects to be modified here were not those affecting relations between capital and labour, and, consequently, the capital intensity of production. Rather, Evans' analysis centers on the way the Brazilian state tried to modify the distribution of profits and market shares among different capitals. Multinational corporations, motivated by world market strategies, would not naturally invest in ways beneficial to local industry, would not necessarily buy from those industries, would not transfer technology, would not take care to avoid disrupting the balance of payments. The MNCs' superior resources would allow them to "denationalize" the economy, buying out real or potential competitors and relegating local firms to economic backwaters. Evans argued that the state could use its political control over access to local markets to redress the problems of MNC behavior, brokering deals in specific industrial sectors among local, state, and multinational capitals. In Brazil, the state sought to force MNCs to contribute to local accumulation. But precisely because MNCs would revert back to "natural" market-driven behaviors in the absence of state action, Evans argued that dependency continued within the triple alliances. Only if indigenous capabilities emerged to replace MNCs, especially in production of capital goods and technology, could the state relax controls.[21] The emergence of indigenous capital

19. P. Evans, *Dependent Development: the Alliance of Multinational, State, and Local Capital in Brazil* (Princeton: Princeton University Press, 1979). F. Cardoso, "Associated Dependent Development," in A. Stepan, *Authoritarian Brazil* (New Haven: Yale University Press, 1973), also analyzes Brazil from this standpoint. I will not discuss in detail Cardoso's argument, which anticipates that of Evans. Cardoso describes a "double" alliance between multinational and state capital, in contrast to Evans' notion of the "triple" alliance of multinational, state and local capital. But, as Cardoso wrote six years earlier than Evans, perhaps this reflects a changing reality rather than substantive disagreement. Other typical examples of this approach are G. Gereffi, *The Pharmaceutical Industry and Dependency in the Third World* (Princeton: Princeton University Press, 1983) and D. Bennett and K. Sharpe, *Transnational Corporations vs. the State: The Political Economy of the Mexican Automobile Industry* (Princeton: Princeton University Press, 1985).
20. Evans, *Dependent Development*, pp. 290, 291. On the "triple alliance" see p. 32, chap. 6, and *passim*.
21. See especially Cardoso, "Associated Dependent Development," p. 163. Evans, and others in this line, also seem to incorporate some of the insights of the external forces line into their concern that the MNCs' capital-intensive production methods exacerbate

goods and high-technology industries in the Asian NICs thus simultaneously challenged and affirmed Evans's observations. Even if it sometimes seemed hard to find a triple alliance in Asian NIC political economies, where the state was *primus inter pares* and not simply *imperator*, the very power of these states went a long way toward explaining why and how indigenous industries had been created.[22]

Nevertheless the lack of specific criteria to pinpoint what was and was not crucial in this bargaining process exposed Evans to two related criticisms. If dependency was simply a matter of control over technologies (and not one of social relations between capitals), why was dependency a long-term problem? First, if the state was simply acting as a broker, bargaining with MNCs over access to markets and technologies, how was dependency internalized in the ways Cardoso and Faletto discussed? Second, if bargaining positions defined dependency and in turn were described by specifics of particular markets and industries, where were the *structural* sources for dependency? These problems gave rise to a vast literature studying the minutiae of bargaining between dependent states or firms and MNCs, all attempting to show various degrees of "dependency" or "autonomy" in the bargaining process, measured by how much each side gave up. A similarly voluminous literature measured monopoly power and thus dependency by looking at the commodity and partner concentration of export economies.[23] Both sets of critics focused on MNCs and on specific trade patterns and so were able to argue that dependency was simply one among several possible outcomes of the bargaining process between state and foreign capital. Why could states not borrow abroad to capitalize local firms, to finance overseas trade, to buy technology from the MNCs, and so to escape dependency? Was Brazil, with a lower commodity concentration in 1981, less dependent than Australia?[24]

---

unemployment in dependent societies. Nonetheless, their key concern is control over the accumulation of capital; marginalization is an outcome of the process of dependent accumulation, not an independent variable.

22. For Evans's auto-critique and analysis of dependent development in East Asia, see "Class, State and Dependence in East Asia: Lessons for Latin Americanists," in F. Deyo, ed., *The Political Economy of the New Asian Industrialism* (Ithaca: Cornell University Press, 1987). The relative absence of inequality in the East Asian NICs also challenged the internal line's assertion that marginalization was a dependent variable.

23. See J. Grieco, *Between Dependency and Autonomy: India's Experience with the International Computer Industry* (Berkeley: University of California Press, 1984), for a typical bargaining study; see V. Mahler, *Dependency Approaches to International Political Economy* (New York: Columbia University Press, 1980), for a typical quantitative exercise.

24. See especially S. Haggard, "The Newly Industrializing Countries in the International System," *World Politics* 38 (Winter 1986), 345–346: "The nature of a country's

Control over Capital Accumulation and Dependency

Where the observations of the external forces line about social relations between capital and labour suggested structural reasons for underdevelopment, observations about relations among capitals lay at the core of the internal forces line. These observations show why dependency is *structural*, and help make sense of Cardoso and Faletto's cryptic and economistic definition of dependency. Although they describe three dependent situations, their definition suggests two possible sources of dependency. With the first, all of a system's economic activity depends on external *demand* or sales and initiative. With the second, a system depends on external *sources of capital* for investment to expand itself. By turning to a variety of analyses based on Marx's concept of the circulation of capital, we can make sense and order out of the many and confusing descriptions of dependency.[25]

This schema traces the differing forms that capital assumes at varying stages in the production process, in order to show the essential unity of what is superficially a chaotic and disorderly process. In its simplest form, $\mathbf{M} \rightarrow \mathbf{C} \rightarrow (\mathbf{M} + \mathbf{m})$. That is, money capital ($\mathbf{M}$) is transformed into commodity capital ($\mathbf{C}$), whose value is realized in sales that transform it back to money capital with an added increment of value ($\mathbf{M} + \mathbf{m}$). But we can expand this to:

$$\mathbf{M} \rightarrow \mathbf{C} \rightarrow \mathbf{P} \{ \mathbf{mp} + \mathbf{l} \} \rightarrow (\mathbf{C} + \mathbf{c}) \rightarrow (\mathbf{M} + \mathbf{m}) \rightarrow \text{etc.}$$

Money capital ($\mathbf{M}$) is transformed into commodity capital ($\mathbf{C}$) via purchases of raw materials and intermediate goods. These materials enter the production site where they are combined with productive capital ($\mathbf{P}$). Productive capital itself is composed of two things, labour power ($\mathbf{l}$, purchased via wages), and means of production ($\mathbf{mp}$). At the

---

links to the international economy, including level and sectoral composition of foreign direct investment, depend on the choice of particular development strategies." Bennett and Sharpe, *Transnational Corporations and the State*, sidestep this question, arguing that local tastes are what forced a dependent position on the Mexican state in its bargaining with multinational auto firms. Data on Brazil and Australia from IBRD, *World Tables*, 3d ed., vol. 1:544–546.

25. My approach both draws heavily on and fundamentally modifies both Palloix and Poulantzas. See C. Palloix, *L'internationalisation du Capital* (Paris: François Maspero, 1975), "Internationalization of Capital and the Circuit of Social Capital," in H. Radice, ed., *International Firms and Modern Imperialism* (Harmondsworth: Penguin, 1975); and Palloix, "Self-expansion of Capital on a World Scale," *Review of Radical Political Economy* 9 (Summer 1977), which abstracts chap. 2 and the appendix of *L'internationalisation*. N. Poulantzas, "Internationalization of Capitalist Relations and the Nation-state," *Economy and Society* 3 (May 1974); see also his *Classes in Contemporary Capitalism*, (London: Verso, 1975), especially part I, which is a revised version of the *Economy and Society* article.

production site, intermediate goods and raw materials are transformed into new commodities. These commodities now contain more value than they did when they entered the production site because they embody the surplus value the capitalist has wrested from the worker.[26] Hence $C + c$, where c is the added increment. The value in these commodities is realized through sales that transform it back into money capital (M), including (the capitalist hopes) the new increment of value (m). The new money capital then can be reinvested to start the whole cycle over again. If this investment includes the increment, then expansion occurs because more commodities enter the cycle; capital, in its tripartite roles of laboursaving devices, claims on surplus, and a form of social relations, accumulates.

Disaggregating the circuit of capital reveals two complementary facts. First, Cardoso and Faletto's three dependent situations can be mapped to specific types of domination within the circuit. These three situations do not exhaust the realm of potentially dependent situations, but because the other situations are less important to the line of argument advanced here, they will not be considered.[27] While Cardoso and Faletto do not themselves do this mapping, their terminology suggests that to do so neither misprizes nor abuses their work. Second, dependency occurs when foreign capital controls any of the steps in this process of accumulation, and uses its control to siphon away the increase in investible surplus, thereby preventing domestically-controlled reinvestment. As different kinds of power are created by control of different parts of the cycle, so different opportunities exist to modify or escape dependency. Politics thus becomes paramount in dependent societies, because political responses to dependency can lessen foreign control, and increase the possibilities for domestically-controlled reinvestment.

In the enclave situation (Cardoso and Faletto's second type), virtually all the capitals come from outside the region in which the production site is located (See Figure 1). Foreign capitals control and

26. By value, I mean value established by the socially necessary labour time involved in production of the goods.

27. Missing from Cardoso and Faletto's typology are situations not historically specific to Latin America. For example, comprador marketing of peasant-produced materials like jute or tea, as found in the Indian subcontinent, is neither an enclave nor a local bourgeoisie situation. Nor is there a local bourgeoisie in situations where colonial merchants totally monopolize marketing of peasant production, as in the West African *économie de traite*. In both, the producers are not clearly "capitalists." See S. Amin, *Unequal Development*, pp. 317–333, and "Underdevelopment and Dependence in Black Africa: Their Historic Origins and Contemporary Forms," *Social and Economic Studies* 22 (March 1973), for a description of the *économie de traite*.

Figure 1. Local control in enclave economy

$$M \rightarrow C \rightarrow \boxed{P \left\{ \begin{matrix} mp \\ \mathbf{l} \end{matrix} \right\} \rightarrow (C + c)} \rightarrow (M + m)$$

Key: **Bold** is local control; boxed areas occur locally.

provide **M**, **C**, and most of **P**, and they dominate the realization of value. The only part of the local economy involved in production are workers, **l**, and such **M** as is channeled to local political elites to secure access to those parts of the natural environment exploited in raw materials enclaves. The sources of dependency here are clear: accumulation is completely controlled by foreign capitals, there is no possibility for local accumulation, and demand is completely external. In this situation only comprador bourgeoisies emerge, generally to mediate between foreign capital and local labour or the local state.

Accumulation by comprador bourgeoisies in an enclave economy depends totally on foreign accumulation, because the comprador bourgeoisie does not control the productive process. Consequently they do not produce surplus value, but instead must appropriate it as revenue from the foreign businesses they deal with. They can do this in a variety of ways, such as brokering access to local political elites, mediating between foreign producers and local sources of labour, and handling commercial transactions. Because they appropriate value as revenue, their accumulation depends on prior creation of surplus value by foreign capitals. Thus compradors are economically, ideologically and politically dependent. Because they do not control production, they cannot increase their own accumulation by increasing productivity (i.e., by increasing the pool of surplus value).[28] Instead they will advocate increasing the number of transactions by the foreign capitals for whom they mediate in order to maximize the number of times they can claim revenue from those capitals. Compradors can rarely dominate foreign capitals, for their structural posi-

28. One could argue that they could increase their revenue stream by increasing wages and so enlarging the (domestic) market available to them. This in turn might lead to development, but would not decrease dependency. Historically, there seems to be evidence of only one such case: Dyster, "Argentine and Australian Development Compared," *Past and Present* no. 84 (1979), makes precisely this case for the behavior of Australian merchants. See my "Foreign Creditors and the Politics of Development in Australia and Argentina," *International Studies Quarterly* forthcoming, for a critique of Dyster.

tion in the cycle of accumulation limits the possibilities for reversing or reducing dependency.

In the local bourgeoisie situation (Cardoso and Faletto's first type), by contrast, there is some local control of the production process (**P**) (See Figure 2). Dependency arises from foreign control of the process of realization [(**C** + **c**) → (**M** + **m**)], from foreign provision of money capital (**M**) to enable local capitalists to begin production, or from foreign control of part of the productive process (**P**) inside the dependent society. In this situation one can speak of the degree of dependency, though Cardoso and Faletto avoid this usage, because dependency here clearly rests on the degree to which local capital is able to finance each new round of accumulation on its own. This in turn depends on how much surplus it loses to foreign financiers and to core monopolies controlling final sales. The "bargaining" school thus is not wrong, but has not looked beneath the surface to understand what it is that structures the bargaining situations.

Where there is local control of the production process, both comprador and local, or interior, bourgeoisies can emerge. (I call Cardoso and Faletto's local bourgeoisies "interior" bourgeoisies, following Poulantzas.[29]) It is now clear why Cardoso and Faletto speak of three *types* of dependency situations but suggest only two *sources* of dependency. Because local or interior bourgeoisies can be dominated at a number of different points, two situations of dependency can envelop them. Cardoso and Faletto's first type of dependency (local bourgeoisie economies) exists when foreign capital lends money capital to start up production in the dependent society ("b" in Figure 2). Their third type of dependency (MNC) corresponds to foreign control of part of the production process, through control over technology, management, or capital goods, or situations where local producers supply goods to foreign MNCs for further transformation before local marketing occurs ("c" and "d" in Figure 2). Cardoso and Faletto's "missing" types correspond to control over realization—marketing and shipment ("a" in Figure 2).

In contrast to compradors, interior bourgeoisies have some (albeit minimal) control of their productive process.[30] Consequently they

29. Poulantzas, "Internationalization of Capitalist Relations and the Nation-state."
30. This distinction between comprador and interior bourgeoisies is a heuristic one, and businesses in dependent societies might conceivably combine aspects of both. For example, a firm might work up imported goods with local labor for resale in the domestic market. The question, for both business and analyst, then becomes one of discerning which activity yields the greatest returns, and so is more important to the business.

Figure 2. Local bourgeoisie, local control

(a) Control over realization

$$M \to C \to \boxed{P \left\{ \begin{matrix} mp \\ l \end{matrix} \right\}} \to (C + c) \to (M + m)$$

(b) Provision of loan capital

$$M \to C \to \boxed{P \left\{ \begin{matrix} mp \\ l \end{matrix} \right\} \to (\mathbf{C} + \mathbf{c})} \to (M + m)$$

or
(c) Provision of capital goods

$$M \to C \to \boxed{P \left\{ \begin{matrix} mp \\ l \end{matrix} \right\} \to (\mathbf{C} + \mathbf{c})} \to (M + m)$$

or
(d) Integration in MNC production circuits

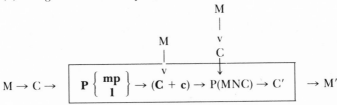

Key: **Bold** is local control; boxed areas occur locally. Note that the initial provision of **M** can be local, though the diagrams do not indicate this.

have some unmediated access to surplus value and, by improving productivity, can increase the amount of surplus available to them for investment and reinvestment. But interior bourgeoisies are ideologically and politically dominated, because of the way their circuit is enmeshed in circuits controlled by core capitals. They may depend on foreign merchants to sell their product overseas (for example, Argentine cattle raisers in the early twentieth century sold their output to foreign owned meat packing plants for processing and sale in British markets). They may depend on foreign loans to start the process of accumulation by providing them with enough capital to purchase raw materials and labour until they can recoup some of this money through sales (Australian wool growers in the nineteenth century relied on loans from British commercial lenders to get through their two-year production cycle). Finally, interior bourgeoisies may produce goods incorporated into multinationals' "commodity groups."[31] Thus a Brazilian firm selling only glass to a multinational auto producer is an interior bourgeoisie. Its accumulation depends on the MNC's prior and posterior success in completing its own cycle. These specific dependencies arising from foreign control of the circuit create the more general political and economic dependency in societies with interior bourgeoisies. Because the glass manufacturer's accumulation is linked to accumulation by the MNC auto firm, the manufacturer will advocate state policies that promote auto sales, and so benefit the MNC. Because the wool growers depend on credit, they will oppose state policies that frighten foreign lenders. Because the cattle are sold through foreigners, foreigners must have access to domestic markets so their ships do not "deadhead" coming to pick up the meat, which would raise outward freight charges. In order to promote their own interests, all these interior bourgeoisies must simultaneously promote those of foreign capital, which internalizes foreign interests in domestic politics. Domestic economic expansion thus serves to expand foreign capital; but foreign expansion, while prerequisite to, is no guarantee of domestic expansion.

Unlike compradors, interior bourgeoisies have an ambivalent relationship with foreign capital. Because interior bourgeoisies control some part of the production process, they can create surplus value, even though they may not have completely unmediated access to it (e.g., because what they produce will be incorporated into a commodity group). Thus they have a partial ability to make investments on their own. By accelerating creation of surplus value, they can gradually expand their control of the entire circuit of accumulation, and so transform themselves into a "national" bourgeoisie.[32] The interests of interior bourgeoisies and foreign capital thus conflict in a way that those of foreign capital and compradors do not. Though

31. Palloix uses the term "commodity group" to denote the combined form that most modern goods come in. Rather than buying the parts of a car separately, as glass, electronics, wheel, etc, the commodities are combined by the MNC final assembler into one commodity group, sold as a package.

32. In contrast to the two dependent types, a national bourgeoisie would control the entire circuit of accumulation in which it is involved and so is autonomous. Ideologically and politically, national bourgeoisies are more unified than either interior or comprador bourgeoisies, because their interests are not divided. They advocate policies primarily supporting their own accumulation, though foreign bourgeoisies may incidentally be helped by these policies.

compradors may fight with foreign capital over shares, they can never attain complete control of the whole process as interior bourgeoisies can.

Transfer of Surplus Value

If control over accumulation circuits is the first aspect of dependency, a transfer of surplus value is its second and may make potential battles into real ones. If foreign capital can bring with it expansion, then foreign capital must also take away part of the benefits of expansion to make dependency an ongoing process. Otherwise dependency would cease, as locally accumulated capital rapidly displaced foreign capital. Again in contrast to compradors, interior bourgeoisies have a conflictual relationship with foreign capital, for transfer of surplus value limits their ability to reinvest and thus to terminate dependency. Transfers create a second source of conflict because of the presence of heterogenous interior bourgeoisies in a given society. The benefits accruing from links to foreign capital may not be evenly distributed among all interior bourgeoisies; a given interior bourgeoisie may benefit more from ending surplus drains than it loses from the exclusion of foreign capital. But before the kinds of conflicts that surplus transfers occasion can be identified, it is necessary to specify what those transfers are and how they operate in dominion-type societies.

The transfer mechanisms benefiting foreign capital of most interest are those loosely called "primitive accumulation," because they operate through mechanisms requiring extra-economic enforcement of claims to surplus. Extra-economic surplus transfer results from the establishment and exercise of claims to surplus value that are not subject to market valorization: valorization is the process of turning commodity capital back into money capital, so realizing the increment to capital created in production. In markets, this process is subject to the uncertainties and vagaries of the market; the value embodied in the commodities is not necessarily always exchanged for an equivalent value of money capital. In such cases, the capital embodied is "devalorized" or lost. In dependency, surplus is transferred through both economic (market) and extra-economic channels. Claims to surplus based on extra-economic surplus transfer are not subject to destruction or diminution by market valorization like "normal" claims. Extra-economic surplus transfer can take many forms, a range illustrated by Spain's pillage of American civilizations to the establishment of foreign-held public debt. The difference between *continual* and *continuous* forms of extra-economic surplus transfer makes it possible to distinguish between contingent and structural forms of surplus transfer.

While contingent forms of extra-economic surplus transfer appropriate value and may be *continual*, they do not establish a permanent claim on future value, that is, they are not "capital." In contrast, such forms of *continuous* transfer as establishing or transferring title to land or establishing public debt creates ongoing—structural—claims to surplus. These structural types of extra-economic surplus transfer are most interesting, for dependency must be a structural phenomenon to make theoretical sense: as, for example, robbery is contingent, a random unique event, it may be a necessary, but it is not a sufficient cause of dependency. The causes of dependency must be continuous and self-reinforcing in nature, rather than contingent.

The external forces theorists recognize the significance of primitive accumulation *cum* surplus transfers in maintaining what they call underdevelopment but see it as another consequence of the factors causing underdevelopment. Although the crux of their argument is about why development does not occur, they find themselves faced with the problem of explaining where all the surplus value created in conditions of low wages and moderate-to-high productivity goes. Why is the periphery not awash in "capital"? External forces theorists claim that surplus transfers occur as forms of unequal exchange, for example, repatriation of superprofits accruing to MNCs using modern technologies in low-wage areas, payment of less-than-lifetime wages to workers producing for export, or Emmanuel's pure form of unequal exchange.[33] This answer begs the question of how surplus transfer is related to *control* over circuits of accumulation, because it reduces primitive accumulation to a simple mechanical consequence of social relations between labour and capital. Surplus transfers occur automatically, as a function of wage levels, through the process of unequal exchange. Emmanuel, once more, provides the purest example, for his unequal exchange only operates when high productivity and low wages are combined in the periphery in export production, a situation typical of enclaves. For Emmanuel, the question of control is essentially irrelevant: "I must confess I have never understood what Canadian workers or the Canadian people would gain if the decision-making centres of their industry and commerce were to be shifted from offices located in the skyscrapers of New York and Chicago to

33. Emmanuel, *Unequal Exchange*; author's discussions with T. Vietorisz, New School for Social Research; I. Wallerstein, W. Martin, and T. Dickenson, "Household Structures and Production Processes," *Review* 5 (Winter 1982).

offices located in the tower blocks of Montreal or Toronto."[34] For Emmanuel, Canada's higher wages mean it exploits Britain; British ownership of Canadian industry is inconsequential. Less extreme versions claim that unequal exchange is a form of primitive accumulation because *political* forces maintain the social relations holding down wages. Thus the external forces theorists habitually point to Giovanni Arrighi's combined study of Rhodesia and critique of W. A. Lewis.[35] Arrighi showed that political mechanisms kept blacks' wages low regardless of the overall level of development of Rhodesian production.

Internal forces theorists also acknowledge the importance of surplus transfers, but as a cause, not a consequence, of dependency. They variously conceptualize transfers as monopoly rents, the effects of MNC transfer pricing, or the transfer of superprofits arising from the subordination of dependent economies.[36] Just as the concerns of the external forces theorists arise from the observation of declining terms of trade, these concepts arise from Paul Baran's original observation of the core's monopolistic control over trade. The locus of monopoly control identified varies from analyst to analyst, depending on the particular case studied; commercial, managerial, technological, financial and other "monopolies" are each singled out for blame.

What both literatures overlook is the way in which foreign debt can create dependency. Most studies of the International Monetary Fund or World Bank tend to focus narrowly on bargaining over austerity regimes, or on *concessional* debt carrying below-market interest rates. But concessional loans seem to imply a surplus transfer *to* the periphery: the opposite direction from the one we seek to understand.[37] Consequently none of these literatures directly addresses the specific problem of understanding the origins of dependency in the Dominions and latterly, in the indebted NICs. In the Dominions, multinationals did not control production; with the key exception of railways, "technology"—in the sense of agricultural technique—quite often was

---

34. Emmanuel, "Myths of Development vs. Myths of Underdevelopment," 74. Amin, who also buys into the unequal exchange argument, in *Accumulation on a World Scale*, sidesteps the question of what happens to peripheral surplus value by saying that it gets "sterilized" through investment in the purchase of rent-producing land rather than in productivity enhancement; pp. 185–189, 217–218.

35. G. Arrighi, "Labor Supplies in Historical Perspective: A Study of the Proletarianization of the African Peasantry in Rhodesia," in G. Arrighi and J. Saul, eds., *Essays on the Political Economy of Africa* (New York: *Monthly Review*, 1973). Here Lewis's "Economic Development with Unlimited Supplies of Labour" is the object of critique.

36. See, for example, the discussion of denationalization and MNC monopoly control of technology in Evans, *Dependent Development*.

37. See C. Payer, *Debt Trap: The IMF and the Third World* (New York: Monthly Review Press, 1974), for a typical study.

locally created; commercial monopolies were nowhere near as strong as in Afro-asia, and were easily displaced during the twentieth century. The key foreign connection, control of loan capital used to initiate production, seemed to be a contractual obligation not conducive to primitive accumulation. The nature of South Korean dependency is similarly opaque, because MNCs are only marginally involved in local production circuits and because state and private trading companies have displaced older commercial oligopolies.

How then does debt create dependency? The next chapter will explore the question in relation to the Dominions, but a brief answer is possible here. Foreign debt created dependency in the Dominions because states used public borrowings to subsidize the expansion of foreign and domestic capitals in a way that did not allow them to capture enough revenue to repay debt. Taxation of other, primarily domestic, sectors to pay for debt service reduced the ability of those domestic capitals to invest and expand, making them and the entire society dependent on more foreign investment for renewed expansion. The absolute level of the transfers is critical, for here a *quantitative* difference constitutes a *qualitative* difference between debt-dependent countries and marginal net debtors. As with unemployment in labour surplus areas, the critical factor is not simply the presence of debt—after all, both debt and unemployment are endemic in capitalist economies—but the sheer magnitude of debt, when combined with subsidy.

In summary, development, underdevelopment, and dependency need to be understood in terms of the different sets of social relations to which they refer. Underdevelopment is a function of social relations between capital and labour, while dependency is a function of social relations among capitals. The critical issue with underdevelopment is the degree to which wage pressures induce labor-saving investment; the key issue of dependency is the question of which capitals dominate the circuit of capital, and, more important, whether or not local capitalists are involved in the creation of surplus value.

CHAPTER TWO

Dominion Dependency and Development

The previous chapter disaggregated Dependency theory into two lines, one concerned with the way in which external forces structured peripheral social relations so as to block development, the other with the way foreign control over accumulation circuits made domestic capitals and the entire domestic economy dependent on foreign capital for expansion. This chapter uses the two concepts arising from that disaggregation—underdevelopment and dependency—to show why it was possible to have coterminous development and dependency in the Dominions. External forces analysts would deny the possibility of Dominion dependency because of the obvious development that has occurred there. For them, dependency is a consequence of the social relations causing underdevelopment and cannot exist without underdevelopment. Internal forces theorists are perhaps more willing to recognize Dominion dependency because they believe that high levels of investment by multinational companies can create dependency. But because they see marginalization and poverty as the natural consequences of dependency, they are at a loss to explain the obviously high standards of living found in the various Dominions. Equally, they are unable to understand why high levels of foreign public debt, as distinct from multinational firms' investments, can create dependency. To demonstrate Dominion dependency I go beyond the abstract discussion of dependency presented in Chapter 1 and create a historically specific model that explains Dominion dependency. This model will provide our guide through the case studies in Chapters 3 through 7.

The external forces line easily explains the absence of under-development in the Dominions. First, the indigenous population disappeared. Natives in what became Dominions had lived in relatively small nomadic societies whose survival depended on an information-rich culture that rationed exploitation of fragile ecologies, in contrast to the more centralized, populous and productive societies in Asia and Latin America. Even where there were no deliberate extermination campaigns, European diseases and European forms of land tenure caused ecological displacement that destroyed the viability of these societies. Australian aborigines and the New Zealand Maori represent opposite extremes of this process. Dispersal of the aborigines in the arid Australian ecology rendered them extremely vulnerable to British settlers; a very low proportion of the original population survived. In contrast, Maori traditions of warfare and agricultural competence, as well as New Zealand's lushness, enabled fierce resistance to the initially light British settlement, so a much higher proportion survived.[1] In all of the Dominions, however, destruction of native populations virtually eliminated the possibility that a labour surplus might emerge, though Maori in New Zealand and Indians in Argentina at times provided pools of low-wage labour for specific sectors.

Second, as demand in the core began to make production of raw materials profitable in these thinly settled areas in the early nineteenth century (see the Introduction to Part II), a shortage of labour emerged. One historic and two structural factors made this shortage of labour unyielding enough to prevent the emergence of underdevelopment, even if, as in Argentina, these factors did not guarantee development later. The major attraction for investing in the Dominions was the possibility of extensive pastoral and agricultural production in contrast to Europe's intensive production. But the presence of surplus land—the absence of a settled population—meant a structural shortage of labour "relative" to the coming flood of much more mobile capital. The Dominions' labour supply always lagged behind the supply of capital; labour rarely came voluntarily on the scale necessary to expand production in advance of capital. Originally, coerced labour prevailed in the Dominions—slaves in Latin America, indentured servants everywhere, convicts in Australia.[2] But mechani-

1. On aborigine population, see N. G. Butlin, *Our Original Aggression: Aboriginal Population of South Eastern Australia, 1788–1850* (Sydney: Allen and Unwin, 1983). In the late 19th century white Australians thought the entire race might disappear. On Maori, see D. Pool, *Maori Population of New Zealand 1876–1971* (Auckland: Auckland University Press, 1977). Estimates of pre-contact Maori population range from an (unlikely) low of 10,000 to a high of 200,000. The nadir of Maori population, 40,000 in 1896, thus represents a decline of as much as 80 percent. For a general survey of the effects of contact, see D. Denoon, *Settler Capitalism* (Oxford: Oxford University Press, 1983), chap. 1. Tasmania is the only place where the autochthonous population was completely exterminated by settlers.

2. Only New Zealand was born "free"; permanent colonial settlement occurred at the same time the labour crises emerged in the 1840s-1850s.

zation of wool textile production in Britain increased demand for wool rapidly in the 1840s and 1850s, creating a general shortage of labour in all the Dominions.[3] Expanding demand revealed the inherently low productivity of coerced labour, motivating producer/owners to search for alternatives. Political conflicts produced regimes that encouraged immigration of free labour and emancipation of coerced labourers in all the Dominions except southern Africa. In principle, any free labour would have sufficed, and capitalists successfully imported small numbers of "low-wage" non-Europeans. But a historical factor interceded. The major source of free labour then available was people "freed" from the land by successive expansions of capitalist agriculture in Europe and in the Dominions themselves. Britain, for her own reasons, suppressed the African slave trade; Manchu China forbade emigration, and Southeast Asia sopped up most of those who left anyway. Though some Indians were available as emigré labour, most went as indentured servants to Burma under British aegis. In any case, bringing Afro-asian labour to the Dominions would probably have meant a continuation of the unprofitable and politically unpalatable coerced-labour regime. Free labour in the 1840s thus meant principally Celts, Basques, and Germans. The English, desiring to rid themselves of the Celts, happily subsidized emigration to the Antipodes and Canada, where disproportionately Irish and Scottish populations are still found. Argentina similarly assisted European immigration. Once majority European populations were in place, working and professional class movements reinforced this tendency to bar all but Western European immigration. Such barriers would have been ludicrous anywhere that the indigenous population significantly outnumbered settlers, but in places with newly created majority European populations, they served as the first line in defense of prevailing wage and consumption levels.[4] In societies where indigenous populations survived in large numbers, but native preference for or access to

3. P. McMichael, *Settlers and the Agrarian Question* (New York: Cambridge University Press, 1984), *passim*; F. Cardoso and E. Faletto, *Dependency and Development in Latin America* (Berkeley University of California, 1979), pp. 55–59; Denoon, *Settler Capitalism*, pp. 25–28; H. Ferns, *Britain and Argentina in the 19th Century* (Oxford: Clarendon, 1960), pp. 289–307. The weakness of an argument which does not delve into local class structures is apparent in Senghaas's treatment of immigration in *European Experience* (Dover, N.H.: Berg, 1985), pp. 122–126, 146–151.

4. On assisted migration to Argentina see Ferns, *Britain and Argentina*, pp. 328–329, 340. In societies with indigenous majorities, the "color bar" took the place of opposition to non-European immigration. Most interesting are the intermediate societies of Algeria, the South African states, and Brazil, where the ratio of native (or, in Brazil's case, natives plus imported slaves) to colonizer was in rough parity. An additional case of European opposition to imported non-European labour is mid- and late nineteenth

traditional subsistence forms of survival caused labour shortages, colonizers imported indentured and bonded labour.[5]

Given European wage expectations (certainly not uniform), were high wages and thus development assured?[6] Clearly historic expectations had an effect, but many migrants were displaced agricultural labourers whose expectations could not have been particularly high; certainly many Irish were fleeing starvation rather than chasing high wages. Later immigrants brought knowledge of Europe's rising living standards and perhaps of trade union activity; wages had to be high enough to overcome ignorance, fear, the breakup of social ties, and transport costs (though the British Dominions subsidized transport to lower this "barrier"). Gold discoveries also drove wages up because prospecting competed with the "normal" labour market. Finally, European wage earners' resistance to the introduction of "tropical" peoples into the labour force set a floor on wages. But an additional structural factor drove up nominal wages and thus made underdevelopment unlikely: because producers wanted free labour to come to the Dominions, they had to cope with two effects that drove up nominal and real wages. First, free labourers in the Dominions had a relatively smaller social network sheltering them from the vicissitudes of unemployment, wage struggles, and old age, especially in terms of the women who traditionally provided uncommoditized household products. Australia had 121 men per 100 women in 1861–1870, 111 as late as thirty years later,[7] while Britain in contrast, had more wom-

---

century California, where proletarianization of mining caused American miners to drive out Asian immigrants to defend wage rates.

5. For example, sugar producers in Cuba imported Chinese to work the cane fields; post-Union South African mine owners imported Chinese; subcontinental Indians were indentured to Malaya, the West Indies, and Pacific Islands to grow rubber, sugar, and palm. Where investors lacked the political power to import indentured workers, as in Turkey, their investments came to grief; C. Keyder, "Small Peasant Ownership in Turkey: Historical Formation and Present Structure," *Review* 7 (Summer 1983), 66–67.

6. Here the classical argument is W. A. Lewis, "Economic Development with Unlimited Supplies of Labour," *Manchester School Journal* 22 (May 1954); and Lewis, *Evolution of the International Economic Order* (Princeton: Princeton University Press, 1978). Lewis distinguishes between temperate and tropical wage expectations based on their different agricultural productivities in 1900: 1600 pounds per acre in temperate areas versus 700 pounds per acre in tropical (*Evolution*, p. 14). But this ignores massive migration by both temperate and tropical producers before 1900; why did not the productivities of 1700 set wage expectations? What were the "wage expectations" of millions of slaves and indentured servants (many of whom were in fact "European")?

7. Normally there are 98 men for every 100 women; E. Boehm, *Twentieth Century Economic Development in Australia* (Victoria: Longman Australia, 1971), p. 40. The United States had 104 men per 100 women as early as 1790, rising slightly to 105 in the period 1850–1900. Canada had 103 in 1871, rising to 105 in 1901 as male emigration

en than men through the second half of the 1800s. Real wages in the Dominions thus had to be high enough to pay the monetized cost of the household services and production generally left unmonetized in Europe.[8] Second, keeping labour free in an environment in which land was readily available meant employers had either to restrict access to the land artificially or to pay wages attractive enough to dissuade workers from taking up independent farming. Following Edward Gibbon Wakefield's suggestions on systematic colonization, the early colonial states in Australia and New Zealand used laws to block access to the land; in Argentina and Uruguay, political insecurity and the colonial legacy had the same effect. Nonetheless, "leakage" of labour occurred, so wage rates rose somewhat in compensation.[9] Dominion wages perforce were always higher than European, for European households still provided part of the lifetime wage, and land was a totally inaccessible alternative.

These factors did not, however, produce uniform outcomes. Class struggles in each of the Dominions determined how much pressure wages put on capital to "develop" above the floor the other factors created. Where immigrant labour comprised a high percentage of peasants who intended to return to a peasant economy, wages stayed at lower levels that were, still, higher than those in Europe. Thus Maori, Quebecois, and *golondrinas* ("Swallows," the nickname applied to Italian migrant harvest labourers) all expected and accepted lower wage rates.[10] In Australia and New Zealand, the relative difficulty of re-migration made workers more likely to fight than leave. But differ-

---

to the wheat fields increased; United States Department of Census, *Historical Statistics of the United States* (Washington, D.C.: GPO, 1972), M. Urquhart and K. Buckley, *Historical Statistics of Canada* (Cambridge: Cambridge University Press, 1965).

8. Employers routinely repatriated indentured workers when demand for labour eased, or when workers got too old or debilitated to work.

9. The comparison with the United States, where access to fertile land was much simpler in the early days of settlement—one had only to walk west a little bit—is instructive. See S. Duncan Baretta and J. Markoff, "Civilization and Barbarism: Cattle Frontiers in Latin America," *Comparative Studies in Society and History* 20 (1978), for information on "leakage" and efforts to both counter and restrict it.

10. Compare the discussion of "peasant workers," C. Sabel, *Work and Politics* (Cambridge: Cambridge University Press, 1983), chap. 3. Remigration was a common phenomenon among Italians. Among those coming to the United States, about half ultimately returned to Italy. Other groups showed the same tendencies, albeit at lower rates. There is some debate on the degree to which Argentina's underdeveloped and "labour surplus" interior hindered development on the Pampas, with B. Dyster, "Argentine and Australian Development Compared," *Past and Present* no. 84 (1979), arguing that displacement competition in the interior in the early and mid-1800s decisively destroyed Argentina's chances for later development. E. Gallo, *La Pampa Gringa* (Buenos Aires: Editorial Sudamerica, 1986), chaps. 2 and 6, presents data that refute this argument.

ences in the outcomes of these struggles between capital and labour do not fully explain or exhaust the differences in the kinds of capitalism and capitalists that emerged in the Dominions. Thus, we must look at relations among different capitals to understand dependency in the Dominions.

DEPENDENCY IN THE DOMINIONS

As Dominion wages are higher than European wages, unequal exchange either does not operate, or, if we take Arghiri Emmanuel's definition seriously, perhaps operates in favor of the Dominions. How and why does foreign debt create dependency in Dominion-type countries? Dependency, as noted above, must rest on two things: a strategic control of accumulation circuits by foreign businesses, and, to perpetuate this control, a transfer of surplus from local firms and the local economy to foreigners that is large enough to hinder autonomous investment by domestic capitalists. Certain criteria must determine whether a particular surplus transfer mechanism causes dependency. Dependency, to be a useful concept, must be a structural phenomenon, for if dependency were a temporary, contingent, one-day affair, it would be of no significance; the events it tries to explain could as easily be handled by Marxist theories of uneven development or by neoclassical location theories. So, too, the identifiable surplus transfers must be structurally determined. Transfers must somehow affect domestic capitals and thereby produce dependency on foreign capital. Transfer must be on a scale large enough to account plausibly for stagnation of domestic accumulation. Internal sources theorists usually point to monopoly power as the source of surplus transfer from interior bourgeoisies and dependent societies to core bourgeoisies and societies. But although Dominion producers did face marketing monopolies, in many cases they were able to overcome them. Australian graziers, for example, easily regained control over wool auctions. Most core capital came as portfolio not direct investment, so Dominion producers were left in control of production. That leaves only capital borrowed via public and private debts as potential sources of dependency, and here it is public debt that bulks largest (see Tables 2 and 3). While foreign debt creates a reverse flow of interest and principal payments, it is not obvious that these are exchanged unequally. Dominion debtors usually bought substantial amounts of capital goods with loan money; borrowing stimulated expansion of both foreign and domestically owned sectors. To a much

35

Table 2. British-held dominion private portfolio and direct debt, 1913

	GDP (mil £)	Debt (mil £)	Service (mil £)	Service as % GDP
Argentina	310	295.2	14.6	4.7
Australia	267	186.9	8.9	3.3
Canada	530	107.5	(4.1)	(0.8)
Chile	—	40.3	2.0	—
New Zealand	65	15.0	0.8	1.2
Uruguay	(46)	21.2	1.0	2.2
USA*	(7100)	(600)	(30)	(0.4)

greater extent than the "classic" periphery, Dominion societies felt multiplier and accelerator effects from foreign investment, even if not on the scale experienced in the core.

But debt alone is an insufficient explanation for dependency. After

Table 3. British-held dominion public debt, 1913

	GDP (mil £)	Debt (mil £)	Service (mil £)	Service as % GDP
Argentina	310	184.6	8.8	2.8
Australia	267	185.9	6.8	2.5
Canada	530	469.8	17.9	3.3
Chile	—	35.8	1.8	—
New Zealand	65	80.6	2.7	4.2
Uruguay	(46)	26.1	1.3	2.8
USA*	(7100)	(25)	(1.3)	(<1)

*U.S. data for comparison only; all estimated. Numbers in parentheses are estimates.

NOTE: GDP estimates for all countries besides Australia should be regarded as at best rough estimates; but since they can be used to judge the order of magnitude of service requirements, they are adequate for the purposes here.

SOURCES TABLES 2 AND 3: All data as of 1913, except Australia, 1907. Canadian data, British holdings only; U.S. holdings equal 206.2 m£, mostly DFI (93%). I. Stone, "British Portfolio and Direct Investment in Latin America before 1914," *Journal of Economic History* 32 (1972) pp. 695, 706; L. Randall, *An Economic History of Argentina in the 20th Century* (New York: Columbia University Press, 1978); *New Zealand Official Yearbook*, 1950; *Statistics of the Dominion of New Zealand*, 1914; M. Urquhart & K. Buckley, eds., *Historical Statistics of Canada* (Toronto: Cambridge University Press, 1965), pp. 141, 169; D. Paterson, *British Direct Investment in Canada, 1890–1914* (Toronto: University of Toronto Press, 1976), p. 10; CWPP 07/08, vol. II, p. 1061; N. Butlin, *Australian Domestic Product* (Cambridge: Cambridge University Press, 1962), p. 6.

all, to make an analogy, a business that starts out debt-financed need not necessarily remain dependent. Firms routinely borrow money to finance their start-up or expansion, repay their debt, and become self-financing. The key is to invest the money in productive activities that generate sufficient funds to pay back the loan, as well as to replace depreciated capital and to buy sufficient labour power and raw material to start production anew. Clearly, if the firm used some of the money to buy expensive executive cars or other unremunerative items, it would risk remaining dependent, for it would have to dip into operating funds and profits to pay the cost of these extravagances. Just so, a country borrowing to fund the "ballet dancers, etc." that statistician Michael Mulhall entered on Egypt's balance sheet would have to dip into investment funds to service debt and so would have less left over to restart production.[11] But, with some exceptions, virtually all the borrowing done by the NICs was invested in remunerative projects, as was virtually all the borrowing done by the Dominions in the 19th century. Why did the revenue streams these projects generated not cover the cost of borrowing and depreciation? Whence came the need to continue borrowing to fund new investment? Whence dependency?[12]

The answer is that the value created by public debt was not completely captured by the state. Borrowed money creates value by purchasing or creating productive assets. For example, all the Dominion states borrowed to build or support the construction of railroads, which opened up land for profitable use. Governments also borrowed to invest directly in productive activities outside the "traditional" social overhead domain of railroads and harbors, much as current-day NIC governments do. This state investment could be quite extensive, as Noel Butlin has noted: "The Queensland government provided a very considerable part of the physical assets that were provided by private entrepreneurs in [New South Wales]: a great deal of fencing and of water conservation was financed as public works, thereby reducing private outlays on new physical assets."[13] All of these productive physical assets, such as railroads and land, generated a flow of

11. Mulhall's balance sheet quoted in A. Fishlow, "Lessons from the Past," *International Organization* 39 (Summer 1985), 400.

12. Here we are concerned with dependency, not with the obvious export dependence that underlies much of the discussion below. Clearly there are dangers in too high an export dependence. But the relatively small share that exports and imports have in Brazil's GNP—lower than for the United States or Japan—does not in any way lessen Brazil's dependency. See World Bank, *World Tables*, 1985 ed., sec. I.

13. N. Butlin, *Australian Domestic Product, Investment and Foreign Borrowing, 1861–1938/39* (Cambridge: Cambridge University Press, 1962), p. 295.

income which could be used to repay the borrowed money and perhaps even return a profit for reinvestment by the debtor. The crucial problem here was not just for the debtor to create enough value to repay the debt, but also actually to capture that value. As the primary borrower or guarantor of debt, the state had three ways to recoup its mortgaged investment in social overhead and other capital. The first two derive from the value its investments create; the third is by taxation. By opening land for productive use, the state created potential claims to surplus—capital—through the absolute and differential rents that could accrue to that "new" land. Land only has value insofar as something can be produced on it, and until land had access to transportation it was worthless. Thus railroads constitute a primary example of this process: by building railroads the state made it possible for "new" land to return a stream of income, which could be capitalized via mortgages. The state could capture the increment to the land values that its rail system created by selling that land. Second, and more obviously, the railways themselves generated a stream of revenue through freight charges.

Dependency arose when the state proved unable to capture the full amount of the value its debt-financed investments created, that is, when political factors made ostensibly remunerative ventures less remunerative. This occurred in two ways. Either the state did not or could not charge the full, real cost of freight on its railways, or the state lost the value of the land that railways made productive.

In all of the Dominions the state either directly built and ran the railroads, or guaranteed a minimum profit for foreign owned railroad firms; the railroads generally were able to pay operating costs out of their charges for transport. But they were not able to pay a return on the capital invested in them that equaled the "cost" of that capital; that is, their revenues did not cover debt service in addition to operating expenses. The major users of the rails, primary product exporters producing on land that the railways opened up, benefited from what in effect were subsidized freight rates. The subsidy there was the difference between actual freight rates and the real cost of transport, including debt service.

The more significant loss came when Dominion states sold, gave or let land be taken away beneath its new market value, as measured by the stream of income it generated. Dominion states' control over land varied from the relatively strong control exerted in New Zealand and Australia (a result of the metropolitan state's strength) to the virtual absence of control in Uruguay (a result of the absence of any state after independence). There are no abstract reasons why Dominion

states should not have been able to recoup the full cost of their investments in railways through either land sales or freight charges. But
there are a myriad of practical reasons, which Michael Cannon cap-
tures nicely: "Much of the money being borrowed by the State [for
railroads] was finally flowing into the pockets of the land profiteers,
many of them actually being members of the governments which
were floating the huge loans."[14] Insiders used advance knowledge to
buy up land from the state in advance of railroads, which they then
resold at now-inflated values to the state for right-of-way, or sold to
other pastoral producers. Consequently the state not only did not
capture the new increment to the land value, but actually paid for that
increment in many cases. Most of these states also were thoroughly
penetrated by the very producers who used the railroads, making
imposition of full-cost freight rates difficult. The Dominion that generated the most revenue through land sales—New South Wales—still
barely broke even when land revenues were lumped in with railroad
receipts.[15] The difference between pre- and post-railroad land values
constituted a kind of "promoters' profit" (Rudolf Hilferding's term)
that helped to create various financial bourgeoisies, domestic and
foreign, in the Dominions.[16] It was they, rather than the state, who
captured the value public debt created, and the state proved unable to
recapture this value so as to pay off the public debt without resorting
to the third, dependency creating method.

As a consequence of these losses, all of the Dominion states resorted
to taxation, the third way of recouping the cost of their investment in
social overhead capital.[17] Unlike the others, this method did not recapture part of the value that railroads and other investments created; instead it redistributed revenue within society as a whole. This
redistribution created dependency, because it fell unevenly. In the
nineteenth century, customs and excise taxes were the major revenue
sources for the Dominions. For example, in New Zealand in 1901,
where both land and income taxes existed, customs still provided 74
percent of tax revenue, and 40 percent of all government receipts

14. M. Cannon, *Land Boomers* (Melbourne: Melbourne University Press, 1966), p. 29.
15. E. Boehm, *Prosperity and Depression in Australia 1887–1897* (Oxford: Oxford University Press, 1971), pp. 164, 175.
16. Hilferding's notion of promoters' profit is, I believe, what lies at the heart of the best piece of work on this subject: A. Wells, "A Marxist Reappraisal of Australian Cap-
italism: The Rise of Anglo-Australian Finance Capital, 1860–1890" (Ph.D. dissertation, Australian National University, 1986). Unfortunately I have not been able to obtain a complete copy and so rely on conversations with the author.
17. In Argentina the presence of paper money meant that at times inflation func-
tioned as a "hidden" tax, replacing overt taxes.

39

(including direct charges for rail use, telegraph and the like). Most revenue came from excise or customs taxes on spirits, tobacco, and textiles, which in New Zealand provided 77 percent of customs receipts.[18] Direct taxes typically came later, for they were anathema to the groups that had a firm grip on political power when the basic decisions on railroad finance were made.

We can divide society into two groups to determine the effects of this taxation: those who directly benefited from the subsidization of export activity ("exporters") and those who benefitted either indirectly or not at all ("domestic producers").[19] Where taxes funded debt service, two factors determine whether the domestic group's taxes subsidized export activity: the relative labour-intensity of the export and domestic sectors, and their relative use of the railroads. (Table 4 summarizes the results of the following analysis.) Because taxes functioned as consumption taxes on workers, both sectors would feel the tax burden through rising wage levels as workers struggled to maintain rough parity in real wages after taxes. The sector with a lower ratio of labour to value added would bear a disproportionately heavier tax burden relative to the amount of surplus it created. In general, capital intensity is a fair measure of this ratio, so if domestic sectors were more labour-intensive than export sectors they would bear a disproportionately high share of taxes. Similarly, a sector that used the rails less than the average use per unit output for both sectors would also bear a disproportionately heavy share of the taxation that bridged the deficit between receipts and debt service. Historically, the domestic sector was more labour-intense and also used the rails less than the export sector; it thus provided a large subsidy to exporters.

Neither factor that creates subsidy is accidental. Exporters faced world market competition and so had to invest to stay competitive. Foreign-owned exporters had easier and preferential access to capital, and so could capitalize to a larger degree than domestic producers. In contrast, domestic producers had small and sheltered markets, and thus had no incentive to capitalize. Dominion domestic sectors were thus typically more labour-intensive than export sectors,

18. M. Lloyd-Pritchard, *Economic History of New Zealand to 1939* (Auckland: Collin, 1970), p. 212–213; Boehm, *Prosperity and Depression in Australia*, p. 192. See N. Butlin, A. Barnard, and J. Pincus, *Government and Capitalism* (Sydney: Unwin & Allen, 1982), p. 160, for a qualitative assessment "that wage earners . . . contributed the major part of the funds" for Australian taxes.

19. However, in the abstract, it matters not at all that the sector exporting is the subsidized one. It could as well be a sector producing goods for the domestic market. However, because the export sector in the nineteenth century Dominions was subsidized, we will use that for example.

Table 4. Railroad use as subsidy to exporters

	Railroad use by domestic capital EQUALS use by Export capital	Railroad use by domestic capital LOWER than export capital use
Equal labour intensity	No or small subsidy to exporters	Medium subsidy
Domestic production more labour-intense	Medium subsidy	Large subsidy

with a hierarchy of labour-intensity from domestic producers, to domestically-owned exporters, and down to foreign-owned exporters. Domestic producers also used the rails less, for their markets by and large were concentrated in the large entrepot cities on the coast; in the nineteenth century the Dominions were among the most urbanized societies in the whole world. Wagon transport could efficiently distribute goods in cities.

This subsidization of export activity by other, primarily domestically oriented sectors, is what created and maintained Dominion dependency. Value was drained via the tax system from other sectors to subsidize the expansion of export, primarily by foreign-owned sectors; this drain weakened the ability of the society to continue funding investment and growth out of its own resources. Subsidy eventually reduced the amount of locally generated capital available for investment, which forced reliance on continued overseas investment to continue growth. Subsidy thus perpetuated dependency on foreign loans. We must look at the specific effects of subsidy to see why.

ECONOMIC EFFECTS OF SUBSIDY AND DEPENDENCY

Subsidy through freight rate underpricing encouraged export activity, but undermined the long-term profitability of exporting in two ways, by encouraging overinvestment and overproduction. The consequence was a private debt crisis as mortgages became illiquid. Subsidy increased the short-term profits accruing to exporters by significantly reducing their operating expenses. Butlin estimated transport charges at between 8 percent and 12 percent of total wool proceeds for the Australian sheep stations for which data are available.[20] Sub-

20. Butlin, *Australian Domestic Product*, pp. 69–74. Comparing Butlin's calculation of total rail transport charges for the pastoral sector with the (not necessarily equivalent) pastoral sector output recorded by T. A. Coghlan, *A Statistical Account of the Seven*

sidies led to overinvestment, by concealing the real rate of return on export activity. More capital was invested in export activity than the flow of profit could sustain if subsidies were removed. Subsidies also encouraged overproduction, thence declining prices, and thus a declining rate of return. In turn, this triggered more overproduction as exporters tried to spread their fixed costs, mostly investments in land, stock and improvements, as broadly as possible. But as everyone, including producers in other Dominions facing the same dilemma, increased production world market prices declined even further as producers glutted their market. Such a fall in prices threatened the capital invested in export activity with destruction. Once liquid capital (money) is invested in a productive asset the value of that capital is determined by the stream of income the asset can produce. If the price of the goods that asset produces falls, and the profit rate for those goods falls, then the value of the capital invested must fall as well. Most of the capital invested in Dominion export activity was secured by mortgages on land. But as the prices exporters received for wool and meat fell, in turn land values fell, and loans to exporters became insecure and illiquid, trapping financiers' investments. In the abstract, this process should drive capital out of the sector; but practically, "capital" as liquid money capital could not leave because the market for land had disappeared. Not all the capital backed by land could be made liquid again at the new, lower level of land prices. Refinance of extant debt became equally impossible, for the land no longer secured even the initial investment.

At the same time that subsidy encouraged overinvestment in export activity, it had paradoxical effects on domestic sectors. Rapid growth in the export sectors created demand for domestic sector producer and consumer goods, creating interior bourgeoisies in manufacturing in the Dominions. Initially the domestic sector expanded even though it was losing surplus via the tax system to the export sector. This induced growth explains why interior bourgeoisies would initially acquiesce in the entire system. But the domestic sector grew more slowly than the export sector because part of the surplus it generated was siphoned off to the export sector and so made unavailable for reinvestment. As the export sector grew faster than the domestic sector, and as subsidies grew in proportion to the expanding export sector, eventually a point was reached where the drain of subsidy from the

---

Colonies of Australasia (Sydney: W. A. Gullick, 1898), gives a lower estimate of 5–6 percent as the share of rail transport costs for *all* pastoral production, including meat, hides, tallow, etc., along with wool.

domestic sector was larger than the growth induced by export sector demand. Whether this value is drawn from the domestic sector's share of surplus, or from workers, by driving down living standards, the domestic sector suffers.

Simultaneously the state's ability to prop up the system through renewed borrowing is undercut by the declining profitability of both sectors, which reduces the state's ability to finance subsidies through increased taxation. Precisely when the state needs to maintain or increase subsidies, it finds it cannot. Exporters faced with declining profits go bankrupt, reducing export revenue, growth, and taxes. Declining or stagnant tax and export revenues hurt the state's ability to refinance. For the state to convince foreign lenders of its creditworthiness, it must be able to point to revenue sources, that is, production that will generate enough revenue to pay back the debt. But if those sources clearly are not growing, or are contracting, the state cannot borrow; if the state cannot borrow, the export sectors' long run growth prospects are hampered, because they depend on continued provision of subsidized "public goods." In a vicious cycle, the state's declining creditworthiness undermines the basis for private prosperity, and declining private prosperity decreases the tax base.

Eventually a crisis is born of the contradiction between the export sector's need for subsidy and the domestic sector's increasing inability to supply it through taxes: to maintain the bloated export sector at its current rate of profitability requires destruction of domestic sectors as their ability to reinvest drops below the level needed even to replace depreciated equipment; but if subsidies are decreased or eliminated then the value of all of the capital invested in the export sector decreases because its rate of profit decreases. Things rarely go so far as to force entire domestic or export sectors, or the state, into bankruptcy, for political conflicts intervene. For example, in Australia in the late 1880s declining prices for wool led to destruction of pastoral entrepreneurs by their creditors. But the process was accelerated when Argentina's 1890 default (discussed in Chapter 6) caused London to choke off new overseas loans to all of the Dominions.

POLITICAL CONFLICTS IN THE DOMINIONS

The underlying economic cause of the crisis suggests its own solution, because the problem is that extant forms of production do not generate enough surplus to maintain all the capital invested in public and private debt at their original values. If some way of increasing

43

productivity could be found, then all those capitals could be saved because the rate of profit could support prior investments at their original values. Some authors, for example Senghaas, suggest that such intensification of production was purely a matter of labour pressures to raise wages and that producers were free to make a transition to more intensive production if they so desired. But since a transition requires renewed investment, the majority of producers were unable to make a transition on their own to new, more profitable markets for different goods. Both public and private creditors, already facing the loss of their outstanding loans, were unwilling to make new investments. For example, while the technologies required for export of refrigerated dairy and meat products for UK markets were available in the 1880s, their widespread adoption in Australia and New Zealand had to await political solutions that made new financing possible and freed the illiquid capital locked up in devalued land; in Argentina, they awaited a political restoration of public credit.[21] In principle this political solution can be positive or zero-sum for the different capitals threatened with destruction, because each will try to shift the burden of repaying public debt or of revaluing land onto other capitals and groups.

The Dominions thus typically find themselves in a three-way conflict. Public debt, private "debt" in the form of investments in export activity, and labour's standard of living are all threatened when domestic sectors no longer can subsidize export activity. The owners of public and of private debt, and labour and the domestic sectors, all struggle to make the others lose their investment or wage level. The unity among capitals that underwrote the whole system of public debt–subsidized expansion disintegrates as each group of capitals tries to save its own investment. Holders of public debt advocate retrenchment (i.e., decreased subsidies) so that the fisc can meet service payments. Exporters and their creditors advocate increased taxes on other sectors so that they can continue at their expected "historic" rate of profit, or they propose state-subsidized buyouts of export land so as to free the capital frozen in devalued mortgages. The increased insecurity of claims to surplus based on mortgages secured by land make those mortgages an acute political issue. Political issues of distributing the "costs" of debt are thus not only over costs as *flows*, the immediate question of who pays this year's interest, but also, more

21. S. Hanson, *Argentine Meat in the British Market* (Stanford: Stanford University Press, 1938), chap. 2 and 3, provides an excellent summary of technological developments.

important, over whose claims to surplus will, in the absence of state intervention, be devalued, and thus who will be unable to appropriate surplus in the future. These issues had elements of "high" politics, as foreign haute financiers attempted to prevent the state from defaulting or stopping debt service, and low politics, in urban struggles over housing rents and rural struggles over rent, access to land, and land tenures.

Debt politics also contributed to labour unrest. Private capitals had an interest in pushing down wages as their profit margins narrowed. Domestic sectors had to make up the increment appropriated by taxes; export sectors had to increase production and productivity to maintain profit levels in a glutted market. Additional pressures arose where the state owned productive enterprises directly, as with Australian and New Zealand state railroads. Ownership of enterprises would impel a state to increase the productivity of its own labour force to make debt service easier. The more surplus that could be squeezed from its own enterprises, the less the state need fund debt out of taxes. Depending on who controlled the state, state enterprises were models for enlightened or for repressive means of exploitation. All these pressures on labour to be more productive provoked resistance from labour, inducing organizing attempts and strikes. These in turn aggravated investor fears for the viability of profitable production, leading investors to shy away from unstable polities, thus aggravating the financing crunch. Labour strife also made it more difficult for capitalists to maintain a united front. Within export capitals, foreign capitals typically were stronger, larger, and more capital-intense operations. They thus had the opportunity and incentive to deal separately with labour, offering higher wages for labour peace in order to continue production and meet their mortgages. This put pressure on their domestically owned counterparts.

To sum, dependency in the Dominions created interwoven political and economic conflicts revolving around public debt, private debt (in the form of investments in export assets), and labour conflict. The failure to make foreign debt–financed enterprises fully pay their way created an unstable situation in which one sector underwrote another sector's rapid growth in an unsustainable way. The result was a crisis in which some of the capital sunk into public and private debt had to be destroyed to make the rest viable once more. Public debt was threatened, for with land values down, no alternate source of revenue to taxation existed, and as economic activity slowed, tax receipts fell too. Export, commercial and financial capitals' claims to surplus from assets in properties rapidly became illiquid. Businesses attempted to preserve their claims from market devalorization, provoking zero-sum battles over taxation and state economic policy. All businesses attempted to protect their capital by pressure on wages. High levels of conflict over these claims were inherent in the system, but specific outcomes were not. Outcomes depended on the relative power of groups to organize themselves into classes to capture the state. In this struggle the state's influence on class formation and the economy through publicly controlled investment is crucial; but the presence of severe capital-labour conflicts, the state's own debt problem, and destruction of domestic capitalist class fractions all limit the state's autonomy and power. The first reduced the state's legitimacy, the second limited the resources available to the state, and the last made it difficult to construct a stable social base. The next Chapters detail four specific crises and their outcomes.

PART TWO

CASES

Introduction

Before turning to the individual cases it is worth examining the global context in which the nineteenth-century Dominions and to-day's NICs find themselves, for both share similar world-historical contexts. Both achieved rapid growth as much because of rapidly expanding markets for the specific types of products they produced as because of their own domestic political economies. Both benefited from the departure of capital from the core in search of places to create claims to surplus.

Divergence in the relative productivity of agriculture and of manufacturing in the nineteenth century both created markets for Dominion produce and motivated capital to invest there.[1] Rapidly increasing manufacturing productivity outstripped core agriculture's ability to provide food for the growing industrial proletariat as well as the raw materials worked up into virtually all manufactured goods of the time. Textiles, the premier product of the early and much of the late nineteenth century, demanded wool, cotton, flax, and fur. Looms to make the textiles demanded wood, leather, and tallow; shipping, timber, pitch, hemp. England's population quadrupled 1800–1914, and although wages may not have increased much in the first half of the nineteenth century, they doubled in the second half.[2] But the hold of the landed classes on most European land through entail inhibited productivity-increasing investment in agriculture. The price of agricultural goods was thus kept high, and surplus was diverted to landholders as absolute rent. Consequently, as Samir Amin wrote, "the [industrial] bourgeoisie attack[ed] private landownership by

1. Cf. K. Marx, *Capital* (New York: International, 1967), Vol. III, Section 6.
2. B. Mitchell, *Abstract of British Historical Statistics* (Cambridge: Cambridge University Press, 1962), pp. 6, 343–344.

opening up to agricultural production new lands where there [were] no landlords, that is, by bringing into competition with the products of agriculture dominated by landownership the products of agriculture where access to the natural conditions of production [was] free, unhindered by monopoly landownership."[3]

Simply put, entrepreneurs found they could make money producing industrial raw materials and food outside western Europe, so they brought or borrowed capital to create highly profitable monocultures producing the materials that manufacturers demanded. Investment started with cotton production in the American south, and accelerated after repeal of the Corn Laws and Navigation Acts. Numerous agencies invested in a wide range of products and a wide range of temperate locales, providing goods for the expanding British market and competition for landlord-dominated agriculture. By 1913 the British held between £3.75 and £4.08 billion in publicly listed overseas securities, roughly 4.5 times what they had held in 1870; this expansion caused the ratio of British domestic to overseas holdings to drop from 1.7 in 1870 to only 1.1 in 1913.[4] Investment went to the American South and old Northwest, Russia, Ireland, Central Europe, and India, but it was oriented predominantly towards the Dominions. Australasia, Canada, South Africa, Argentina, Uruguay, and Chile received at least 36 percent of British overseas investment. Investment in Dominion government issues, railways, and temperate pastoral and agricultural production, respectively, absorbed 17.9 percent, 8.1 percent, and 6.5 percent of *total* British overseas investment.[5]

Investment enabled production of vast quantities of food and raw materials; technological innovations expanded both the range of items produced and location of production. Consequently world trade expanded by over 50 percent per decade 1835–1914. By 1900, per capita meat consumption in Great Britain was the highest in Europe, and 20 percent higher than 20 years previous. Thirty-seven percent of the beef and 47 percent of mutton consumed was im-

3. S. Amin, *Unequal Development* (New York: Monthly Review, 1976), p. 65.
4. See M. Simon, "The Pattern of British Portfolio Investment," 40; and B. Thomas, "International Capital Movements to 1913," p. 14, both in J. Adler, ed., *Capital Movements and Economic Development* (New York: St. Martin's Press, 1967); M. Edelstein, *Overseas Investment in the Age of High Imperialism* (New York: Columbia University Press, 1982), p. 48.
5. Thomas, "International Capital Movements to 1913," pp. 13–14. Other calculations put the Dominion share as high as 46.2 percent of total investment. Including investment in U.S. railroads (because they facilitated movement of grain to export markets) would increase the "dominion" share to well over half of British investment.

Table 5. Productivity growth in Britain, 1859–1914

Year	Per capita industrial production, price constant	Real wages	Wages relative to production
1859–68	51	63	124
1869–79	66	74	111
1880–86	83	80	96
1887–95	96	91	95
1896–1903	105	99	94
1904–08	104	95	91
1909–14	106	93	88

NOTE: All numbers are indices; 1900 = 100.
SOURCE: J. Kuczynski, *A Short History of Labour Conditions under Industrial Capitalism in Great Britain and the Empire* (New York: Harper & Row, 1972), p. 81.

ported, as was 4.8 million metric tonnes of wheat per annum. Virtually all imported meat and half of imported wheat came from the dominions. Britain imported 740 million tons of wool, with 80 percent coming from the Dominions, of which fully half was from Australia.[6] Investment bought two generations of rising British productivity and wages, and thus social peace (see Table 5).

Though all the locations to which investment went benefited equally from British demand, different social conditions made investments in the Dominions more likely to prosper than elsewhere. The Dominions had only sparse nomadic populations, whereas Ireland, Russia, India, and Central Europe all had large peasantries and landlords. The absence of these two social classes in the Dominions allowed relatively faster accumulation by capitals investing there, and, through an evolutionary, market-driven process, facilitated a shift in the locale of raw material production from the core to the Dominions. Investments in the Dominions returned more profit to their owners than those in the tropics, allowing higher rates of reinvestment and drawing fresh capital both from the core and from other temperate areas with lower rates of return.[7] The absence of monopoly land rents elsewhere accruing to the nobility and the presence of superprofits

6. P. Katzenstein, "International Interdependence: Long-term Trends and Recent Changes," *International Organization* 29 (Autumn 1975), 1024; D. C. M. Platt, *Latin America and British Trade* (London: Adam and Charles Block, 1972), pp. 260–261, 264, 272–273.
7. Direct political control in the Dominions surely also facilitated a more rapid expansion there than in Eastern Europe. But as the cases of India and Argentina show, such control was neither a guarantee nor a prerequisite of investment. Contingent events, like the "cotton famine" caused by the American Civil War, also affected the rate of investment.

accruing to previously uncultivated and therefore superfertile land made it more than profitable for capitals to bear the cost of opening new land, transporting labour to, and administration in the Dominions.[8] Furthermore, as sea transport is always the cheapest form of long-distance bulk transport, European agricultures would gain little from investment in transportation innovations unless they were in close proximity to urban areas.[9] Core agricultural areas needed rails for overland bulk transport, just as Dominion areas did, and the higher cost of right of way in the core was not fully offset by the fact that much smaller rail systems were needed there.

Simultaneously the absence of a settled population in the Dominions diminished the possibilities for resistance to a shift to capitalist monoculture agriculture. Except for Maoris and Araucanians (in Chile), both of which were instead confined on a fraction of their former territory, the nomadic societies of the Dominions were swept away by European guns and disease. In the European periphery, in contrast, settled peasant populations were better able to resist shifts. The Celtic fringe of Britain and Ireland provide the best examples of resistance in the nineteenth century. The Irish "land war" of the 1870s and 1880s, a response to displacement of peasants by cattle, intensified from antilandlord terror into a low-level anticolonial guerrilla war in 1916 and 1919–1922. Foreign agricultural investments in Turkey came to grief because peasant landownership was so secure that it was hard to get peasants to work for any wages, least of all low wages.[10] Because investments in the Dominions were more likely to

8. These are technically called absolute rent and differential rent I, respectively. See D. Bedggood, *Rich and Poor in New Zealand* (Sydney: Unwin & Allen, 1980); and J. Macrae, and D. Bedggood, "Development of Capitalism in New Zealand," *Red Papers on New Zealand* no. 3 (Summer 1978/9), for more extensive analyses of the significance of these Dominion advantages. "Since ground rent is very low or purely nominal, owing to the large amount of free land resulting either from the bounty of nature or from the forcible expropriation of the native population, costs of production are low." R. Hilferding, *Finance Capital* (London: Routledge & Kegan Paul, 1985), p. 316. The lease rents for Crown lands in Australasia are an example of "nominal" rents.

9. Superprofits accruing from transportation advantages are technically called differential rent II. Local areas did move to higher value added and higher quality products, such as dairy and vegetables, as production of their former staples migrated to more distant areas. Ireland, which shifted from wool, to grain, to meat, to dairy, is perhaps the clearest example. Students of the German economist von Thunen would not find this very surprising; see J. R. Peet, "Spatial Expansion of Commercial Agriculture in the 19th Century," *Economic Geography* 45 (October 1969), for an analysis following von Thunen.

10. C. Keyder, "Small Peasant Ownership in Turkey," *Review* 7 (Summer 1983), 66– The Ottoman state had for centuries protected peasant ownership rights to prevent the emergence of a landed aristocracy in opposition to the central state.

prosper than those made elsewhere, in areas with peasants and land-lords they either drove competing capitals out of the market or limited their growth. The rise of Australian (or New Zealand, or Argentine) wool paralleled the decline of Silesian (or Spanish, or Scottish) wool; North American and Australian wheat drove European grain producers to seek protection. Protection and the social tension arising from increasing uncompetitiveness only increased the Dominions' advantage, attracting even more capital.

Investment in the NICs and other less developed countries runs generally parallel to the process of transfer of agricultural activity to the Dominions, with the NICs inheriting the Dominions' role. In the late twentieth century the difficulties in the core areas that paralleled the nineteenth century's land shortage was a relative shortage of labour, and not the political power of landlords but the political power of organized workers in the core. Confronted with labour's power after the climactic strikes of 1967–1970, core businesses made concerted attacks on wages, work conditions, and unions.[11] The limiting condition on expansion in the core seemed to be wages and the political and economic power of labour. Capital thus went in search of politically and economically weaker labour, which it found in the NICs, in other, less successful, LDCs, and in labour reserve areas at home. Continuation of core fordist mass markets even as fordism collapsed provided places for the NICs to sell low-cost manufactures, or even mandated them, because the breakup of fordist industry in the core led to wage stagnation. Only the NICs' low wage rates and thus low production costs made possible continued mass consumption elsewhere of the goods they produced.

Meanwhile the displacement of standardized manufacturing processes to low wage areas created a market in which all LDCs could participate to some degree, just as all agricultural areas participated in supplying Britain and Europe during the nineteenth century.[12] By

11. The dating runs roughly from the Ford strike (1967) through the French May (1968) and Italian "Hot Autumn" (of 1969) to Lordstown (1970).

12. Here the logic driving displacement is not the increased rents nearer urban areas, the factor von Thunen identifies. In the twentieth century the logic driving the displacement of manufacturing from core to periphery is not increased rents nearer urban areas, the factor von Thunen identifies as crucial in the location of agricultural production. Instead, the standardization and simplification of industrial production as well as the ability of multinational companies to capture oligopolistic rents both enable and induce displacement. Historical, political, and cultural forces of course modified investment patterns: American textile producers could move south within their own country or could import illegal aliens to find a pool of low wage labour, and German firms could "bring the south north" by importing legal guestworkers, but Japanese

encouraging direct foreign investment by multinational corporations or by borrowing Eurofunds for on-lending to domestic firms, LDC states could, with varying degrees of success, build up local industry. As with the Dominions, those LDCs with better control over their labour forces and better state direction created competitive forces that drove core producers out of their original markets and hindered the efforts of other LDCs producing for similar markets. These more successful LDCs became the NICs. As the Dominions dominated world markets for temperate agricultural products, so too the NICs dominate world markets for standardized low-cost manufactures, at times providing over half of LDC exports of manufactures. Just as rapidly expanding demand for agricultural goods absorbed increased Dominion production in the 1800s, so 70 percent increases in world trade per decade helped absorb increased NIC exports.[13]

firms, with no recourse to a south, and with xenophobic proscriptions against immigration, had to go overseas.

13. Katzenstein, "International Interdependence," p. 1029.

CHAPTER THREE

Australian Federation

"It's a quare, quare country, anyhow," sadly soliloquized [Rory] the exile of Erin, after he had thought the matter over. "Wondhers 'll niver quit saisin'. At home, iv a body hed twenty English acres o' good lay lan', at a raisonable rent—let alone a graat farrum like thon—he need n't do a han's turn the year roun', beyant givin' ordhers; an' he would hev lavin's iv iverything, an' a brave shoot o' clo'es till his back, an' mebbe a gool' watch, furbye money in his pocket. Bates all! Bates all!".

But the anomalous and baffling nature of Australian conditions made Rory all the more reluctant to tear himself away from his present asylum—though its shelter seemed to resemble the shadow of a great deficit in an insolvent land.

Joseph Furphy, *Such Is Life*.

Australian history after 1890 seems to have three parts: 1890 to 1900 saw a long but ultimately successful effort to federate the six Australian colonies. The years 1900–1914 saw two things: first, the rise of a national Labor Party and its efforts to institutionalize and enlarge a system of juridicized collective bargaining called Conciliation and Arbitration. Then, unlike the depressed 1890s, the early 1900s saw rapid economic growth with considerable domestic expansion, including, ultimately, establishment of an iron industry. Though there are many and diverse explanations for these events, the next two chapters show how the issues of public and private debt and labour control lay at the heart of events. All of the bargaining positions of Australian class fractions then struggling for domination reflect a preoccupation with the three dominion issues. These struggles eventuated in greater development and lessened dependency for Australia compared with the other dominions, largely because federation created a political space in which an interior bourgeoisie in manufacturing could assert itself. Chapter 3 concerns the creation of dependency in Australia and thence the politics of Australian Federation as a response to the emergence of dual debt crises. Chapter 4 details the efforts of the interior bourgeoisie in manufacturing to transform itself into a national bourgeoisie in the context of the new Federal state and complex tripartisan politics.

FEDERATION IN THE CONTEXT OF AUSTRALIAN HISTORY

Most explanations of the Federation movement of the 1890s treat it as an organic outgrowth of previous efforts at federation, as a natural outcome of a maturing political system, or as the natural solution to the Colonies' difficulties. But Federation ultimately was a decade-long process whose success rested as much on the failure of other proposals as on its own merits. Enmity among the colonies was as strong as the "crimson thread of kinship running through [them] all," and the distances to be surmounted greater than any other extant federal or confederated system.[1] The real question is not "Why Federation?" but "Why a political solution?" and "Why, among all possible political solutions, amalgamation?" Why did Federation seem an appropriate solution to enough groups that it could be instituted as a new political regime, outlasting other proposed and attempted solutions to Australian problems?

The next section of this chapter will answer the question "Why

1. There were five efforts at federation before 1890: 1870, November 1880, January 1881, December 1883, and 1885. Examples of traditional approaches to Federation history are Manning Clark, *A History of Australia*, 5 vols. (Victoria: Wilke & Co., 1981); and W. Hancock, *Australia* (Brisbane: Jacaranda Press, 1964). Another is the Parker-Blainey debate of the 1950s, which sought to explain Federation's "success" at the polls by looking at voters' own short-run economic benefits. See G. Blainey, "The Role of Economic Interests in Australian Federation," *Historical Studies, Australia and New Zealand* (hereafter HSANZ) 4 (November 1950); R. Parker, "Australian Federation: The Influence of Economic Interests and Political Pressures," HSANZ 4 (November 1949) and "Some Comments on 'The Role of Economic Interests in Australian Federation'," HSANZ 4 (November 1950). See also A. Martin, ed., *Essays in Australian Federation* (Melbourne: Melbourne University Press, 1969). My interpretation is similar to that of B. Fitzpatrick, *The British Empire in Australia 1834–1939* (Melbourne: Macmillan, 1949, rep. ed. 1969) in that I also point to labour control, debt, and depression as the motivations for political change. Where I differ is in the weighting of these issues and in the exposition of the mechanisms translating these motives into actions, in both following the theoretical scheme laid out above. Fitzpatrick also tended to assume a unified capitalist class dominated by foreign financial capital, which is not quite accurate. *Tocsin*, May 12, 1898, mocked the "crimson threads" as "golden chains."

politics?" by showing how British investment created dependency and dual debt crises in Australia. Markets having created the Colonies' problems, markets could not solve them. The two sections following discuss how debt and labour control issues intertwined with the Federation movement. Ultimately debt was the major impetus behind Federation. Colony-level efforts to resolve the crises deserve more coverage than they can here be afforded; Federation's appeal waxed because colony level solutions proved unsatisfactory and tardy to the groups affected by the crises.[2] The final section of this chapter details the influence of the crises on specific features of the draft constitution.

DEPENDENCY: THREE CRISES IN AUSTRALIA

Strategic concerns, not economic, created Australasia, as well as the other Dominions. Rebellion in America forced Britain to turn to Botany Bay as a dumping ground for convicts in 1788. Though the colony exported whale and seal products, most economic activity on the mainland centered on production of subsistence goods, under a regime of forced labour replenished by periodic shipments of transportees from industrializing England.[3]

The wool economy began in 1810, when the crossbred merino was firmly established. But wool production expanded slowly, hampered on the one hand by laggard demand, and on the other by the limited availability of capital and labour. Woolen and worsted manufacture were not mechanized in Britain until the 1830s, a period of relative economic stagnation. Financially the industry depended on merchant entrepreneurs in Sydney, who advanced short-term credit against extant, or, less often, future wool production. But crop sizes limited credit, and credit costs rose when the City tightened money supplies after Mississippi's default in 1838. Convicts proved intractable workers whose supply depended more on English law than Australian demand. Australian pastoralists and merchants turned to politics to remove the constraints of expensive capital and an inelastic coerced-

---

2. See J. Rickard, *Class and Politics: NSW, Victoria and the Early Commonwealth—1890–1910* (Canberra: Australian National University Press, 1976), and Fitzpatrick, *British Empire in Australia,* for overviews of efforts at Colony level political and economic solutions.

3. See D. Denoon, *Settler Capitalism* (Oxford: Clarendon Press, 1983), chap. 1, for comparison of the Dominions. The following paragraph draws from P. McMichael, *Settlers and the Agrarian Question* (Cambridge: Cambridge University Press, 1984).

labour supply. England terminated convict transportation and assignment, and assented to a series of laws enabling mortgages to be written on pastoral freehold and leases. The former made Australia more attractive to immigrants while rising wages spurred technical innovation. Mortgages gave graziers access to greater masses of capital for longer time periods, freeing them from some of the constraints imposed by short-tern credit.[4] Corn Law Repeal removed the final check on expanded wool production. British demand created a large class of colonial capitalists who pushed wool production farther and farther inland. But in 1851, gold strikes in Victoria introduced a factor that caused Victorian and then Australian history to diverge slightly from that of the other dominions.

Gold had three effects, most of which flowed from Victoria's roughly tenfold population increase between 1851 and 1857. First, it accelerated the emergence of an interior bourgeoisie in manufacturing. Second, it indirectly accelerated the destruction of the Australian pastoral interior bourgeoisie. Third, it permitted significant increases in public and private debt. Alluvial gold mining, which could be done by individuals or small groups, attracted 62,428 miners to Victoria and generated £125 million in specie in a short time. Much of the money stayed in Victoria, flowing to Victorian graziers and farmers as miners bought meat. Meat sales allowed graziers to substitute capital for labour, a necessity as many workers went prospecting. Victoria's pastoral industry thus diversified much earlier than that of NSW, which primarily continued to export wool. In six years, to 1857, the number of farmers septupled, and by 1866 nearly 14 percent of freehold Victorian land was plowed, compared with just 3 percent in New South Wales. Graziers' social weight decreased as pastoral employment fell from 66 percent of employment to about 10 percent, while mine employment increased from nil to 63 percent during this six-year period.[5]

---

4. I use "squatters," "pastoralists," and "graziers" interchangeably to indicate direct producers of wool and, later, of mutton. Expansion inland ran mostly along natural waterways; see N. G. Butlin, *Investment in Australian Economic Development, 1861–1900* (Cambridge: Cambridge University Press, 1964), pp. 63–65.

5. E. Shann, *An Economic History of Australia* (Cambridge: Cambridge University Press, 1930), p. 184; G. Wood, *Borrowing and Business in Australia: A Study of the Correlation Between Imports of Capital and Changes in National Prosperity* (London: Oxford University Press, 1930), pp. 39–40. See I. McLean, "Rural Outputs, Inputs and Mechanization in Victoria, 1870–1910" (Ph.D. thesis, Australian National University, 1971), p. 65 and *passim*, for data on Victorian diversification; S. Roberts, *History of Australian Land Settlement* (Melbourne: Macmillan, 1924), p. 216, on employment. Victoria's lead continued, and by 1892 it still possessed three times as many cultivated acres as NSW, with approximately the same population.

As alluvial mining petered out, unemployed miners became a major political problem, for one third of Australian adult males were miners. The problem was nowhere more acute than Victoria.[6] Some miners were absorbed back into the pastoral sector to do improvements, but the short-lived Ballarat (Victoria) Rebellion revealed the potential volatility of the rest. Largely for fiscal reasons, the Victorian government laid on slightly protectionist tariffs that had the effect of absorbing ex-miners by engendering a vast number of micro-enterprises producing for the domestic market.[7] These enterprises in turn demanded more state intervention, so the Victorian government ordered state railways to buy local goods. Resulting contracts for locomotives created engineering and metallurgical firms. Despite a later start and a smaller population, manufacturing output in Victoria soon exceeded neighboring New South Wales. Led by Victoria, manufacturing's share of Australian GDP jumped from an average of 5.3 percent in 1861–65 to 11.0 percent in 1875–77; by 1883 over 100 locomotives had been built in Victoria.[8] Victoria's more domestically-oriented and diversified economy thus became the cradle for Australia's manufacturing interior bourgeoisie, and Victorian-controlled capital moved along with British capital to exploit other areas of Australia.[9] Subsequently Victoria's lead increased because of its control of the Broken Hill silver and lead mining complex in New South Wales, which yielded up £17.6 million in dividends from 1883 to 1914. The period 1861–1877 saw a mostly locally-financed round of expansion with rapid growth in overall productivity—3.1 percent per annum increase in GDP per worker.[10] The gold rush thus pushed Victorian development along lines differing from the other, more export-oriented colonies.

Gold also drew British investment in two related ways. First, customs on the imported consumer goods gold paid for made colonial governments very liquid, permitting rapid growth in public debt.

6. Butlin, *Investment*, p. 39.

7. Revenue needs were in most circumstances "the prime, if not the only, reason for tariff increases." G. Patterson, *The Tariff in the Australian Colonies, 1856–1900* (Melbourne: F. W. Cheshire, 1968), pp. 164–165.

8. On state intervention, see T. Parsons, "Government Contracts and Colonial Manufacture," *Australian Journal of Politics and History* (hereafter AJPH) 26 (August 1980), *passim*; Butlin, *Investment*, p. 22. NSW made no efforts to encourage locomotive building until after Federation.

9. B. R. Wise, *The Making of the Australian Commonwealth* (London: Longmans Green, 1913), p. 334.

10. *Official Yearbook of the Commonwealth of Australia* 1915, p. 411; Butlin, *Investment*, p. 14.

New Zealand was the first to make use of this opportunity, borrowing £10 million during the 1870s.[11] By 1877, New Zealand's emerging fiscal difficulties shifted British attention to the Australian continent, where borrowing ballooned. T. A. Coghlan best summed the result:

> The mild and beneficial stream of capital flowing into the country up to 1880 was changed into a flood during the five years 1881–85, when . . . £69,000,000 reached Australia, and to a deluge in 1886–90, when the sum introduced overpassed £100,000,000. The various Governments during these ten years jostled one another in the London market in their anxiety to get money. . . . After [1881] . . . the inflow was much in excess of what could be properly assimilated . . . and there arose a demand [in Australia] for [speculative] investments.[12]

But private borrowing preceded public, as unemployed miners and urban capitals, bypassed by the pastoral industry's expansion, agitated for land to farm.[13] Their agitation led to a series of Land Acts starting in 1860 in Victoria and 1861 in NSW. The Land Acts opened crown lands, formerly held only by lease, to outright purchase, presumably so individuals and the unemployed could establish family farms. Agitation certainly was genuine, especially in Victoria, where it forced some pastoral activity to shift north to NSW. But this agitation mainly served the interests of the colonial states and financiers.

The threat of free election by farmers under the Land Acts forced pastoralists to buy up huge chunks of land to protect their investment in improvements and livestock and to control water sources. Compelled to buy, they in most cases were compelled to mortgage. And if they were to borrow to buy land, then they might as well borrow to fence it and improve its productivity. Fencing costs ran from £23,500 to £50,000 for typical runs. Financial capitals gained a new outlet for funds, and a tighter hold on pastoral activity via mortgages. Since the mortgagee typically held the actual title or lease as security, the indebted pastoralist in default on his loan could be chucked out at the mortgagee's will. With British and Victorian funds providing equal

---

11. New Zealand will be examined in more depth in chap. 5. Gold was discovered there in 1857.

12. T. Coghlan, *Labour and Industry in Australia* (repr. ed., Melbourne: Macmillan, 1965; orig. 1918), pp. 1635–1636.

13. See S. Roberts, *History of Australian Land Settlement* (Melbourne: Melbourne University Press, 1924) for the best general discussion of land and land laws. A. Wells, "A Marxist Reappraisal of Australian Capitalism" (Ph.D. thesis, Australian National University, 1986), is the best analysis of this period, but I have not been able to obtain a complete copy; the following text draws on an unpublished chapter from that ms.

shares, pastoral finance companies invested about £25 million, banks another £30 million. Simultaneously the colonial states gained a new source of revenue from land sales, which they used to fund the expansion of debt-financed railways. These railways in turn vastly enlarged the land area available for grazing; for the small scale and high cost of ox-cart transportation was now the limiting factor in wool production.[14] The Land Acts seemingly created a magic circle: the state forced pastoralists to buy land, used land sale revenue to service the debt incurred by building railroads, used railroads to open new land for use and sale, and borrowed more money to build more railways to open more land for sale, thus creating more revenue. Politicians naturally accelerated this cycle, for, as Michael Cannon wrote, "much of the money being borrowed by the State was finally flowing into the pockets of the land profiteers, many of them actually members of the Governments which were floating the huge loans." Foreign loans provided an increasingly larger share of gross domestic capital formation: from 4.4 percent in 1870–75 to 13.4 percent in 1876–1880; to 49 percent in 1880–85 and 51.7 percent in 1886–90.[15]

But as Chapter 2 argued, this "magic circle" was also a treadmill. Expanding public and pastoral debt both ultimately rested either on wool prices via the value wool production gave to otherwise worthless land, or on the fiscal base. Neither of these was certain to rise in proportion to debt service, and debt service for the railways was inimical to an expanding fiscal base. We will deal with public debt first, then pastoral.

Origins of the Public Debt Crises

As the colonies borrowed heavily to finance and subsidize railways, the magic circle soon developed gaps: chronic fiscal deficits in the 1880s. Australian public debt levels and debt service increased 60 percent per capita and as a proportion of GDP in 1880–1890.[16] (See Table 6). NSW ran budget deficits in seven years of that decade. Loans financed mid-decade deficits, but they were creating future demand for debt service in years when loans would not be forthcom-

14. J. Bailey, *A Hundred Years of Pastoral Banking: A History of the Australian Mercantile Land & Finance Co., 1863–1963* (Oxford: Clarendon Press, 1966), pp. 52–53, 55–56; Butlin, *Investment*, pp. 60, 93, and especially pp. 299–320, for a discussion of transport costs.

15. Quotation from M. Cannon, *Land Boomers* (Melbourne: Melbourne University Press, 1966), p. 29; data from Butlin, *Australian Domestic Product*, pp. 18, 424.

16. Butlin, *Australian Domestic Product*, pp. 10–11, 416. It is misleading to deal with Australia as an integrated whole. It was not regarded as such by investors, and the

Table 6. Australian colonial government borrowing, 1861–1900

Years	Flow of govt. borrowing (mil £)	Interest paid in 5-year period (mil £)	Interest as % of borrowing	Public debt service as % of exports
1861–65	6.4	3.0	45.3	3.3
1866–70	9.6	5.8	60.0	6.1
1871–75	9.2	8.8	95.7	6.9
1876–80	15.6	12.3	78.8	12.3
1881–85	50.8	17.6	34.6	12.5
1886–90	43.2	25.7	59.5	22.9
1891–95	28.9	35.5	122.8	29.8

SOURCE: Butlin, *Australian Domestic Product,* pp. 410–411, 416, 424.

ing, without making any productive investment (e.g. in railways) that might pay back the charges. Thus interest payments, as a percentage of NSW gross revenue, rose from 10.2 percent to 19.6 percent, 1881–1890, while per capita revenues fell from £8.9 to £8.4 1881–1890.[17] Victoria was in a slightly different position. Debt service as a percentage of revenue actually had declined slightly over the decade to 17.9 percent, because Victoria had borrowed heavily in the late 1870s and then tapered off in the early 1880s. In the late 1880s, as the speculative bubble seemed to be reaching its natural limits, politicians mooted a massive increase in rail building to sustain the boom, proposing to borrow £41 million in 1890.[18] But London's discovery that only Victoria's budgetary handwaving had turned a large deficit into an imaginary surplus in 1889 soured it on Victorian issues. London critics claimed that the "official earnings of the [Victorian] railways [were] open to grave suspicion," describing Victorian balance sheets as "the annual lie."[19] With Argentine default in the foreground in 1890, Victoria appeared no more honest than Argentina, and therefore no better a risk.[20]

---

several rail systems were not compatible. Wide variation in investment occurred; long after investment ceased in the eastern Colonies, gold-rich Western Australia drew capital. We can, however, use the fiction of "Australia" for gross estimations of motive, especially since federation came to be seen as Australia's salvation.

17. E. Boehm, *Prosperity and Depression in Australia, 1887–1897* (Oxford: Oxford University Press, 1971), p. 174.

18. H. Turner, *History of the Colony of Victoria* (London: Longmans Green, 1904), 2:275–277.

19. J. Fortescue, "Guileless Australia," *Nineteenth Century* 30:175 (September 1891), p. 432; *Australasian Insurance and Banking Record,* December 18, 1891, p. 894.

20. See especially the 1891 debate in *Nineteenth Century* between Fortescue, "Guileless Australia," and H. Willoughby, "The Seamy Side of Australia—A Reply, *Nineteenth Century* 30 (August 1891).

Table 7. Real interest rates on new colonial loans, 1876–1898

Years	Victoria	NSW	Queensland	New Zealand
1876–80	4.53	na*	4.37	
1881–85	4.16	4.01	4.14	3.46
1886–90	3.69	3.66	3.86	3.84
1891–94	4.20	3.96	4.01	
1895–98	nl*	3.16	3.35	

*na = not available; nl = no loans.

SOURCES: Victoria Yearbook 1902, p. 51; OYBNSW 1904–5, p. 468; Statistics of Queensland 1909, pp. 106–107d; NZOYB.

By London's rule of thumb for determining public creditworthiness, the smaller colonies represented even greater risks than the two larger ones; Queensland for example was spending 32 percent of its revenue on debt service.[21] The London market's loss of confidence pushed up the real interest rate on new loans to the Colonies (see Table 7). But the Colonies could not stop borrowing, for interest payments began exceeding new loans at the same time revenues were contracting—they needed to borrow simply to service and refinance old loans.

At the heart of the problem lay the colonial rail systems' continual deficits, and behind this, as Chapter 2 argued, was colonial states' inability to capture the full rise in land values. As reproductive works, the railways represented the securest form of loan, for in theory they ought to have been self-financing. But rail receipts never covered the cost of interest, thus exports were being subsidized. Raising freight rates was no solution, for pastoral activity had come to depend on and expect subsidy. If rates rose, pastoral profits would fall, in turn causing decreases in land sale revenue. In any case, as falling wool prices drove down pastoral profits, land prices did fall; the contribution of land sales to NSW revenue fell from a high of 42.1 percent in 1880 to 23.6 percent in 1889.[22] Freight rate increases would only aggravate the fiscal crisis. Here, then, was the contradiction: debt service required profitable pastoral production to generate the "foreign ex-

21. "The true rule by which the incidence of colonial borrowing, from a public point of view, is to be determined is . . . the *interest charge per head* of population." AIBR, May 18, 1891, pp. 312–313; emphasis in original. See also the *Economist*, April 12, 1890, p. 455: "There is grave danger of even the most prosperous of the Australian colonies borrowing in [London] out of proportion to their increase in population, and their remunerative expenditure on public works." Boehm, *Prosperity and Depression*, p. 174.
22. *New South Wales Statistical Register*, various dates.

change" used to service debt.[23] Profitable pastoral production required either expanding debt to subsidize exports further or squeezing domestic sectors for additional revenues. But pastoral retrenchment and rising taxes both reduced domestic growth. To get revenue the colonies needed to build railways to increase exports and economic activity; but without revenue they could not borrow at economic rates or, in some cases, could not borrow at all. Both paths risked political conflict and economic disaster. Aggravating the fiscal crisis was a parallel crisis of private pastoral investment.

Pastoral Investment and the Crisis in Private Debt

Slower rates of growth in demand for wool and falling wool prices underlay the private crisis. British wool consumption slowed in the late 1880s and began to drop off early in the 1890s. Wool prices fell in the 1880s to 77 percent of the 1870s' average, bottoming at 63 percent of 1870 prices in 1894.[24] While short-term advances to pastoralists doubled, and long-term investment increased 75 percent from 1880 to 1887, falling prices limited the increase in the mass of profits to only 10 percent. The 3.1 percent per annum productivity increases of the self-financed period gave way to 1.1 percent per annum growth.[25] Declining profits motivated some graziers, especially Victorians, to diversify into meat and dairy production, while the pastoral finance companies began shifting investments to urban areas. But falling wool prices trapped the majority of pastoralists between declining receipts and growing debt obligations. By 1887, interest was claiming 40 percent of the value of Australian wool production, up from 20 percent in 1881. Financial capital felt the squeeze as well, as the pie they were eating from became smaller. A typical firm, Australian Mortgage Land and Finance, saw its rate of return drop 40 percent between 1880 and 1890.[26] (See also Table 8.)

Creditors reacted to declining returns by eliminating the Australian

23. In the case of Britain's formal colonies, merely a surplus of exports over imports was necessary since the colonies used Sterling as currency.

24. J. Clapham, *Woolen and Worsted Industries* (London: Methuen, 1907), p. 271; *Votes and Proceeding of the Legislative Assembly of NSW*, 1901, 4:v–ix.

25. Butlin, *Australian Domestic Product*, p. 14. Butlin notes that "the rapid increase in 'productivity' occurred before 1877, before the great investment boom, and while the Australian colonies relied primarily on their own resources."

26. See, on interest, Bailey, *One Hundred Years of Pastoral Banking*, pp. 108–110; ibid., pp. 147–149 for problems with freezing technologies that limited diversification; ibid., pp. 121–122, on the rate of return, which fell from 5.1 percent in 1880 to 3.1 percent in 1890.

Table 8. Pastoral debt burden for 10 representative Australian sheep stations, 1881 and 1889

	Central NSW		Western NSW	
	1881	1889	1881	1889
Wool earnings (£ '000)	57.6	76.5	54.9	41.3
Interest (£ '000)	16.0	27.3	11.0	28.0
Interest as % earnings	28	36	18	67
Debt per sheep (£)	0.71	1.08	0.68	1.42

SOURCE: Bailey, *One Hundred Years of Pastoral Banking*, p. 112.

pastoral interior bourgeoisie. Steadily narrowing profit margins forced finance firms to foreclose or to impose supervision amounting to foreclosure on the properties they held paper on if they were to have any chance of recouping their capital.[27] Theoretically their investments were secured by land, but the market value of that land was determined by the value of the production occurring on it. As Coghlan commented:

> Advances had been made against stock and stations on the basis of values existing prior to 1884, and in 1889 these values had to a great extent disappeared. . . . The banks found themselves in possession of a great number of pastoral holdings, which could not be disposed of except at prices much below the advances made against them; these the banks were compelled to work as if they were their own property.[28]

From being enterprises largely owned and managed individually and domestically, sheep stations increasingly became businesses controlled by banks or corporations. (See Table 9.) In 1890 in NSW alone, 1200 stations were foreclosed upon.[29] Where individual owners or small groups of owners retained ownership, banks or financial companies often held legal title to their lease or land as security, effectively turning them into paid managers. The threat to foreign investors was even greater: besides being the creditor for much of the industry,

27. N. G. Butlin, "Company Ownership of NSW Pastoral Stations 1865–1900," HSANZ 4 (May 1950), *passim*; Coghlan, *Labour and Industry in Australia*, p. 1644; Bailey, *One Hundred Years of Pastoral Banking*, pp. 82–83, 114.

28. Coghlan, *Labour and Industry in Australia*, p. 1644. Urban land speculation will be discussed below.

29. On foreclosures, see Butlin, "Company Ownership of NSW Pastoral Stations," pp. 94–95; and Roberts, *History of Australian Land Settlement*, pp. 292–293. See N. Cain, "Companies and Squatting in the Western Division of NSW, 1896–1905," *Economic Record* 37 (June 1961), 200 for a discussion of proletarianization of owners.

Table 9. Ownership patterns of pastoral land, 1866–1897

A. Ownership Distribution, All NSW Lessees

	1866	1871	1879	1889–90
Absolute number of holdings by type of lessee				
Banks and corporations	37	313	734	611
Group of individuals	795	983	1122	283
Individuals	2689	2314	2467	719
Total	3521	3610	4323	1612
Holdings as percentage of total number of leases				
Banks and corporations	1.0	9.1	17.0	38.1
Group of individuals	22.5	27.3	25.8	17.5
Individuals	76.5	63.6	57.2	44.4
Total	100	100	100	100

B. Ownership by District (%)

	1866	1871	1879	1889/90	1896/97
Eastern Division					
Banks and corporations	0.2	4.5	12.9	31.9	n/a
Individuals and groups	99.8	95.5	87.1	68.1	n/a
Central Division					
Banks and corporations	1.0	7.8	19.4	38.6	50.8
Individuals and groups	99.0	92.2	80.6	61.4	49.2
Western Division					
Banks and corporations	1.6	9.5	16.9	47.6	64.6
Individuals and groups	98.4	90.5	83.1	52.4	35.4

n/a = not available.
SOURCE: Butlin, "Company Ownership of NSW Pastoral Stations," pp. 94–97.

their direct holdings generally were larger and in more marginal areas than domestic investment and, being newer, had been amortized less.

This increasing bank pressure on station owners had two political effects. First, it undercut any basis for accommodation between graziers and the labour unions that emerged in shearing and shipping in the late 1880s. Owners, domestic or foreign, could not afford significant concessions, for they needed dramatic increases in productivity to stay profitable. When workers began demanding that owners hand over traditional managerial prerogatives—e.g. accept closed shops—owners faced a no-win situation. Banks were demanding tighter managerial control to squeeze out the last shilling of profit;

workers were attacking stricter controls. Owner-managers were under attack from both sides.[30]

The second effect was that as steady elimination of pastoralists stabilized the financial position of the foreign creditors, it also reduced their ability to make alliances with local class fractions, which isolated them from domestic groups. Their natural allies were domestic pastoral and export capitalists, and of these the station owners had the greatest political power, for they controlled their rural legislative districts by disenfranchising workers through property and residential qualifications. In contrast, the other domestic capitals had to contend with the enfranchised urban labour and petit bourgeoisie. The elimination of the grazier class by banks thus immediately affected labour relations, and hurt financial capitals after Federation.

Labour and Investment

Both fiscal crises and pastoral illiquidity exacerbated tense capital-labour relations. As foreign investment concentrated the control of shipping, shearing, and mining, it also concentrated labour in those industries. Workers in these highly capitalized industries existed as homogenous bodies of labour confronting employers to whom they had no social ties. When labour was itinerant, as in shearing, this homogeneity was especially prevalent where it was not itinerant, as in mining, workers lived in compact communities conducive to organizing.[31] Workers were acutely aware of the fragility of their working conditions and the instability of wages and employment.

An anomaly observed by Francis Castles, in his interesting comparative monograph *The Working Class and Welfare*, allows an entry point into Australasian labour's reaction to growing foreign control of grazing and concomitant efforts to lower wages.[32] Castles observes, without explanation, that Australasian workers typically have focused their efforts on the short-run maximization of wages through juridicized collective bargaining rather than on creating state-run universal social welfare programs along the Western European model. Castles is unable to say why, because he presumes that labour reacts

30. See *Australasian Pastoralists Review*, March 16, 1891, pp. 2–3, for a jeremiad.
31. I. Turner, *Industrial Labour and Politics* (Canberra: A.N.U., 1965), pp. 4–6. But Coghlan, *Labour and Industry in Australia*, p. 1598, says that many shearers were also "selectors"—small holders—in 1890. Although this would not necessarily reduce their antipathy towards graziers—indeed, might amplify it—it has different implications for union organizing strategies.
32. F. Castles, *The Working Class and Welfare* (Boston: Allen & Unwin, 1985).

similarly to foreign and to domestic capitalists. But the Australian workers with the greatest economic and, later, political power all confronted foreign capitals.[33] Workers and capital can be thought of as bargaining over futures in wage negotiations.[34] Workers' long run wages depend on future investments by capitalists, which workers cannot control. Workers thus must defer current wage gains to gain (discounted) future wages, hoping capitalists will turn deferred present wages into investment. Where workers can see that capitalists are likely and willing to make the investments necessary to assure future employment, workers are more willing to make concessions on present wages. But foreign capitalists are not perceived as having any commitment to future investment in the workers' locale because they remit profits overseas and so can invest elsewhere. Absent guarantees of reinvestment, workers have to maximize short-run wages to assure themselves of a lifetime subsistence wage. Australasian workers, especially pastoral workers, thus typically bargained for increased current wages, and increased control of day-to-day operations. If "capital" ever did leave, the increase in day-to-day control would allow production to continue.[35]

In this context, growing pressure to increase productivity in the late 1880s led to growing militancy by established industrial unions like the Australian Miners Association and Seamens Union, and the organization of mass unions among other unskilled workers, beginning with wharf workers in 1885 and shearers and station hands in 1886. Eighty-four unions formed between 1888 and 1892. These unions experienced immediate successes in raising wages, but their success provoked shippers to band together in the Victorian Employers Union (VEU) in 1885 and the NSW Employers Union (NSWEU) in 1888, and pastoralists to "unionize" in 1889.[36] Nonetheless, unskilled labour was well ahead in the race to form colony- and continent-wide organizations, and so they continued to best employers.

33. For those who may doubt that workers from the British Isles could view capitalists from the British Isles as foreign, I recommend a leisurely tour of labour newspapers from the 1880s and 1890s. This sentiment existed even outside the groups, such as the Irish, who had particular reasons to doubt the kinship of the English; see especially *Brisbane Worker*, June 1890, p. 8.
34. See A. Przeworski and M. Wallerstein, "Structure of Class Conflict in Democratic-capitalist Societies," *American Political Science Review* 76 (June 1982), pp. 215–238.
35. See *Brisbane Worker*, January 10, 1891, and April 22, 1893, for particularly salient examples of this thinking.
36. The Australian Miners Association and Seamans Union formed in the 1870s. Fitzpatrick, *British Empire in Australia*, pp. 206–207, 212–213; OYBCWA no. 20, p. 580. On employer organizations, see T. Matthews, "Business Associations and the State," in B. Head, *State and Economy in Australia* (Oxford: Oxford University Press, 1983), p. 117.

Urban workers' situation differed. Urban craft unions traditionally were cooperative. They saw a community of interest with their largely petit entrepreneur employers, who could not take their "capital" and flee. Indeed, social mobility and economic growth leavened the ranks of employers with former workers. So long as the "dignity of labour" was preserved and progress was made towards a minimum wage and eight-hour day, craft unions had no urge to fight; until the mid-1880s, real wages rose steadily as the price of food, housing and consumables dropped. Falling shipping costs cheapened imports; domestic production achieved economies of scale as urban markets grew. But all these trends reversed by 1885. According to Coghlan, "the expenditure of the Governments [on railways] counteracted, so far as the working classes were concerned, the effect of the great drop in prices, which all the important producing classes felt as far back as 1881."[37] Pastoral companies' growing investment in urban areas drove housing costs up astronomically. Stagnating real wages coincided with increasing pressure from larger employers in the newly concentrated construction and food processing industries. In mid-decade, in the heat of bootmakers' and other strikes, amity between craft labour and the larger urban capitals evaporated.

Both labour groups had peak organizations: craft unions via six annual Intercolonial Trade Union Congresses between 1879 and 1889, and industrial unions under the "Maritime Council" formed in 1884. But fears that "the unskilled would cut the tradesman's throat" divided craft unions from industrial unions. Only in Queensland, one of the most mono-industrial areas in a continent of mono-industrial areas, did all unions join together under the Australian Labour Federation.

While increased organization encouraged increased labour militancy, it had no corresponding political effects. Politics generally were seen as corrupt and corrupting, and residency requirements disenfranchised itinerant rural workers. Economic organization was a prerequisite to political organization; thus disorganization of the unskilled reinforced by disenfranchisement, dictated a strategy of direct action.[38] The few candidates who ran as "labour" men in urban work-

37. Coghlan, *Labour and Industry in Australia*, p. 1635. See W. A. Lewis, "Economic Development with Unlimited Supplies of Labour," *Manchester School Journal* 22 (May 1954), 163–166, for a theoretical explanation of why government borrowing leads to inflation and a drop in workers' consumption.

38. See Turner, *Industrial Labour and Politics*; R. Gollan, *Radical and Working Class Politics* (Melbourne: Melbourne University Press, 1960), and Fitzpatrick, *British Empire in Australia*, for this fairly standard interpretation. For differing interpretations of

ing-class districts generally abandoned labour slogans once in the Assemblies. In contrast, economic struggle promised and seemed to deliver immediate results.

The Maritime Strike

In 1890 the struggle latent in the increasing economic pressure from graziers' creditors and increased unionization erupted. As the timing of this struggle is important for understanding the origins of Federation, it is worth elaboration. In May 1890, the Queensland Shearers Union (QSU) forced the owner of Jondaryan, a medium-sized sheep station, to accept a union contract by getting dockworkers and wool carriers to blacklist his wool. Both sides thereafter rushed to organize alliances for a larger conflict seemed inevitable when the QSU announced its intention to unionize the 20 percent of stations still nonunion in July 1890.[39] Afraid of the dockside-shearer link, pastoralists organized a continental association with shipowners and mine owners. The alliance with the shipowners proved pivotal, for the conflict was sparked when negotiations between shipowners and their officers' union collapsed. Officers had organized a union and affiliated it with the Melbourne Trades Hall Council, but owners demanded disaffiliation as a precondition for any negotiation. The officers refused and walked out on August 16, 1890; coalminers, shearers, and others struck in solidarity to stop export of nonunion goods, starting an Australasia-wide strike.

Traditionally the Maritime strike is explained as an unintentional outcome of a smaller strike. But Rickard's revision is more reasonable: capitalists felt they had no alternative to fighting and had picked their moment.[40] As Coghlan noted:

> This immense combination [of labour] was threatening in its very nature.
> It was pledged to support the claims of any of its sections, not only by

---

unions' political activity, see the debate between J. Phillip, "1890—The Turning Point in Labour History?" and J. O'Connor, "1890—A Turning Point in Labour History: A Reply to Mrs. Phillip," in *Historical Studies: Selected Articles*, 2d ser. (Melbourne: Melbourne University Press, 1967).

39. Shann, *Economic History of Australia*, pp. 321–322; Fitzpatrick, *British Empire in Australia*, p. 221; *Melbourne Age*, May 13, 1890.

40. Rickard, *Class and Politics*, pp. 7–29. See also Archive of Business and Labour mss no. (ABL) 78/1/63, pp. 347–351, J. Gregson to AAC/L, July 18, 1890; and p. 362, July 15, 1890; p. 370, July 21, 1890; pp. 384–386, August 15, 1890; all describing Gregson's fears of united unions.

finding money, but by the use of the "sympathetic strike." But beyond this it was well known that the ulterior aim of the [Australian Labour] Federation was a change in the basis of society, 'something in the nature of a revolution,' as one trade unionist afterwards declared.[41]

Given growing animosity, the ship officers' union affiliation meant that owners might lose the loyalty of the technical cadres needed to break a strike. If officers sided with owners, ships could be run with scab labour; if not, ships could not sail, wool did not sell, and the whole rickety financial structure of Australia might collapse. Any officers' union thus had to be broken immediately. Employers' groups, backed by the banks and, some have suggested, by the British shipowners' federation, set out to destroy the new unions in a pitched battle, and succeeded with the help of the Colonial states' military and quasi-military forces.[42] By August 1891, shearers and seamen agreed to open shops and nonunion contracts. Other unions were systematically broken. The Broken Hill mining companies inconclusively locked out their workers in 1890, setting the stage for a bloodier, more decisive defeat of the miners in 1892.

Graziers and banks gained some economic breathing time by defeating workers, though price declines continued to offset their savings from wage reductions. More threatening, Broken Hill shares lost £8 million in value on the Melbourne stock exchange from strikes and falling silver prices during 1891–92; goldmining shares lost £4 million.[43] Despite the scale and violence of the strikes, investment continued at fairly high levels through 1891, because the strikes only minimally affected investor perceptions of Australian credit. In 1887–1889 the British had invested £3.88 million in pastoral enterprises, while 1890–1892 saw disinvestment of £1.14 million, part of an 80 percent fall in net pastoral investment. But most of this fall came after 1891, which actually saw the highest levels of pastoral investment gross and net, since 1877. From 1891 to 1894 net foreign investment fell 71.5 percent from its average 1888–91 level; all gross

41. Coghlan, *Labour and Industry in Australia*, p. 1839.
42. Rickard, *Class and Politics*, p. 22; B. Fitzpatrick, *A Short History of the Australian Labour Movement* (Melbourne: Melbourne University Press, 1940), p. 66; *Melbourne Argus*, July 31, 1890; *Sydney Daily Telegraph*, August 2, 1890; *Melbourne Age*, August 19 and 26, 1890, September 4, 1890. Banks suspended mortgage and loan payments, and increased overdraft for graziers and shippers. Coghlan, *Labour and Industry in Australia*, pp. 1579–1599.
43. Coghlan, *Labour and Industry in Australia*, p. 1725. Overall, £20 million in value evaporated on the Exchange.

pastoral investment fell 50 percent. It was not the strikes themselves but their *political* consequences that disturbed British capital.[44]

Like the bank foreclosures of pastoralists, the Maritime strike had profound political consequences. Whereas prestrike unionism had stressed direct action over politics as the primary road to ending capitalist exploitation, this strike demonstrated the state-reinforced dominance of capital in those struggles. As growing unemployment steadily eroded labours' hopes for direct struggle, the very unions defeated in the strike turned to politics to undo their defeats.[45] At the same time the open intervention of the colonial states on behalf of capital exploded any claim they might make to neutrality. To labour, the difference between the extant parties appeared to be that the Ministry ordered Gatling guns to the mines while the Opposition protested its dilatoriness. Strikers viewed the locally recruited military as an "army of occupation," and later heckled anti-Labor candidates with "Fire low and lay them out!"—the orders given to soldiers in Melbourne during the 1890 strike.[46] By forming specific labor parties, labour could use its numeric strength to move the state at least to a truer neutrality. Labour thus changed colonial politics from elite struggles over distribution of surplus among capitals into an explicit arena for class struggle. One of the first labor members of the Legislative Assembly in NSW declaimed: "We have *not* come into [the NSW Assembly] to make and unmake Ministries. We *have* come into this House to make and unmake social conditions."[47]

Though Labor parties formed in all six Australian colonies, only the NSW party had immediate electoral success, returning 36 MLAs to a 141-member house in the 1891 elections.[48] This success proved

44. Boehm, *Prosperity and Depression*, chap. 6.6; Butlin, *Australian Domestic Product*, pp. 20, 294–296, 424; but Fitzpatrick, *British Empire in Australia*, p. 214, notes that the threat of a railway strike was taken seriously by investors. Railwaymen threatened work stoppages when the rails were used to transport scabs and militia, and contributed heavily to strike funds.

45. W. Spence, *Australia's Awakening* (Sydney: The *Worker* Trustees, 1909), p. 220; Turner, *Industrial Labour and Politics*, p. xix.

46. *Brisbane Worker*, July 25, 1891; Gollan, *Radical and Working Class Politics*, pp. 134–135; O'Connor, "1890—A Turning Point in Labour History," p. 147; *Sydney Morning Herald*, July 21, 1891.

47. G. Black, Labor Electoral League Member of the Legislative Assembly (hereafter MLA), 1891, quoted in P. Loveday, "Support in Return for Concessions," HSANZ 14:55 (October 1970), 376. Emphasis in original.

48. See Turner, *Industrial Labour and Politics*, p. 22; R. Gollan, "Industrial Relations in the Pastoral Industry," in A. Barnard, ed., *The Simple Fleece: Studies in the Australian Wool Industry* (Melbourne: Melbourne University Press, 1962), pp. 610–611. Queensland's Australian Labor Party quickly moved into a position of permanent opposition to the remnants of the older parties by the mid-1890s, but was unable to form a majority

its short-run undoing but its long-term strength. With other parties urging both positions on it, it fragmented almost immediately over the question of free trade versus protection. The party, re-formed, "agreed to disagree" on fiscal matters, but members were pledged to abide by caucus decisions on all matters spelled out in the party platform, and to vote as a coherent bloc.[49] Thus Labor pioneered the modern, disciplined political party in Australia, shortly after Parnell did so in Ireland. Against the backdrop of the Baring crisis and Argentina's semi-default, these parties raised the specter of nationalization and default in London, discouraging new investment. Investment dropped not following the 1890 strike but after the emergence of these Labor parties in 1891.

CRISIS, CLASSES, AND THE FIRST FEDERATION MOVEMENT

> It has been said that finance lies at the root of all political questions, a proposition which is aptly illustrated whenever Australasian political questions come to the front.
>
> *The Economist,* 1890[50]

The Debt Crisis and the 1890 Melbourne Conference

By 1890–91, then, all the dominion crises were present in Australia. But when thirteen senior politicians met in Melbourne to discuss Federation in February 1890, the strikes and their political aftermath were still to come. Traditional histories usually claim that it was a British military mission in 1889 that sparked the 1890 meeting. The mission's report emphasized the weakness of the divided colonial militaries in the face of a hypothetical invasion.[51] But the extant, if moribund, Federal Council of 1885 could have served as the basis for military integration, which thus did not necessitate the uncertainties of an attempt to federate Australasia.[52] More plausibly, labour historians usually see the strikes as behind the meeting's hidden agenda:

---

ministry until well into the 1900s. Craft unionist adherence to the Liberal Party, a protectionist group based in manufacturing capital, hampered Victoria's Progressive Political League until after 1899. Similarly, South Australia's United Labor Party found a ready but limiting ally in the farmer-based Radical Party.

49. P. Loveday, "Labor," in Loveday et al., eds., *Emergence of the Australian Party System* (Sydney: Hale and Iremonger, 1977), p. 203.

50. *Economist,* February 8, 1890, p. 168.

51. At the time, fear focused on Russia, France, and Germany.

52. As contemporary observers knew; see *Melbourne Age,* February 7, 1890.

Federation was a pre-emptive effort at labour control. Even taking the defense issue at face value, the specter of divided militaries facing continental unions cannot have been entirely out of politicians' minds.[53] But why then in October 1891, after the big strikes, did the NSW Legislative Assembly reject a proposal for a centralized military by a vote of 92–10 even as it assented to a Constitutional Convention? This suggests that labour control is unlikely to have been the only or primary motive for the Federation meeting.

The British military mission's report was catalytic because it provided an excuse to meet. As LaNauze points out, NSW Premier Parkes, who arranged the meeting, had been making arrangements to meet with other Premiers prior to the report.[54] All the pressures—the emergence of national unions, the foreclosure of local pastoralists, and the deterioration in public credit—were present in NSW, whose economy depended more on debt-financed growth than the other colonies' in the late 1880s, more on pastoral exports than Victoria, and had more industrial unionism than anywhere save Queensland. But for Parkes the most proximate problem was public credit. As early as 1888 B. R. Wise, a prominent politician-attorney, had warned Parkes of NSW's impending fiscal crisis, and had urged adoption of a range of revenue-gathering devices aimed at splitting the political opposition while increasing NSW's tax take.[55] Imperial authorities also pushed Parkes, for "all the [British appointed Colonial] Governors went out of their way warmly to advocate the cause of Federation" during the 1890 meeting.[56] The content of this advocacy may be judged from Wise's description:

> [Parkes] was pressed by the then Governor, Lord Jersey, with an urgency which was almost a command, to remain at the head of affairs, in order to

53. See Fitzpatrick, *British Empire in Australia*; Turner, *Industrial Labour and Politics*; and L. Crisp, *Australian National Government* (London and Croydon, Victoria: Longmans Green, 1965), p. 17. Military fragmentation proved no obstacle to smashing the 1890 strike. But the absence of intercolonial military cooperation reflected legal difficulties and coincident crises, not an absence of desire. Queensland did request military aid from NSW during the strikes, but Premier Parkes demurred, expressing his lack of authority to do so; see *Brisbane Worker*, April 25, 1891.

54. J. LaNauze, *The Making of the Australian Constitution* (Melbourne: Melbourne University Press, 1972), pp. 8–9; Coghlan, *Labour and Industry in Australia*, pp. 2337–2339.

55. Wise, *Making of the Australian Commonwealth*, pp. 83–86; *Melbourne Age*, February 12-14, 1890; Mitchell Library, Sydney, manuscript no. (hereafter ML MS) A912, pp. 310–313, B. Wise to H. Parkes, August 8, 1888.

56. *Economist*, February 8, 1890, pp. 166–167.

avoid a danger to the public credit. Rumblings of the coming financial crisis could be heard already by experts; and loan negotiations were in progress, which depended for their success upon the confidence of London lenders in the Administration . . . Lord Jersey . . . a partner in [a local] Bank . . . urged Sir Henry Parkes to remain in Office until the loan was floated.[57]

Meanwhile the *Economist* hammered away at the issue of the creditworthiness and credibility of the other great colony, specifically questioning Victorian solvency four times in the first five months of 1890, while blandly suggesting on the convention's eve that "steps should be taken to secure public credit at a time when great political and fiscal changes are in contemplation."[58]

As self-appointed representatives, those meeting in 1890 could pass only notional resolutions in favor of general Australasian Federation and call on the Colonial Legislative Assemblies to pass bills enabling a full scale constitutional convention. But they made explicit agreements on the utility of Federal resumption of colonial debts, while avoiding any statement on taxation.[59] As the strikes had not yet happened, no specific labour control proposals surfaced. Meantime, "there was as yet no *popular* impetus behind the movement."[60]

The Legislative Assemblies debated the 1890 conference's recommendations shortly after the Jondaryan affair, while pastoral and shipping capitals were busy preparing for the upcoming struggle. From May 7 to July 15, 1890, five Assemblies assented to a convention of forty-five nominated delegates from all seven colonies in Sydney, to be held in March and April of 1891. Western Australia, essentially ruled by Colonial Office nominees, agreed to attend; so, reluctantly,

57. Wise, *Making of the Australian Commonwealth*, pp. 160–161. Parkes was a "Free Trader," the group (one dare hardly call it a party) supported by Sydney mercantile and financial interests against the protectionist (manufacturer, farmer, labour) group headed by Dibbs. Three representatives of the Sydney softgoods importers and financial circles—W. McMillan, J. Brunker, A. Bruce Smith—met with Parkes in advance of the conference to berate him for taking up the issue prior to discussion designed to avoid "future misunderstandings." ML MS 2958, pp. 23–24, W. McMillan to Parkes, November 20, 1889.

58. *Economist*, January 3, 1890, p. 9; January 18, 1890, p. 72; February 1, 1890, p. 141; May 31, 1890, p. 693. Quotation from February 22, 1890, p. 235.

59. *Melbourne Age*, February 6, 1890.

60. J. Quick and R. Garran, *Annotated Constitution of the Australian Commonwealth* (Sydney: Legal Books, 1976; orig. 1901), p. 122, emphasis added. See AIBR, January 16, 1890, p. 1, and May 19, 1893, p. 293, for examples of continued boundless optimism on the part of capitalists.

did New Zealand.[61] In the meantime, the Maritime Strike and the first bank failures had created a "popular impetus" for a new level of government.

Labour and the 1891 Sydney Convention

The 1890 strike's influence on Federation is clear but limited. The Labour Defence Council, which directed the 1890 strike, was composed of those unions who could completely stop export production were they to strike successfully.[62] Transport unions and the Maritime Council could paralyze shipping; miners, mineral exports and the coal used by ships and rails; shearers, the golden fleece. All these unions and the employer groups confronting them were continental bodies or looked soon to be; it was only political power that remained fragmented. At the 1891 Sydney convention, South Australian Premier Playford moaned: "Labour has federated, and capital has federated all throughout the Colonies, and the experience of the late strike shows most unmistakably . . . that as far as our local laws are concerned we are practically powerless to deal with the question."[63] The 1891 Convention was also reminded constantly of the prior year's strikes by word of new strikes in Queensland. But even the Melbourne *Age*, which had consistently called for arbitration of these disputes, saw that strife would first "seriously affect the *credit* and prosperity of Australia."[64] Between the 1890 meeting and the 1891 convention, all of the strikes had failed, but meanwhile the first labor member of the Legislative Assembly in NSW had been elected in October 1890, five "labor" MLAs became part of a reform ministry in New Zealand, and discussion had started about forming the Labour Electoral League in NSW.[65] Thus labour control powers at the 1891 Sydney Convention got only contentious and cursory consideration. The "labour problem" now was not so much one of preventing strikes, for labour demonstrably was cowed, as it was a problem of convincing London that the new Labor parties would not take control of government and renege on overseas public debt obligations. Consequently, three-fourths of the delegates favored plural voting and property

61. Even as early as the 1890 meeting, it was clear that New Zealand had serious reservations about federation with the Australian colonies; *Melbourne Age*, February 12, 1890.
62. Fitzpatrick, *British Empire in Australia*, p. 214.
63. *Official Report of the National Australasian Convention Debates* (Sydney: Government Printer, 1891), pp. 784–785.
64. *Melbourne Age*, March 19, 1891; see also March 23, 26, 1891. Emphasis added.
65. Rickard, *Class and Politics*, pp. 42, 54.

restrictions on a federal franchise.[66] Though manufacturers proposed extensive Federal labour control powers, the victorious exporters voted them down 25–12. The exporters' assessment proved correct. By 1892 both shearers and miners were in full retreat, and the
Melbourne Trades Hall Council and the Sydney Trades and Labour
Council were crumbling from financial pressures.[67] The issue of arbitration powers reversed, with labor taking up the cry in order to win
back politically the economic power that striking had lost. Arbitration
of labour issues then became a local political issue.

The rise of Labor parties could not be shrugged off as easily as the
crumbling unions, for it immediately affected credit. South Australian and Queensland bond issues in London in February and May
of 1891 were only 33 percent and 10 percent subscribed; a Victorian
issue on the eve of the Sydney Convention was only 60 percent subscribed; and NSW, the most creditworthy, going to the market at a
relatively favorable time, managed only a 90 percent subscription.[68]
Financiers and their pastoral subalterns blamed the Labor parties for
the erosion of public credit. The *Australasian Pastoralists Review* complained:

What is the main cause of . . . financial insecurity? . . . The real reason is
undoubtedly to be found in the political unrest that is being engendered
throughout the colonies by a certain segment of the labouring classes. . . .
Investors in England have found out . . . the liability [*sic*] of colonial
legislatures to fall under the control of men who are quite prepared to
undermine the foundations of national prosperity by passing laws of a
reckless and revolutionary character.[69]

Meanwhile articles attacking Australian credit were rebutted by declarations of the inevitable and "beneficial" aspects of Federation.[70]

66. *Official Report of the National Australasian Convention Debates*, pp. 634–637.
67. See Rickard, *Class and Politics*, pp. 36–37, and generally, for the argument that
"middle class" fears that capital-labour conflict would expand into social revolution led
that class to push arbitration. See *Economist*, August 15, 1891, p. 1049, for fears of the
Labor Parties. See *Official Report of the National Australasian Convention Debates*, pp. 780–
785, for debate over labour control powers.
68. A. Hall, *The London Capital Market and Australia, 1870–1914* (Canberra: ANU
Press, 1963), is the best study for general background and a retrospective analysis of
Australian borrowing; see also *Economist*, October 18, 1890, for British perceptions of
the problem of political labour; Coghlan, *Labour and Industry In Australia*, pp. 1714–
1716; *Melbourne Age*, April 14, 1891; Boehm, *Prosperity and Depression*, p. 177.
69. APR, December 15, 1891, p. 377.
70. J. Fortescue, "Seamy Side of Australia," *Nineteenth Century* 29 (April 1891), and
"Guileless Australia"; R. Hamilton, "Lending Money to Australia," *Nineteenth Century* 32
(August 1892).

The Draft Constitution

It is thus unsurprising that the Sydney Convention drafted a constitution largely addressing the fiscal and political threats to public credit. It called for a minimalist central government whose only extraneous power was debt resumption and whose conservatism was assured by an upper house nominated by the state (i.e. Colonial) Legislatures; a strong Governor-General; and a High Court subordinated to the legislature. The controversies (e.g., the tariff) were given to the first Federal parliament to resolve. Just after the power to tax was listed the power to raise loans on the credit of the "Dominion of Australasia," taking precedence over defense, law, commerce and a host of other federal powers.[71] The Federal state's power to resume and convert extant loans removed control over borrowing from colonial governments, where Labor was strong, to a higher, more secure level of state. Creditors saw the strong nominee upper house and the restricted franchise as guarantees against the possibility that a Labor government in any given state would undermine not only that colony's credit but also that of the others, and as a dam against "the shallow surface opinion of the mob."[72] But despite their desire for Federation *cum* debt resumption, and their strong ties to the various colonial governments, they could not simply ram Federation down Australian throats. First, dealing with seven distinct governments meant accommodating a range of particularist interests. Second, the legacy of the Reform Act and the absence of strong military forces made any repressive solution (as in Argentina) difficult, even though individuals within the financial community might have preferred something along those lines.[73] The Irish-Australians were citizens and could not be openly disenfranchised like syndicalist Italians in Buenos Aires who lacked Argentine citizenship. Both labour and

71. LaNauze, *Making of the Australian Constitution*, p. 292. The U.S. Senate was still appointed at this time.

72. Quote in *Melbourne Argus*, April 27, 1891. Twenty-seven percent of the population was eligible to vote in NSW in 1891; Loveday, "Labor," p. 176. For contemporary perceptions and declarations of intent about the Senate and franchise, see *Official Report of the National Australasian Convention Debates*, pp. 589–593, 625, 630–637.

73. See, for example, W. McMillan's correspondence with Parkes: McMillan to Parkes, September 1890, ML MS A925, pp. 796–808; McMillan to Parkes, September 24, 1895, ibid., pp. 824–825; and McMillan to Parkes, June 21, 1893, ML MS A884, pp. 383–384. *Melbourne Argus* called for an imposed, nonplebiscitary constitution; April 27, 1891. By contrast, see comments in *Melbourne Age* February 4–5, 1895, on the Premiers' Conference. Civil liberties were routinely suspended during major strikes; strikers were arrested without warrants and held without habeas corpus; *Sydney Daily Telegraph*, August 30, 1894; *Brisbane Worker*, September 6, 1894.

manufacturers thus had a say on the draft constitution's fate. The popular forces, shut out of the Sydney Convention so that it could determine how best to control them, proved the draft constitution's undoing.

Labour opposed the draft constitution, an opposition that by demonstrating Labor's political power, actually increased the need for Federation while blocking it. Labour correctly assessed the constitution as an effort to contain local reforms and block their spread to more retrograde colonies. The *Brisbane Worker* complained that: "Political federation of the colonies without one-man–one-vote is a huge piece of political chicanery. . . . A huge propertied federal parliament will be created into whose hands certain important functions, *including the maintenance of order*, will be surrendered. . . . This federal parliament is evidently designed to be the stronghold of Australian Capitalism."[74] The proposed franchise limited participation; the nominee upper house was even more insulated than the nominee Colonial Legislative Councils. Nationalist opinion—an amalgam of Labor, Irish, and small producers—similarly suspected the draft's intent: "Time and popular opinion have been filing away the Imperial connection to a shadow but the Constitution has renewed its substance."[75] If labour's strike in part inspired the Sydney Convention, Labor's political "strike" scuttled the constitution. The other Legislatures waited on NSW to accept the constitution, for Federation would be a hollow shell without NSW participation. But the NSW Labor Electoral League used its control of the NSW Parliamentary balance to table the Bill, and then combined with anti-Federation farmers and manufacturers threatened by intercolonial free trade to turn out pro-Federation Premier Parkes.[76] Subsequently the other Colonial Legislatures left the draft in limbo.

This demonstration of the Labor Party's power only aggravated fears about Australian credit. One London banker warned that:

A notable factor, more and more recognised here as working with augmenting power against the financial *prestige* of the Australasian colonies

74. *Brisbane Worker*, May 16, 1891, original emphasis. See ibid., November 3, 1894, February 23, 1895, and March 2, 1895, for similar statements. See Gollan, *Radical and Working Class Politics*, pp. 176–177, for an account of Labor Party attempts to extend the local franchise.
75. *Bulletin*, April 18, 1891, quoted in LaNauze, *Making of the Australian Constitution*, p. 76. See also Gollan, *Radical and Working Class Politics*, pp. 119, 194–196: "Australian national feeling was an essential part of class feeling."
76. LaNauze, *Making of the Australian Constitution*, pp. 86–89; Quick and Garran, *Annotated Constitution*, pp. 145–150.

generally, is the present and prospective ascendancy of working men, not only in the electorates, but in the Legislative Assemblies. The balance of power is now regarded as in the hands of the strong Labour Party in the NSW Parliament; and it is considered only a question of time before other Australian parliaments are similarly dominated. *Added to this is the indefinite postponement of inter-colonial federation.*

Six months later he echoed his warning in stronger terms: "It is the wildest delusion for English capitalists to lend scores of millions to so evanescent a corporation as a colonial government (whose members are incessantly liable to be displaced), without having available sources of Government revenue in every case pledged against public loans."[77]

Divisions among business also prevented an imposed constitution. Had financiers had more allies, they could perhaps have simply ignored labour and imposed a solution. But Victoria's interior bourgeoisie in manufacturing inclined against an imposed solution favoring financial interests.[78] At the 1891 Sydney Convention a small group of "liberals," originating in manufacturing capital, proposed a number of democratizing measures, including an elected Senate.[79] Their failure contributed to the manufacturers' lack of enthusiasm

77. First quote, AIBR, December 18, 1891, p. 894; emphasis added. Second quote, AIBR, May 18, 1892, 16:5, pp. 332–333. See also Hall, *London Capital Market and Australia*, p. 203.

78. Manufacturers were not united, however. NSW manufacturers were split into those working up imported goods for re-export to other colonies and those manufacturing local goods, the former desiring free trade and the latter fearing it. A. Martin, "Economic Influences in the 'New Federation' Movement," HSANZ 6 (November 1953), 69. South Australian manufacturing districts that elected the radical C. C. Kingston showed anti-Federation majorities in two referenda to approve the constitution. R. Norris, "Economic Influences on the 1898 SA Federation Referendum," in Martin, ed., *Essays in Australian Federation*, pp. 137–166. Western Australia, with virtually no established industries, resisted imposition of intercolonial free trade to the last, extracting a five-year exemption from it as the price for joining the Federation. A prominent Western Australian publisher wrote to Deakin: "It would be unwise for us to enter the federation until . . . [we] consolidate our embryo industries." National Library of Australia, Manuscript no. (hereafter NLA MS) 1540/11/ 54–5, J. W. Hackett to A. Deakin, May 23, 1898.

79. "Liberal" is LaNauze's term. Deakin, Kingston, and Cockburn moved to establish machinery for the arbitration of industrial disputes, to create a federal franchise without plural voting (at the time, multiple residency or ownership conferred multiple votes), and to require popular referenda for adoption and amendment of the constitution at the 1891 convention. LaNauze, *Making of the Australian Constitution*, p. 72. The only "liberal" motion to pass, and that narrowly, was abolition of appeal from a future Australian High Court to the British Privy Council. The significance of this is discussed below. On the Senate, see *Melbourne Age*, March 9, 1891. Victoria's Chief Justice lambasted Federation as "really a plutocracy and not a democracy." NLA MS 1540/11/7–8, G. Higgenbotham to A. Deakin, April 4, 1891. For Deakin's similar feelings see A. Deakin, *Federal Story* (Melbourne: Robertson and Muellens, 1944), p. 55.

for the draft constitution; they feared that a nominee Senate, composed largely of pastoral largeholders and mercantile capitalists, would use what even the *Economist* called "despotic powers" to block political reforms aimed at expanding manufacturers' political base, to block protection, and to block state economic intervention to widen the local market.[80] Though not all went as far as Charles Kingston, who proposed negotiating with the new NSW Labor Party to outflank NSW financial interests, manufacturers saw popular consent as a weapon they could wield against both labour and financiers. Alfred Deakin first suggested using plebiscitary approval of the constitution as a way to rally public support for Federation while assuring manufacturers' goals.[81]

Nevertheless, manufacturers had one important stake in the Federation process and so were willing to bargain with the financial interests they opposed. They desired "free trade throughout Australasia," as the Victorian Chamber of Manufacturers telegraphed the 1891 convention.[82] Victoria was a net exporter to the rest of the Colonies, but tariffs blocked further expansion. "Under the fostering influence of Protection, numerous manufacturing industries were established on a sound footing" in Victoria, according to B. R. Wise. "The time was approaching, however, when, unless there were a large influx of immigrants, the local market would be oversupplied, and it would be imperative to seek new outlets for the surplus [production]."[83] As Victorian manufacturers largely produced consumption goods for labour, declining wage levels after the strikes motivated fresh demands for a customs union. But manufacturers saw little gain from full scale Federation, because markets, not guarantees for public debt, concerned them. They preferred the simplest possible political solution to their problem, a mere customs union with economic but not political amalgamation with its attendant risk of a nominated Senate. When Federation was first discussed in 1890, the *Melbourne Age* craftily urged that "instead of advancing toward Federation *per saltum*, we advance toward it step by step, and allow a Customs

---

80. *Economist*, April 11, 1891, p. 491.

81. NLA MS 1540/11/167, C. C. Kingston to A. Deakin, July 16, 1891. ML MS A930, pp. 693–696, H. Parkes correspondence, A. Deakin to H. Parkes, July 23, 1891. Note that the three senior Premiers, Parkes (NSW), Munro (Victoria), and Playford (South Australia), met privately to discuss ways to obtain popular support; *Melbourne Age*, April 27, 1891. See also *Melbourne Age*, January 29, 1895; Coghlan, *Labour and Industry in Australia*, p. 2343; Deakin, *Federal Story*, p. 55; and NLA MS 1540/11/10, H. Parkes to A. Deakin, May 26, 1892.

82. *Official Report of the National Australasian Convention Debates*, p. 108.

83. Wise, *Making of the Australian Commonwealth*, p. 334.

Union."[84] And at the 1891 convention, Victorian Premier Gillies expressed manufacturers' misgivings at the political integration that Federation implied: "I imagine that we all understood in the formation of this federation that it was not such a federation as would be a complete legislative federation. . . . We are gradually going beyond that idea."[85] The full fledged Federation proposed in 1890 and written up in 1891 thus exceeded their needs.

So while Labor continued to block a federal solution, Victorian manufacturers' organizations pursued a sustained extra-parliamentary campaign in favor of a customs union. This campaign started before the 1893 bank crash, under the aegis of the Australian Natives Association (hereafter ANA), a group of nationalist manufacturers with a disproportionately large Catholic membership.[86] After the crash, agitation increased. The president of the VEU saw "incalculable" benefit to "industrial enterprise if a customs union were arranged," and the Victorian Chamber of Manufacturers declared its "unanimous opinion . . . to see a customs union established."[87] Both, however, still called for a customs union rather than for the further political integration Federation implied. But graziers and merchants continued to argue for the "great advantages to be gained from complete consolidation. For instance," said the APR in 1893, "Federation would reestablish Australian credit to an extent which a Customs Union could not reach, and lead to further, but wiser, output of British enterprise throughout the continent. . . . What Federation tends to promote is that confidence which is so conspicuously absent in Australia now."[88] With capitals unable to compromise, and Labor

84. February 6, 1890. The *Melbourne Age*, champion of manufacturing interests, continued to proclaim the virtues of intercolonial free trade in the next five years, although it also said that protection was more important than federation (March 5, 1891). See Deakin, *Federal Story*, p. 89, for the *Age*'s motivations. The *Melbourne Argus*, more reflective of financial interests, cautiously advocated Federation when it spoke on the issue at all.

85. *Official Report of the National Australasian Convention Debates*, p. 624. Gillies also wrote Parkes urging him to propose a Canadian style confederation; J. Neasey, "Andrew Ingles Clark Sr. and Australian Federation," *Australian Journal of Politics and History* (AJPH) 15 (August 1969), 4; see also Quick and Garran, *Annotated Constitution*, pp. 143–147, on Victorian social groups involved in the Federation movement.

86. Roman Catholic membership in the ANA was disproportionately large relative to overall Roman Catholic control of capital in Australia, but not to the population in general. See Deakin, *Federal Story*, pp. 4, 90, and generally, for the ANA's role in Federation. *Melbourne Tocsin*, February 24, 1898, claimed that the ANA spent £80,000 promoting Federation. The Melbourne Trades Hall Council supported the ANA's campaign; Gollan, *Radical and Working Class Politics*, p. 141.

87. *Melbourne Age*, June 21, 1893.

88. *Australasian Pastoralists Review*, May 15, 1893, p. 68.

set against it, the movement for political or economic amalgamation seemingly died in the Legislative Assemblies in late 1891. To contemporary observers, political amalgamation seemed a dead issue, and politicians turned to local solutions. But these solutions needed time to work, and time proved lacking, first because the Labor Parties waxed, second because the whole financial system was at the edge of collapse.[89]

Conflicts among Capital and the Second Federation Movement

Growth of the Labor Parties

After 1892 the threat posed by unions continued to recede, and with it exporters' desire for political solutions to strikes. Labor sought arbitration as an alternative to direct action and, in combination with some manufacturers in Victoria, succeeded in legislating minimum wages and working conditions in four Melbourne trades in 1896. In 1900–1901, the NSW Labor Party combined with various segments of NSW business to pass an Act prohibiting strikes and imposing binding arbitration on both business and labour. While these Acts served to contain the renascent labour movement of the late 1890s, the "solutions" were too tardy and tiny to affect the rise of *political* labour.

The ebbing of the labour threat only aggravated conflicts between capitals, each trying to assure its own survival at the expense of another's bankruptcy. This conflict opened up a space in which political labour flourished. In elections from 1892 to 1895, Labor expanded its parliamentary representation to control about 11 percent of Legislative Assembly seats by 1896.[90] Labor polled 35 percent of the vote in South Australia and Queensland. Labor's attraction for Irish Catholics led Sydney's Cardinal Moran to declare: "I regard Federation as the only means of preventing one or the other of the Colonies from going right over to extreme Socialism."[91] Rising unemployment after

89. See LaNauze, *Making of the Australian Constitution*, pp. 88–90, on contemporary perceptions. Only in New Zealand were local "solutions" successful, but New Zealand lacked the pressures that independent Labor Parties created, and success came at the cost of increased debt.

90. C. Hughes, B. Graham, *A Handbook of Australian Government and Politics, 1890–1964* (Canberra: ANU Press, 1968), *passim*.

91. *Sydney Daily Telegraph*, July 17, 1894. For Irish and Catholic support of Labor, see C. Hamilton, "Irish Catholics of NSW and the Labour Party, 1890–1910," HSANZ 8 (November 1958), 127–128.

the strikes fed discontent and Labor's prospects, which alarmed creditors. For the *Economist*, "The condition of . . . the working classes in Melbourne first excite[s] commiseration and then (because of their crude and badly advised political views) apprehension for the future."[92] And Australian financiers pondered the "deeply rooted fear in well-informed [London] circles that while the insane system of protection continues to extend, population will neglect the boundless resources of the country, and fill the towns with a dangerous unemployed element, which must sooner or later become a chronic source of evil."[93] A. Bruce Smith, the Sydney shipper who helped form both the Melbourne and the Sydney employers' unions, declared at the 1897/98 convention that "this growth on our body politic [i.e. Labor], can only be removed for all time by the proposed Federation of the Colonies."[94] But by this time, the second wave of pressure for Federation had achieved a new, popularly elected convention. The issues motivating groups to push for political amalgamation continued to be the central crises of public and private debt, reflected and aggravated by the 1893 bank crash.

The 1893 Bank Crash

Behind the wave of pastoral foreclosures had come another and greater wave of urban defaults culminating in a general bank failure in 1893. This crash triggered intense conflict among capitalists about whose investments would be protected and whose would disappear. The vast expansion of pastoral activity in the 1880s had engendered a secondary boom in the major entrepot cities, fed by pastoral sector labour purchases, by an enlarged middle class based in government bureaucracy (especially the rails), and by rail systems' local purchases. Peculation and speculation had created a mad scramble to buy suburban land and erect housing for the growing population, especially along inter- and intra-urban railways.[95] This strategy seemed infallible, given insider knowledge and an urban population that was growing at an annual rate of 5.2 percent. Capital came from Britain and

92. *Economist*, March 19, 1892; see also *Economist*, May 18, 1895, p. 650, for similar fears. P. Macarthy, "The Living Wage in Australia and the Role of Government," *Labour History* 18 (May 1970), quotes a NSW grazier as saying that wages had fallen by half.

93. AIBR, May 18, 1892, p. 332.

94. Quoted in H. Evatt, *Australian Labour Leader* (Sydney: Angus & Robertson, 1945), p. 97.

95. See Cannon, *Land Boomers*, for a sometimes droll compendium of misfeasance and malfeasance.

Table 10. Patterns of ownership of Melbourne housing, 1880–1890

Year	Total holdings (£ mil)	Index total holdings	Bldg societies (%)	Life Insur. Cos. (%)	LMCs* (%)	Index, LMC holdings
1880	4.5	100	45.9	31.5	19.5	100
1885	8.7	193	50.4	20.6	19.1	189
1887	12.3	272	52.5	17.7	21.7	303
1888	17.2	380	45.7	14.5	32.2	628
1890	23.3	515	36.9	15.4	38.0	1007

*LMCs = Land mortgage companies.
SOURCE: Calculated from Silberberg, "Institutional Investors," p. 169. Residual percentage held by savings banks.

Australia's own pastoral areas. Falling wool prices and profits after 1885 moved land mortgage firms to redirect their investment activity into urban areas. Soon their investments in Melbourne housing increased at double the average rate for other investors.[96] (See Table 10.) British deposits in Australian banks also rose dramatically after 1885, with the total increase in deposits from 1887 to 1890, £13.2 million, slightly exceeding the net investment in Melbourne mortgages, £11.8 million.[97]

Victoria's faster rate of growth and more urbanized population—43.1 percent compared to the 33.0 percent Australian average—intensified the speculative boom there. In Melbourne alone, 52,000 new dwellings were constructed in the 1880s, and landlords may well have been the single largest urban class.[98] The wealth generated by the Broken Hill mining complex and by local manufacturing drew a disproportionate share of British investment; about half the British capital invested in Australian banks was channeled through Victorian banks. Even so, this base proved too narrow, for bank loans in Victoria totaled £100 million, twice the per capita average in Australia; in NSW they totaled £43 million in 1890.[99]

But the flight of both domestic and foreign capital from faltering

96. R. Silberberg, "Institutional Investors in the Real Estate Mortgage Market in Victoria in the 1880s," AEHR 18 (September 1978), 169.

97. *Economist*, November 22, 1890, p. 1474.

98. Coghlan, *A Statistical Account of Australia and New Zealand*, 1903/4 (Sydney: Government Printer, 1904), pp. 149, 155; Dingle and Merrett, "Homeowners and Tenants in Melbourne 1891–1911," AEHR 12:1 (March 1972), 22, 33. For data on investment in housing, see N. G. Butlin, *Private Capital Formation in Australia* (ANU, Canberra: Department of Economics, 1955), p. 51.

99. Fitzpatrick, *British Empire in Australia*, p. 254; Coghlan, *Labour and Industry in Australia*, p. 2141; *Official Yearbook of New South Wales* (OYBNSW) 1915, p. 332.

pastoral investments to urban investments defeated its purpose, for it created no new growth to sustain the prices paid for land and housing. As increasing unemployment and shrinking pay packets in the stagnant pastoral sector decreased demand on the housing market, landlords failed to meet payments to their land company creditors; in turn, beginning in 1890, those companies failed when they no longer could pay the banks and bondholders holding their paper.[100] Between 14 and 20 percent of all new housing built in Melbourne in the 1880s was repossessed in a situation precisely paralleling that in pastoral landholding. "Financial institutions, which had underwritten much of the suburban expansion of the 1880s, were forced to repossess much property through default on the part of borrowers," as Dingle and Merrett wrote. "Institutions and their creditors were unable to sell without suffering substantial capital loss on a depressing housing market, and so became unwilling landlords."[101] From July 1891 to March 1892, forty-two building societies and mortgage firms failed; they represented 47 percent of such institutions and locked up 82 percent of their deposits.[102] Insolvency percolated up, and in the first half of 1893 thirteen mainly Melbourne-centered banks suspended, locking up 45 percent of deposits in what became known as the 1893 Bank Crash.[103] Only a handful of the major banks continued operations. Major pastoral firms, like Goldsborough Mort, failed. The crash liquidated British stockholders and depositors, who were forced to ante up capital to replace the estimated £11.5 million lost. British depositors fled, their deposits falling more than 75 percent at two representative banks. By 1900 British deposits had largely disappeared from Australia.[104]

The bank crash revealed what had been latent for four years: vast amounts of capital had been trapped in illiquid and worthless pastoral and urban property. By 1894, banks' urban mortgages were completely illiquid, and financial publications complained that "Rents . . .

100. *Economist*, September 12, 1891, applauded the elimination of "this cancerous growth on the otherwise sound financial business of Victoria."

101. Quotation from Dingle and Merrett, "Homeowners and Tenants in Melbourne," pp. 32–33; AIBR, November 19, 1894, p. 748.

102. S. Butlin, *The Australia and New Zealand Bank* (London: Longmans Green, 1971), p. 286; G. Blainey, *Gold and Paper* (Melbourne: Georgian House, 1958), p. 145, gives the figure of £18 million by December 1892.

103. *Economist*, May 13, 1893, p. 566; Butlin, *Australia and New Zealand Bank*, pp. 301–303.

104. Wood, *Borrowing and Business in Australia*, p. 71, citing Coghlan, *Labour and Industry in Australia*; Butlin, *Australia and New Zealand Bank*, pp. 316–317; Blainey, *Gold and Paper*, pp. 150–170; R. Holder, *Bank of NSW: A History*, 2 vols. (Sydney: Angus & Robertson, 1970), p. 496.

Table 11. Profit volume and rate for Australian banks, 1885–1909

Year	Volume (£ thous.)	Return on assets (%)
*1885–89 (ave.)	—	12.85
*1890–92 (ave.)	—	12.40
*1893	—	7.20
ˆ1899	908.1	2.64
*1900	—	4.05
ˆ1902	1579.5	4.10
ˆ1909	2479.4	5.41

SOURCES: *from Wood, *Borrowing and Business in Australia*, p. 70; ˆ from AIBR, January 21, 1909, p. 5; AIBR September 20, 1912, p. 758.

have generally become next to nominal." "At the moment real property in Melbourne possesses next to no marketable value."[105] Forty-two percent of National Bank of Australia loans paid no interest in 1895; Blainey says that stockholders who "for twenty years . . . had received dividends ranging from 10 to 15 percent . . . now receive[d] no more than 4.5 percent a year." Pastoral finance companies held equally illiquid assets for as the *Economist* noted: "squatting property is not at present marketable." Neville Cain tells us that only in "rare cases stations paid interest from current earnings."[106] Although Table 11 mixes data from two sources, the numbers tell a consistently depressing story.

Public Debt, Private Debt, and Federation

The crash unleashed a struggle among the different capitals invested in Australia over whose wealth would be lost, whose preserved. This contest generally pitted City of London holders of public debt against the mainly Scottish and Victorian holders of private, largely pastoral debt. Examination of the public situation, then the private, reveals the contours of this conflict and why capitals sought refuge in Federation.

105. First quotation, AIBR, November 19, 1894, p. 748; second quotation, *Economist*, October 20, 1894, p. 1282. *Economist*, May 13, 1893, p. 566, worried, "What employment is to be found for the money locked up at present in real property?"
106. First quotation, Blainey, *Gold and Paper*, pp. 164, 186. Second quotation, *Economist*, July 8, 1893, p. 817. See also *Economist*, June 13, 1896, p. 759. Third quotation, Cain, "Companies and Squatting in the Western Division of NSW," pp. 200–206. Goldsborough Mort, a major pastoral finance firm, wrote off £1 million of bad loans, 1896–1902. Ten typical stations representative of those Goldsborough financed had debt-asset ratios of 182 percent.

Declining wages, pastoral unprofitability, and the Bank Crash all stressed colonial budgets as revenue decreased. Colonies retrenched, hoping to create room in the budget to meet debt obligations. By 1894, though, the "shadow of a great deficit over an insolvent land" had become substance. Despite significant declines in expenditure, Victoria ran major deficits from 1890 to 1896 as depression lowered Victorian customs receipts by 25 percent (1890–95) and railway receipts by 18 percent. NSW managed a razor-thin surplus in one year as customs fell from their peak in 1892 by 50 percent, and total revenue by 10 percent. Though both Victoria and NSW cut staff, wages, and rail expenditure—Victoria by 32 percent, 1890–1896, NSW by 9.8 percent, 1891–FY 1897/8—the railways continued to show deficits.[107] Customs duties fell after the strikes, as lower wages led to a one-third reduction in consumption of the four goods contributing the most customs and excise revenue—beer, liquor, tobacco, and wine. Contracting revenues meant that debt service bulked larger in the budget: 24 percent up from 18 percent for NSW; 28 percent up from 18 percent for Victoria, 1890–95.[108] The London market made the situation worse, raising interest rates on new loans because, said the *Economist*, "the derangement of the finances is greater than the public know, and ministers shrink from stating the real position."[109]

If British capital had been more or less evenly distributed over the range of Australian investments, conflict over public debt might not have occurred. But City of London investment houses largely held Government debt, while pastoral companies drew their capital from thousands of small rentiers, especially Scots.[110] The City preferred its own security to that of other capitals, and demanded balanced budgets as a sign of willingness to meet public debt obligations. But the only way to increase revenue as customs and rail receipts declined was

107. *Victorian Statistical Register* (VSR) 1900, 301; *New South Wales Statistical Register* (NSWSR) 1900, pp. 933–939. Note that monetization of deficits was not a possibility in Australia, unlike Argentina or modern times, for the Australasian colonies used sterling. Victorian deficits averaged 8.6 percent of revenue, NSW deficits, 2.9 percent; Butlin, *Australian Domestic Product*, p. 184.

108. VSR 1899, Statistical Summary, p. 57; Boehm, *Prosperity and Depression*, p. 192; VSR 1914, Statistical Summary, pp. 2, 10, and elsewhere; NSWSR 1900, pp. 937, 939, and elsewhere. Victorian imports per capita fell almost by half between 1891 and 1895; *Victorian Yearbook*, 1895–98, p. 497.

109. *Economist*, June 18, 1892; see also July 30, 1892, March 4, 1893. Wise, *Making of the Australian Commonwealth*, p. 167, confirms prevarication by NSW treasury: "There was a very large deficit, although this was not admitted . . . by the treasurer."

110. Bailey, *Hundred Years of Pastoral Banking*, pp. 62, 64–65. Wood, *Borrowing and Business*, p. 52.

to impose direct taxes on land and income. Both of these would hurt the crippled pastoral industry further, driving more and more private capital into bankruptcy. Even before the imposition of direct taxes, eight million acres of leased pastoral land was abandoned in NSW in 1893.[111]

The domestic—largely Victorian—and Scots mortgagees of pastoral and urban land made every effort to preserve their own investments at the expense of increased unemployment and insecure public debt. They first tried a positive strategy of revalorizing pastoral land by selling it for subdivision into farms, since farm land carried a higher price per acre because of agriculture's greater productivity. Pastoralists' mortgagees could capture part of the difference between the land's value for pastoral and for agricultural use when they sold the land. But they needed state intervention thus to raise the value of pastoral land. As no one could afford to buy land, pastoralists and their bankers proposed *Crédit Foncier* subsidized mortgage schemes, which attempted to loan the unemployed money to buy land. On the continent, South Australia made the greatest efforts, but all emulated her and New Zealand.[112] The London bankers, however, took a dim view of these efforts to revalorize pastoral property, fearing that they would come at the expense of public debt service and that they courted default. The *Economist* said in February 1895: "All these imitations of the *Crédit Foncier* system have at bottom two aims, viz., 1st, the maintenance of the reputed value of land, and 2nd, the introduction of fresh British capital. Australian land is to retain a fictitious value by the help of the British investor. Otherwise, there is no necessity for the intervention of the State in mortgage business." It explained that "loans are no longer regarded only as instruments of 'development' but as necessary to provide employment for workmen, to enable the Government to repurchase land at exorbitant prices, and generally 'to keep things going'. It is hard to ignore the fact that

---

111. Roberts, *History of Australian Land Settlement*, pp. 292–293.

112. Chapter 5 examines the social bases and consequences of New Zealand's extensive resettlement scheme. See AIBR, October 19, 1894, pp. 673–674; and May 18, 1895, p. 284, on the NSW Land Bill; Fitzpatrick, *British Empire in Australia*, pp. 173–174, on Victorian efforts to stimulate dairy production; R. Walker, "Ambiguous Experiment: Agricultural Cooperatives in NSW, 1893–1896," *Labour History* 18 (May 1970); and R. Shlomowitz, "The Search for Institutional Integrity in Queensland's Sugar Industry," AEHR 19 (September 1979), for information on those Colonies. VSR 1899, vol. 10, p. 59, provides data about the differing scale of *Crédit* operations. Victoria, with a population of roughly 1.1 million, by 1899/1900 had loaned £896,000; New Zealand, with 700,000 people, loaned £1,747,000; South Australia, with 350,000 people loaned £455,000.

restoration of confidence in Australian finance in London is a most pressing need." London feared *Crédit* bonds would end up as valueless and unmarketable as the Argentine mortgage bonds called *cédula*.[113] While local borrowing was possible, local lenders had a better appreciation of the precariousness of colonial finances and demanded even higher interest rates than the London market. Without access to new loans, the *Crédit* schemes remained limited. Only in New Zealand, where London was more forthcoming with loans, did *Crédit* systems have major success freeing capital from land.

Unable to revalorize land, domestic financiers settled on a defensive strategy of severe retrenchment. The core of these policies was similar to the IMF's typical austerity regime and indeed could be interpreted as being in the interests of the City, not of the domestic financiers. The *Australasian Insurance and Banking Record* (AIBR), which generally reflected domestic financial interests, demanded reductions in imports and public spending, and asked labour to accept lower wages for the good of the community. All were solutions to the imbalance of payments and revenue that threatened public default. AIBR also attacked the major source of budget deficits, the railways, claiming: "The financial rehabilitation of the Colonies cannot be completely achieved without an absolute cessation from public borrowing and the construction of public works for the present," and that "The development of the [railway] traffic is the problem of the hour and until it is solved there should be no more railway construction. . . . The local form of borrowing is as objectionable . . . as floating loans abroad.[114]

But the City's call for direct taxation to balance the budget explains why domestic financiers demanded decreased borrowing and retrenchment as the path to increased net rail revenue. Direct taxes on

113. First quotation, *Economist*, February 9, 1895, p. 185; second quotation *Economist*, January 3, 1892, pp. 9–10. For an explicit comparison with Argentine mortgage bonds called *cédula*, *Economist*, August 4, 1894, p. 953. See also Coghlan, *Labour and Industry in Australia*, p. 2067, for a description of South Australia's difficulties with its *Crédit Foncier*; and Roberts, *History of Australian Land Settlement*, p. 336 and *passim*. Australian financiers preferred revaluation of pastoral land to urban; AIBR, November 1897, p. 803.

114. Quotation from AIBR, December 18, 1893, pp. 1083–1084. See AIBR, September 19, 1892, p. 641, for evidence of AIBR's understanding of the links between stagnant wages and stagnant customs revenue. Clearly they hoped that the increased exports engendered by lower wages would offset lost customs revenues. AIBR continuously linked its concerns about export production, debt service, and public debt to Federation; see AIBR, October 19, 1892, pp. 715–716; September 19, 1893, p. 849; and April 19, 1894, p. 218. See APR, May 16, 1898, p. 112, for an obfuscatory rationale for pastoral support for Federation.

land and income put fresh burdens on pastoral production, on devalued urban property, and on the rich. As early as 1893, pastoralists
railed against direct taxes: "Before additional taxation is granted in
any of the Colonies the several Parliaments should insist upon much
severer retrenchment . . . reducing borrowing to a minimum. . . .
Nothing would do more to retard recovery than . . . levying special
burdens upon the landholders."[115] Because the rail deficit was in most
years larger than the overall budget deficit—i.e., was the cause of
budget deficits—reducing that deficit removed the necessity for direct taxes. While railway expansion would create some new opportunities for grazing, it would not help the profitability of *existing* pastoral investments, and these were banks' first concern.[116] Domestic
and Scots financiers thus tried to preserve what profit flow they could
from the enterprises they dominated.

The outcomes of these struggles among capitals depended, of
course, on the specific balance of power in each colony.[117] In NSW,
where the old "free trade" party of domestic and foreign financiers
and pastoralists had fragmented, George Reid's 1894 coalition of Labor and London attacked the weakened pastoral complex.[118] Domestic financial interests were much weaker in NSW than in Victoria, and
extensive foreclosures had stripped Scots lenders of their pastoral
allies. Reid, whose ties to London were always close, replaced a regime
of regressive tariffs protecting rural interests with free trade and
direct taxes on land and income. London approved of Reid's direct
taxation, and lowered interest rates on NSW issues after Reid raised
taxes. But, notes Coghlan, "Reid's . . . proposals for direct taxation
were vastly disliked by the [pastoralist-dominated] Legislative Council, which lost no opportunity of obstructing him."[119] In Victoria,

115. APR, July 15, 1893, pp. 219–220.
116. *Economist*, December 17, 1892, p. 1580, recognized and argued that the extension of railways was likely to decrease revenue.
117. See Rickard, *Class and Politics*, and various articles in Loveday, *Emergence of the
Australian Party System*, for more extensive descriptions of these alliances.
118. See *Sydney Daily Telegraph*, July 16–17, 1894 and October 10-13, 1894; ML MS
3039, p. 83–86, J. Ashton to P. Morton, July 10, 1895, and pp. 87–90, P. Morton to G.
Reid, July 31, 1895, for Reid's strategy and political realignments. See also J. LaNauze,
Alfred Deakin, 2 vols. (Melbourne: Melbourne University Press, 1965), p. 136; A. Martin, "Free Trade and Protectionist Parties in NSW," HSANZ 6 (May 1955), 316–319;
and Martin, "Legislative Assembly of NSW, 1856–1900," AJPH 2 (November 1956), 64.
See Patterson, *Tariff in the Australian Colonies*, pp. 144–151 on NSW tariffs. See ABL
78/1/68, pp. 426–427, J. Gregson to AAC/L, October 4, 1895, for graziers' reactions to
the land and income tax. NSW also tried to tax foreign dividend payments, which
would have hurt land companies; see ABL 78/1/69, pp. 429–430, J. Gregson to AAC/L,
October 3, 1896, and p. 448, November 2, 1896.
119. Coghlan, *Labour and Industry in Australia*, p. 1946.

pastoralists were more resilient because they had diversified production much earlier, while domestic financiers were politically more salient than in NSW because of the great wealth that Broken Hill had generated. Instead of a London-Labor alliance, Victoria's coalition government linked all domestic interests behind a policy of muddling through and hiding prior political malfeasance.[120] Victoria tried a *Crédit Foncier* scheme to a much greater extent than NSW, but nowhere near as extensively as New Zealand or South Australia. Despite direct taxes on income, London remained wary of Victoria and interest rates stayed higher than for the other colonies.

Thus colonial-level efforts, after the Maritime Strike and the bank crash, to resolve the public and private debt crisis and to control labour yielded no solutions. If anything, these efforts intensified the two debt crises as capitals followed *sauve qui peut* policies. In this context Federation began to look attractive even on the terms that manufacturers were demanding, for it offered a way to restore both public and private credit while containing labour politically. As colonial efforts looked less and less fruitful, more and more financial groups, beginning with Victorian financiers, added their voices to those of the manufacturers.

Almost immediately after the crash, pro-Federation leagues formed in NSW and Victoria in 1893, holding unofficial conferences in Corowa, NSW in July–August 1893 and Bendigo, Victoria, in January 1894. Australian Natives Association (ANA) members were particularly visible at these meetings, but representatives of Victorian financial capital attended Bendigo.[121] Both conferences resolved that the Colonial Legislative Assemblies should pass laws enabling a constitutional convention to take place; provisions for popularly elected convention delegates and plebiscitary approval of the constitution would remove the Federation process and its outcome from the Assemblies' control. That way neither Labor nor the grazier- and financier-dominated Legislative Councils could obstruct the process. The adhesion of Victorian financiers to the side of the manufacturers

120. Rickard, *Class and Politics*, p. 111. In any case, Victoria was much more dependent on tariffs for government revenue than was NSW; Patterson, *Tariff in Australian Colonies*, pp. 145–146. See also W. Sinclair, *Economic Recovery in Victoria, 1894–1899* (Canberra: ANU Press, 1956), for economic data.

121. Quick and Garran, *Annotated Constitution*, pp. 102–103. According to Quick and Garran, ANA members proposed popularly elected delegates, while a caucus of ANA members, Victorian MLAs, and Imperial Federation Leaguers approved it. See Deakin, *Federal Story*, for the ANA's role in Federation; see also *Melbourne Age* editorials on January 29, 1895, February 4, 1895, and February 5, 1895. For a critical view of the ANA see *Tocsin*, February 24, 1898.

doomed any lingering hopes of an imposed constitution and assured
that the Corowa/Bendigo proposals would govern any future conventions.

Because highly exposed Victorian banks would benefit if a customs
union brought a revalorization of *urban* property in Melbourne, they
were the first to move closer to the manufacturers' position, retreat-
ing from demands for complete Federation, and supporting a customs union as a stopgap measure. In early 1894 AIBR declared that
"the remedy [for the 1893 crash] is either Federation, or failing that, a
Customs Union."[122] Still, specific problems revealed or exacerbated
by the crash impelled financiers to seek a more complete form of
Federation. The lockup of small depositors' money in the crash had
engendered a "spirit of distrust" among depositors that imperiled the
"safety of financial institutions." When British depositors holding only
a minority of deposits prevented banks from helping small depositors, bank prestige sank lower.[123] Banks thus feared a hodgepodge of
hostile local legislation if the individual colonies attempted to tighten
banking regulation, especially over their important and highly profitable trans-colonial branches.[124] Bankers also desired publicly issued
currency, as "there was no longer any worthwhile profit in note issue,"
but as with branches, they "preferred uniform legislation and note
issue."[125] Thus fear of hostile local legislation made Federation *qua*
national legislation preferable to a mere customs union. A meeting of
bank managers in 1895 probably confirmed a policy of support for
Federation and federal laws, and after the 1897–98 conventions,
bankers lobbied for national legislation. "Legislation such as we want
can only be undertaken by a Federal Parliament," editorialized H.
Turner, Manager of the Commercial Bank of Australia.[126]

Despite these narrow concerns, public debt remained the banks'
primary worry as conflicts between capitals heated up. By March

122. AIBR, January 18, 1894; see also AIBR, June 19, 1894, p. 367. See Martin,
"Free Trade and Protectionist Parties in NSW," p. 321, on motivations for pro-federation activity by other elite groups.

123. Quoted in AIBR, January 18, 1894: Blainey, *Gold and Paper*, pp. 168–170.
Bankers probably welcomed the liquidation of British deposits forced by the crash; see
AIBR, January 19, 1895, p. 1, for veiled remarks about this.

124. AIBR, March 18, 1893, p. 164. The five largest banks did 42.5 percent of their
business at branches, the top ten, 32.4 percent; the five largest banks' branch activity
equalled 21.3 percent of all Australian bank activity.

125. Butlin, *Australia and New Zealand Bank*, pp. 324–325; Crisp, *Australian National
Government*, p. 15.

126. Quoted in AIBR, May 19, 1900, p. 366: On the 1895 meeting, see Fitzpatrick,
British Empire in Australia, p. 257; and Butlin, *Australia and New Zealand Bank*, pp. 324–
325.

1895, AIBR put its worries about debt ahead of its worries about hostile legislation:

> The great questions in the work of federating Australia are naturally the consolidation of the public debts and the nationalization of the currency. Such a state of affairs [as existed in the United States, where Bryan was leading his crusade against the "Cross of Gold"] does not at present exist in Australia, but, with an unreasoning and often unreasonable class legislation the danger is one which cannot too strongly be pointed at.[127]

AIBR also feared the burden that new direct taxes were placing on devalued pastoral and urban property, especially in NSW. Consequently, as conflict between City holders of public debt and everyone else increased, those domestic financiers who still rejected a plebiscitary constitution in 1893–94 finally accepted the Corowa/Bendigo scheme in 1895. By then, Federation seemed the only way to prevent fratricidal conflict between capitals. The director of the Sydney Joint Stock Bank lectured his fellows: "The federation of the Australian Colonies would meet and finally settle the difference of opinion that now exists between us and the English Capitalist. Securities resting on the asset of United Australia could no longer be flouted by a pack of London brokers . . . but . . . would take their place among the best securities . . . in any part of the world."[128]

To the 1897 Elections and Conventions

By 1895, then, the consequences and limitations of colony-level solutions led to a convergence of the previously conflicting interests of Victorian manufacturers and financiers, London financiers, and pastoralists around some sort of continental political solution. As in 1891, NSW remained the key colony. In NSW the protectionist Dibbs ministry, whose social base centered on manufacturers and farmers threatened by Victorian and South Australian producers, had obstructed Federation proposals through 1894. At one point Dibbs had proposed complete unification in place of Federation, but groups favoring Federation saw this as his way of asking for everything in hopes of getting nothing.[129] In 1894, Reid successfully outbid Dibbs

127. AIBR, March 19, 1895, p. 154.
128. Barton Lodge, "Federation and the English Investors," *Journal of the Institute of the Bankers of NSW*, January 16, 1893, quoted in Martin, "Economic Influences in the 'New Federation' Movement," p. 68.
129. Wise, *Making of the Australian Commonwealth*, p. 105; Quick and Garran, *Annotated Constitution*, p. 156.

for Labor Party support, offering arbitration, franchise and social reforms and, of course, direct taxation. Reid then proposed a meeting of premiers, which the other premiers, except for New Zealand's, reluctantly attended in 1895. At this meeting the premiers acceded to enabling acts. In late 1895 and early 1896, as the deficit issue and direct taxation became increasingly salient, five Colonies passed enabling acts along the plebiscitary lines proposed at Corowa-Bendigo.[130] Uncertain about the kind of constitution an elected convention might produce, pensive MLAs in NSW and Victoria set a threshold of 50,000 yes votes (about one-fifth of registered voters) to accept the constitution. Pressing their advantage, manufacturers via the ANA then held a conference at Bathurst NSW in December 1896, which demanded that the constitution provide for an elected Senate.[131]

BARGAINING OVER THE FORM AND CONTENT OF FEDERATION

> We are here to make a bargain!
>
> Isaac Isaacs, 1897 Sydney Convention

A broad range of delegates from Australian and Anglo-Australian capitals, as well as one Victorian labour delegate were elected in March 1897. Delegates met in Adelaide, South Australia that month. This first convention retained the draft written in 1891, but made several decisive changes favoring Labor and manufacturing interests, providing for an elected senate, prohibiting plural voting (which had been based on multiple residence or property ownership), and creating a fully independent judiciary. In September 1897, the convention reconvened in Sydney NSW; the major issues were taxes and the type and power of the Senate. The question whether to have equal state representation, as in the United States, or representation proportional to population divided populous and sparse states. Whether to give the Senate control over money bills and larger powers in deadlocks between the two houses split financiers and manufacturers. Upset over the decision in favor of equal state representation, and fearing unfavorable outcomes in the unsettled issues of control of rivers and

---

130. Queensland could not pass an enabling act because sectional and Labor-capital conflicts in the Legislative Assembly and Council prevented any agreement on participation in federation. Northern areas wanted to secede from the south; conservatives wanted appointed delegates because Labor was likely to win delegate elections.

131. *Melbourne Age*, November 19–23, 1896.

scale of tariff, the NSW Legislative Assembly amended its enabling act to raise the acceptance threshold to 80,000.

January 1898 saw the third and final sitting in Melbourne. Here a number of major compromises permitted agreement on points of narrow and immediate economic interest, such as control of rivers. The convention also gave the Federal government power to intervene in interstate labour disputes and made high court decisions final by restricting appeals to the Privy Council in London. The constitution then was returned to the five prospective states for plebiscite.[132] The following sections examine the conventions and constitution in the context of the dominions' three major issues.

Labour Control Problems and the Conventions

As in 1891, labour control powers were a contentious issue, and ultimately were created only because of their utility in dealing with public debt concerns. Initial efforts by H. B. Higgens, a radical Victorian lawyer, directly to grant the Federal government arbitration powers were overwhelmingly rejected. NSW exporters had just crushed a coal miners' strike, and Victorian manufacturers, distressed by the 1896 Victorian Factory Act, gave only hesitant support to Higgens's efforts. Unions were at the nadir of their power, then in the middle of the "fifteen years [in which the ASU] was a shadow of the militant organization of 1890," so these powers seemed unneeded.[133] Higgens persevered and at the last Convention proposed that the constitution permit the Federal government arbitration powers if Parliament passed an enabling act. Financiers again opposed the measure, claiming that unions could in no way be legally compelled to obey a decision. As force inevitably would be needed, why clutter the issue? With seamen (the most important of the transport unions) controlled by navigation powers previously approved in the draft, the question of specific labour control powers seemed moot.[134] But advo-

132. Queensland still remained aloof from the process. Although some "bloc" voting by Colonies occurred, most delegates seem to have voted according to their interests; see P. Loveday, "The Federal Conventions: A Voting Analysis," *AJPH* 18 (August 1972).

133. Gollan, "Industrial Relations in the Pastoral Industry," p. 605. See statements by McMillan, p. 783, and Wise, p. 786, in *Official Record of the Debates of the Australasian Federal Convention*, Adelaide, March 22–May 5, 1897 (Adelaide: Government Printer, 1897 [hereafter *Adelaide Official Record*]), on responses to Higgens; see *Adelaide Official Record*, p. 787, for the vote.

134. *Official Record of the Debates of the Australasian Federal Convention*, Melbourne, January 20, 1898–March 17, 1898 (Melbourne: Government Printer, 1898 [hereafter *Melbourne Official Record*]), p. 180; see interchange between Higgens and McMillan on

cates countered with two arguments that split the opposing ranks. William Trenwith, the Victorian labour delegate, countered arguments about enforcement, saying that threats to union funds—then a major source of health "insurance" and pensions—and the force of public opinion—vital to labour—would both compel obedience.[135] This argument, and the absence of Federal arbitration powers over shearers, moved representatives of pastoral interests like J. Abbott to support arbitration powers. Later Higgens pointed out "one great advantage which employers appear not to recognise. [Arbitration] gives them . . . certainty for the for the next two or three years . . . as to the conditions under which they are to work." And then he linked arbitration to the debt problem: "The State [i.e., Colonial governments] . . . cannot afford to stand idle and to allow these disputes to be carried out to their bitter consummation";[136] "afford" literally, for the strikes and subsequent depression had brought the governments into seemingly perpetual deficit and near default. Labour control per se thus yielded to the larger question of debt service. These arguments persuaded John Forrest, the deeply conservative premier of Western Australia, to swing his puppet delegation in favor of the proposed powers. Forrest's delegation and the pastoral delegates gave the proposal a three-vote margin (22–19).[137]

The Labor Parties, Public Debt, and the Conventions

While Federation in part was intended to control political labor, political labor had to be accommodated to get the constitution accepted. Labor and unions had laid out the minimum concessions they expected in return for accepting and participating in a Federal state in 1891: manhood suffrage and an elected Senate.[138] At the 1896 Bathurst "People's Convention," manufacturers and some pastoralists had in effect grafted Labor's demands for an elected Senate and a

---

the enabling act; see statements by McMillan and Glynn, ibid., pp. 181–182, Zeal, p. 183, and Downer, pp. 186–188, on compulsion; see statements by Quick, ibid., pp. 182–183, on control of seamen.

135. *Melbourne Official Record*, pp. 193–194. See Rickard, *Class and Politics*, for arguments on the importance of public opinion.

136. Quoted in Higgens, *Melbourne Official Record*, p. 212. J. Abbott was brother of the W. E. Abbott who helped found both the NSW Pastoralists Union and the Pastoralists Federal Council, and who ran both for many years.

137. See *Commonwealth Parliamentary Debates* (CWPD) 2:1, vol. 18, pp. 594–595, March 16, 1904, for Forrest's retrospective explanation of his decision; see *Melbourne Official Record*, p. 215, for some perceptive commentary by Braddon on Forrest's behavior.

138. See *Brisbane Worker*, May 1, 1897.

broader franchise onto their own. Evidence of a broad acceptance of the need for an elected senate is nowhere more visible than in an interchange between a conservative Tasmanian delegate, Dobson, and George Reid, ever London's man, at the first convention. Dobson attacked an elected senate: "You all know how strongly sociology [*sic*] is making its way among the people. . . . The country belongs to the people; but the people who are most entitled to our consideration are the people who are thrifty and intelligent and have something to pay our liability [to Britain]."[139] Precisely because Federation seemed the only viable solution to debt problems, creditors were willing for its sake to accept an elected senate.[140] The clause was not even put to a vote, indicating broad consensus on the need to gain popular support for a plebiscitary constitution. Westralian Premier Forrest's behavior shows the close relationship between debt problems and willingness to compromise: Westralia had temporarily sound finances on the basis of vast gold discoveries. In the absence of overt debt problems and debt-induced direct taxes, Forrest saw no need to compromise with Labor for the sake of Federation, declaring "I believe in the Bill of 1891 on these questions [of suffrage]."[141] But an elected senate was all Labor won for domestic and foreign financiers closed ranks against additional Labor demands for a unicameral legislature, elected ministries, and initiative and referendum, all of which would have weakened the Federal state's ability to contain Labor.[142]

Private Debt, Export Activity, and the Conventions

The draft constitution did little directly for private solvency. One could argue with Fitzpatrick and others, that capital as a unified class came away from the conventions with a deeply conservative constitution capable of thwarting any labour attempts to seize the means of production. But it is not clear that labour, especially the conservative craft unions, desired or had the power to seize. Furthermore, the rapid ascent of the Federal Labor Party to control of the Federal Senate demonstrates that "capital" had been mistaken about the likely

139. *Adelaide Official Record*, pp. 195–197. Dobson also favored a franchise that gave every man "as many votes as he deserves"; quoted in *Melbourne Tocsin*, February 24, 1898. On Reid's connections with London, see B. deGaris, "The Colonial Office and the Commonwealth Constitution Bill," in Martin, *Essays in Australian Federation*.

140. *Adelaide Official Record*, pp. 670–671.

141. NLA MS 296/1, J. Forrest to W. H. James, March 8, 1897. James was a delegate to the 1897–98 conventions, and later became Westralian Premier. Under Forrest, Westralian debt went from £1.4 to £12.2 million.

142. Wise, *Making of the Australian Commonwealth*, p. 219.

effects of parts of the constitution, just as the most conservative capitals, which opposed a strong and independent High Court, were later to find this branch their salvation many times over.

The extensive debate over Federal control of rivers, though, does reveal the delegates' concern for the problem of revalorizing pastoral mortgages. The colonial *Crédit Foncier* programs to revalorize pastoral holdings by subsidizing subdivision and sale to agriculturalists depended in part on irrigation schemes to increase the value of agricultural land. Reid, typically unsubtle, is our best guide:

> In the interests of the people to whom we have sold the land in [freehold] . . . we must vindicate our rights to the water of those rivers. . . . NSW has sold enormous quantities of land, based on the rights which the people possess in this water under the New South Wales law and Government. Millions of money have been received by the New South Wales Government for land sold within the watershed of the Murrumbidgee. . . . It is not a light question for us to nullify the things we have sold. . . [Should] the Federal Parliament [have] . . . the power of irrigation and water conservation . . . we would change the position of our landowners . . . very seriously.[143]

This threat to water rights, and thus to revalorization, occasioned the successful effort of NSW pastoralists to raise the threshold acceptance vote in NSW to 80,000.

Public Debt and the Conventions

The debates over public debt provide the clearest examples of the conflicting interests of manufacturers and financiers, illuminating a hierarchy of compromises between them. Contemporary and later observers believed manufacturers essentially came to the convention powerless. As Deakin observed, the Victorian, thus mainly manufacturing, delegates "found themselves in an unpopular minority and almost in isolation from the first. [They] had little or nothing to yield . . . and [were] regarded as committed to any scheme of union [the convention] might please to frame."[144] Isaac Isaacs similarly commented that Victoria accepted a Federation with equal State representation in the Senate and with larger legislative powers than a simple customs union might have had because it was better to take amal-

---

143. *Melbourne Official Record*, p. 444; see also Isaacs's concern "to make it perfectly clear that irrigation shall be the first consideration," p. 592.
144. Deakin, *Federal Story*, p. 77.

gamation now than to have it imposed later on worse terms.[145] But these interpretations overlook manufacturers' agenda-setting successes. Acting in concert with Labor, manufacturers won their greatest victories *before* the Conventions commenced, when financiers acceded to the delegate elections and plebiscitary approval demanded at Corowa-Bendigo, and the wider franchise and elected senate demanded at Bathurst.

Second, manufacturers fought a successful rearguard action against the efforts of financiers to secure public debt. Having secured intercolonial free trade simply by attending the Conventions, manufacturers blocked financiers from achieving their major goal of writing direct and immediate Federal resumption of colonial public debt into the Constitution. AIBR wailed:

> It is to be feared that the adoption of the recommendations of the Finance Committee by the Convention will in no wise improve the financial arrangements of Federation. Much larger powers have to be conceded to the Commonwealth Government [including] . . . the guaranteeing and the administration of the public debts of the Colonies. . . . In short, the public finances of the federating Colonies should be unified.

Right down to the installment of the first cabinet, the financial community "keenly regretted . . . that the [Constitution] does not provide absolutely for a consolidation of the public indebtedness of the Colonies."[146] Financial notables privately echoed public lamentations. The chair of the huge pastoral finance firm Dalgety wrote the editor of APR:

> It looks after all as if the immediate advantages [of federation] are rather doubtful and that instead of a saving in the expense the boot will on the other foot. In legislation also the leading points which made federation apparently desirable seem to attract less attention than matters which might well be left alone until matters as to debts, tariff, etc. were finally attended.[147]

145. *Official Record of the Debates of the Australasian Federal Convention*, Sydney, September 2–24, 1897 (Sydney: Government Printer, 1897 [hereafter *Sydney Official Record*]), p. 304.

146. First quotation, AIBR, February 19, 1898, p. 167. AIBR repeated this demand March 19, 1898, and June 20, 1898. Second quotation, AIBR, February 20, 1899, p. 76; see also February 19, 1900, p. 96, and June 19, 1900. Labor supported manufacturers, afraid that resumption would "make the lien of the foreign bondholder on our souls and bodies and those of our children more secure"; *Melbourne Tocsin* March 24, 1898. After Labor came to control the Federal Government, and anti-Labor to control the States, AIBR's tune changed.

147. ABL N8/28/353–354, E. T. Doxat to R. W. Twopenny, September 18, 1901.

Manufacturers also won a major, if temporary, victory by prohibiting appeals from Australia's nascent High Court to England's Privy Council. In both the 1891 and 1897 drafts, the constitution limited all appeals to the High Court. But all realized that "the grave result of [appeal's abolition] is that . . . the British creditor . . . suing or being sued in Australia may . . . be at a disadvantage," as a Colonial Office minute said, after the 1891 convention restricted appeals.[148] Financiers mounted a coordinated but unsuccessful effort to reinstate appeal. "The Colonies," noted AIBR, "owe the Mother Country on public and private debt something like £250,000,000. With the large financial interests at stake . . . the final court of reference should be at the centre of the Empire, so that the conditions upon which loans are granted in London under British law shall be unquestionably paramount."[149] By the Conventions' end, all financial capital had won was the *potential* for Federal debt resumption, and lesser goals like uniform banking laws.

The Draft "Goes to the People"

In remarkably low turnouts, the draft received majority yes votes in the four states where referenda were held. In Victoria, where Federation had tremendous popular support, only one in two voters bothered to vote. Overall, only 69 percent of those voting supported Federation, meaning only 30.1 percent of registered voters voted yes. NSW had the lowest proportion of yes voters to registered voters at 23.2 percent, and thus failed to muster the required 80,000 minimum. Coghlan as usual has the most vivid comment on the nature of popular support for Federation. "The majority of the people were well satisfied to go on as they had been going on in the past, and had to be educated to adopt the Federal idea."[150] George Turner provides

148. Quoted in LaNauze, *Making of the Australian Constitution*, p. 89; see p. 190 on the importance of no appeal to Deakin.

149. Quotation from AIBR, May 19, 1897, p. 287; see also March 19, 1898, p. 139; January 19, 1899, p. 5; April 19, 1900, pp. 252–253; May 19, 1900, pp. 330–331; and June 19, 1900, p. 460. On financiers' efforts, see *Melbourne Official Record*, pp. 4, 17, 33, 322, 338, 345–347 (division), 1355, 1865–1866, 2287, 2297–2298, 2304–2306, 2320–2322, 2422, and C. Grimshaw, "Australian Nationalism and the Imperial connection," AJPH 3 (May 1958).

150. Western Australia, again preferring the wisdom of its Legislature to that of the people, did not hold a referendum. The electoral statistics are drawn from Parker, "Australian Federation," who took them from Quick and Garran, *Annotated Constitution of the Australian Commonwealth*, p. 213, except where noted therein. The lowest turnout was South Australia's 39.5 percent. Quotation from Coghlan, *Labour and Industry in Australia*, p. 2543.

us with an understanding of that education in a private letter to Deakin: "I would like if possible to point out some advantages the country producers will receive from Federation but I confess I cannot see any—it is all apparently the other way—can you suggest anything to help me?"[151] When the selective disenfranchisement practiced routinely in pre-Federation Australia is considered, the notion of overwhelming popular support quickly fades. In NSW only 23 percent of the adult male population was registered, even after registration reforms promulgated by the Reid Government to win Labor support.[152] "Owing to the intricate provisions of the Electoral Act and their stringent interpretation by the [NSW] government," noted Wise, "a large number of electors . . . were disenfranchised. Also there was considerable delay and confusion in fixing the polling places in the [largely anti-Federation] country districts, which contributed to diminish the number of votes recorded."[153]

Thus yet another Premiers' Conference was held in January 1899 to decide what to do; Westralia's absence was tolerable, but Federation without NSW was hollow, geographically impossible, and demographically senseless. NSW Premier Reid thus was able to get the Federal capital placed in NSW in exchange for a second referendum; and, in a pregnant change, the clause guaranteeing to the States 75 percent of Federal customs revenue was set to run only ten years. Queensland had by then passed an enabling act and planned to vote with the others, albeit on a constitution not of its making.[154] With higher turnouts (60.7 percent of registered voters voted, 42.9 percent of those registered voted yes), NSW managed to muster the requisite 80,000 yes votes. Western Australia continued to hold out for better terms, fearing economic subjection and an agrarian future.[155]

The Draft Goes to Britain

The Bill then went to Britain's House of Commons for what was hoped to be *pro forma* Imperial approval. Elimination of appeal to the Privy Council proved a sticking point for the Colonial Office, however. The C.O. had covertly used Reid as a channel into the Conven-

151. NLA MS 1540/11/49, G. Turner (Premier, Victoria) to Deakin, April 4, 1898.
152. Loveday, "Labor," p. 176.
153. Wise, *Making of the Australian Commonwealth*, p. 282.
154. Here there were irregularities too. 46,000 voters were disenfranchised in Queensland on the eve of the referendum. *Brisbane Worker*, July 22, 1899.
155. See NLA MS 1540/11/54–55, J. W. Hackett to A. Deakin, May 23, 1898, and NLA MS 1540/11/99–106, W. James to A. Deakin, July 20, 1899.

tions, with Reid making amendments using language the C.O. provided him. But it was unable to insure covertly either Privy Council appeal or a first lien on the customs for bondholders.[156] Consequently the C.O had overtly to reestablish Privy Council appeal for all but strictly constitutional questions. Chamberlain played off the more export- and foreign capital–dependent colonies of New Zealand, Queensland, and Western Australia against the others to win his point.[157] The desire to secure British investments in Australia was the primary consideration. As the *Worker* put it: "This allegedly self-governing continent, if it wants to [federate], first has to obtain the consent of the gang who engineered the present South African war in the House of Commons. These financiers . . . will probably insist on the right to alter the conditions under which it was proposed to federate. . . . The demand of Chamberlain and Co. is that federated Australia shall not be allowed to have any right of finality in its judicature, but on all matters alike the appeal to the Privy Council shall remain intact."[158]

Western Australia, unable to extract concessions from the other five colonies following Chamberlain's maneuvers, held a referendum just after Lords approved the Bill in July 1900. On January 1, 1901, the new federal government was installed under a caretaker cabinet until elections could be held.

Federation imperfectly addressed the problems the Australian Colonies faced and thus created a new arena in which conflicts over foreign claims to surplus could be fought out, rather than definitely resolving those conflicts. Nevertheless, Federation and its associated struggles set the parameters for future conflicts in important ways.

156. See deGaris, "The Colonial Office and the Commonwealth Constitution Bill," pp. 105, 109. Discovery of Reid's actions probably cost him a seat in the first cabinet; AIBR, January 19, 1901, p. 4. The Colonial Office (C.O.) apparently dealt with Reid rather than Kingston, President of the Conventions, because Kingston was regarded as "disloyal" by South Australia's Governor-General. Perhaps mindful of what the Commons and the C.O. would do to any Constitution Bill, at the 1895 Premiers' Conference Kingston had proposed that Commons pass an imperial enabling act, and so give up its ability to control the outcome in Australia; *Melbourne Age*, February 1, 1895. See also *Commonwealth of Australia Bill: Reprint of Debates in Parliament, The Official Correspondence with the Australian Delegates and other papers* (London: Wyman & Sons, 1904), pp. 37–38, 44, 153.
157. See Deakin, *The Federal Story*, pp. 139–142; Deakin and Kingston, CWPD 1:2, p. 5464. Deakin, *Federated Australia*, March 27, 1902, reports that after 1902 Deakin tried to seduce litigants away from the Privy Council by appointing a series of respected, and conservative, jurists to Australia's High Court.
158. *Brisbane Worker*, April 21, 1900. See Deakin's comments on the negotiations, which alienated Deakin considerably from Chamberlain and Great Britain; Deakin, *Federal Story*; also *Brisbane Worker* June 8 and July 20, 1901.

The alliance between Labor and City against a financial bail out of graziers meant that their political importance continued to decline, while Labor achieved time in which to consolidate its gains. Labor would use this time to make another strategic alliance with manufacturers against the City and graziers. Manufacturers' agenda-setting successes at the conventions set the stage for an assault on overseas public debt and a positive program of self-transformation. Chapter 4 details the struggles of these groups within the new arena.

CHAPTER FOUR

Origins of an Australian National Bourgeoisie

> The Liberal Protectionists are fully aware of the immense importance of preferential trade. To them it represents something more than a policy; it is a faith in itself.
>
> Isaac Isaacs, Victoria Liberal Protectionist Party

Federation paved a political road out of the overlapping debt crises of the 1890s. But while it made renewed expansion possible, it did not specify for whom. Conflict over that issue gives Australian Federal politics from Federation until World War I the appearance of confusion and deadlock. In Australian historiography, the period 1901–1909 is one in which three numerically equal parliamentary parties—one Labor and two bourgeois—were unable to form any lasting coalitions. Most analyses claim that the deadlock was caused by disagreements between the two bourgeois parties over the tariff and suggest that once the tariff issue was settled, towards the decade's end, the way was clear for a bourgeois fusion against Labor. Consequently they view politicking by the Liberal Protectionist Party (LPP) as unsuccessful, incoherent, and irresolute attempts to move either left or right to fuse with one of the other two parties, and the politics of the Free Trade Party (FTP) as a resolute and successful anti-Labor stand.[1]

1. On contemporary Australian usages of "Liberal" and "Conservative": "A Colonial Liberal is one who favours State interference with liberty and industry at the pleasure and in the interest of the majority, while those who stand for the free play of individual choice and energy are classed as conservatives." A. Deakin, December 11, 1900, quoted in J. LaNauze, ed., *Federated Australia: Selections from Letters to the Morning Post* (Melbourne: Melbourne University Press, 1968), p. 3. See *Brisbane Worker* February 6, 1904, for a typical contemporary view of this "either-or" choice. For examples of the

CASES

My argument differs from these views in two respects. First, dead-lock emerged because sections of the bourgeoisie had fundamentally divergent political and economic visions about these problems and the future. All of the fundamental conflicts generated by the prior period of debt-financed export-oriented expansion persisted through this period, defining the contours of political conflict. Deadlock in this period was not simply a function of division over the tariff among an otherwise homogenous bourgeoisie. The tariff was only one of sever-al issues separating a nascent national bourgeoisie in manufacturing, represented by the LPP, from the pastoral-financial complex repre-sented by the FTP; resolution of the tariff issue in 1908 still left a host of other differences. Needless to say, Labor also possessed its own political and economic vision.

Second, I argue the LPP, far from "irresolute," was the only party possessing a coherent economic and political vision of how to acceler-ate its members' own accumulation during this period.[2] Although it failed to implement this vision completely, its efforts laid the founda-tion for manufacturers' transformation from an interior bourgeoisie to a national bourgeoisie, which inevitably reduced Australian depen-dency and increased development. In contrast, the pastoral-financial FTP had only a negative political strategy of decrying Labor to com-plement its economic project of rebuilding rural export industry—a strategy illustrated by its 1904 name change to Anti-Socialist Party (ASP). Meanwhile Labor, despite a highly viable and positive political defense of workers, small farmers and the petit bourgeoisie, was split between free traders and protectionists, and between socialists and petit bourgeois utopians in its economic policies. Precisely because of the incompleteness of their projects, it was impossible for either party to supplant the LPP between 1900 and 1909. The LPP thus governed for most of the decade, interrupted only by a four-month coalition of Labor and the most left members of the LPP in 1904, an eleven-month coalition of Free Traders and LPP members from agricultural districts in 1904–05, and a Labor ministry for seven months in 1908–09.

Depictions of LPP irresolution typically focus on the LPP and its leader, Alfred Deakin, and on their partially instituted Preferential

"inevitability" argument see J. Rickard, *Class and Politics* (Canberra: Australian National University Press, 1976), chap. 8; and J. LaNauze, *Alfred Deakin* (Melbourne: Melbourne University Press), 1965, 2 vols., chap. 24.

2. B. Jessop, "Accumulation Strategies, State Forms, and Hegemonic Projects," *Kapitalistate* 10/11 (1983), provides the most precise terminology for what I call "accumula-tion strategies" or "hegemonic projects," as well as a turgid but interesting analysis.

Trade (with Britain) and "New Protection" (which linked tariffs and wages) policies. Thus Deakin's biographer J. A. LaNauze notes the perplexity of Deakin's ally David Syme:

> Deakin's main personal anxiety was the fate of the provision for British Preference. He was pledged to it by repeated commitment in Australia, and he felt a further obligation after his advocacy in England. Privately he spoke of resigning if it were lost, an attitude which [Melbourne *Age* editor] David Syme thought utterly foolish. To [Syme] the tariff was everything, Preference merely a gesture; he could only suppose that Deakin's aberration, and, what was more, his persistence in it despite remonstrance, must be explained by his illness.[3]

LaNauze leaves this issue unresolved, calling Deakin a "colonial nationalist" whose passionate advocacy of his country's rights, aspirations, and autonomy coexisted with a desire to retain all the ties binding Australia to England.[4] But it is hard to see an unambiguous emotional attachment to England in the Deakin who fought bitterly and determinedly in England against amendment of the Constitution Bill and who perceived England as "effete and rotten"; it makes even less sense that Deakin, whose civility was sorely tried by Colonial Secretary Joseph Chamberlain in the negotiations over the Constitution Bill, would tie his political fortunes to Chamberlain out of loyalty to either the person or the Empire.[5] Their negotiations over Preferential Trade (discussed below) are devoid of any such sentiment.

Deakin and the LPP are better explained as representatives of an interior bourgeoisie in manufacturing striving to transform themselves into a national bourgeoisie. The social base of the LPP was the medium-sized manufacturers, who used imported capital goods to produce consumer goods for Australian markets, generally workers. Deakin, after becoming Prime Minister in 1903, pursued coherent political and economic strategies designed to transform these manufacturers into a national bourgeoisie. Politically, he did not pursue

3. LaNauze, *Alfred Deakin*, p. 425. For his part, Deakin felt that by 1904 Syme was out of touch with events outside Victoria; see National Library of Australia mss. no. (NLA MS) 2822/8, A. Deakin to O. C. Beale, September 27, 1904.

4. Most follow LaNauze's lead. See, *inter alia*, C. M. H. Clark, *A History of Australia* (Melbourne: Melbourne University Press), 1981, vol. V; Clark, while labeling Deakin and others "Australian-Britons," also notes, pp. 279–280, Deakin's efforts at the 1907 Colonial Conference to "rescue Australia from the last vestiges of colonialism."

5. See A. Deakin, *The Federal Story* (Melbourne: Robertson & Muellens, 1944), especially pp. 117–120, 133, 139–142. A study of Deakin's efforts to gain a voice for Australia in Imperial decision-making, which for reasons of space must be omitted from this study, reveals a similar determination to make the best of a bad situation.

the "either-or" fusion most analysts perceive, but instead the unmentioned alternative: he tried to split off specific class fractions from Labor and the FTP and adhere them to the LPP, aiming to destroy both Labor and FTP as significant political entities and to leave them as mutually antagonistic fractions unable to recombine against a hegemonic, centrist LPP bloc.[6] The LPP's economic and political visions dovetailed, for the economic flows and state institutions they desired would bind together the groups Deakin desired to steal away from the FTP and LPP. Preferential Trade—"a faith in itself"—was mainly bait for the groups to be stolen from the Free Traders—farmers, some pastoralists, and domestic financiers. The Conciliation and Arbitration issue was bait for the groups to be stolen from Labor—urban and skilled labour. Both were intended to expand domestic manufacturers' ability to accumulate capital. The LPP sought to centralize control over old debt and limit new overseas debt, sought to create a domestically controlled iron industry, sought Conciliation to have a stable and large market for consumer goods producers, and sought Preferential Trade to channel the backward linkages from export activities exclusively to Australian manufacturers. The unity of these projects is clear in Deakin's speech launching his campaign for Preferential Trade:

> [The] Liberal . . . in this country is associated with the development of our own industries by our own people. To us this is the foundation of political unity. . . . With us the necessary beginning of national unity is a binding together [of the Australian colonies] by commercial ties. . . . The first duty of Australian citizenship is to ensure that the interchange of the products raised should take place within ourselves. . . . The first condition for the transaction of business in this country is to lay down once and for all the conditions upon which Australian investments and Australian labor shall be employed in this country.[7]

Not lack of vision, but rather failure to achieve what they desired, produced political deadlock between 1900 and 1909. The LPP's partially implemented policies had unintended but negative political consequences that undermined their ability to construct a mass political

6. See NLA MS 1540/1/1032, O. C. Beale to A. Deakin, August 16, 1904: "We believe there is a general desire among the old workers [i.e. trade unionists] to come to a working understanding. Afterwards a rapprochement with the [FTP] upon what many call a Canadian basis."

7. Deakin, Pre-sessional Speech, 1903, NLA MS 1540.

Table 12. Australian parliamentary strength by party, 1901–1914

House of Representatives

	1901	1903	1906	1910	1913	1914
LPP	31	26	16 ⎫	31*	38*	32*
FTP/ASP	28	25	27 ⎭			
Labor	14	23	26	43	37	42
Independent	2	1	2	1	—	1
"Corner"	—	—	4	—	—	—

Senate

	1901	1903	1906	1910	1913	1914
LPP	11	8	5 ⎫	14*	7*	5*
FTP/ASP	17	12	15 ⎭			
Labor	8	14	15	22	22	31
Independent	—	2	1	—	—	—

*Post LPP-ASP Fusion = "Commonwealth Liberal Party"
SOURCE: Hughes and Graham, eds., *Handbook of Australian Government*; Crisp, *Australian Federal Labour Party.*

base beyond their manufacturing core. Consequently their parliamentary representation decayed after 1901 (see Table 12), and in 1909 they fused with the ASP in a losing effort to contain Labor. Manufacturers lost their party until World War I conscription issues caused Labor to "blow out its brains," yielding precisely the coalition between domestic financiers, manufacturers, and centrist unions that Deakin sought.[8]

This chapter examines this three-sided fight through four LPP ventures central to manufacturers' self-transformation: the Bonus for Manufactures Bill, which proposed a domestic iron industry; efforts to federalize control over overseas borrowing; Preferential Trade, an attempt to create backward linkages; and Conciliation and Arbitration, a primitive Keynesianism. Each reveals the contours of the three parties' competing projects; each shows how the golden thread of debt bound each side to a position antagonistic to the others.

8. The best short account of post-World War I Australian politics is found in P. Cochrane, "Dissident Capitalists," pp. 122–148 in E. Wheelwright and K. Buckley, eds., *Essays in the Political Economy of Australian Capitalism*, vol. IV (Sydney: Australia and New Zealand Book Co., 1980).

MANUFACTURERS' FIRST INITIATIVE: THE BONUS BILL

> The Americans and the Germans are determined to have the Australian Iron trade.
>
> William Sandford, 1905[9]

For the manufacturing interior bourgeoisie, Federation presented new opportunities and new problems. If a continental market created more opportunities for domestically controlled accumulation, it also attracted more foreign producers than its fragmented predecessor. This was nowhere more true, and more threatening, than in iron and steel production. Memories of the 1890s made manufacturers see Australia's "sole hope of progress" as the "pursuit of diversified industry," for which "the manufacture of cheap iron and steel [was] the very basic element of our hopes." But 1901–1902 saw a flurry of foreign proposals to build ironworks.[10] Manufacturers felt this inevitably would result in foreign domination not just of iron manufacturing and machinery, but of the whole economy, because virtually all modern industries lay downstream of metals production. The LPP thus proposed a £250,000 bonus to encourage private pioneers in domestic iron production. In May, 1902, C. C. Kingston, Minister for Trade and Customs, moved a bill for the "encouragement of manufactures," arguing that: "The Bill is intended to complete the scheme of encouragement of local manufactures. . . . The chief idea of the proposals is to encourage the establishment of the iron industry . . . the backbone of all manufacturing enterprises."[11] Privately he noted: "We have the destinies of our people to mould and we do not want Australia to be the retail shop for the wholesale manufacturers of

9. NLA MS 1540/15/473 W. Sandford to A. Deakin, November 4, 1905.
10. Quotation from NLA MS 1540/1/991, O. C. Beale to A. Deakin, May 10, 1904. See also H. B. Higgens (LPP Vic), Commonwealth of Australia Parliamentary Debates (CWPD), June 10, 1902, 13,522; and NLA MS 1540/16/274, A. Chapman to A. Deakin, June 9, 1905, on the urgency manufacturers felt. Mercantile interests had previously stifled domestic efforts to create an industry. A. Chapman (LPP NSW), CWPD, October 18, 1904, pp. 5686–5687; and *Melbourne Age*, September 9, 1904. The best history of the industry is H. Hughes, *Australian Iron and Steel Industry* (Melbourne: Melbourne University Press, 1964). Foreign Proposals in: Australian Archives, Commonwealth Record Series no. (AA CRS) AA A589 unnumbered folio, Department of Trade and Customs files. U.S. Steel, Graphitic Steel of New York, and the British and Colonial Agency all made offers in 1901–02; see also, Commonwealth of Australia Parliamentary Papers (CWPP) 1906, vol. IV, p. 92.
11. C. C. Kingston (LPP SA), CWPD, May 27, 1902, pp. 12,581–12,852.

other nations who may gain all the profit."[12] But the Bill bogged
down precisely because of the critical position iron production oc-
cupied. Debate centered on the nature of the industry's ownership
and of government subsidies, because of their implications for control
of the industry. Three groups emerged, advocating a "market plus
tariff" decision, state ownership, and government subsidy via a
"bonus."

Foreign and domestic financial interests argued that the market
should decide the question of ownership, and that the government
should pass a tariff to attract the necessary capital into the industry.

> *C. C. Kingston (LPP South Australia):* You . . . favour a protective duty?
> *W. Jamieson (BHP):* Yes. . . . Financiers at home [i.e. England] felt they
> would be more satisfied with a Tariff without a bonus. . . . It is evident
> that a Tariff would . . . last for a certain number of years. . . . We cannot
> raise the money to create the company or erect the works unless we have
> a [tariff].[13]

Even a multiyear bonus was a terminal subsidy, for any renewal would
require active legislation. In contrast, ending a tariff would require
active legislation, and with a clearly fragmented Parliament this
seemed unlikely. The likely outcome of a market-plus-tariff decision
was a British-owned monopoly with an interminable tariff. But the
financiers' normal allies defected. A tariff would hurt both pastoralists and Sydney manufacturers working up imported raw materials.
Pastoralists' imports of fencing wire and galvanized plates for construction accounted for 44.6 percent of nonmachinery iron imports
and 27.5 percent of total ferrous imports.[14] Pastoralists demanded
state control, protesting that: "If this Bill is carried, the money . . . can
only come from the producing classes of the community [who] already have a sufficient burden on them. . . . There is no doubt that
the profits [of] the manufacturer of iron are infinitely greater than
those enjoyed by any farmer. . . . If the Commonwealth is going to
help [iron manufacturers] we must exercise the right of controlling

12. AA CRS A589, Department of Trade and Customs, internal memo on the Bonus
for Manufactures Bill, p. 8. Kingston seems to have actually preferred state control to
private ownership; see AA A589 unnumbered folio, Department of Trade and Customs 02/8709, letter from W. Jamieson to C. C. Kingston, June 21, 1902.
13. CWPP 1904, vol. II, p. 1473 and 1475. See p. 1564 for wage guarantee desires,
pp. 1540–1545 for a discussion on the level and duration of the tariff desired.
14. CWPP 1904, vol. II, pp. 1614–1617.

them in their works."[15] Sydney manufacturers using imported raw iron and machinery made similar protests: "It is necessary to replace most of the up-to-date machinery every three or four years, and consequently by the imposition of machinery duties we are periodically penalizing enterprise. I would rather [nationalize iron], and have full control."[16] Consequently both groups joined Labor, in Parliament and on the tripartisan Royal Commission established to settle factual questions, to recommend and vote for state ownership.[17]

The Labor Party advocated state control on grounds of principle and economy; as state-owned railroads were the single largest consumer of iron, iron production should be state-owned too. If the government were to advance and risk £250,000, it might as well end up with equity in an industry as central as iron.[18] A desire to prevent renewed borrowing or at least to insure local investment also underlay Labor proposals for state control. Labor's chairman felt that were state control blocked, he "would prefer that [the industry] were an Australian one, because there would be some probability of whatever is owned being spent or invested locally."[19] And others preferred no industry at all if it involved overseas borrowing: "Under the present circumstances, State monopoly would simply mean a monopoly of financiers in London, seeing that we should have to borrow the money in order to undertake the enterprise. That would simply be handing the industry over to capitalists in London, and leaving us as far as ever from a state monopoly."[20]

Although manufacturers wanted an Australian industry, they

15. A. Conroy (FTP NSW), CWPD, June 11, 1902, pp. 13,542–13,545.

16. G. Edwards (FTP NSW), CWPD, June 11, 1902, pp. 13,519–13,520.

17. CWPD, June 12, 1902, pp. 13,624–13,825. See also the Fourth Division on the Bill, where many Free Traders again lined up with Labor. See CWPP 1904, vol. II, for the Royal Commission's report.

18. J. Watson (LP NSW), chair of the Labor caucus, first proposed state ownership; CWPD, June 10, 1902, pp. 13469–13470. For other representative statements, see J. Batchelor (LP SA), CWPD, June 11, 1902, p. 13,535, and J. Watson, CWPD, July 31, 1902, p. 14,789. See also the minority report of the Royal Commission, CWPP 1904, vol. II, pp. 1502–1505. A few Labor members supported the bonus option; see CWPP 1904, vol. II, p. 1415 and 1562–1563. Union officials in the iron industry itself supported a tariff; see CWPP 1904, vol. II, pp. 1546–1547. From 1898 to 1902, rails accounted for approximately 9 percent of iron imports by value; CWPP 1904, vol. II, pp. 1614–1617.

19. J. Watson (LP NSW), CWPD, June 12, 1902, pp. 13,624–13,625.

20. J. Ronald (LP Vic), CWPD, September 2, 1902, p. 15,621. See also W. Spence (LP NSW), CWPD, October 20, 1904, pp. 5883–5884: "This bounty, if given to private individuals, will really benefit British capitalists. . . . At least one fourth of it would be paid to the British moneylender, who has already done well out of Australia, because he has had from us more money that we have ever borrowed from him, while we are as much in debt as ever."

feared that a state-owned iron monopoly would lead inevitably to socialization of all manufacturing. They were willing to trade guarantees to Labor on wages and conditions to get a privately owned industry.[21] Manufacturers also opposed the tariff proposed by financiers because it placed the costs of the subsidy directly on the manufacturers themselves, especially those who were heavy users of iron. Unlike a tariff, a one-time bonus would expose a monopolist iron producer to world market competition, keeping prices down. The manager of Mort's Dock, then Australia's largest engineering firm, told the Royal Commission on the Bill that "the Government should guarantee the promoters of an iron industry as much work as would enable them to establish their business, but I would not compel the manufacturers who have to buy iron to pay the whole amount. A bonus is contributed to by every taxpayer in the country, where as a duty is paid only by those who have to buy the article upon which it is imposed. [A] duty is paid only by a few firms."[22] Downstream manufacturers desired that *machinery* imports be dutiable, so that they in turn could capture the superprofit involved in protected machine manufacture. Some also advocated repayment of the bonus to reduce long-term revenue needs and with it taxation. "Why should any subsidized company be [allowed to] declare dividends out of public money? . . . Any company which makes a big success of an industry will not be crippled by being compelled to return . . . the money which has been advanced to it."[23] The desire to reduce taxation was also mixed with a desire to minimize foreign participation, including state borrowing, so that dividends stayed at home—i.e., Australia— instead of Home—i.e., Britain. The *Sydney Daily Telegraph*, organ of Sydney's manufacturing interests, railed against borrowing money to set up an industry: "Whether trade was good or bad . . . an annual dividend of over £30,000 a year, secured on the resources of the state, would have to be paid to the British investor. This is a kind of State Socialism which would suit the private enterprise of the London money lender admirably, but it seems rather more doubtful that anyone else would benefit by it."[24]

21. For fears, see AA CRS A589, unnumbered folio, letter from O. C. Beale, representing the NSW Chamber of Manufacturers, to C. C. Kingston, May 14, 1903, and the resolutions of the Federated Chambers of Manufacturers, reported in *Melbourne Argus*, January 18, 1906.

22. J. Franki, Mort's Dock and Engineering Co., CWPP 1904, vol. II, p. 1501.

23. J. Quick (LPP Vic), CWPD, June 10, 1902, p. 13,466; see also S. Mauger (LPP Vic), CWPD, June 12, 1902, p. 13606.

24. *Sydney Daily Telegraph*, August 29, 1902; see also C. C. Kingston, CWPD, June 12, 1902, p. 13,619.

A coalition between Labor, Sydney importers, and pastoralists could arguably have pushed through a state-owned industry. But the community of interest here was more apparent than real. The latter two groups had no desire for any *Australian* industry, but if one were to be forced on them they were determined to nationalize it so as to control prices. Labor, in contrast, had a genuine desire to construct a state-owned, Australian industry.

Thus a Labor-LPP majority in the House passed a revised bonus bill in 1905, but the Senate once more rejected it over the question of ownership. With Parliament and social groups so divided, the Bonus Bill languished until 1909, when the Labor Party finally guaranteed a bonus for whichever State erected an ironworks. When NSW, under a Labor government, looked ready to exercise its option and claim the bonus, BHP preempted it, demanding a variety of state subsidies to build an ironworks. In 1913 BHP began building a local iron industry that was consolidated during World War I.[25]

The fight over the Bonus Bill set the pattern for the next six years. Unable to advance their interests alone, the LPP learned the necessity of cleaving fragments from the other parties to itself. The debates had shown precisely were cleavage lay. Labor had shown signs of splitting over free trade vs. protection.

> *J. Ronald (LP Vic)*: In Germany protection is for the capitalist pure and simple; there has never been any attempt at industrial legislation. There must be Conciliation and Arbitration combined with protection.
> *W. Spence (LP NSW)*: Protection does not raise wages.
> *J. Ronald*: Protection, and Conciliation and Arbitration, does raise wages, and maintain them—one is the complement of the other.[26]

Ronald's meld of protection and higher wages prefigures Deakin's efforts to woo Labor with the "New Protection." Distinct groups also appeared in the FTP as direct producers split from financiers. Some

25. The Constitution seemed to preclude Federal ownership, so it is likely that Labor passed the Bill as part of a last-ditch effort to keep the LPP from fusing with the Anti-Socialist (*née* Free Trade) Party. NSW attempted to preempt Federal initiatives by giving guaranteed contracts in 1906 to Sandford, a small local producer, and later by creating a massive market for steel by double tracking its rail system. See H. Evatt, *Australian Labour Leader* (Sydney: Angus and Robertson, 1945), p. 303; Hughes, *Australian Iron and Steel Industry*, p. 46.

26. J. Ronald (LP Vic) and W. Spence (LP NSW), CWPD, October 18, 1904, p. 5700. The free trade–protectionist division in labour seems to have pitted unskilled workers in export industry against skilled workers in manufacturing. See *Brisbane Worker*, September 17, 1892; V. Childe, *How Labour Governs* (Melbourne: Melbourne University Press, 1923), pp. 34–37.

could be wooed if the LPP found export markets for them, or guaranteed an expanding internal market. If manufacturers could weld enough of these subgroups to their party they would have a natural and permanent majority. The Bonus Bill fight thus revealed a political terrain on which an LPP centrist project was a plausible goal. Conciliation and Arbitration, and Preferential Trade were the central positive features of this quest; debt, to which we now turn, a key defensive feature.

Control over the Public Debt

> It is the interest payments of this Country that are for the most part now crippling its progress. Any scheme . . . which will overcome the vampire of interest is surely worthy of careful study.[27]
>
> J. Hume Cook, 1900

At the Federal Conventions, manufacturers successfully blocked automatic Federal resumption of State debts. But Federation reestablished State credit. From 1900 to 1902, NSW and Victoria borrowed over £10 million.[28] Simultaneously, political realignments in Victoria and NSW defused Labor's strength and installed governments hostile to the LPP federal ministry. First in Victoria, then in NSW, a number of conservative movements coalesced around the issues of retrenchment and rural relief. These parties, which at the State level represented the core of the FTP/ASP, successfully carried out an accumulation strategy resembling the old strategy based on wool, but now including meat, wheat and dairy exports.[29] They provided a "substantial financial discrimination in favour of private non-wool rural farming" amounting to 0.3–0.5 percent of GDP in 1901–12.[30] These subsidies extended to rail transport as the *Australiam Pastoralists Review* complained: "A settled policy of Australian railway managers seems to be that it is desirable at all costs to foster the

27. ABL E97/7/22–3, J. Hume Cook to Ballarat Trades Hall Council, 1900.

28. In response, B. R. Wise resigned from the NSW government when borrowing exceeded what was needed to roll over existing loans. NLA MS 1540/1/1004, B. R. Wise to T. Waddell, NSW Treasurer, June 14, 1904.

29. The best overviews of these movements and their origins are Rickard, *Class and Politics*, chap. 6; and B. Graham, *Formation of the Australian Country Parties* (Canberra: ANU Press, 1966).

30. N. Butlin, A. Barnard, and J. Pincus, *Government and Capitalism* (Sydney: G. Allen & Unwin, 1982), pp. 57–58. The conservative Wade government in NSW also reduced land and income taxes in 1907, thus shifting the tax burden off pastoralists; Evatt, *Australian Labour Leader*, pp. 245–248.

growing of wheat, even at the expense of the wool grower, miner, or other primary producer. [I]t is a fact that [freight] rates for wool . . . sent down to the coast for export are four times as high as those for wheat."[31] As in the past, subsidy and infrastructure investment threatened to increase debt. The LPP thus tried to centralize control over borrowing. Economically, Federal control would limit any increases in the "vampire of interest" manufacturers feared. Politically, limits on state borrowing would make farmers clients of the LPP-controlled Federal government, instead of the increasingly hostile State governments.

Unfortunately, the Federal government lacked the power to order an immediate halt to State borrowing. All it could do was assume pre-Federation State debts, which paradoxically would improve State credit further. Section 89 of the Constitution compelled the Federal Treasury to hand over three-quarters of its customs receipts to the States so they could service their debt; this money provided roughly half of State revenues. But Section 89's writ only ran until 1910, as Deakin recognized: "The real power under the Constitution is that of the purse, and it is possessed by the Commonwealth, not fully at present, but assuredly, and after ten years, absolutely."[32] So long as the LPP controlled the Federal government, and borrowers the States, a bargaining situation existed. Conservatives, for their part, lacked the ability to capture the Federal Parliament, first because their "States' Rights" orientation undercut efforts at cooperation, and second because the LPP and Labor constituted a solid anti-borrowing bloc. Without a settlement by 1910, the States faced massive fiscal crises, but they could trade away their power early in return for financial concessions from the Federal government. The LPP could also wait, but huge debts could be and were run up in ten years.

By 1904 conservatives controlled both NSW and Victoria; therefore, parallel with his efforts to gain Conciliation and Arbitration and Preferential Trade, Deakin began looking for ways to centralize debt control, proposing to resume debt and give the States a fixed per capita allotment instead of a share of customs. The LPP felt that

the alteration of the Constitution merely to permit of the 1901–06 debts being handled by the Commonwealth is insufficient. When the alteration *is* made it should provide for the absolute control by the Commonwealth of all Australian financial operations and finally determine the terms and conditions under which future borrowings are to be conducted. The

31. APR, May 15, 1907, p. 196.
32. A. Deakin, in J. LaNauze, ed., *Federated Australia*, August 12, 1902.

ultimate aim of Australia should be to get out of debt entirely; but in any case to be relieved of obligations outside the Commonwealth.[33]

In 1906, Deakin sent Treasurer Forrest to London to explore the attitudes of English bankers and investors to Commonwealth conversions of existing State loans. According to Forrest, the Bank of England, Treasury, and Nivison Co. (which underwrote most Australian issues) "all say we should convert [existing loans] when reaching maturity . . . all seem [more] favourable to Commonwealth than [to] States and all say it would attain a better price."[34] But the London banks expected the Commonwealth to acquiesce in the States' demands for total financial security and thus the ability to continue borrowing. This clashed with LPP domestic proposals calling either for a complete cessation of State borrowing following Federal assumption, or limiting State borrowing to local sources and then only for projects not requiring subsidy.[35]

The States, backed by the London banks, rejected these proposals. Instead, both the 1906 and 1907 Premiers' Conferences called on the Federal government to assume all State debts while leaving the States "financially independent, each within its own sphere," a formula implying no restriction on State borrowing.[36] The States also demanded that Section 89 be extended ten years, thus removing the time pressure on them. The financiers' position reveals that the struggle to control borrowing went beyond a simple turf struggle between two levels of government, for they reversed their pre-Federation stance. Rather than supporting debt consolidation, they "hoped that the

33. Quotation from NLA MS 601/5/1–2, J. Hume Cook (LPP Victoria) to J. Forrest (LP WA), 1906. Forrest was then Treasurer. See AIBR, February 20, 1904, p. 91 on LPP proposals. Deakin also made efforts to use the States' Agents General in Britain for Commonwealth purposes, and so isolate the States from their allies in the C.O. On the Agents General, see B. Atkins, "The Problem of Representation of Australia in England" (MA thesis, Melbourne University, 1959); on Deakin's efforts, see NLA MS 1540/1/1955, 1989, 2182, T. Coghlan to A. Deakin, April 9, 1908, May 15, 1908, and November 5, 1908; and generally Deakin's correspondence with A. Cockburn, T. Coghlan, and Leo Amery.

34. NLA MS 1540/15/509, J. Forrest to A. Deakin, March 23, 1906; R. Gilbert, "London Financial Intermediaries and Australian Overseas Borrowing 1900–1929," AEHR 11 (March 1971).

35. NLA MS 1540/15/509, J. Forrest to A. Deakin, March 23, 1906; see also 1540/15/480, 482, 487, 515. See CWPP no. 35 of 1906, by T. Coghlan, for the first proposal, and CWPP no. 52 and 119 of 1906, by R. Harper (LPP Vic), a starch manufacturer, for the second.

36. On 1906, CWPP no. 2 of 1907 (Minutes of Premiers' Conference) p. 9; see also the counterproposal of W. Knox (FTP Vic), CWPP no. 118 of 1906. On 1907, CWPP no. 13 of 1907, vol. III, p. 411.

States will decline to assent to any [restriction on borrowing]. . . . The only role for the [Commonwealth] Government to fill is that of administrator of the debts, simply registering and obeying the decrees of the States with respect to new loans."[37]

By 1907 the clock was running down for both sides, for two reasons. First, several huge renewal loans were scheduled to come due, including £12,339,000 in 1907, and £8,039,000 in 1908.[38] Second, the manufacturers' hold on the political center and the balance of power between Labor and financial capital was slipping rapidly. Deakin desired a settlement before the LPP completely lost its grip. But he was unwilling to compromise on the key issues: "We want the conference [on debt] and we want it soon, but to summon one which we cannot control . . . creates an awkward situation."[39] Deakin hoped that eventually enough capital would be available in Australia to fund the bulk or the whole of public borrowing. Even so, when Forrest and others suggested in compromise that States be allowed to borrow locally while the Commonwealth controlled external borrowing, Deakin regarded this with suspicion: "There [is] little difference between Melbourne and London or New York." At most, Deakin was willing to allow local borrowing only if done through the Commonwealth Treasury, thus effectively preserving a federal veto on borrowing. "I don't like any State borrowing in London on any terms at any period. . . . The Commonwealth [needs] an efficient brake upon all borrowing anywhere not undertaken through its Treasury."[40] Unable to get a conference on his terms, Deakin moved to retain control over as much revenue as possible. Customarily, the Federal government gave

37. AIBR, March 20, 1906, p. 181. NSW and Victoria's Premiers, themselves and through their Agents General in London, went out of their way to attack not only debt centralization but also Preferential Trade, Conciliation, Deakin, and the LPP. The NSW Premier contacted the Colonial Office about the fight over borrowing; see AA CRS A2 06/2318 and 3186, June 6, 1906, Prime Ministers' General Correspondence, Annual Single Number Series.

38. *State Public Debts*, CWPP no. 783 of 1906.

39. Quotation from AA CRS A49, "Papers Relating to Public Debts, 1904–1908," typed memo from J. Forrest to A. Deakin, February 28, 1907, Deakin's handwritten comments on memo. AA CRS A49, memo from J. Forrest to A. Deakin, March 4, 1907, Deakin's handwritten comments on memo.

40. First quotation, AA CRS A49, A. Deakin to J. Forrest, March 4, 1907; see also memo of May 5, 1907 and NLA MS 1540/1/1984, A. W. Jose to A. Deakin, May 7, 1908. Among other things, Deakin also feared that external creditors might precipitate another 1893-style bank crash by withdrawing funds; see NLA MS 1540/1/1913–1915, W. H. James to A. Deakin, March 10, 1908, advocating default as a solution. Second quotation, AA CRS A49, memo from J. Forrest to A. Deakin, May 5, 1907, Deakin's handwritten comments on the memo. Even Forrest, who later led the first wave of defections from the Liberals to the Anti-Socialists, desired, despite his willingness to sanction local borrowing, to repatriate or eliminate debt. At the 1907 Premiers' meet-

the States any unspent revenue from its quarter share of the customs. Under the Surplus Revenue Act, which the High Court upheld on challenge from the States, the Federal Government began to store away unspent revenue for the future.[41] Deakin also threatened to cut the States off from Federal funds as soon as he legally could.

But time ran out on Deakin rather than the Premiers. By 1909 the LPP had been reduced to a rump supporting a Labor Ministry. Labor was even more opposed to borrowing than manufacturers: "The benefits of foreign capital, even when publicly introduced, are absolutely *nil*. The [Brisbane] *Worker* is pleased to see an attempt made to raise capital [for the State] by borrowing on the local market and by doing so to retain the interest in the State, yet it fails to see why the State should pay any interest at all."[42]

At the 1909 Federal-State conference, Labor chose to wait out the States, offering three-fifths of customs in perpetuity without resumption of debt, while Prime Minister Andrew Fisher warned, "I view with horror another borrower in Australia." But in mid-1909 the LPP finally fused with the only slightly less bedraggled ASP. Deakin chose to head this new "Fusion" party, so as to preserve as much for his core demands in any future agreement as possible.[43] In August 1909, the Fusion's Parliamentary majority approved an agreement guaranteeing the States grants on a per capita basis from the Federal Treasury after 1910. The States ended up with 30 percent less revenue yearly than under Section 89, while still being responsible for their entire debts.[44] This combination of non-resumption and smaller disbursements forced the States to slow their borrowing after 1910.

Although Deakin tried to control debt as part of his political and

---

ing, he admonished the State Premiers, "I am wedded to the idea of a sinking fund," CWPP no. 13 of 1907, vol. III, p. 495.

41. D. Wright, "The Politics of Federal Finance: The First Decade," HSANZ 13 (April 1969), 466–478.

42. First quotation, *Brisbane Worker*, October 20, 1900; second quotation, March 2, 1901. See also (Sydney) *Australian Worker* January 31, 1903, and comments by K. O'Malley (LP WA), CWPD, October 21, 1904, pp. 5956–5957. The LPP itself acknowledged Labor's stronger position on debt; see NLA MS 2822/8, A. Deakin, presessional speech at Ballarat, June 24, 1905, p. 9.

43. Quotation from CWPP no. 48 of 1909, vol. II, p. 23. See p. 17 for Fisher's praise of Deakin's no-borrowing policy. A. W. Jose wrote Deakin before fusion: "A Forrest-Irvine-Cook ministry . . . cannot mean anything but . . . a complete surrender to the States in financial matters." NLA MS 1540/16/573, May 16, 1909.

44. CWPP no. 48 of 1909, vol. II, pp. 57–59; CWPP no. 50 of 1909, vol. II, p. 55. See also H. G. Turner, *First Decade of the Australian Commonwealth* (Melbourne: Mason, firth, & M'Cutcheon, 1911), p. 236. The States asked for 31 shillings per capita, Deakin countered with 23; they settled at 25, which represented double the decrease the States had offered.

economic strategy, the constitutionally-imposed ten-year guarantee on federal disbursements to the States meant that the other pieces in their scheme took precedence in LPP strategy. Debt reduction, given extant debt levels, necessarily took longer to effect and be noticed than did Preferential trade and Conciliation and Arbitration, which promised more immediate political and economic payoffs.

PREFERENTIAL TRADE, DOMESTIC ACCUMULATION, AND A CENTRIST COALITION

> Joe C[hamberlain] is done. . . . What are we preferential traders to do?
>
> W. H. James, 1906[45]

In many ways Preferential trade, though never consummated, represented both the political and the economic centerpiece of LPP strategy. Deakin intended Preferential Trade to fracture the opposing parties, and, by means of farm exports, to drive manufacturing growth. Expecting the British to sponsor Imperial Preference, Deakin and the LPP set about constructing the Australian side of Preferential Trade in 1904. But Chamberlain's failure turned this into construction of a Preferential Trade manqué, designed to salvage as many of Preferential Trade's benefits as possible. The key elements of Preferential Trade manqué were the New Protection, linking protective tariffs to "fair and reasonable" wage levels, and the Australian Industries Protection Act, an antitrust measure aimed at foreign monopolists. In contrast to the original scheme, the manqué version delivered benefits more to labour than farmers, for the Conciliation and Arbitration provisions that accompanied it parallel the "popular alliance" and co-optation of workers in Latin America during the 1930s. Like the "popular alliances," Conciliation linked accumulation by local industry to the level of domestic wages. Consequently both elements ran afoul of legal challenges from rural and financial interests, despite Deakin's belief that he could "probably force [FTP head Reid] to adopt preferential proposals."[46]

Economically, Preferential Trade would have functioned like the import substitution industrialization strategies adopted in Latin America during the Great Depression. Agricultural exports to a

---

45. NLA MS 1540/1/1528–9, W.H. James to Deakin, September 28, 1906.
46. NLA MS 2822/8, A. Deakin to O.C. Beale, December 10, 1903.

growing and guaranteed British market would drive the economy, providing the "foreign exchange" needed for capital goods imports. Contemporary estimates of potential Australian exports to a preferential British market ran as high as £200 million, four times 1900's export level (and more than twice the pre-war export peak of £80 million in 1911); thus Preferential Trade looked like a powerful engine of growth.[47] Even without Preference, exports had increased 60 percent from 1900 to 1911. It was expected that the state would subsidize growth of domestic manufacturing through tariff policies that shut out imported consumer goods. Tariffs on goods demanded by agricultural exporters would increase domestic manufacturers' profits and investment, especially in the nascent domestic agricultural machinery industry. Second, some of these extra manufacturing profits could be diverted to increased wages, gaining not just labour peace, but also a further extension of the market for consumption goods. The LPP tried to institutionalize this diversion through Conciliation and Arbitration and, later, the New Protection. Third, despite reliance on agricultural exports, Preference would tend to reduce dependency by creating and enlarging domestic circuits of accumulation, especially if public debt were held constant and an iron industry were created, because the pool of domestically-created capital would increase. Ideally, mining, manufacturing, pastoral production, and agriculture would all be tied together by product and capital flows. Linking up these circuits inside Australia would allow Keynesian multiplier and accelerator effects to expand the economy to a greater degree than before. Even without Preference, but with protection, between 1900 and 1907 Victorian "exports" to the other States rose from £1.7 million to £6.4 million (from 8 percent to 19 percent of the value of all Victorian production), indicating increasing integration in the economy.[48] Finally, Preferential Trade dovetailed with LPP efforts to reduce the deleterious effects of foreign debt. Deakin was aware of the burden placed on the "community" by the unprofitable rails: "The States, having all embarked on undertakings which in the Old World are in the hands of private corporations, suffer whenever the country suffers. Our railways, which rarely make a profit even in good years, plunge us into heavy losses with every general drought. These with us are public deficits."[49]

47. Turner, *The First Decade of the Australian Commonwealth*, p. 145; N.G. Butlin, *Australian Domestic Product* (Cambridge: Cambridge University Press, 1962), p. 436.
48. C. Foster, *Australian Economic Development in the 20th Century* (London: Unwin Allen, 1970), p. 145.
49. Deakin, *Federated Australia*, September 3, 1901.

He wanted the rails to become legitimately profitable operations for the first time since their inception, as wheat and dairy would increase the density of traffic on the extant rail net.[50] Because Preference's prohibitive tariffs implied decreased customs revenue, and thus smaller disbursements under Section 89, there would be additional pressure on the States to restrain their borrowing and to rationalize rail operations. Instead of public debt draining surplus from manufacturers, agriculture would have to pay its full share of rail fares, though the more intensive use of the rails might obviate any increase in rates. Preference thus would restructure the way that State fiscal policies would affect manufacturers.

Politically, Preferential Trade was the key to drawing farmers out of the arms of conservative retrenching parties and to the LPP in a *coup de main*, for the gains to farmers from a huge and guaranteed British market would outweigh the costs of the tariff. In 1900–1904, most Australian agricultural production went to urban domestic markets, especially in NSW, so any domestic prosperity resulting from Preferential Trade meant more sales for farmers. Precisely this connection had partly underpinned the labour-farmer alliance in pre-Federation NSW. Second, as Australian farmers were expanding their debt after 1900 to mechanize and buy land, the stable export market provided by Preference was a huge benefit (see below). The LPP also targeted the smallholders and partially-proletarianized farmers likely to benefit most from rapid growth: "The Australian National League here is considered by so many to be too conservative a body that it appeared to some of the leading farmers here absolutely necessary, if the small holders of land and those who are practically working men were to be brought into an organisation, to have something entirely separate from either the A N League on the one hand or the Labor Party on the other. The result has been the formation of this [Farmers and Producers] union."[51] Finally, Deakin explicitly linked irrigation projects to Preferential Trade in his first speech calling for Preference and in pre-session speeches in 1903. Irrigation would require borrowing money, but Deakin had been a major proponent of self-financing irrigation during his ministerial tenure in pre-Federation Victoria.[52] Here lies the connection between Deakin's

50. In other words, the rate of return on capital invested in railways would be equal to or greater than the interest rate on monies borrowed to create that capital stock.
51. NLA MS 1540/1/269–271, Farmers and Producers Political Union, South Australia, to A. Deakin, March 4, 1906. Emphasis added.
52. Deakin, *Federated Australia*, November 2, 1903. H.G. Turner, *History of the Colony of Victoria* (London: Longman, Green, 1904), vol. II, p. 255.

debt control efforts and Preferential Trade, for Federal control over borrowing would make farmers beholden to the Federal, not State, governments, while manufacturers would not pay taxes to subsidize irrigation schemes.

Conversely, the LPP sought to use Preferential Trade to split the fractious capitals within the FTP. O. C. Beale, an LPP partisan, wrote Deakin that: "If [FTP leader] Reid declares against preference he will have all the papers here with him, which means a good deal, but the old free-importers are divided on the subject, and all protectionists are against him."[53] Importers stood to lose the most, since imports would shrink as domestic production expanded. The mercantile-oriented *Sydney Morning Herald* blasted Preference eight times in the six-week period after it was floated.[54] But pastoralists might gain, for after 1897 graziers increasingly feared Argentine competition in world meat and wool markets. Although the *Australasian Pastoralists Review* called for reductions in wages as the only road to restored competitiveness it was willing to countenance Preference as an alternative if Britain promised to buy as much as Australia could produce.[55]

Creating Preferential Trade Manqué

Before he could use Preference, Deakin first had to safeguard manufacturers' basic interests, which Chamberlain's initial terms had attacked. Chamberlain offered a market for Australian primary products only, in return for an expanded market in Australia for British manufactures: "If England imposed very substantial preferential duties favour Colonial wool, wheat, meat, wine etc. would Australia reduce present protective duties on British imports, instead increasing taxes foreign imports—seems probable Canada, South Africa adopt that policy."[56] But Deakin preferred that Britain increase its share of the Australian market at the expense of foreign, not Australian producers: "Free trade press hostile preference could not rely on Free Trade support—even for reductions, preference by increases neces-

---

53. NLA MS 1540/1/1043, O.C. Beale to A. Deakin, October 6, 1904.
54. *Sydney Morning Herald* January 26, to March 4, 1904.
55. APR, August 15, 1901, p. 387–388; see also November 15, 1902, p. 613; July 16, 1903. Financial circles echoed these sentiments; AIBR, September 20, 1901, p. 720.
56. NLA MS 1540/14/361, P. Mennell to A. Deakin, June 21, 1903. Chamberlain contacted Deakin initially through Philip Mennell, one of Deakin's informal but extensive network of contacts in England. Mennell was Editor of the *British Australasian and New Zealand Mail*.

sary ensure Australian success."[57] Chamberlain rejected this, but offered a compromise:

> The Colonies will no doubt take steps to guard their growing manufactures from extinction. On the other hand our people will not assent to a tax on . . . articles of primary necessity unless they are satisfied that they will have something substantial in return in the share of increased exports of manufactures. This cannot be secured entirely by a mere increase of the differential rates against foreign nations. . . . It seems to me that what we both want is possible. *You* may preserve your present industries, but give *us* a full share in your future expansion. If you have . . . decided to establish . . . the great primary industries of Ironmaking and cotton spinning, and require a small protection against us to prevent them from being overwhelmed, such a course might be taken while . . . you would leave to us the smaller industries not yet established in your country in regard to which there is no vested interest and which together will make up a large business.[58]

Australian manufacturers' sights were set on iron and wool spinning, the ambition that Chamberlain was prepared to allow.[59] On these terms a deal was possible, and Deakin launched his campaign, only to have Preferential Trade in his lifetime doomed by Chamberlain's incapacitating stroke and electoral failure in England. Absent full-blown Imperial Preference, the LPP attempted to construct as much of the Australian aspects as possible. These efforts consisted of a Preferential tariff, the antimonopoly Australian Industries Protection Act, revival of the Australian Imperial Federation League, and, most important, the "New Protection."

To keep sentiment for Preferential Trade alive, Deakin attempted to revive the Australian Imperial Federation League, which had existed in the 1890s as a creature of the Anglo-Australian and Australian banks. But nationalists (who made up the core of the LPP) rejected the cry for Imperial Federation. One LPP lawyer reported

57. NLA MS 1540/14/361, handwritten response on obverse of folio.
58. Quotation, NLA MS 1540/14/372–373, J. Chamberlain to B. R. Wise, July 31, 1903, copy in Deakin papers. By "smaller" we must presume Chamberlain means bicycles, chemicals, electrical goods—in short, all the goods of the future. For his objections to Deakin's offer, see NLA MS 1540/1/885, (Chamberlain's secretary) J. Wilson to A. Deakin, July 28, 1903: "[Chamberlain] say[s] that the answer is unsatisfactory. He does not see how Australia can expect substantial preference unless her government is willing to make larger concessions."
59. See minutes of a 1906 meeting of the Federal Chamber of Manufacturers which linked bounties for iron and wool production to Conciliation. *Melbourne Argus*, January 18, 1906.

the typical response: "I'd rather support an Australian Separation League."[60] Deakin met similar resistance trying to sell Preferential Trade and an Imperial Secretariat for the Dominions to Britain and Canada at the 1907 Colonial Conference.

More practically, Deakin began to construct the Australian side of Preference by raising rates for non-British goods in the 1905 preferential tariff and by introducing antitrust legislation intended to control foreign cartels operating in Australia. The antimonopoly Australian Industries Protection Act (AIPA) was especially concerned with competition in the agricultural machinery industry. Victorian producers controlled roughly half the Australian market, but their "exports" to other colonies were threatened by foreign firms. North American firms had been evading the Australian tariff by underinvoicing their products at dockside, then raising the prices at point of sale.[61] Australian manufacturers had tolerated this, benefiting from a quasi-cartel with the North Americans. But when the cartel collapsed into competition, the Australians cried for help. The LPP, for its part, was not loath to impose controls on this vital industry: "If we have any desire to make this country what I think it may well become . . . a great manufacturing country, a country [holding] its millions of people as other continents do," wrote Isaac Isaacs, "then I say that it is necessary to see that its manufacturing industries and its natural resources . . . are not stifled . . . by the power of numbers and the power of aggregated wealth wrongly used to the repression of honest individual effort."[62] The AIPA gave the state sweeping powers to control industry, allowing it to remove tariffs selectively to force cartel prices down, to subpoena virtually any record, and to decide cases on substantive criteria rather than merely technical judicial considerations.[63] But the shipping cartel successfully limited the state's powers in a High Court appeal that gutted critical AIPA clauses.

The final, and most important part of Preference manqué, though,

---

60. Quotation, NLA MS 1540/12/5, E. O. Shann to Deakin, September 26, 1907. On the AIFL, see NLA MS 1540/12/6–7, 32, 53, and especially 76; *Melbourne Argus* September 30, 1905; C. Grimshaw, "Australian Nationalism and the Imperial Connection 1900–1914," AJPH 3, (May 1958).

61. I. McLean, "Rural Outputs, Inputs and Mechanization in Victoria, 1870–1910" (Ph.D. dissertation, Australian National University, 1971), pp. 349, 361; CWPP 1906, vol. IV, pp. 97, 124–125, 140–146.

62. Isaac Isaacs (LPP Vic), CWPD 1906, vol. 31, p. 376. See also similar comments by Deakin, in his pre-sessional speech, June 22, 1905, Ballarat Victoria (NLA MS 2822/8), and in a speech accepting the presidency of the Imperial Federation League, June 14, 1905.

63. Acts of Parliament of Australia, no. 9 of 1906, pp. 19–27.

was the "New Protection." A Deakin-authored parliamentary paper made clear the New Protection's purpose:

> The "old" Protection contented itself with making good wages possible. The "new" Protection seeks to make them actual. It aims at according to the manufacturer that degree of exemption from unfair outside competition which will enable him to pay fair and reasonable wages without impairing the maintenance and extension of his industry, or its capacity to supply the local market. It does not stop here. Having put the manufacturer in a position to pay good wages, it goes on to assure the public that he does pay them.[64]

Economically, New Protection was very similar to Preferential Trade. Manufacturing was to be protected both by tariffs and by the AIPA, but this protection was explicitly tied to maintenance of labour stability by the Excise Tariff Act, which removed protection for firms failing to pay "fair and reasonable wages".[65] As well, higher wages would expand the domestic market for the consumer non-durables that local manufacturers produced. Politically, the New Protection tried to weld skilled labour and manufacturing capital together rather than placating agriculture. Ruling on the basis of this Act, the Commonwealth Conciliation Court established a 7 shilling per day minimum wage for unskilled labour (the "Harvester" Decision; see next section). The "New Protection" cemented a political alliance between Labor and the LPP that permitted a fairly high tariff to be passed in 1908. But in 1908 the High Court ruled that the Excise Tariff Act exceeded Federal constitutional powers.[66] Though this disallowed the 7 shilling minimum wage per se, the amount set the minimum in all federal awards afterwards and spread to other industries. After the Labor Party victory in 1910, this wage was indexed to the cost of living, thus avoiding the problems that New Zealand's Conciliation system later encountered with falling real wages. The essence of the New Protection thus persisted, although the lack of an institutional link between wages and protection was a crucial political obstacle for

64. CWPP no. 16 of 1907–08, vol. II, p. 1887. See I. Isaacs' comments, CWPD 1906, vol. 34, pp. 4215–4217, for a similar articulation of the link between wages and the tariff, and NLA MS 1540/10/318, E.O. Sullivan to A. Deakin, May 26, 1905, which suggested the political utility of such a plan in NSW.

65. See CWPP no. 147 of 1907, also on "New Protection." The law was embodied in the "Commonwealth Excise Tariff Act," no. 16 of 1906.

66. Deakin believed there would be no problem with the High Court, because he had just appointed two like-minded LPP lawyers—H. B. Higgens and Isaac Isaacs—to the bench.

the LPP. The only piece of legislation the LPP succeeded in implementing was Conciliation and Arbitration.

CONCILIATION AND ARBITRATION

If Preferential Trade started as an LPP effort to wrest the farmers away from alliance with the financiers, Conciliation was an effort to split Labor. Encouraged by State level Arbitration Acts 111 new unions formed from 1900 to 1903, in contrast to only four in the four years preceding.[67] Labor was once more a growing political and economic threat. The Liberal Barton government first introduced an Arbitration Bill on June 5, 1901, but it was lost in the blizzard of housekeeping legislation passed to set up Federal departments.[68] Deakin reintroduced the Bill on July 28, 1903, hand in hand with his Preferential Trade proposals.

The Conciliation and Arbitration Act of 1904 institutionalized collective bargaining between employers and unions under the supervision of a special federal court. This Court ruled on work conditions, wage levels, and contracts. Strikes and lockouts were prohibited for unions and firms seeking awards or rulings from the court. The act made unions legal, while regulating their operations. As the only LPP proposal enacted early and fully, and because of its importance for the development of Australian unionism, a literature has grown up concerning Conciliation and Arbitration.

Traditional Explanations for Conciliation

The standard interpretation for conciliation, by Brian Fitzpatrick, is that capital and the state jointly imposed Conciliation on the weakened unions as a new mode of labour control. Revisionist John Rickard argues that a significant and substantial middle class, occupying positions *outside* labour and capital, enforced its will upon them through the instrumentality of the state, with the help of a decidedly

---

67. *Official Yearbook of the Commonwealth of Australia* (OYBCWA) no. 20, p. 580. A stronger version of the Victorian Factory Act passed in 1900; the NSW Industrial Arbitration Act passed late 1901.

68. Turner, *First Decade of the Australian Commonwealth*, pp. 22–23. The Governor-General's speech for the first session of the first parliament contained fourteen agenda items, eight of which were to establish various government departments. Of the remaining six, only one (restricting immigration) passed. Conciliation was taken up in the next session, while the others languished.

centrist Labor Party. In contrast to Fitzpatrick, Rickard argues that capital to a large extent had to be dragged unwilling to the altar of Conciliation by Labor. Rickard also deprecates the notion that conciliation was a piece of deliberate policy, asserting that Deakin, and by extension the LPP, regarded Conciliation as *lagniappe* to Labor for its support of their program.[69]

My interpretation differs on three key points. First, no one knew what to expect from the actual functioning of Conciliation. Second, "capital" was not as united as either Rickard or Fitzpatrick suggest.[70] Manufacturers went willingly, and dragged the rest of capital behind them. Finally, as my arguments above suggest, Conciliation was a strategic move by the LPP. Rickard's *lagniappe* argument understates both the depth of conflict over Conciliation and the extent of contemporary fears about its potentially significant effects on the economy. As Deakin said, introducing the Bill: "We are touching some of the springs upon which the working of society depends. We are seeking to control them without interfering with what may broadly be described as legitimate business methods."[71] Much conflict over the Bill and later Court battles came from trying to define the "legitimate business methods" Rickard (and perhaps Deakin?) took for granted.

Small and Manufacturing Capitals

Manufacturers clearly articulated the four things they desired from Conciliation. First, Conciliation assured—as Rickard asserts—that social anarchy would not erupt out of a general strike centering on export industries: "The central purpose of this Bill is to prevent strikes and lockouts. . . . These are modes of war which rend our industrial system to pieces, and will be found . . . to have cost . . .

69. As evidence for this argument Rickard points to an article by Deakin in the *London Morning Post* and to Deakin's resignation when Labor tried to extend the Bill's ambit. But Deakin pitched the *Morning Post* articles for the ears of those in London who invested in Australia. It was to his advantage to minimize the significance of Conciliation for this audience while portraying the LPP as firmly in the governmental saddle. Deakin's decision to resign his government has to be understood in terms of the specific proposal—to extend Federal Arbitration powers over State employees. As lawyer Deakin surely knew, this would never be accepted as constitutional. Resignation signaled Deakin's sense of the limits of the possible to the Labor Party. Rickard, *Class and Politics*, pp. 207–209; for Deakin's article, see *Federated Australia*, April 11, 1906.

70. Rickard, despite an extensive and excellent discussion of the difficulties employer groups faced in trying to aggregate businesses into one political organization, treats them as if they had more or less unified interests vis-à-vis labour and Labor.

71. Deakin (LPP Vic), CWPD 1:2, July 30, 1903, p. 2863.

many millions sterling." By legitimating unions nationally, Conciliation would preempt a major cause of the 1890s strikes, preventing an isolated dispute from expanding into a devastating general contest.[72]

Second, Conciliation would keep domestic capitals from being squeezed, as Hume Cook feared, between sweated labour on the one hand, and the banks and larger capitals on the other. "What we want is a measure which will get at the sweater and compel him. . .to submit to proper conditions. . . It will weed out employers who have not sufficient capital."[73] In the 1890s small sweatshops created considerable competition for Victorian manufacturers; with wages regulated in Victoria, they needed nationwide standards to level conditions in Australia.[74]

Third, Deakin's need for Conciliation dovetailed with his desire to wrest Preferential Trade concessions from the British. Deakin needed to assure them that Australia would be able, literally, to deliver the goods. Conciliation meant that wool and other exports would leave the docks, unlike in 1890.[75] This expanded export activity dovetailed with manufacturers' final concern.

More unionization would actually help manufacturers' business. The prospect of more, stronger, and legal unions did not deter manufacturers, for it was the larger export capitals in mining and wool that already confronted industrial unions, while small and medium-sized firms faced craft organizations amenable to personalistic and

72. Quotation, Deakin (LPP Vic), CWPD 2:1, March 22, 1904, p. 765. See also CWPD 7:2, August 11, 1903, pp. 3362–3363, quoting B.R. Wise on the utility of removing unionization as a *casus belli*, and J. Hume Cook in the *Melbourne Age*, May 2, 1903, on "disastrous social and commercial consequences" of general strikes. See *Melbourne Age* editorials August 11 and 19, 1890, for evidence of an early acceptance of unions.

73. J. Hume Cook (LPP Vic), CWPD 1:2, August 20, 1903, p. 3981; see also CWPD, April 13, 1904, p. 899. Such competition had led to the 1896 Victorian Factory Act; see Rickard, *Class and Politics*, chap. 4.

74. Deakin conflated the need for uniform conditions in the national market with conflict prevention: "The measure aims at a gradual, slow, but sure achievement of fair hours, fair wages, and fair conditions of labour. . . . Its object is to place employers on the same footing one with another so that the most scrupulous and the most generous . . . shall not be hampered by such qualities in the struggle to maintain themselves against the competition of less worthy men. It aims at placing employees under obligations and control that will prevent the rebellious breaking away of unruly unionists." CWPD 1:2, July 30, 1903, pp. 2882–2883.

75. Aside from Deakin's remarks above, see also J. Hume Cook (LPP Vic): "An Arbitration Act . . . shall for ever get rid of the disastrous strikes and locks-out which have . . . disgraced our industrial affairs. Industrial peace will do more to attract capital to this country, and set the wheels of progress in motion, than will anything of which I know." CWPD 2:1, April 13, 1904, p. 900. J. Wilks (NSW FTP), CWPD 1:2, August 11, 1903, p. 3357, also discusses the utility of Conciliation for preventing capital flight.

paternalistic control. The higher wages likely to emerge from union activity were more than just a bribe for Labor's support for the tariff; more money to wages overall meant increase in the domestic market for precisely the kinds of things Deakin's peers manufactured, largely at the expense of the export sectors.[76] Arbitration would reverse the situation of the nineteenth century, for export sectors would subsidize manufacturers' domestic accumulation. As J. W. Hackett, a West-ralian publisher, noted: "Even on the goldfields we get little more spent on the country than what the Arbitration Court, or some similar means, has been able to extract from the pocket of the joint stock owner."[77] Thus, Conciliation seemed the key to continued prosperity for the capitals that had suffered the most in the 1890s.

Labor versus Labour?

The reactions of the Labor party and labour to Conciliation best show its political ramifications: the points of division the LPP hoped to exploit. Labor's statements reveal both its immediate strategy to-wards Conciliation proposals and its analysis of Australian capitalism. The latter underlay its electoral and economic strategy up to World War I, and showed the degree to which Labor politicians, in contrast to unionists, more readily accepted capitalism as a system of produc-tion.[78] Let us start with what labour accepted.

Workers were less impressed with Arbitration's utility and with capitalist production relations than were Labor politicians, but they understood the trade-offs involved in the proposed regime. The Im-migration Act of 1901 had set a floor on wages by excluding "colored" labour. The industrial section of the labour movement wanted Ar-bitration to provide a rise from this floor:

> The *[Brisbane] Worker* is not looking for the millennium from [arbitra-tion]. . . . It is a palliative only. . . . Labour's share is the whole, and that no Arbitration court will ever give us. . . . Arbitration will take from us the power to cease work. But while we have the power to vote that will not matter a great deal. We can hit Capitalism harder at the ballot box than

76. See T. Ewing (LPP NSW), CWPD 2:1, April 13, 1904, p. 921, for a clear statement.
77. NLA MS 1540/16/508–510, J. W. Hackett to A. Deakin, February 24, 1909.
78. See Clark, *A History of Australia*, vol. V, chap. 7; Rickard, *Class and Politics*, chap. 11; and I. Turner, *Industrial Labour and Politics* (Canberra: ANU Press, 1965), on "embourgeoisment" of the Labor movement.

we ever did on strike. The point that decides this paper in favour of arbitration is that it will give us more than we have got at present.[79]

The *Worker* had long since announced the concession it expected for abandoning strikes:

> A pertinent question in regard to arbitration and conciliation is this: Supposing . . . the Conciliation Court decided against the men, how is it to enforce its decision? What guarantee is there that the men may not disagree with the decision and leave the job? . . . By giving preference to trades unionists [and providing that] Courts shall only be available to workmen [through the] medium of their unions. Organization and the Union funds are a guarantee that the mandates of the Conciliation Courts shall be adhered to by Labour.[80]

If, unlike the party, the *Worker* was more committed to socialism, it clearly delineated the acceptable short-run tradeoffs: exchange the right to strike for juridically-enforced unions to protect workers, and judicial amelioration of conditions; accept a draw on point-of-production struggles and transfer the struggle to politics in hopes of a victory there. The original logic of abandoning direct for political action after the 1890s strikes culminated, in essence, in this position. The unemployment and wage reductions of the 1890s made workers set their sights on today's bread rather than tomorrow's socialist pastry; but workers were unwilling to countenance increased exploitation unmatched by increased wages.[81]

In contrast, Labor politicians and the craft section of the labour movement liked the emphasis Conciliation gave to politics and also Labor gave explicit guarantees to capitalists in their pursuit of a winning electoral coalition. The chair of the Federal Labor Party Caucus, J. C. Watson, believed that: "in the long run the average gain under the decisions of the court will be higher than that obtained under the old system" of strikes. He also made explicit guarantees to encourage

79. *Brisbane Worker* March 26, 1904. See *Brisbane Worker* March 30, 1901, on the prerequisite nature of "White Australia." As Queensland unions were predominantly industrial unions, the *Brisbane Worker* is a good guide to the thinking of that section of the labour movement.
80. *Brisbane Worker*, June 16, 1900; see also January 8, 1898, November 24, 1900, July 27, 1901, and August 20, 1904 on the importance of political action. See APR, February 15, and November 15, 1898 for pastoralists' thoughts on the link between unionization and Arbitration's effectiveness.
81. See *Brisbane Worker* June 1890, p. 8.

investment by capital, illustrating the potential for fusion between elements of Labor and the LPP.[82] Labor implicitly accepted the continuation of capitalist relations of production, holding up craft production as a model. As Watson said:

> In the old days, individual employers gave far greater consideration to the fair claims and necessities of their employees than has ever been done by the vast trusts and corporations which now conduct industrial concerns. . . . The companies have absolutely changed the conditions, have introduced sweating [i.e. increased the intensity of work] as far as possible. . . . While competition lays its iron hand upon the employer, he is, in many cases against his own desire, constrained to reduce wages far below what he believes to be a fair rate.[83]

Watson saw trusts as the ultimate cause of strikes where workers tried to hold the line on wages and conditions; was this not the lesson of 1890, when strikes raged in precisely the sectors dominated by large and foreign capital?

This opposition to trusts also drew urban and rural petit entrepreneurs to Labor. As in the United States and Canada, cartelized shippers and suppliers forced down basic commodity prices to reap monopoly profits at farmers' expense.[84] The urban self-employed, one eighth of all employed Australians, perceived themselves as being gobbled up by trusts, and in absolute terms their numbers in Victoria and NSW fell 31 percent in the decade after 1901.[85] Both farmers and urban petit owners preferred a responsive public master to the unresponsive, voracious private owners castigated by Labor. Labor consistently advocated nationalizing trusts, while leaving petit entrepreneurs alone.[86] Labor's position seemed more authentic than the

82. Quotation from J. C. Watson (LP NSW), CWPD 1:2 August 6, 1903, vol. 15, p. 3211. See NSWPD, vol. 36, 2nd series, November 30, 1909, for Holman's comments during the coal strike. See also D. Watkins (LP NSW), CWPD 1:2 vol. 16, August 26, 1903, p. 4245: "I hope [conciliation] will . . . tend to bring about security of investment throughout Australia."

83. J. C. Watson (LP NSW), CWPD 1:2, vol. 15, August 6, 1903, p. 3207. See also W. Hughes' comments in the *Sydney Daily Telegraph*, February 8 and 29, 1908, and November 27, 1909; Turner, *Industrial Labour and Politics*, pp. 33–34.

84. For a contemporary view, see T. Wilkinson, *The Trust Movement in Australia* (Melbourne: Critchley Parker, 1914).

85. OYBNSW 1900/1, p. 701. As W. Hughes, *Policies and Potentates* (Sydney: Angus and Robertson, 1950), p. 35, put it: "In my own electorate shops were as the sands of the seashore."

86. By 1908 the Commonwealth was pursuing fifteen separate antitrust actions against, among others, tobacco producers; CWPP no. 9 of 1908, vol. II, pp. 1571–1572. NSW Labor proposed nationalizing food distribution in Sydney, to eliminate the whole-

LPP's AIPA, which seemed designed more for the protection of manufacturers.

Where Labor departed from the LPP was in its determination to bring public servants of all kinds under the ambit of the Federal Conciliation and Arbitration Act. Historically public servants had served as the vanguard for improved conditions, establishing before 1900 the principles of minimum wages, the eight-hour day, and pensions. The Federal Court could be used to defend this pattern from retrenchers and the conservative state Governments, especially after the unsuccessful 1903 Victorian railway strike showed their anti-labour bent.[87] Victorian Premier W. H. Irvine provoked and then smashed a strike by railway workers. As in 1890, the immediate issue was the workers' right to affiliate with the Trades Hall, for this affiliation threatened export transport and the movement of scab labour. The situation was aggravated by other efforts to roll back labour gains through retrenchment, union-busting, and an elegant gerrymandering scheme.[88] Irvine pushed through a coercion act that deprived strikers of civil liberties and was so worded as to outlaw striking, picketing, loitering, and any activity in support of the strikers. Strikers were fired, scabs hired, and the strike collapsed in short order.[89] In light of this, Conciliation for public servants seemed a necessary defensive measure to Labor.

Extension of Arbitration to railway workers also had positive political aspects, because huge numbers of Australians were public employees. The Labor Party advocated development led by government spending (funded by a land tax, not more borrowing), in contrast to the Anti-Socialist call for retrenchment.[90] The importance of state spending in economic development was clear to all, especially Western Australians. There the relative lateness of development (even for Australia) made the State's role even more prominent than elsewhere: railways, urban public works, agriculture, and infrastructure for min-

---

salers and agents disliked by farmers. *Australian Star*, March 2, 1909. See Graham, *Formation of the Australian Country Parties*, for farmer conflicts with middlemen.

87. Butlin et al., *Government and Capitalism*, p. 153; B. Mansfield, "The State as Employer: an Early Twentieth Century Discussion," AJPH 3 (May 1958), *passim*. Victoria cut public expenditure for wages and salaries 20 percent between FY1900/1 and FY1903/4; Butlin, *Australian Domestic Product*, p. 190.

88. *Australian Worker*, May 9, 1903. See L. Benham and J. Rickard, "Masters and Servants: The Victorian Railway Strike of 1903," *Labour History* 24 (May 1973), for a full description of the strike.

89. See also AIBR, September 20, 1902, p. 732, and May 20, 1903, p. 298, congratulating Irvine on his electoral victory and for cutting the railway unions down to size.

90. CWPD 4:3, vol. 49, June 27, 1909, p. 289.

ing all came from the State simultaneously. The Westralian elite recognised this, for as publisher Hackett wrote Deakin: "What [the Australian Women's National League] consider[s] the strongest plank in [its] platform—the denunciation of socialism—falls on absolutely dry rock here in [Western Australia]. From its circumstances, and no one knows it better than [Premier] Forrest, we have had to be socialistic all along. Almost our only capitalist was the State. Certainly almost the only one of whose honesty and capacity we could assure ourselves. We are a state-created community." Australia's relatively high proportion of employment in services also made this Labor initiative electorally attractive.[91]

Free Traders, Anti-Socialists, and the Haute Bourgeoisie

Just as the Conciliation debates reveal Labor's positive political and negative economic projects, they illumine the FTP's negative political and positive economic projects. The LPP hoped that Conciliation, like Preference, would split the FTP. Mercantile, financial, and pastoral capitals (to the extent to which these were distinct) desired the security of no strike-no lock out provisions, but feared that government intervention might expand into wage regulation.[92] Debt concerns underlay their desire for no strikes, as their stand on Labor's efforts to include agricultural labor shows.

Labor twice tried amending the Conciliation and Arbitration Bill to include virtually unorganized agricultural labour, fearing they would provide most of the scabs used to break strikes. In the House the first attempt failed, with the FTP voting as a bloc against the motion, along with all but the most étatist of the Liberals—Hume Cook, Higgens, Deakin, Samuel Mauger, and Charles Kingston. After the 1903 elections, the now Labor-dominated Senate restored agricultural labour to the Bill. The House again rejected this measure on party lines.

FTP voted en masse against the proposal because of their public and private debt concerns. Allen Robinson, a Victorian largeholder and representative of the Central Council of Employers of Australia, argued against inclusion of agricultural labour because "by adopting

91. Quotation from NLA MS 1540/16/508–510, J. W. Hackett to A. Deakin, February 24, 1909. The proportion of Australian employment in services consistently exceeded the proportion in services in, for example, the United States; J. A. Dowie, "The Service Ensemble," in C. Forster, ed., *Australian Economic Development* (London: Unwin Allen, 1970), p. 221.

92. See, for example, ABL 78/1/78, pp. 53–54, February 27, 1905, J. Gregson to London Board of the Australian Agricultural Co. (AAC).

[Labor's] proposal [to include agriculture] we shall check our export trade. The interest of the huge debt of Victoria is paid largely by the export of wheat and other farming product which is sold in the London market. Our producers have to compete there against the whole world, and consequently should be allowed to carry on their vocations with as little restriction as possible."[93] Private debt—graziers' debt in the form of mortgages on land—also motivated the FTP. The value of production occurring on the graziers' land determined its value, and if land values were to rise sufficiently to revalorize their mortgages, then more profitable products than grazing had to be found, at least for some of the land. Those products were wheat, dairy and fruit—precisely the activities most affected if Arbitration extended to seasonal and low-paid agricultural labour. If Conciliation depressed the profitability of these essentially infant industries, then revalorization of mortgages would depend either on meat sales—a market dominated by New Zealand and Argentina—or an unlikely rise in wool prices.

If FTP/ASP desires for economic stability and continued debt service unified the party on exclusion of agricultural labour (which, significantly, did not include shearers), those desires caused splits over the question of railway workers. All of the exporters wanted assurances that the rails would always function to move goods to port and scabs to work. The question of regulating rail workers centered on whether ultimate control should be vested in the States or the Commonwealth. Some argued that there was no need for federal jurisdiction, since the Victorian railway strike had seemingly demonstrated that conservative governments made the State railways secure. Others, however, observed the lasting enmity Irvine garnered for his efforts, and worried that a "frontlash" would create a resurgence of Liberal-Labor government at the State level.[94] Federal powers might then serve as a final line of defense when a State was too "soft" on strikes. Furthermore, unions clearly had come to stay, so it was bad

---

93. A. Robinson (ASP Vic), CWPD 2:1, April 2, 1904, p. 1916 and April 13, 1904, p. 895.

94. As Hume Cook said when Irvine was mooted for a cabinet position in the "Fusion" ministry: "Re Irvine: this man *must be excluded* at all costs. When one thinks of the thousands and thousands of railway men and the relatives in every state, as well as all the other civil servants, his inclusion would spell disaster" NLA MS 1540/16/581–584, J. Hume Cook to A. Deakin, May 22, 1909, original emphasis. See also NLA MS 601/1/170–173, 176, Hume Cook papers, for correspondence between Hume Cook and the union, and Hume Cook and S. Mauger, on Liberal efforts to woo the strikers and to reduce the political and human costs of the strike.

policy to antagonize labour needlessly.[95] Thus large domestic capitalists, who, unlike foreign capital, could not move offshore, were
willing to let unions exist in exchange for no strikes. As B. R. Wise,
then NSW Attorney General, had argued when introducing the NSW
Arbitration Act, the costs of fighting over unionization *per se* were too
high. The Victorian Employers Federation (VEF) secretary, R. Wal-
pole, said that employers "had no objection to the working classes
organising, and they were prepared to accept the legislation for sani-
tation and hours and conditions of labour. But they drew the line at a
government stepping in and fixing wages."[96] While these larger
capitalists typically could afford somewhat higher wages to buy labour
peace, they were vulnerable to any strikes triggered by weaker exporters who preferred to fight. The NSW Pastoralists' Union president
said: "It never occurred to us to pay low wages. If there is a person
down on wages it is the man with the small shed; the small sheds could
fight you easily if they liked, but it is the big sheds that lose heavily,
where they have a large number of men employed. A man with a
small family to feed doesn't care whether he shears this month or
next."[97] The strong needed mechanisms to control the weak and each
other, and conciliation seemed one way to do this. Conciliation also
offered a broader stability, which insurance magnate and member of
the NSW Legislative Council A. Meeks foreshadowed in the debates
over the NSW Industrial Arbitration Act: "If provision were made for
collective agreement being carried out, say for a period of two-three
years, anyone could with some certainty start a factory and enter into
contracts."[98] Small domestic producers and foreign financiers were

95. Rickard, *Class and Politics*, p. 195. Bentham and Rickard, "Masters and Servants,"
p. 6.
96. *Sydney Daily Telegraph*, April 18, 1903. See also ABL E256/1663, p. 21, August 4,
1902, Report of a Conference between the NSW Pastoralists Union and the Australian
Workers Union, where W. E. Abbott (Pastoralist Union President) supported arbitration so long as wages were not dictated; and similar and oft-quoted remarks of M.
McEachern (FTP Victoria) on behalf of the shipping industry; CWPD 1:2, August 11,
1903, p. 3340.
97. ABL E256/1663, "Minutes and Verbal Report of a Conference between the
NSWPU and the AWU," August 4, 1902, p. 20. For similar sentiments by other export-
oriented businesses see ABL 78/3/16, October 29, 1897, p. 330; June 10, 1898, p.442;
ABL 78/3/17 February 17, 1899, p.34; ABL 78/1/80, January 10, 1907, pp. 80–81, on
the AAC's willingness to raise wages to avoid a strike; ABL E217/3 March 12–13, 1908,
p. 228, Australian Ship Owners Federation (ASOF) meeting minutes; ABL E203/1,
January 10, 1907, ASOF Sydney branch meeting minutes.
98. A. Meeks, NSWPD vol. 108, November 20, 1900 p. 5428. C. Hall *The Manufacturers* (Sydney: Angus and Robertson, 1971), pp. 93, 152–155, asserts that the NSW
Industrial Arbitration Act passed only because of the absence of explicit provisions for
wage regulation.

less sanguine than export producers and their domestic financial allies about conciliation. Reid surely spoke for the large number of Sydney manufacturers involved in working up imported raw materials when he blithely asked: "How are we going to compete with these underpaid and sweated countries until our own labour is underpaid and sweated too?"[99] Foreign financiers feared that the Bill meant out-and-out socialism, and, more concretely, they worried about increased wage bills in mining and pastoral production.[100] They threatened capital flight, as they had only a few years earlier when West Australian Liberals tried to pass a Conciliation Act.[101] "Capitalists . . . view their investments [in Western Australia] with uneasiness and a sense of insecurity," complained the London Chamber of Mines, "and if this Bill becomes law without substantial modifications to protect the interest of the mine owner, it is feared that it will be impossible to obtain English capital to protect or further develop the mining industry."[102]

Like Preference, Conciliation split the capitals represented outside the LPP, and thus was able to pass. The deal between the LPP and the FTP fragments was closed in a revealing exchange between Deakin and Melbourne shipping magnate Malcolm McEachern. McEachern offered Deakin this "hypothetical" case: Supposing shearers and pastoralists to be in conflict, but the shearers had not actually accepted work yet, and so were not technically striking, what could the state do? Deakin framed his response in terms of Section 69 of the Bill, which allowed the Court to register an unregistered organization. "The employers' organization could bring the matter before the court, and if

99. G. H. Reid (FTP NSW), CWPD 1:1, vol. 7, October 31, 1901, p. 1800. See also *Melbourne Age*, August 21, 1906.

100. See comments by E. T. Doxat, chair of the large pastoral firm Dalgety and of the Australasian Chamber of Commerce in London, in his letter to R. Twopenny, editor of the APR, in ABL N8/29/475–478, January 2, 1905; and J. A. Cockburn (SA Agent General) to A. Deakin, NLA MS 1540/1/1303–1304, January 19, 1906. The LPP worried about these fears but saw them as unfounded; see, for example, NLA MS 1540/15/773–774, A. W. Jose to A. Deakin, January 29, 1908.

101. "If the measure is pushed to extremes, it will force employers to emigrate from Australia," was a typical comment offered when Labor tried to include railway workers. J. G. Wilson (FTP Victoria, a big farmer), CWPD 2:1, April 13, 1904, p. 929; see also W. Knox (FTP Vic), CWPD 1:2, vol. 16, August 26, 1903, pp. 4245–4253, for the views of financial and mining capital, and W. McMillan (FTP NSW), CWPD 1:2, August 20, 1903, p. 3967, for importers and mercantile capital.

102. "Petition of the London Chamber of Mines to the Western Australia Legislative Assembly on the Occasion of their Promulgation of a Conciliation Bill in 1900," Western Australia Legislative Assembly, *Votes & Proceedings 1900* session 6, vol. II, no. A32, November 22, 1900. See also Carruthers' comments on the utility of Conciliation for stopping capital flight; NSWPD, vol. 1, 2nd series, pp. 922–923, August 29, 1901.

the shearers belonged to a registered organization, as they no doubt would, they could be dealt with. If they were not organized, the court could compel them to register as an organization, and then deal with them [using its power to fine]."[103] But this also implied a potential to coerce employers and their organizations under Section 69, so McEachern asked: "Would that provision [for penalty for defying the court's decree] apply if a man is determined to close his business rather than comply with the decision of the court?" Deakin replied, "I do not suppose it would."[104] At bottom then, the court would guarantee the availability of labour, even if labour had to be coerced. Labour organizations could be fined into bankruptcy (pensions and sick benefits depended on union funds) if workers did not work. But disinvestment was not the court's concern. On this basis, Conciliation became the only measure the LPP was able to pass, indeed the only measure for which the LPP was able to construct a grand coalition supported by political Labor on the one hand, and by domestic financial and pastoral interests on the other. In the absence of a fully articulated scheme of Preferential Trade, however, Conciliation proved to be the LPP's undoing.

COLLAPSE OF THE LIBERAL PARTY

In mid-1909 the LPP disintegrated. All but four of sixteen Liberals joined the ASP in what is known as the "Fusion"; the four left behind joined Labor.[105] Why did this happen? Most accounts point to either fatal splits within the LPP, a natural polarization between bourgeois and Labor parties, or both.[106] The cumulative effects of poor organization by the LPP and increasing class conflict all played their part in the disintegration. But these factors in turn were caused by the LPP's partial implementation of its policies. In the absence of a fully articulated scheme of Preference Trade to complete the triad of debt repatriation, Preferential Trade, and Conciliation, LPP policies acted to polarize its own political base, even as the economic pieces of its ac-

103. A. Deakin (LPP Vic), CWPD 1:2, July 30, 1903, p. 2872.
104. CWPD 1:2, July 30, 1903, p. 2883.
105. Lyne, Chanter, Storrer, and Wise all went to the Labor Party in mid-1909; Higgens had been appointed to the Conciliation Court. Forrest's "corner" already was in open alliance with the ASP. The curious thing here, of course, is that it was the NSW LPP that rallied to the Labor Party, while their Victorian cousins chose "Fusion".
106. See for example C.M.H. Clark, *A Short History of Australia* (New York: NAL/Penguin, 1987), p. 194; or the longer analysis in C.M.H. Clark, *A History of Australia*, vol. V, chap. 8.

cumulation project came together. The purpose of the following sections is to show that the LPP's partial success ultimately doomed its political project, but not its economic project. Thus we will first look at the usual explanations for political failure to show how they related to LPP policy.[107]

Organizational Arguments

Perhaps the LPP's relatively weak party organization caused its political failure. Labor was the best organized of the three national parties, as contemporaries noted: "The Senate [election] I despair of, because the state as a whole can only be canvassed by an omnipresent organization such as the labour people can alone give effect to."[108] The unions provided a permanent manpower and organizing base for the Labor Party. Despite members' differences over the degree of socialism, protectionism, and labour activism desired, biannual conferences tended to produce binding, if occasionally less-than-amicable, agreements on policy and strategy. Unions used Conferences and the associated Caucus and pledge tactics to limit, with varying degrees of success, the ability of Labor politicians to cut individual deals with other parties.[109] Although the politicians disagreed, in the end most

107. Another possible explanation comes from Douglas Rae, who argues convincingly that single member districting inevitably leads to a two-party system. *Political Consequences of Electoral Laws* (New Haven: Yale University Press, 1971). Australia had single member districts for virtually all House seats and what amounted to the same thing for Senate seats until 1919. But the pattern of mono-cultural and mono-industrial production in Australia meant that three-way elections (at least between official parties) were rare. In the three elections before Fusion, 87 percent of elections were two-way; in the three-way contests, Labor typically came out worst, winning only one-fifth to the other two parties' respective two-fifths. This, and the presence of various semi-official electoral truces, makes the question of the timing and causes of LPP disintegration even more salient—why could not such truces have postponed polarization indefinitely? After 1909 the Fusion itself fell victim to preferential voting, which created a new three party system. After 1911 the States started to adopt preferential voting; in 1919 it spread to Federal elections. See J. Rydon, "Electoral Methods and the Australian Party System 1910–1950," AJPH 2:1 (November 1956), 75–76. As early as March 1, 1904 the *Melbourne Age* called for compulsory voting, presuming it would work against Labor. In 1906, L. Groom (LPP Vic) introduced (and the *Age*—August 21, 1906—supported) a preferential voting bill for the same reasons.

108. NLA MS 1540/15/519, J. W. Hackett to A. Deakin, April 2, 1906. The best studies of Labor's organization are Childe, *How Labour Governs*; and L. Crisp, *The Australian Federal Labour Party* (London: Longman Green, 1955).

109. The Caucus was the official group of Labor MPs in the Federal or State assemblies. The "pledge," given by a candidate to get on the Labor ticket, affirmed that he (they were all men in those days) would vote the Party line on all issues for which the Conference and Caucus set policy. On all other issues the MP could vote his conscience. See Childe, *How Labour Governs*, for the degree of freedom each side actually experienced.

unions agreed with the *Australian Worker* that "coalition is corruption said softly."[110] There is no doubt that some Labor Members of the House, prominent among them William Hughes and George Pearce, were amenable to, indeed actively sought, some kind of permanent arrangement with the LPP.[111] Conference and pledge imposed major constraints on the LPP's ability to split Labor. Furthermore, the LPP's Deakin was hampered by the partial success of his strategy in Victoria, where the more congenial unions had already allied with "Liberals" before Federation.[112] This early success left a radical rump Labor party in Victoria that consistently opposed electoral immunity for and cooperation with the LPP, thus pulling Labor leftward. If this split had occurred in the context of a general move to the LPP by Labor elements, then the rump's intransigence would not have mattered, but occurring "prematurely" as it did, it prevented a tighter coalition between Labor and the LPP federally. However, Labor's solidity is no complete explanation for the LPP's disintegration. Solidity and organization explain only why Labor could resist and outlast LPP inducements—and, after all, the unions that made possible such solidity were products of the LPP's Arbitration Act.

The organizational base of the FTP and the ASP was similar to that of Labor. Like Labor, the ASP was relatively well organized; the National Citizens' Reform League (Victoria), People's Reform League (NSW), various Farmer, Property Owner, and Producer Associations, and Australian Women's National League provided a constant year-to-year operational and organizational base, financed by the Victorian Employers Federation (VEF).[113] The ASP also seems to have had

110. *Australian Worker*, June 24, 1904. In 1906, the Labor Conference firmly ruled out a permanent electoral alliance, a stand reiterated in 1909 before the Fusion; see Childe, *How Labour Governs*, p. 37.

111. See Hughes's correspondence with Deakin, NLA MS 1540, various series; especially 16/33–34, 15/661, 15/705. See also P. Weller and B. Lloyd, eds., *Caucus Minutes, 1901–1949*, vol. I (Melbourne: Melbourne University Press, 1975), for April 23, 1904 and May 15, 1904. A look at the formal articles of alliance between Labor and those Liberals who aligned with them during the brief Labor Ministry of April-August 1904 shows the limits that the caucus imposed on freedom of action, even for those angling for a better deal. *Caucus Minutes*, pp. 468–469, has a transcript of these articles.

112. See D. Rawson, "Victoria as the exception," in P. Loveday, A. Martin and R. Parker, eds., *Emergence of the Australian Party System* (Sydney: Hale and Ironmonger, 1977), p. 47, on Victorian Labor's weakness. See also R. Gollan, *Radical and Working Class Politics* (Melbourne: Melbourne University Press, 1960), pp. 141, 170; and T. A. Coghlan, *Labour and Industry in Australia* (Melbourne: Macmillan, 1965), pp. 1494–1495.

113. See T. Matthews, "Business Associations and Politics" (Ph.D. thesis, Sydney University, 1971), pp. 220–233, and *passim*; Rickard, *Class and Politics*, pp. 168–172; and P. Loveday, "Labor," in Loveday, *Emergence of the Australian Party System*, pp. 411–412.

external funding, as Wise warned Deakin in 1906: "After the election appoint a Royal Commission to enquire into the expenditures of the Reid [Anti-socialist] party; and call the Sydney and Melbourne actors of the Banks and Mortgage Companies having head offices in London. You would—to my knowledge . . . learn some startling facts."[114] But antagonism between State and Federal parties, and between the mass organizations and the VEF, debilitated the ASP. The mass organizations were factious and determined to avoid the VEF's domination. The "States' Rights" nature of the Federal party eliminated the possibility of positive policies infringing on State powers, leaving only attacks on Labor that had little mobilization potential. "Anti-socialism, yet once again, the other fellow's program and nothing but that," commented a Liberal when the ASP debuted in 1906. "Can a leader really believe that any considerable and sane body of men can be 'enthused' into a state of meningitis just to save the tobacco combine and old Julius Kronheimer (whose self and palace in Hamburg I know well) or the International Harvester Company with its aristocratic MacCormick or even the British Salt Union or the Westphalian Iron Syndicate?"[115] Indeed, the state-level "anti-socialist" parties were virtually independent of and often indifferent to the Federal party. Consequently ASP representation decayed almost as fast as the LPP's (see Table 12, above). But unlike the LPP, the ASP's strong grounding in state-level organization meant it could outlast the LPP in a race against fragmentation.

Unlike both Labor and the ASP, the LPP lacked continuous organizations providing a day-to-day base. By converting Australian Natives Association (ANA) chapters, the LPP established a national organization barely in time for the first Federal elections in 1901.[116] Five years later little had changed, and one NSW LPP member complained "so far nothing absolutely nothing has been done by [ASP head] Reid or ours. There is no organization here [in NSW] excepting the 'People's Reform League' and 'Labour.' The latter are well organized and are making every effort to increase their strength. . . . The protectionists here are as usual doing nothing."[117] At each election, organizations were formed from scratch, with new names, only to disappear soon

114. NLA MS 1540/15/645, B.R. Wise to A. Deakin, November 26, 1906.
115. NLA MS 1540/1/1165, O. C. Beale to A. Deakin, June 4, 1905.
116. Rawson, "Victoria as the Exception," p. 47, and Loveday, "Labor," pp. 391–393; Matthews, "Business Associations and Politics," p. 221.
117. NLA MS 1540/1/1283, A. Chapman (LPP NSW) to A. Deakin, n.d. (c. 1905); see also NLA MS 1540/1/1615–1616, W. H. James to Deakin, January 11, 1907, on West Australian LPP disorganization. The Political Reform League was the state anti-socialist party base.

after the election. Organizations that might have formed a permanent base for the LPP either vacillated or were weak—e.g., the Imperial Federation League dismayed as many as it attracted. This organizing failure did not reflect a lack of material, for pro-LPP groups were emerging spontaneously as late as 1908. Westralian Premier James wrote to Deakin that:

> Some young Australian Natives . . . desire to start—indeed have started—a political organization called the "Australia League." The promoters desire to meet the need for an organization which shall voice the body of public opinion between Labour and Conservatism. I [James] have found out that this need is a well recognized one in every state: the perplexing difficulty is to supply it satisfactorily. These promoters are strong supporters of [Deakin] . . . [but] believe every word of the gospel according to the [nationalist] "Bulletin."[118]

Unlike the VEF, the Victorian and Sydney Chambers of Manufacturers failed to sustain a number of mass front organizations. Disorganization had some socio-economic origins. The LPP tried to hold the middle in all senses, but the "middle class" as such was composed of a wide variety of sub-units without shared interests. Lack of common interests meant that other parties could exploit cleavages to draw groups from the center. Both Labor and the ASP (as well as their components) engaged in such divisive politics. Labor attacked Britain and Empire; the ASP was full of Orangists and "Drys." Even the ANA was torn by these divisions.[119] Wherever cleavages lined up, support for the LPP could disappear—as when Catholics in the ANA plumped for wet, nationalist, pro–small capital Labor, which supported state subsidy of parochial schools, and, eventually, protection. But the key question is why the LPP's own core group, the manufacturers, divided. To understand that we need to look at Conciliation's effects, but first we must consider whether in fact capitalists sided with their own against Labor.

118. NLA MS 1540/1/1913–1915, W. James to A. Deakin, March 10, 1908.
119. See Loveday, "Labor," p. 429, and Rickard, *Class and Politics*, pp. 199–203, 249–250, for activities of the Loyal Orange Lodges and their ilk. On the ANA, see NLA MS 1540/16/469, J.N. Hume Cook to Deakin. On Catholics' political proclivities, see C. Hamilton, "Irish Catholics of NSW and the Labour Party, 1890–1910," HSANZ 8:31 (1958), "Catholics' Interests and the Labour Party," HSANZ 9:33 (1959), and her "Irish-Australian Catholics and the Labour Party" (MA thesis, Melbourne University, 1957). About 25 percent of the Australian population was Catholic.

Capital versus Labor

What about that most significant of cleavages—the one between capital and labour? Perhaps unification of the bourgeois parties was inevitable, given a coherent Labor Party. Certainly protectionist editor Syme felt this might happen: "Between Watson's socialism and Reid's anti-socialism where are we?"[120] But mere opposition to Labor was the frailest of foundations for the Fusion. "If you read our daily papers," O. C. Beale wrote Deakin, "you will perceive that we're not so much a Fusion as an Exclusion, and if there wasn't a Restless Worker to shake us up we'd soon separate," if only because many capitalists apparently preferred Labor to an anti-socialist party. As W. James pointed out, "It is an irony is it not that the so-called 'fat man's' party suffers from the want of means: all the capitalists are on the Labour side."[121]

Clearly the tariff and debt concerns of part of the LPP's social base outweighed its fears of the Labor Party's dilute socialism; but the LPP rejected mid-decade ASP offers to compromise on the tariff. One manufacturer approached by ASP head Reid before the 1906 election rejected Reid's overtures:

> I explained that . . . our people, [manufacturers] and protectionists, will not join [Reid on his tariff-less terms]. *They will prefer Labour rule and take their chances.* [Reid] is willing to concede what he offered before, a referendum:
> A: revenue tariff
>   low tariff
>   high tariff   which?
> B: protection, yes or no?
>   I told him that the former [tariff] proposal by itself will suffice to shake industry and enterprise to its bedplates, would mean the cessation of whole ranges of investment.[122]

---

120. NLA MS 1540/15/505, D. Syme to A. Deakin, March 14, 1906. See also AIBR, May 20, 1905, p. 306, and August 21, 1905, p. 652.
121. First quotation, NLA MS 1540/1/2491, O. C. Beale to A. Deakin, January 19, 1910; second quotation, NLA MS 1540/1/2462–2463, W. H. James to A. Deakin, December 27, 1909.
122. NLA MS 1540/1/1165, O. C. Beale to A. Deakin, June 1905. Emphasis added. Reid also told David Syme that were Reid Prime Minister he would appoint a committee of businessmen to consider the tariff and make any suggestions they pleased; moreover that Syme could pick the chair and one of the four other members, while vetoing a certain number of ASP appointees to the committee. Syme rejected this offer. Turner, *First Decade*, p. 96. See also Loveday, "Labor," pp. 406–407; NLA MS 1540/16/131–133,

In 1905 Hume Cook, who saw debt as a "vampire," advocated fusing the LPP with Labor; in 1906 the Victorian Chamber of Manufacturers made similar overtures to Labor.[123] Clearly a significant group of Australian capitalists found their workers a more congenial set of allies than their fellow capitalists.

Since organization problems and grand class conflict tell an incomplete story, we need to turn to LPP policies to understand what lay under the LPP's disintegration. Of the LPP's policies, Preference and Conciliation had the most profound effects. Preference as instituted actually tended to weaken rather than strengthen the LPP's hold over farmers, for it imposed a burden (tariffs) without any offsetting benefit (a captive British market). Conciliation was perhaps even more important, for though it brought labour stability, it also forced manufacturers to become increasingly capital-intense. Economically this represented an advance that created the material foundation on which manufacturers could constitute themselves as a national bourgeoisie. But politically it pushed some manufacturers closer to the ASP, and, along with resolution of the tariff issue, enabled the disharmonious "fusion" to take place.

Preferential Trade and Agriculture

The LPP's political failure to "deliver" a protected British market through Preferential Trade, increased capitalization of production, and an increasing orientation to world markets, all pushed farmers away from the LPP. Most important was the shift from domestic to export markets, which brought no political credit to the LPP (see Table 13). From 1890 to 1911, butter and wheat went from negligible fractions of NSW nonmineral exports to, respectively, 8 percent and 13.4 percent; in Victoria, butter, wheat, and flour exports went from 3.3 percent to 44.4 percent of nonmineral exports. By 1911, 64 per-

---

F. Wegg-Horne (NSWEF) to A. Deakin, August 26, 1904, offering to bury "fiscalism" and to fuse; NLA MS 1540/16/142–143, National Citizens Reform League (NCRL) to A. Deakin, September 19, 1904; NLA MS 1540/16/144–145, G. Reid to A. Deakin, September 24, 1904, offering to split the NCRL off from the VEF.

123. NLA MS 1540/16/400–403 J. N. Hume Cook to A. Deakin, June 22, 1905; Loveday, "Labor," p. 473; *Melbourne Argus*, March 5, 1906, reporting the VCM's withdrawal from the VEF over the tariff issue. See also MS 1540/1/2277–2278, A. Chapman to A. Deakin, January 21, 1909, implying that as late as 1909 Deakin could still move either left or right politically. Rickard, *Class and Politics*, pp. 232–233, sees the tariff as the key issue: it was set too low in 1902 for manufacturers' interests, and they soon joined with other capitalists after a much higher tariff passed in 1908.

Table 13. Australian wheat production and exports

	1896–00	1901–05	1906–10	1911–15
Annual average wheat production, 1896–1915 (million bushels)				
Victoria	11.63	16.43	22.05	23.76
NSW	9.49	15.27	19.14	27.25
S. Australia	5.99	10.17	20.25	17.33
W. Australia	0.53	1.32	3.21	7.08
Average % of crop exported, quinquennia				
Victoria	26	53	51	50
NSW	3	27	25	38
S. Australia	24	54	73	67
W. Australia	—	9	21	40

SOURCE: Graham, *Formation of Australian Country Parties*, p. 33.

cent of Victorian agricultural production was exported, compared to about 3 percent in 1890; 33.9 percent of NSW production went abroad, versus 2.7 percent in 1890.[124] This shift in markets had profound effects.

Economically, competition in world wheat and dairy markets forced farmers to mechanize to remain profitable, as the average cost of production per acre on a small undercapitalized farm was almost double that of a large one. Thus the value of machinery used per unit labour rose from £18.5 in 1900-01 (virtually identical to the 1880-01 figure) to £38.3 in 1910-11 even as machine prices fell 21 percent. Investment in machinery and implements grew four times as fast as other forms of reproducible rural capital from 1900/01 through 1910/11, doubling their share of all rural capital. Although the harvest increased only 8 percent in Victoria, the number of engines almost quadrupled, from 2,424 in 1905 to 9,295 in 1914, with 91 percent of the increase in more efficient, oil-fueled engines.[125] Debt-financed machinery and land buys increased; at the Bank of NSW advances for agricultural purposes tripled 1906–1910, from 11 percent to 21 percent of outstanding loans. By 1914 farmers alone owed

124. NSWSR 1914/5, pp. 1264–1265; OYBNSW 1905, p. 342; OYBNSW 1915, p. 787; VSR 1914, p. 5 and Statistical Summary. These are true exports, not "exports" to other Australian colonies.

125. Production costs (27 shillings per acre vs. 15 shillings 6 pence), OYBNSW 1900/1, p. 303; machinery data, I. McLean, "Analysis of Agricultural Productivity: Alternative Views and Victorian Evidence," AEHR 21 (March 1981), 6; and McLean, "Rural Outputs, Inputs and Mechanization," pp. 145, 167; *Victorian Statistical Register* (VSR), various dates.

£18 million.[126] The banks in turn desired mortgages as security. "Everybody knows that while there was a certain sentiment behind the cry for freehold," wrote the chairman of the NSW Labor Party, "the practical strength of the movement to convert to freehold was this: that the man with freehold has a more attractive security to offer to the money-lender than the man with a leasehold. . . . The demand, although it has taken the form of a demand for freehold, has really been for an attractive form of tenure from the standpoint of the financier."[127] Farmers in turn desired stable markets and secure land tenures. Exposure to world markets also forced farmers, especially those in Victoria, to mix production of meat, wool, dairy, and wheat to moderate the effect of declining prices for one commodity. Diversification made their interests overlap those of graziers.[128] Without preferential access to the British market, the LPP had little to offer farmers to offset the burden of the tariff. The benefits of an expanding domestic market declined as farmers exported more and more of their production, as a telling exchange in the debates over Conciliation shows:

W. Spence (LP NSW): The Honourable member's constituents are producers, and if the wages of . . . employees were cut down the income of his constituents would be reduced.
J. Wilson (FTP Vic): No.
Spence: If the purchasing power of the consumers be reduced, the demand for the goods of the producers must likewise be reduced.
Wilson: The product of the farmers of my district is sent to England.[129]

126. R. Holder, *Bank of NSW* (Sydney: Angus and Robertson, 1970), pp. 546–547. Outstanding mortgages (both pastoral and agricultural) in NSW rose from £8.8 million to £21.7 million, 1900–1911; OYBNSW 1905, p. 587; OYBNSW 1915, p. 355. Graham, *Formation of the Australian Country Parties*, p. 34.

127. W. A. Holman, NSWPD, 2nd series, vol. 33, p. 314, July 8, 1909. Holman chaired the NSW Labor Party.

128. The eleven-month Reid-McLean government August 1904–July 1905 prefigured this alignment, for McLean, nominally an LPP member, represented Victorian agricultural and pastoral interests. *Victorian Yearbook* 1902, p. 217, suggests the following degree of diversification: 82 percent of all farmers owned some dairy cows but only 6 percent were exclusively dairying operations. The land sale issue caused tremendous conflict within Labor in 1905 and 1907. Diversification, the freehold issue, and Labor's land tax all caused massive rural defections from Labor in the 1913 election, though this gave the Fusion CLP a bare majority in the House. See Graham, *Formation of the Australian Country Parties*, pp. 53–63; Childe, *How Labour Governs*, pp. 22–24, 31–32; G. Sawer, *Australian Federal Politics and Law* (Melbourne: Melbourne University Press, 1956), p. 112.

129. CWPD 2:1, June 1, 1904, p. 1798.

The more established farmers thus fled the LPP for the ASP. The middle also cleared out because of movement in the opposite direction. The Labor Party's policy of breaking up large pastoral holdings attracted sharecroppers—the "smaller men" mentioned above—who produced between one-fifth and one third of NSW wheat.[130] The LPP's partial success thus ended up driving away the farmers and farmers' organizations they had initially hoped to attract. Simultaneously, diversification and world market conditions polarized rural areas anew, as the land-hungry once more lined up against the landed.

Effects of Conciliation and Arbitration

Despite fears that Conciliation was galloping socialism, the courts affirmed and maintained capital's control over investment, hiring, and production technique, within, of course, the limits necessary to prevent strikes. Higgens—the judge who broke trail for much of the system—presented this understanding of the system:

> I conceive it to be my duty to leave every employer free to carry on his own business on his own system, that he may make the greatest profit within his reach, so long as he does not perpetuate industrial trouble . . . and that means, so long as he satisfies the *essential* human needs of his employees, and does not leave them under a sense of injustice. . . . In the strain of competition, the pressure on the employer is often very great, and he ought to be free to choose his employees on their own merits and according to his own exigencies, free to make use of new machines, of improved methods, of financial advantages . . . free . . . to put the utmost pressure on anything and everything, except human life.[131]

The conciliation courts formalized the bargain articulated by the Brisbane *Worker*: higher wages and better conditions but no interruptions of production. All of the courts explicitly framed their role in assuring continued production in terms of a "public interest" in conti-

---

130. E. Dunsdorfs, *The Australian Wheat Growing Industry* (Melbourne: Melbourne University Press, 1956), p. 246; OYBNSW 1909/10, p. 198. In NSW an alliance between Labor and the Farmers and Settlers' Association ran joint candidates in rural areas. See Loveday "Labor," pp. 218–220; Hughes, *Policies and Potentates*, p. 33; and Rickard, *Class and Politics*, pp. 158–160.

131. 4 CAR p. 18, 1910. Emphasis added. (Citations to *Commonwealth Arbitration Reports* are in the standard Australian format: Volume CAR page, year). Higgens also explicitly ruled out profit sharing in the "Harvester Judgment."

nuity.[132] Thus the Courts' structure, consciously or unconsciously, inhibited strikes.

Conciliation and Labour. Union's participation in conciliation molded organization, finances and membership in ways reducing their ability and desire to strike. Registration under the Federal Act involved re-vamping internal rules to conform with a large number of regula-tions, a time-consuming process; in one extreme case, it took seven years.[133] Registration exposed a union to a £1000 fine for an illegal strike—a heavy penalty for unions whose members had been im-poverished by the unemployment of the 1890s, and a major threat to workers' only source of benefits.[134] Filing for awards required signifi-cant and expensive paperwork. The financial burden was so heavy that NSW unions actually got poorer in the years 1902–10, with aver-age funds—and potential strike pay—per member dropping from £3.5 to £1.05. Without money for strike benefits, unions waited for the courts to deliver wage increases and better conditions. The courts also checked the trend towards industrial unionism by segmenting labour under different conciliation acts.[135] Coastal seamen and ship-ping were regulated by the Navigation Act, federal public servants by

132. The NSW Industrial Arbitration Court judge declared in his first judgment: "The basic principle of the [NSW Industrial] Arbitration Act is continuity of industrial employment and operations." *NSW Industrial Gazette* 1901, vol. I, p. 7. The NSW Act required 21 days' notice by either side if a strike or lockout was intended. This gave the businesses directly or indirectly affected time to prepare for disruption. Isaac Isaacs also saw a public interest in continuity: "The real *raison d'être* of the arbitration power in the Constitution is not the mere decision between two contesting parties as to industrial conditions . . . but the desirability, sometimes amounting to public necessity, that the community may be served uninterruptedly." 11 CAR p. 83, 1917.

133. See J. Merritt, "A History of the Federated Ironworkers Association of Aus-tralia: 1909–1952" (Ph.D. thesis, Australian National University, 1967), pp. 50–53, 56–57, and *passim* for a detailed presentation of one union's experiences. The Act was amended regarding registration eleven times from 1904 to 1929. Butlin et al., *Govern-ment and Capitalism*, p. 72, for the extreme case.

134. Merritt, "A History of the Federated Ironworkers," p. 126; G. Anderson, *Fixa-tion of Wages in Australia* (Melbourne: Melbourne University Press, 1929), p. 64. There was no Federal Old Age Pension until 1910.

135. In 1905–07, the Australian Workers Union prepared and executed a case costing £4000; W. Spence, *Australia's Awakening* (Sydney: The Worker, 1909), pp. 138–139. See P. Macarthy, "Labor and the Living Wage," AJPH 13 (May 1967), 70–71, for data on union finances. NSW Justice Heydon admitted "litigation in the courts is very much feared by the men . . . [as] expensive and caus[ing] delay." *Sydney Morning Herald*, October 12, 1907. Note that the drop in per capita funds occurred even as union membership, and therefore collected dues, rapidly expanded. See 6 CAR p. 73, 1912, where Higgens remarks that union leaders "are always found to exert their influence in favour of peace" by holding "out the prospect of relief from this court." See also APR, February 16, 1903, p. 852, applauding the proliferation of the number and type of unions.

a special arbitrator outside the formal conciliation system, state public servants and railways by state systems, and agricultural and household labour excluded altogether. The number of Victorian wage boards increased from six in 1899 to 135 in 1914, while the number of manufacturing workers covered by these boards only tripled.[136] Administratively then, Conciliation created division among unions and prevented the reemergence of the universal unions of the 1880s. Why then was it the LPP, not the Labor Party, that disintegrated?

Labour received substantial political and economic gains from acquiescing in a capitalism without strikes. Although unions remained relatively fractionalized, they grew absolutely; even without formal preferential hiring, unionization went from 5.1 percent of wage and salary earners in 1901 to 34.3 percent in 1914.[137] 1907 saw a seven-shilling minimum wage award, and unionization and demonstration effects pushed up all wage levels. The average manufacturing wage in NSW increased 41 percent between 1905 and 1913.[138] As a result, recent studies suggest, working class living standards rose, with a substantial redistribution of income after 1900 that raised *median* though not *average* income per capita.[139] Redistribution permitted significant rises in working class consumption, particularly in housing. Substandard housing as a percentage of housing stock fell from 8 percent in boom year 1891 to only 3.3 percent in depressed 1933. In

136. P. Macarthy, "Wages for Unskilled Work, and Margins for Skill, Australia, 1901–21," AEHR, 12 (September 1972), 143, and "Wages in Australia 1891–1914," AEHR, 10 (March 1970), 59.

137. Butlin et al., *Government and Capitalism*, p. 72. Consider the contrast with the United States, after the Homestead Strike, which waited until the 1937 Wagner Act for legally binding collective bargaining.

138. Most scholars agree that the minimum wage was not universal until 1921, for a three-tiered system of workers emerged. At the bottom were women, who only got 44 percent of the minimum, and unskilled labour that had not organized to claim the legal minimum, getting about 5 to 6 shillings per day; unionized unskilled labour got 7 shillings; skilled labour got 7 shillings plus court-awarded margins for skill. Seven shillings per day, roughly £105 per year, was reckoned enough to support a family of five persons. Although most agree this was a bare minimum, it represented a significant increase over current wages. Anderson, *Fixation of Wages in Australia*, pp. 188–189. The logic behind the lower award for women was that they didn't have families to support, so employers need not pay them the five person "family" wage males got; 6 CAR p. 70, 1912. This encouraged employers to displace males from low productivity jobs such as sorting, packing and labeling; see OYBNSW 1909/10, p. 299. Wage data from NSWSR 1914, pp. 1011–1013. OYBCWA no. 9, pp. 484–492, records a 35 percent increase for all Australia from 1907–1913; data are unavailable before 1907.

139. I. McLean and J. Pincus, "Living Standards in Australia 1890–1940: Evidence and Conjectures," ANU Working Papers in Economic History no. 6 (August 1982), p. 18; see also N. G. Butlin, "Trends in Australian Income Distribution: A First Glance," ANU Working Papers in Economic History no. 17 (September 1983).

Melbourne, 66 percent of new housing starts were owner-occupied, compared to pre-1900 when 68 percent were rented. Finally, the number of hours worked per week also fell gradually even though wages were rising, allowing workers to capture some of the productivity gains being made.[140]

Consequently, organized labour in general remained committed to Conciliation, which enhanced the power of political Labor. Unlike New Zealand, where declining wages and increasing union dissatisfaction caused unions to defect wholesale from the conciliation system after 1907, and culminated in a wave of strikes and a general strike in 1913, most Australian industrial unions continued to live with the system. William Spence, who had helped precipitate the 1890 strikes, in 1909 reiterated the *Worker*'s delineation of the trade-offs arbitration involved. Arbitration, he said, "provide[s] a peaceful means of avoiding strife, leaving the Labor unions free to devote their time, their money, and their energies to securing permanent and lasting reform by means of political action."[141] The NSW Trades Union Congress, even after the 1909 coal strike led to the virtual dismantling of the NSW Industrial Arbitration Act, still was "in favour of obtaining its ideals, and redressing its grievances by constitutional methods, and is of the opinion that strikes should only be resorted to when every possible hope of conciliation has failed."[142] With Labor majorities in the NSW and Federal assemblies after the 1910 elections, this faith seemed borne out.

Conciliation and Exporters

> I attended Mr. Fairbairn's address at the Australasian Chamber of Commerce [in London]—a body of men full of wealth but too mean to do things properly.
> W. H. James, Western Australian Agent General[143]

The export-financial complex benefited economically and politi-

140. McLean and Pincus, "Living Standards in Australia," pp. 12–13; A. Dingle and D. Merrett, "Homeowners and Tenants in Melbourne," AEHR 12 (1972), pp. 22–25, 34; Anderson, *Fixation of Wages in Australia*, pp. 510–511. Miners got a 44-hour week in 1911, builders in 1913. These benefits allow us to accept Castles' argument that arbitration, not welfare, has been workers' first line of defense, providing "welfare wages" to the organized and employed. Accepting arbitration appears a strategic choice that over the long run has significantly benefited the employed in Australia to the occasional discomfort of the unwaged.

141. Spence, *Australia's Awakening*, p. 489.

142. *Sydney Australian Worker*, April 14, 1910.

143. NLA MS 1540/1/1155, W. H. James to A. Deakin, May 26, 1905.

cally from Conciliation, which enforced the peace and united previously divided capitals. The firms that stood to lose the most from a prolonged strike were not small local firms, whose markets would quickly reappear, but those firms selling in volatile international markets, and their financial backers. When coal mine owner H. Forsyth claimed that "the Arbitration Act has twice saved the situation . . . from a ruinous strike," he had in mind the costs that the manager of the Australian Agricultural Company accounted to his board: "The strike may last for some weeks yet, but when ever work is resumed the damage to our foreign trade has been irrevocably done and much of it will be forever lost to us. It will take years of industrial peace and constant coaxing of the trade to enable us to regain what we have lost."[144] The 1909 NSW coal strike occurred because exporters were content to accept the no-strike benefits of Conciliation without giving the wages and work conditions labour demanded in exchange. Despite considerable gains in productivity from mechanization of production, exporters attacked the second half of the bargain, and the structure of the various Conciliation Courts aided their efforts by uniting otherwise unallied businesses.[145]

In contrast to the way the courts divided labour, they promoted aggregation of business in the financial-export complex. NSW insurer A. Meeks supported the NSW Industrial Arbitration Act precisely because bitter animosities between and among various firms had weakened them politically: "In regard to Employers' Unions, the difficulty has always been that we could never get the whole of the employers . . . to join it; . . . the result was that the combination was of no value."[146] "Common rule" provisions in the Conciliation Act ex-

144. Forsythe quoted in *Brisbane Worker* January 30, 1904. Second quotation, ABL 78/1/83, p. 21, January 8, 1910, F. L. Learmonth to AAC/London. Notwithstanding its name, the AAC mined coal and raised sheep.

145. By 1911 30 percent of coal was mechanically cut. See R. Gollan, *Coalminers of NSW* (Cambridge: Cambridge University Press, 1963), pp. 115, 128–132, and J. Turner, "Mechanisation of Coal Cutting in Pelaw Main Colliery, 1902–05," *Labour History* 18, (May 1970), for discussions of mechanization and productivity.

146. NSWPD, vol. 108, p. 5428, November 21, 1900; see also Macarthy, "The Living Wage in Australia and the Role of the Government," *Labour History* 18 (May 1970), p. 183; T. Matthews, "Business Associations and the State," in B. Head, ed., *State and Economy in Australia* (Oxford: Oxford University Press, 1983), pp. 117–119, 143. On conflicts among exporters see ABL 78/2/2, W. E. Abbott (NSWPU) to A. P. Blake (director of the AAC), December 17, 1906, asking him not to pay wages above amounts the NSWPU had negotiated with the ASU; ABL E207/31 and 78/2/2, letters of C. Hall to A. P. Blake; and 78/3/18, letters of A. P. Blake to C. Hall on struggles between ASOF and the colliery owners for control of the coal trade (Hall was sent by Blake to defeat ASOF). For examples of sectoral strategies to cope with organized labour, see, inter alia, ABL 207/25, on the Hunter River Collieries Defense Association's efforts, and ABL E207/29 on ASOF's efforts.

tended any court decision to all firms in a sector, compelling capitalists to register and band together despite their conflicts of interest. When the London Board of the Australian Agricultural Company (AAC) ordered their Australian manager, Jesse Gregson, not to register with the NSW Court, he admonished them: "In self protection it is necessary that every employer should be registered under the Act because, although he is subject to the orders of the Court whether he is registered or not, he has no right to appear before the Court or appeal or for any other purpose unless he is registered."[147] Where employers resisted the logic of combination, at least one State resorted to coercion to create sectoral blocs: "Acting under the direction of [Attorney General] Wise," wrote Gregson, "the registrar is endeavouring to force employers into as few combinations as possible. He aims at placing all the different Coal Mining Companies . . . in one Union, and all pastoralists are to be treated similarly."[148]

State and Federal conciliation acts provoked formation of unified State- and Federal-level employer organizations. On the VEF's initiative, the Central Council of Employers of Australia (CCEA) formed in 1903 to fight the impending Federal Conciliation Act, and then to challenge Conciliation Court rulings in appeals to the High Court. They successfully blocked inclusion of agricultural labour, closed financial records to the court except where germane to the case at hand, and blocked preferential employment for specific unions unless they already had a majority of workers in an industry.[149] After the Act passed, the CCEA coordinated legal challenges to the Federal Court's rulings. Of eight key cases limiting the power of the Court, four were financed by the CCEA: the Barger Case of 1908, which declared the "New Protection" Excise Tariff Act, linking wages and protection, unconstitutional; the Union Label case of 1908, which removed trademark status from the Union Label; the Sawmillers case

147. ABL 78/1/75, p. 34, February 14, 1902. The AAC's legal counsel was quite emphatic on this point, and urged Gregson to register immediately. ABL 78/2/2, no page, private correspondence of the AAC director, E. P. Simpson, to J. Gregson. Similarly the ASOF central committee urged the NSW branch of the Federation to register with the NSW Court so that they could participate in the selection of arbitrators. ABL E217/2, ASOF minutebook, February 6, 1902. Later, Simpson tried to amalgamate all the collieries into one firm because "consolidation is the only way in which the anti-trust laws can be avoided and the men kept in their place." ML MS 516 item 5a, p. 11, letter from E. Simpson to A. P. Blake, February 4, 1909.

148. ABL 78/1/75, p. 33, February 14, 1902, J. Gregson to AAC/London. The AAC avoided registration as a member of either union, on the grounds that as a producer of both coal *and* pastoral products it was *sui generis*.

149. Matthews, "Business Associations and Politics," pp. 165–172. The CCEA failed to block the "common rule" provision in the Federal Act.

of 1909, which attacked preferential employment of unionists; and the Whybrow case of 1910, which killed the Common Rule provision extending rulings to all firms in a sector.[150] As we will see below, the top tier of manufacturing firms, whose interest in the labour situation was rapidly converging with that of exporters, joined these challenges, creating the community of interest behind the LPP-ASP Fusion in mid-1909 (see below).[151]

In the meantime, class conflict increased. One of Deakin's correspondents described the dynamic that culminated in the 1909 coal strike brought about by exporters' failure to "do things properly." A. W. Jose, said that in NSW: "Our labour troubles . . . are likely to evolve into something of wider and more dangerous import. The State Government and the employers have consistently belittled the Arbitration Court, and a hostile Supreme Court has so mutilated its decisions and hedged about its powers, that it has become almost useless. Now, of course, the employers are abusing the men for having lost trust in it."[152] Decay of the bargain underlying conciliation led first to "luddism" against the new mining machines, and then to the strikes by miners at Broken Hill and in the NSW coal fields in 1909 that temporarily destroyed arbitration in NSW, removing the basis for any centrist bloc there.[153] Conciliation thus united exporters and gave them a reason to stay united. What then of manufacturers?

Conciliation and Manufacturers. The Conciliation courts forced "development" on manufacturers, and in doing so polarized the social base of the LPP. By protecting unions and setting minimum wages, the courts encouraged labour saving-investment. Labour peace and an expanding domestic market reinforced this tendency. The Federal Court refused to lower the minimum for the sake of marginally prof-

---

150. All told, the CCEA spent some £10,000 on legal challenges; Matthews, "Business Associations and Politics," pp. 183–191.

151. See Hall, *The Manufacturers*, p. 225, on the positive response of the Australian Chamber of Manufacturers to the High Court's ruling on the Excise Tariff Act. The mediating role of Forrest's "Corner Party" in Fusion arose from Western Australia's lack of manufacturing. Illustrating this, LaNauze, *Alfred Deakin*, p. 561, says: "Behind Forrest . . . could be discerned the suave figure of G. Fairbairn, President of the Employer's Federation." The Westralian economy was highly dependent on primary product exports, especially gold, because its "development" had just started in the 1890s. But many Westralians felt the need to create domestically controlled businesses, including some manufacturing, and this led them to favor both protection and *dirigiste* construction of wheat farming. This placed them between the LPP and ASP.

152. NLA MS 1540/15/777, A. Jose to A. Deakin, February 18, 1908.

153. See ABL 78/1/82, pp. 438 and 470, F. Learmonth to AAC/L, October 16, and November 8, 1909, for accounts of Luddism.

Table 14. Capital intensity in Australian manufacturing, 1901–1913*

Year	Commonwealth		NSW		Victoria	
	hp/emp	hp/fact	hp/emp	hp/fact	hp/emp	hp/fact
1901	n/a	n/a	0.96	18.8	0.60	10.9
1903	0.92	15.7	1.24	23.5	0.58	10.3
1905	0.93	18.3	1.26	24.6	0.54	10.2
1907	1.04	21.0	1.25	24.4	0.58	11.6
1909	1.04	21.6	1.58	31.7	0.66	13.4
1911	1.10	23.8	1.70	36.7	0.71	15.5
1913	1.31	28.5	1.84	41.3	0.86	18.7
% increase, 1901–07			31.3	47.2	(neg)	6.3
% increase, 1907–13			46.0	68.3	48.3	61.1

*hp/emp = horsepower per employee; hp/fact = per factory.

itable employers, saying: "If a man cannot maintain his enterprise without cutting down the wages which are proper to be paid his employees . . . it would be better that he should abandon the enterprise."[154] As the courts raised the price of unskilled labour relative to skilled, employers responded by introducing machines and taylorism to increase the intensity of work as much as possible. The courts encouraged these efforts to expand productivity, by steadfastly refusing to award extra pay for skill to the unskilled machine operators who displaced skilled craftsmen, even though productivity increased by factors of two to seven.[155] Higgens said: "I do not think it is my duty to prop up a falling system, to encourage an antiquated process by prescribing a higher minimum [wage] for it,"[156] Data on horsepower per employee and horsepower per factory illustrate the change in capital intensity. (See Tables 14 and 15) Both increased qualitatively and quantitatively; horsepower supplied by electric machinery rose from 3 percent of the 1903 Commonwealth total to 19 percent in 1914; gas- and oil-fueled engines also displaced steam.[157] A parallel measure, the value of installed machinery and plant, rose less dramatically, but as electricity driven engines were cheaper,

154. 2 CAR p. 32, 1909; see also p. 65, praising "up-to-date appliances."
155. Anderson, *Fixation of Wages in Australia*, p. 319; 6 CAR pp. 75, 470, 1912; 12 CAR p. 427, 1918.
156. 5 CAR p. 73, 1911; the document quoted dealt with the introduction of machine shearing: See also 7 CAR p. 139, 1913; 8 CAR pp. 163–164, 1914; 13 CAR p. 70, 1919. P. Macarthy, "Wage Determination in NSW," *Journal of Industrial Relations* 10 (1968), 197, reports that NSW decisions on minimums and increasing productivity paralleled Federal decisions. Victorian wages boards also were usually reluctant to award any margins for skill to existing bodies of unskilled labour; see Macarthy, "Wages for Unskilled Work and Margins for Skill," pp. 154–156.
157. OYBCWA 1915, p. 472.

Table 15. Machinery and plant values (£) per factory in Australia, 1902–1913

Year	Commonwealth	NSW	Victoria
1902	na	1741	1270
1903	1748	2048	1207
1905	1861	2171	1451
1907	2019	2065	1495
1909	2052	2255	1502
1911	2186	2482	1626
1913	2498	2780	1786
% increase, 1901–07		18.6	17.7
% increase, 1907–13		25.7	19.5

SOURCES: VSR, NSWSR, OYBCWA. Percentage increase, author's calculations.

smaller rises in value nevertheless indicate significant rises in installed horsepower.[158]

Capital intensity accelerated after 1907, when the federal minimum wage was established, but the minimum cannot have been a direct cause; at best it was fear of the minimum, and the real presence of more unions, that propelled manufacturers. There are other plausible explanations: that favorable terms of trade for primary products led indirectly to increased investment in manufacturing, with demand for labour in the primary sector making labour scarce in manufacturing; or that cash from the export sector created increased demand for labour. But terms of trade for exports peaked in 1903–07 and then fell back to depression levels. Second, labour was more plentiful after 1907 than before, for net migration to Australia was positive only after 1902 and was slower during the years of relatively slow growth in mechanization. Finally, agriculture, too, was increasingly capital-intense in this period and so drew few workers, if any, from urban areas.[159]

158. See also Butlin et al., *Government and Capitalism*, p. 23.

159. Labour tried to keep wages up by discouraging immigration, by publicizing Australian unemployment in British newspapers. In response, British financiers actually offered to subsidize an Australia-wide Labour daily paper, on condition that the Labor Party encourage immigration as strongly as it had been discouraging it; see NLA MS 1540/16/447, A. W. Jose to A. Deakin, November 19, 1908. Exporters fairly consistently preferred to link wages to world market prices (the practice in coal mining in the 1890s) and to use immigration to provide a constant pool of fresh workers, while setting minimum wages high enough to assure reproduction of the labour force. See, for example, AIBR, March 20, 1909, pp. 175–176; APR, March 16, 1907, p. 37; ABL 78/1/77, pp. 42–44, January 28, 1904. This policy was later reversed when exporters began seeing immigrants as a source of unemployment and of decidedly radical workers. See ML MS 516 item 5A, pp. 116–117, E. P. Simpson to E. W. Knox (Colonial Sugar Refineries), July 6, 1909: "19/20ths of the immigrants who are now coming to the state . . . are swelling the ranks of the Labour Party."

These judicially prompted increases in capital intensity polarized manufacturers, pushing the larger and more politically active manufacturers towards the ASP as their labour situation increasingly resembled that of the ASP's social base. Bigger firms got much bigger, while the number of small firms exploded. The share of manufacturing employment in factories employing over 100 employees increased from 35.5 percent in 1906 to 41.3 percent in 1914; the largest firms' average size increased 19.3 percent, from 207 employees per unit to 247.[160] Increased taylorization made both employers and workers, for different reasons, less inclined to live with Conciliation. Workers tried to get the courts to mandate wage increases and to control work conditions, but this only increased owners' reservations about Conciliation, especially as larger firms needed more control over the production process and closer supervision of labour to make the new investments profitable. Larger firms thus had increasing incentives to make common cause with the financial-export interests attacking the Conciliation process through the High Court. Since large firms dominated the Chambers of Manufacturers, the organizational backing of the LPP drifted toward the ASP even though much of its constituency did not.[161] Though manufacturers as a class benefited from the expanded domestic market created by court-imposed minimum wages, a "free-rider" logic led individual capitalists to oppose court-mandated minimums and conditions. Only the manufacturers' political leadership saw both the practical and political drawbacks to this "free-rider" activity, and so persisted in "radical" politics and accommodation with Labor. The larger, more capitalized NSW firms, which employed far fewer (low wage) females than Victorian firms, naturally moved first to the ASP. Smaller Victorian manufacturers moved only after any chance of independent action evaporated. LPP strength thus declined first in NSW, and then Victoria. Once direct wage reg-

160. See P. Brown and H. Hughes, "Market Structure of Australian Manufacturing Industry," in Forster, ed., *Australian Economic Development*, p. 475, for a general discussion of industrial concentration; data from OYBCWA 1915.

161. The increased capitalization that occurred did not go far enough to produce the fusion of financial and manufacturing interests termed "finance capitalism," but, since that particular fusion did occur after World War I, the instant situation can be seen as prefiguring it. Before World War I it was unusual for banks to have direct interests or participation in manufacturing activity. See C. Forster, "Economies of Scale and Australian Manufacturing," in Forster, ed., *Australian Economic Development in the 20th Century*, p. 165, and R. Nash, *Australasian Jt. Stock Cos. Yearbook* (Sydney, various dates), for details on directorships. See Matthews, "Business Associations and Politics," for details on the composition of the EFNSW, VEF, VCM, and SCM. Before 1914 fewer than 18 percent of factories were represented in the VCM or SCM; ibid., p. 60.

ulation became a reality in 1907, more and more manufacturers and LPP supporters were like J. M. Joshua, who wrote Deakin:

> Guided by the necessities of the situation from a national standpoint . . . you will lose no time in completing the negotiations for an honorable union of the [LPP and ASP. As for] the prospects of successfully organizing a Center Party. *Briefly there are none.* In every port I am in touch with businessmen of standing. I talk politics generally with 'em all. You haven't a friend—one is tempted to think Australia hasn't a friend among them. . . . Don't think there is hope for the *old* Deakin party.[162]

PERSISTENCE OF LPP POLICY GOALS AFTER FUSION

Thus the LPP's economic policies ended by undermining its own social base, destroying its ability to exist as an independent political force. Nonetheless, Deakin and the manufacturers were less than wholehearted about joining forces with the ASP. In negotiations with J. Farleigh of the NSW Employers Federation, Deakin declared that he would only consent to lead the new Fusion party if "certain essentials" were maintained. These were the LPP's original goals: federal control over borrowing, debt assumption and Commonwealth-State financial relations; supremacy for the Federal Conciliation Court; and retention not only of protection but of the New Protection.[163] As a result, the new Commonwealth Liberal Party's (CLP) short life was marked by sharp conflict between the old ASP and the LPP fragments over control of party funding, and thus of the future of Deakin's essentials.[164] Two of these conflicts are particularly revealing of the continuity in Deakin's policies.

As mentioned above, Deakin worked out a compromise on Federal-State financial relations that was relatively unfavorable to State and financial interests. On the question of renewed borrowings, though,

162. NLA MS 1540/15/702–703, J. M. Joshua (President of the Victorian Chamber of Manufacturers, VEF, Associated Chambers of Manufacturers of Australia, LPP, and friend of Deakin) to Deakin, undated, probably after January 1907. Emphasis in original.

163. NLA MS 1540/16/575–576, A. Deakin to J. Farleigh, May 18, 1909. By then the Labor Party had passed a Bonus Act for iron manufacture, obviating any need for Deakin to pass one.

164. See Rickard, *Class and Politics*, chap. 8, for an excellent discussion of these conflicts; NLA MS 1540/1/2474, O. C. Beale to Deakin, January 6, 1910; Matthews, "Business Associations and Politics," p. 240–260; and B. Graham, "The Place of Finance Committees in Non-Labor Politics 1910–1930," AJPH 6 (May 1960).

Deakin gave ground. The September 1909 budget involved Federal borrowing of £1.2 million, inciting vigorous denunciation by both Labor members and ex-Liberals.[165] The budget also included a £3.5 million loan to buy warships from the United Kingdom. But this money had to be authorized before it could be borrowed, and perhaps Deakin hoped that Labor would scuttle the loan, as it in fact did. Labor intended that any Australian Navy would be built in Australia, by Australian workers, using Australian steel and money.

Deakin also moved to centralize Conciliation powers under the Inter-state Commission (ISC) that he and the premiers had agreed to at the 1909 Financial Conference. The ISC was intended to institutionalize the New Protection, as a Deakin ally makes clear: The "Commission will assist in supervising the working of the existing customs tariff in its operation upon the investment of Australian capital and labour . . . and also with the view of developing Preferential and other trade relations with the Empire."[166] Despite Fusion, manufacturers continued to defend and press for extensions to the New Protection. The same Joshua who had urged Fusion upon Deakin declared that "not only was the New Protection a just policy, but it was in [manufacturers'] interests, as well as the interests of their employees. Further, manufacturers had already admitted its necessity, and demanded its imposition, though not in the form of a federal excise."[167] Deakin looked to a constitutional provision permitting the Federal government to regulate interstate commerce for the authority to amalgamate the State and the Federal courts. But Deakin's effort to establish the ISC led to a replay of the old politics within the new CLP. Deakin's old LPP followers lined up behind him to support the measure, while hostile conservative State premiers delayed action until the Federal Parliament was adjourned.[168] While Fusion represented the failure of the LPP's political ambitions, it is clear that they continued to fight for the economic aspects of their project.

In light of Labor's electoral victory in 1910 (the first in the world), the ASP's political project looks as weak as the LPP's had been. Diatribes on the "dangers" of Labor fell on deaf ears. Deakin had to admonish his own partisans: "Why if the Labor Party is as bad as you

165. Turner, *First Decade*, pp. 238–239.
166. Senator Millen (CLP NSW), CWPD 3:4, vol. 49, June 23, 1909, pp. 266–267.
167. *Melbourne Age*, May 11, 1909. He also attacked anti-socialism as something "which nobody could define, and which meant anything, or everything, or nothing."
168. NLA MS 1540/1/947, A. Deakin to all State Premiers, December 10, 1909. See also letters in AA A60 I 651, and Wade's comments at the 1909 conference, CWPP no. 50 of 1909, vol. II, p. 97, and *passim*.

paint it . . . do we find it so hard to get a majority of our fellow citizens to realize our infinite superiority to that Party?"[169] The answer was that Labor's dilute socialism rang all the right political bells for the mass of Australians. Attacks on graziers, monopolies, and banks drew petit entrepreneurs (who sold in domestic markets, after all), share-croppers and small farmers, and most government employees to Labor's core working class groups. Denunciations of "socialism" did not deter small capitals from clinging to Labor, for most realized that "every advance of the State in Australia, every attempt to extend its domain—Railways, Tramways, Waterworks, Agricultural Banks, Closer Settlement—has been denounced as socialism though afterwards endorsed by those who denounced it. Every class and calling has clamoured for state aid . . . under some guise or another but attacked it when sought by others."[170] But the consequence of such a successful electoral project was that the Labor Party's economic policies strongly resembled those that the LPP had advocated. The Labor Party restricted new borrowing, strengthened the AIPA, built a railroad to West Australia to consolidate the internal market, expanded conciliation, created a Commonwealth Bank and introduced a land tax. Thus, manufacturing investment and production continued to expand rapidly up to 1914.

ASSESSING THE LIBERAL ECONOMIC PROJECT

Clearly the LPP did not achieve its ambitious goal of making manufacturers into the hegemonic fraction of a coalition whose economic project centered on domestically controlled accumulation and growth. How then to assess its achievements? Given that it had less than a decade to overcome the residues of 50 years of pastoral exports and growing debt, its policies were fairly successful. Conciliation institutionalized mechanisms that expanded the domestic market from the demand side, despite its negative political consequences for the LPP. The New Protection and the AIPA sheltered that market from the leviathans of the international market. Both the average wage and the capital intensity of production increased.[171] The economy continued to be state-led, but the larger pool of domestically controlled surplus made it possible to finance much of the new increment to

169. NLA MS 296/27, A. Deakin to W. H. James, April 18, 1909.
170. NLA MS 1540/15/396, W. H. James to A. Deakin, July 10, 1905.
171. OYBCWA 1915, pp. 484–492, 547–557.

Table 16. Who held Australian public debt, 1901–1913?

Year	total debt (£ '000)	London (£ '000)	% all debt	Australia (£ '000)	% all debt
1901	203,588	174,816	85.9	28,708	14.1
1907	240,150	185,579	77.3	54,570	22.3
1913	294,472	204,395	69.4	90,077	30.6

SOURCE: OYBCWA 1915, p. 856.

public debt from local sources, thus slowing surplus drains abroad and reinforcing growth. (See Table 16 for public debt; 17 for growth figures; 18 for net national accumulation.)

Though Deakin's efforts to centralize control of borrowing were only partially successful, domestic growth created a large pool of surplus for investment in both new public and private issues. Thus during this period the economy grew rapidly (not just by comparison with the depressed 1890s), but without a proportional increase in foreign public debt, which grew more slowly than in any other period save 1870–80, the period before capital influx. New foreign public debt increased by only £29.7 million from 1901 to 1910, compared to £51.2 million in the depressed 1890s, for though the States continued to borrow, their borrowings were primarily local. In absolute terms new issues were double overseas issues, raising the share of locally held outstanding public debt to almost a third of public debt while the overseas share fell by one-fifth (Table 16). Australian insurance companies held much of the domestically-issued debt, with 32.1 percent of their assets taking the form of government securities.[172]

When the private side of investment is included, the domestic "takeover" is even more noticeable. While it is impossible to make a precise calculation of British holdings of private Australian securities and firms, estimates suggest a range of zero to 20 percent growth in total British holdings.[173] Fitzpatrick suggests that domestic investment in

172. P. Cochrane, *Industrialisation and Dependence, Australia's Road to Economic Development: 1870–1939* (St. Lucia: University of Queensland Press, 1980), p. 62. Insurance companies, it should be remembered, had a greater tendency to invest in domestic manufacturing, and politicians with ties to insurance helped pass the NSW Arbitration Act.

173. Nash shows no growth from 1899 to 1912/13; Wilson about 5 percent growth over a similar period; Wood a 20 percent increase. Nash, *Australasian Jt. Stock Cos. Yearbook*, various dates; R. Wilson, *Capital Imports and the Terms of Trade, Examined in the Light of Sixty Years of Australian Borrowing* (Melbourne: Melbourne University Press, 1931), pp. 45–46; Wood, *Borrowing and Business*, pp. 154–158. See Butlin, *Australian Domestic Product*, pp. 435–441, for a summary of conflicting data.

Table 17. Growth of Australian GDP and GDP per capita, 1887–1938

Year	GDP (1966/7 A$ mil.)	GDP per capita (1966/7 A$)	
1887	2632.0	928.40	(Pre-Crash peak)
1897	2591.0	722.73	(Post-Crash low)
1900	3127.0	835.87	
1903	3106.0	802.17	
1907	3707.0	906.14	
1911	4721.0	1066.81	
1913	5076.0	1070.43	(Pre-War peak)
1925	6331.0	1076.88	
1938	7549.0	1099.00	(Depression peak)

SOURCE: McLean and Pincus, "Living Standards in Australia," pp. 29–31.

all publicly listed firms and bonds, public and private, went from approximately 26.8 percent of all (domestic and foreign) investment in 1899 to 43.3 percent in 1912/13.[174] Subtracting the official public debt component gives an admittedly crude estimate of the growth of private holdings. The ratio of domestically held to British-held publicly issued private securities went from roughly 0.7 : 1 in 1899 to between 1.3 and 2.3 : 1 in 1912/13.[175] No doubt liquidation of British holdings accounts for part of this shift, for there was a net capital outflow for much of the decade; but given that total capitalization increased and that many domestic firms did not issue stock or bonds, this suggests a remarkable reversal in control of the Australian economy.

Stagnant British holdings combined with overall economic growth to reduce public and private debt service from a high of 8.5 percent of GDP in 1894 (for comparison, it was 5.1 percent in pre-depression 1888) to a pre-War low of 1.9 percent in 1912/13; the average was 2.8 percent over the period 1900/01 to 1912/13. In real terms, per capita overseas debt fell from £60.7 in 1904 to £45.5 in 1914 and per capita debt service from £2.2 to £1.7.[176] The result was lessened dependency

174. B. Fitzpatrick, *British Empire in Australia* (Melbourne: Macmillan, 1969), p. 300.
175. Calculation from data in Fitzpatrick, *British Empire in Australia*, p. 300; *Statistics of New Zealand*, various dates; OYBCWA, various dates; Nash, *Australasian Jt. Stock Cos. Yearbook*, various dates.
176. For percentage of GDP: E. Boehm, *Prosperity and Depression* (Oxford: Oxford University Press, 1971), p. 181; Butlin, *Australian Domestic Product*, pp. 11, 440. For per

Table 18. Net national capital accumulation
as a percent of net national product in Australia,
1881–1914

Period	NNCA as a percentage of NNP	Period	NNCA as a percentage of NNP
1881–85	5.7%	1901–05	6.8%
1886–90	6.9	1906–10	15.7
1891–95	5.3	1911–14	12.4
1896–1900	0.1		

SOURCE: Butlin, *Australian Domestic Product*, pp. 6–7.

and faster capital accumulation and growth. McLean and Pincus's revision of Butlin's GDP figures suggest that a considerable amount of growth occurred under the Liberal regime (and even more under Labor), despite generally adverse terms of trade.[177] Growth thus occurred despite, indeed perhaps because of a slowdown in borrowing. Economic growth centered on domestic consumption, was fairly evenly distributed because of Conciliation, and continued to occur precisely because the benefits of growth were distributed, thus expanding the domestic market. Development also proceeded, as described in the discussion on mechanization in agriculture and industry above. In addition Michael Edelstein has calculated from Butlin's data that output per capita grew 28.4 percent in the decade 1900–1910, compared to 20.9 percent for the decade 1870–1880 (just before the capital influx); 4.2 percent for 1880–1890 (during the capital influx); and -9.2 percent from 1890 to 1900 (depression).[178]

Thus Australian manufacturers laid the economic and political foundations for their transformation from an interior bourgeoisie into a national bourgeoisie in this period. Despite the LPP's disintegration, World War I brought about almost exactly the political arrangements Deakin hoped for, in a body titled, appropriately enough, the National Party, albeit under the leadership of the quondam head of the Labor Party, William Hughes. This coalition used wartime conditions to pursue aggressively *dirigiste* policies of econom-

---

capita figures in constant 1914 values: G. Wood, *Borrowing and Business* (London: Oxford University Press, 1930), pp. 128, 154; and E. Dyason, "Australian Public Debt," *Economic Record* 3 (November 1927), 163–165.

177. McLean and Pincus, "Living Standards in Australia."

178. M. Edelstein, *Overseas Investment in the Age of High Imperialism* (New York: Columbia University Press, 1982), p. 218.

ic development, creating a national steamship line, destroying German monopoly control of the base metal industry, and expanding Australian metalworking capacity. The politics of the 1920s and 1930s consolidated all these gains.[179] By the 1920s, the internal bourgeoisie of pre-Federation days had converted itself into a self-conscious national bourgeoisie, again complete with its own party and rhetoric. The basis for this achievement is to be found in the first decade of the Commonwealth.

179. The National Party combined domestic financiers, large manufacturers and the petit bourgeoisie formerly attracted to Labor. The best exposition of the politics of the depression is in Cochrane, *Industrialisation and Dependence*. He argues that British financiers and Australian manufacturers deliberately created one of the most protected markets in the world, the former to assure sufficient export receipts to service Australian debts and the latter to continue "development".

CHAPTER FIVE

New Zealand

Comparing New Zealand with Australia demonstrates the utility of analyzing development and dependency issues separately, as outlined in Chapter 2. To those who conflate dependency and development, or who focus solely on development questions, Australia and New Zealand present similar "success" stories. Dieter Senghaas, for example, sees both countries making identical transitions from extensive agriculture to the intensive production he views as both prerequisite for and part of development.[1] He argues that in both countries labour pressures helped drive the transition from extensive to intensive production. But Senghaas ignores the different forms labour pressure took in New Zealand and Australia, and the large foreign debts of both. In New Zealand, as in Australia, intensification waited on a *political* solution to the debt problem. And since labour pressure and debt took different forms in each, different political solutions in turn meant the emergence of different types of export agriculture and manufacturing sectors. Unlike Australian exporters, who were intimately involved in the private debt crisis and eventually foreclosed upon by it, New Zealand estate owners suffered relatively little; their problems arose from their increasingly restive labour force. Struggles between estate owners and speculators and between estate owners and their workers ultimately created the petit bourgeois intensive farming on which a new round of accumulation rested. The persistence of largeholders meant that New Zealand manufacturers faced a fairly united and strong rural bloc, and so were unable to transform themselves into a national bourgeoisie. Because of this, and because New Zealand actually increased its foreign debt in the process of intensification, dependency increased.

1. D. Senghaas, *European Experience* (Dover, N.H.: Berg, 1985), pp. 122–126, 146–151.

164

HISTORICAL BACKGROUND

The 1856 Compact and Round One of Expansion

Britain annexed New Zealand in 1840 when the New Zealand Company tried to settle a smallholders' colony on the North Island. Native Maori resisted British rule, but in a series of wars steadily lost control of the land.[2] War costs ran up a modest public debt of about £800,000 by 1862—about £6 1s per capita. Though the last British troops left in 1870, settlers dominated the South Island by the mid-1850s, the North by the late 1860s. In 1852–53, Governor-General G. Grey established the preconditions for pastoral expansion. He halved the minimum price for land and liberalized its sale. As in Australia, graziers bought water holes and leased surrounding areas. About three million acres were alienated 1853–56, and grazier debt increased correspondingly. Following Lord Salisbury's practice of permitting self-rule for "white" colonies, Grey also created a colonial parliament, dividing the islands into six provinces, each with a provincial council. The graziers and merchants who dominated the provincial councils convened them in advance of the parliament to arrogate all significant powers to themselves. The "1856 Compact" between central and provincial government gave the latter control of immigration, public works, debt issues, half of the customs revenue, and all revenue from land sales.[3]

Provincial arrogation of power gave graziers control of the provincial economies. They embarked on bootstrap growth programs, selling land to themselves, using land receipts to sponsor immigration, and employing the mostly poor and landless immigrants to open more land. This process accentuated differences among the provinces for the rich got richer. The two richest provinces, Canterbury and Otago, could afford to buy more immigrants, build more roads, and open more land than poorer provinces. Canterbury and Otago became the leading exporters of wool, between them accounting for

2. See J. Condliffe, *New Zealand in the Making* (London: Unwin & Allen, 1936), pp. 64–65; R. Dalziel, "Politics of Settlement," in the *Oxford History of New Zealand* (Oxford: Oxford University Press, 1981), p. 87, and *passim*; B. Jesson, "British Imperialism and the Crown in Early New Zealand," *Red Papers on New Zealand* no. 2 (May 1977), for a variety of interpretations of annexation. Jesson, pp. 53–59, argues that the Maori disliked English rule more than English settlers. However, English fencing and property law conflicted with Maori customary usage and tenure.

3. Condliffe, *New Zealand in the Making*, pp. 64–65, 114–118; Dalziel, "Politics of Settlement," p. 99. Leases had 14-year tenures.

Table 19. Distribution of sheep
by province, New Zealand, 1851 and 1861

	1851	1861
Total	223,000	2,761,000
Auckland	4.8%	3.0%
Taranaki	1.2	0.5
Wellington	27.5	12.0
Nelson	39.5	9.0
Canterbury	12.2	44.0
Otago	14.9	31.0

SOURCE: Lloyd-Pritchard, *Economic History of New Zealand*, p. 78.

two-thirds of the £7.6 million of land sale revenues up to 1876, and leading the other provinces as the number of sheep in New Zealand increased tenfold between 1851 and 1861.[4] (See Table 19.) Both were on the South Island, where graziers had fewer Maori to contend with. The other provinces specialized too: Nelson in gold; Auckland in agricultural goods for the food-short gold and wool provinces. Though gold was discovered in time to offset rapidly declining timber and food exports to Australia, by the late 1860s fiscal crises emerged as the American Civil War ended and textile producers shifted back to cotton.

First Crisis, First Change

By 1866 the five wealthiest provinces (of what now were nine) had accumulated an £11.9 million deficit on current account, of which roughly two-thirds was public debt. Central government spending on transport had increased the £800,000 war debt of 1862 to £5.2 million by 1869. Provincial debt stood at £2.7 million in 1866, of which Canterbury and Otago owed 40 percent. But land sales, which provided 83 percent of provincial revenues in 1864, fell 50 percent between 1864 and 1867. Aware of New Zealand's increasing insolvency and the widening balance of payments deficit, the London market

4. Sheep in Canterbury increased 3000 percent; in Otago 2000 percent. J. Dowie, "Studies in New Zealand Investment, 1870–1900" (Ph.D. dissertation, Australian National University, 1965), pp. 179–180; M. Lloyd-Pritchard, *An Economic History of New Zealand* (Auckland: Collins, 1970), pp. 78 and 136; W. Sutch, *Colony or Nation?* (Sydney: Sydney University Press, 1966), p. 8.

Table 20. New Zealand exports and immigration, 1861–1876

Year	Total imports (£ '000)	Total exports (£ '000)	Gold exports (£ '000)	Wool exports (£ '000)	Immigration cumulative to end years
1861	2494	1339	753	524	16,222
1864	7001	3051	1858	1071	64,638
1867	5345	4479	2700	1581	24,367
1870	4639	4545	2158	1704	−7,303
Post-vogel borrowing spree:					
1873	6465	5478	1987	2702	18,570
1876	6904	5489	1269	3396	75,331

SOURCE: *Statistics of the Dominion of New Zealand.*

raised interest rates on new issues from 4 percent in 1856 to 6 percent in 1860, and finally to 8 percent in 1864.[5]

To placate London lenders, graziers and politicians reformed local finances in a remarkable anticipation of Australian Federation. Reversing the 1856 Compact's delegation of fiscal power, the central government reclaimed the fisc with three acts reducing the provincial share of customs and tax revenues, prohibiting provincial borrowing, and converting outstanding provincial debt by raising £7 million at 6 percent.[6] As in Australia, London's unwillingness to float new debt stimulated fiscal centralization to bail out the weakest debtors.

Although this new regime permitted continued borrowing—£1.3 million in 1868—the situation continued to deteriorate. By 1870 land revenues were at one-eighth of their 1864 level, driving a 54 percent absolute decline in provincial revenues, and the magic circle collapsed as graziers spent more money on interest and less on land. (See Table 20.) By the late 1860s, seventy out of one hundred sampled Canterbury pastoral leaseholders had been sold or mortgaged to the lessees' disadvantage; Marlborough politicians claimed that 90 percent of their runholders were insolvent in 1869.[7] Export growth and immigration leveled off. New Zealand and individual producers both faced a similar problem: land sales underwrote debt by providing revenue,

5. Lloyd-Pritchard, *An Economic History of New Zealand*, pp. 105, 117–118. *New Zealand Official Yearbook*, 1895, broadsheet.
6. The Public Revenues Act (no. 84), Public Debt Act (no. 89), and Consolidation Act (no. 90) of 1867. Lloyd-Pritchard, *An Economic History of New Zealand*, p. 119.
7. Lloyd-Pritchard, *An Economic History of New Zealand*, p. 105. Sutch, *Colony or Nation?* p. 7; the sample represented 10 percent of all Canterbury leases.

but land only had value if loans were forthcoming to open and develop land.

The Vogel Plan and Renewed Expansion

With fiscal crisis impending, the Stafford ministry from the peripheral provinces found itself displaced by an Otago-Canterbury alliance; Julius Vogel as Treasurer. This ambitious new ministry proposed to borrow £10 million over ten years to buy railroads, roads, and immigrant labour. The balance of payments situation had improved, but to further reassure London and local taxpayers, a centrally controlled land reserve of six million acres would back the debt. Sale of this land, whose value undoubtedly would rise with access to transport, would cover the costs of servicing and redeeming both old and new debt.

The scheme was both economically and politically viable. Rich and poor, large and small would benefit from the scheme. Public works would employ the urban unemployed. The newly built rails would connect poorer provinces to pastoral ones, while opening interior areas to the sea. Roads would connect smallholding farmers with pastoral estates, giving those estates access to cheap inputs from local agriculturalists, and making estates more profitable. Small farmers' new markets would allow them to share in the prosperity of the increasingly specialized pastoralists. The fact that wool never rose above 5 percent of railroad haulage between 1880 and 1900, while grain averaged a 19 percent share, shows the importance of rails to development of *internal* markets for both produce and land.[8]

Even if agreed on the benefits of borrowing to build railroads, the provinces were not in accord over the costs. Anxious to cream off the speculator's profits latent in a railroad-generated rise in land values, the graziers controlling Canterbury and Otago refused to sanction the centrally controlled land reserve.[9] Instead the provinces retained control until 1876, when the central parliament was finally able to abolish

8. Dowie, "Studies in New Zealand Investment," p. 324; see also J. Dowie, "Business Politicians and Railways," AEHR 5 (February 1965). Dowie questions the need for railways, noting that no point in New Zealand is more than 75 miles from the ocean, and that few places on the plains are more than 20 miles. He argues that multiple ports with roads radiating to the hinterland would have served to move wool.

9. It is not clear, given the propensity of Julius Vogel and other politicians to engage in speculation themselves, whether the land reserve was a serious proposal. Vogel, for example, was involved in shady dealings over the "Brodgen contracts," in which an English firm was let contracts for railways in New Zealand at 20 percent over market rates.

Table 21. New Zealand land sales and revenues, 1854–1895

Years	Acres sold (mil.)	£ raised (mil.)	Acres given away (mil.)
1854–71	5.6	3.1	0.8
1872–76	2.5	4.5	1.4
1877–95	2.7	4.3	3.4

SOURCE: *New Zealand Official Yearbook,* 1895, broadsheet.

provincial councils. From 1872 to 1876, the years of the greatest borrowing and greatest increases in government expenditure, the provinces sold or gave away land three times as fast as in the previous or the next eighteen years. (See Table 21.) As expected, rail-building immediately increased land values, in some places by a factor of ten.[10] But unable to hypothecate rail debt with land sales, the state resorted instead to increased taxation, setting up the subsidy and tax dynamic outlined in Chapter 2.

The Vogelian borrowing spree restored the circular prosperity of loans, land, and public works, creating a decade-long boom in the 1870s. Between 1870 and 1878, banks increased their outstanding mortgage loans by over £10 million (£3.5 million of which was borrowed from Britain), roughly four times their previous rate of lending. From 1871 to 1876 New Zealand borrowed a mere £76,000 less than the £10 million Vogel had suggested in 1870, roughly twice Vogel's planned rate of absorption. Public debt service more than doubled from 1870 to 1876, to £1 million, and tripled by 1879 to £1.3 million. Though exports grew 31 percent, imports grew even faster— 50 percent—from a higher base. Again alarmed by the growing gap between revenue and service and between exports and imports, and troubled by failure of the City of Glasgow Bank in 1877, London markets restricted access to credit after 1875, despite Vogel's able and active lobbying in London. London's restriction caused a brief recession in 1876.[11]

10. *New Zealand Official Yearbook* 1894, p. 134.
11. *New Zealand Official Yearbook,* 1895, broadsheet; Sutch, *Colony or Nation?* p. 12; W. Sutch, *The Quest for Security in New Zealand* (Wellington: Wright & Carmen, 1966), p. 86; W. Rosenberg, "Capital Imports and Growth: The Case of New Zealand," *Economic Journal* 71:281 (March 1961), 109; C. Simkin, *Instability of a Dependent Economy* (Oxford: Clarendon, 1951), p. 190.

THE CRISIS OF THE 1880s

At this point the conflict underlying New Zealand politics for the next two decades crystallized. As in Australia, the conflict was grounded in the capital locked up in land. The terms of the conflict revolved around the speed of borrowing and its alter ego, taxes, pitting working estate owners, more cautious borrowers, against speculators, banks, and urban interests, bold borrowers.[12] The cautious borrowers had already benefited from infrastructure improvements; the bold hoped to draw sufficient capital and immigrants to New Zealand to sell off their land speculations profitably. Estate owners resisted extravagant borrowing and public works spending, severely retrenched public employment and expenditure whenever they had the chance, and shifted taxes to urban property. They borrowed largely to refund debt. All these measures decreased the likelihood that graziers' taxes would rise. The reverse course was taken by the speculators, who boosted debt during their tenures, built railroads, and proposed "radical" land taxes benefiting land companies and urban firms during their tenures.

The cautious borrowers are best exemplified by Harry Atkinson, who participated in the "Continuous" and "Conservative" ministries that alternated during the 1880s with those of the bold.[13] Atkinson systematically limited borrowing and spending. From its 1875 peak of £3.1, Atkinson cut loan expenditure to £1.8 million by 1877, producing a meager budget surplus that year. He typically warned: "If pressure is brought . . . upon the Government to push forward the public works . . . you will not only have to face increased taxation, but also a financial crisis of a very serious character."[14] In the struggle over taxation, Atkinson consistently opposed attempts by speculator and urban interests to pass land taxes, preferring instead more general taxes on property, which fell more heavily on urban holdings and firms.

A variety of speculators and urban radicals inhabited the bold and

12. See W. Armstrong, "Politics of Development" (MA dissertation, Victoria University at Wellington, 1960), p. 35, for these terms. See also Sutch, *Colony or Nation?* p. 106. D. Bedggood, *Rich and Poor in New Zealand* (Sydney: Allen and Unwin, 1980), p. 54, sees the split as between protectionists and free traders.

13. Other conservatives were W. Rolleston, a Canterbury pastoralist, C. C. Bowen, and E. Hall.

14. Quoted in J. Bassett, *Sir Harry Atkinson* (Auckland: Auckland University Press, 1975), p. 41. See pp. 37–42 for Atkinson's anti-debt position generally, p. 51 for retrenchment efforts, and p. 83 for his view of the link between debt and taxation.

"radical" ministries that alternated with Atkinson and the conservatives.[15] Their "radical" or "liberal" appellation came from advocacy of state-sponsored subdivision of estates for closer settlement by the landless, and of land taxes as a tax on wealth. But this "radicalism" was immensely attractive to businessmen involved in land speculation because it would increase the value of their holdings. Thus in their interruptions to the cautious ministries, the bold tried to borrow money to settle the land they held more rapidly than "neutral" market conditions warranted.

The bold Grey-Macandrew ministry (October 1877 to October 1879) turned Atkinson's razor-thin budget surplus into a deficit, spending money from a £5 million loan yet to be raised and emptying the fisc. Grey borrowed at twice the rate of the preceding Atkinson ministry and encouraged private rail construction by guaranteeing profits. The ministry made an electoral reform, halving the property qualification for voting while retaining both plural voting and automatic registration for householders. This "reform" increased the number of votes that speculators could cast in rural districts, because plural voting turned each of their holdings into a vote. An estate owner had but one vote, by virtue of his single holding. The smallholders enfranchised by this act apparently were not encouraged to register. Grey's treasurer, John Ballance, put forward a land tax of a halfpenny per pound for holdings valued over £500. This burdened estate owners and prosperous farmers, leaving small farmers and urban land untouched, and touching lightly speculation companies whose land was valued less than already-settled estates even after their improvements were subtracted. Ballance's concern was not primarily fiscal, for he *reduced* customs simultaneously, to the benefit of Auckland and Dunedin business. The land tax led to the ministry's demise in 1879.

But 1878 through 1880 the failure to provide for a land reserve to back public debt made itself felt through another credit contraction. Increasingly apprehensive about New Zealand's fiscal difficulties, English and Scottish investors turned to the seemingly sounder Australian colonies, producing the 1880s boom in Australia and compounding New Zealand's difficulties. By 1881 public debt was roughly quadruple 1870 levels in absolute terms (£29.2 million vs. £7.8 mil-

15. Among them were George Grey, the former Governor-General, who represented Auckland agricultural interests; Robert Stout, the interests of urban-based land speculation companies and their middle class employees; Julius Vogel, land speculation companies in Canterbury: William Larnach, Auckland and Dunedin business; James Macandrew, Otago land speculators; and John Ballance.

lion) and double per capita (£59.2 vs. £31.6). After floating the 1880 loan to cover Grey's deficit spending, what became the cautious Hall-Whitaker-Atkinson ministry promised to stay off the London market for two years.[16] The boom over, the new ministry embarked on a campaign of severe retrenchment. It used land grants, which required no borrowing or spending, to encourage rail building. It substituted labour for capital on the railroads, the amount of fixed capital per rail worker falling from £2,563 to £1,982 between 1881 and 1884. Public service salaries were cut 10 percent.[17] Customs were reintroduced, but, as in Australia, retrenchment led to reduced imports and thence to a fall in customs revenue. As the *Economist* later described it: "When New Zealand's borrowings were checked, we at once found that depression followed, that the imports, and therefore the Customs Revenue, declined, and that property fell seriously in value."[18] The land tax was replaced by a property tax of one penny per pound on the capital value of all possessions, falling heavily on high-priced urban property and buildings. W. Rolleston, Minister for Land, allowed graziers to buy the land they leased at its original low price, and introduced the perpetual lease in 1886. Both lowered costs for working estates.[19] The Atkinson Ministry also tried to restrict speculator purchases of Maori lands. And again reversing Grey's course, the franchise was requalified by a length-of-residence requirement—thus excluding nonresident speculators—and by a quota system increasing the newly cleansed rural districts' parliamentary representation.[20]

Capital Flows and Public Retrenchment

Decreases in borrowing and public spending combined with falling export prices to inaugurate what became known as the "black '80s." In 1876, the value of exported wool peaked at £3.7 million, then stagnated between £3.0 million and £3.3 million from 1880 to 1888. Agricultural exports fell 50 percent from 1880 to 1887 as Australia be-

16. Dalziel, "Politics of Settlement," p. 108; Basset, *Sir Harry Atkinson*, pp. 66, 77, and *passim*; *New Zealand Official Yearbook* 1894. Per capita debt levels in 1881 were ten times the level they had been in 1861 after a generation of war against the Maori.

17. Dowie, "Studies in New Zealand Investment," p. 377; R. Irvine and O. Alpers, *Progress of New Zealand in the Century* (Philadelphia: Linscott, 1902), p. 293.

18. *Economist*, August 2, 1890, p. 987.

19. Condliffe, *New Zealand in the Making*, p. 124.

20. Dalziel, "Politics of Settlement," p. 107; R. Stone, "Thames Valley and Rotorua Railway Co. Ltd., 1882–1889," *New Zealand Journal of History* 3 (April 1974), 30–32.

Table 22. Growth of New Zealand overseas public debt, 1881–1906

Ministry and year	Absolute increase (£ '000)	Ministry and year	Absolute increase (£ '000)
Hall-Atkinson 1880–84	4278	Liberals, part I: 1891–94	1531
Stout-Vogel 1884–87	5365	Liberals, part II: 1895–1900	8056
Atkinson 1888–90	192	Liberals, part III: 1900–1906	12,740

SOURCES: *Statistics New Zealand* 1909, vol. II, p. 478; *New Zealand Official Yearbook*, 1895, broadsheet.

came more self-sufficient.[21] While frozen meat and dairy goods made their debut as exports in this period, their absolute increase barely cancelled the fall in agricultural exports. All of these factors caused the gradual increase in public debt service (from £1.3 million in 1880 to £1.9 million in FY 1890) to contract the domestic economy. From 1887 to 1906 public debt service totaled £43 million against £21 million in new borrowing.[22] But against this ledgerbook accounting of borrowing must be set a political one, for the new £21 million came during the Stout-Vogel Ministries in 1884–1887, and after the Liberal Party, electorally victorious in 1890, had purged its urban/labour allies in 1895–95. (See Table 22.)

A flight of private capital from New Zealand paralleled the cessation in public borrowing in the 1880s. It took longer for private capital imports to turn around into a real outflow of principal, but when it did, private money flowed out at a faster rate than public funds did. A variety of calculations exist for private capital flows, but all agree they turned unfavorable around the middle of the 1880s (Table 23). Most of this capital was transferred by Anglo-Australian banks, as Steven Butlin notes: the Union Bank of Australia "was, in the Eighties, treating New Zealand as a net source of funds for investment in . . . Australia."[23] Even a New Zealand–owned firm like Auckland's Bank of New Zealand moved almost £2.25 million to Australia 1881–85. Out-

21. *New Zealand Official Yearbook* 1892, p. 69.
22. Rosenberg, "Capital Imports and Growth," *passim.*
23. S. Butlin, *Australia and New Zealand Bank* (London: Longmans Green, 1961), p. 231. British capital tended to use their extant and larger Australian operations as a base for investment in New Zealand.

Table 23. Private capital inflows to New Zealand, three estimates

Coghlan	Gross (£ mil.)	Simkin	Net (£ mil.)	Rosenberg	Net (£ mil.)
1840–1885	19.9	1840–1885	11.4	1840–1886	29
1886–1890	0.6	1886–1902	−17.9	1887–1906	−15
1891–1902	−8.1				

SOURCES: T. A. Coghlan, *A Statistical Account of the Seven Colonies of Australasia* 1903/4; Simkin, *Instability of a Dependent Economy,* pp. 83–84; Rosenberg, "Capital Imports and Growth," pp. 94–95.

standing bank loans rose from £4 million in 1871 to £13.1 million in 1879, grew much more slowly to £15.8 million in 1886, and then declined to £11.4 million in 1891.[24]

The Crisis and the Financial and Landed Groups

As in Australia, New Zealand's crisis centered around public debt, mortgages on private land, and labour struggles. But an understanding of politics in the 1880s and 1890s requires understanding the effects of private and public investment flows and the burden of debt service on different groups.

In the 1870s, railroad building created expectations of increased land values. Speculators and land companies bought up huge tracts of land ahead of actual construction during the 1870s, mostly with money borrowed at the prevailing 10–12 percent rate of interest.[25] Many small and large plots were bought from speculators at inflated values with money borrowed at the same high rates of interest. When cessation of borrowing cut short rail expansion, land values fell. This fall affected speculators and large and small landholders differently.

Speculators had the greatest problem. With no intention of using the land themselves, they could not generate enough of a cash flow to meet their mortgages. For a while they were able to continue operations, because the private capital still flowing into New Zealand allowed functioning estates to continue to expand. But after the turn-around in private capital flows in 1886, the bottom fell out of the land market. By 1888/9, foreclosure of 500 bankrupt properties, some

24. Sutch, *Colony or Nation?* p. 25; *New Zealand Official Yearbook* (various dates). Bank lending did not recover to the 1886 level until 1905.
25. Simkin, *Instability of a Dependent Economy,* p. 88; Sutch, *Colony or Nation?* p. 33.

262,954 acres, made the Bank of New Zealand the country's largest landholder. These estates had a putative value of £1.1 million; but the market for land had evaporated, forcing the Bank to write off £1.2 million in the period 1885–1889, and to acknowledge £3,450,000 in bad debts in 1887. By 1892 the Bank had been forced to double its holdings, to 457,084 unprofitable acres. All told, land companies held £4.2 million of land in 1888.[26]

More direct speculators cannot have been much better off.[27] They had only two ways out of their bind, both involving more borrowing. The first involved returning to the old policy of borrowing for railroad construction. The New Zealand Agricultural Company would probably have been liquidated in the mid-1880s if not for the timely and personally-interested intervention of the Robert Stout–Julius Vogel government, which propelled itself into power by holding out to Canterbury and a variety of speculators (including Stout and Vogel) the prospect of a Canterbury–West Coast railway.[28] But the social base for such a solution was narrow, for only speculators stood to benefit overall. London lenders would not tolerate the borrowing necessary to liquidate all speculator holdings because the proposed railroads would never be profitable, and neither the current balance of payments deficit nor the extant forms of production could support the service burden. While the direct benefits of a railroad in Canterbury could swing enough Canterbury estate owners over to the speculators' camp, the tax burden inherent in a second massive rail program would alienate both urban interests and estate owners, who in any case were increasingly unable to buy the new land opened up by the railroads.

The second option involved borrowing to finance subdivision of speculator-held lands into small farms—with the government either buying out speculators and reselling to family farmers or subsidizing mortgages to family farmers. This too was tried under Stout-Vogel

26. Sutch, *Colony or Nation?* p. 26; see also Condliffe, *New Zealand in the Making*, p. 125; A. Ward, "The New Zealand Gentry 1890–1910: Twilight or Indian Summer?" *Australian Economic History Review* (AEHR) 19 (September 1979), 171; Simkin, *Instability of a Dependent Economy*, pp. 165–167; *Australasian Insurance and Banking Record* (AIBR) July 10, 1890, p. 941. Land company holdings represented about 15 percent of all mortgages; the Bank's own foreclosures about 1 percent.

27. See H. Hanham, "New Zealand Promoters and British Investors 1860–1895," in R. Chapman and K. Sinclair, eds., *Studies of a Small Democracy* (Auckland: Auckland University Press, 1963), for an analysis of speculator groupings.

28. D. Hamer, "The Agricultural Company and New Zealand Politics, 1877–1896," *Historical Studies Australia and New Zealand* (HSANZ) 10 (May 1968), *passim*.

when Minister for Lands Ballance attempted to settle workers on the land.[29] The social base for this program was broader than for the railroad program. If export markets could be found for family farmers, then debt service problems would disappear, alleviating London's distaste for renewed borrowing and reducing estate owner (i.e. tax-payer) opposition. The large agricultural proletariat desired land, and the rural village–centered petit bourgeoisie stood to gain from an enlargement of their market if rural living standards rose. As we will see, precisely this coalition underlay the Liberal Party victory in 1890. The costs of such a program would largely be borne by the very farmers who gained land. But for them the acquisition of land outweighed the disguised costs that mortgages and the world market imposed.

In the short run, though, retrenchers stymied speculators. When government revenues declined in 1887, a renewed cry for retrenchment arose, institutionalized itself in the newly formed Political and Financial Reform Association, and propelled Atkinson back into power. On both the North and South Islands a coalition of large farmers and runholders called for increases in customs on labour consumption goods—tobacco, tea, and sugar—while advocating cuts in public services like education. For them, like the state-level conservative parties in post-Federation Australia, there was "no alternative between crushing taxation and rigid retrenchment." Atkinson's resurrected tariff was distinctly regressive, even as the ministry lowered pastoral rents.[30]

Largeholders working estates producing wool for export were not affected as adversely by decreased borrowing as were speculators, nor were they foreclosed upon like their Australian cousins. First, they benefited from extant transport networks, which gave them access to local agricultural intermediate goods and to export markets. Though estate owners saw their (borrowed) capital locked up by falling wool and land prices after 1886, just as in Australia in the 1890s, their estates remained fairly profitable, for they had several advantages over their Australian counterparts. Climate, the course of prices, and diversification all favored New Zealand wool exporters in the 1880s. New Zealand graziers enjoyed relatively high productivity from their

29. Only 1000 people were settled under this Act by 1892; Condliffe, *New Zealand in the Making*, p. 124.

30. Quotation from *Hawkes Bay Herald*, quoted in K. Sinclair, "The Significance of the Scare-crow Ministry, 1887–1891," in Chapman and Sinclair, *Studies of a Small Democracy*, p. 109–111, 116; Condliffe, *New Zealand in the Making*, p. 124; Lloyd-Pritchard, *Economic History of New Zealand*, p. 139.

superfertile land and fairly abundant rainfall, as well as several more good seasons before wool prices bottomed out in the 1890s. Many estate owners also had investments in mercantile activity and, occasionally, manufacturing, unlike the typical Australian grazier.[31] New Zealand graziers' profitability and alternative sources of income prevented the wholesale foreclosure experienced by the Australian graziers.

Despite these advantages, New Zealand estate owners suffered from the reversal of capital flows and declining prices in the mid-1880s. John Gould argues that only newly sown pastures balanced a tendency toward overstocking and declining fertility on the land, but without continuing inflows of capital, pasture formation had to be financed out of profits precisely when profits were declining.[32] Further extension of estates thus would only reproduce *in extenso* an already extensive method of producing wool and would not change the relative private debt burden on any given piece of land; given declining fertility, it might even increase it. Furthermore, smallholders surrounded many estates, and their displacement would be politically and financially costly.

Alternatively, estate owners could switch to intensive methods and products by increasing the number of workers on their estates. Intensive production would increase the amount of surplus produced on any given acre and so reduce the relative burden of fixed debt. Here too there was a political obstacle. Estate owners had already encouraged the formation of an itinerant workforce, numbering in the thousands, by various forms of charity during the winter off-season, and intensive production on estates would require even more of these "swaggies." But small farmers, who did not need seasonal workers and who often worked off-farm themselves, saw swaggies as "alien, predatory, and parasitic." They wanted to integrate swaggies into the community through marriage and settlement as smallholders.[33] So estate owners would have faced resistance from smallholders had they tried

31. S. Eldred-Grigg, "Whatever Happened to the Gentry?" *New Zealand Journal of History* 11 (April 1977), 8, 10–11, 20; see also D. Bedggood's arguments on this point in "New Zealand's Semi-colonial Development," *Australia–New Zealand Journal of Sociology* 14 part II (October 1978); and Bedggood, *Rich and Poor in New Zealand, passim.*

32. See J. Gould, "Pasture Formation and Improvement in New Zealand, 1871–1911," AEHR 16 (March 1976), for information on pasturage and capitalization of estates.

33. J. Martin, "Development from Above: God Made the Country and Man the Town," in I. Shirley, ed., *Development Tracks* (Palmerston North: Dunmore Press, 1982), pp. 106–109; see also M. Fairburn, "Local Community or Atomised Society?" *New Zealand Journal of History* 16 (October 1982), 149–153.

to increase the number of swaggies (or *pari passu*, further to proletarianize smallholders). Instead owners attempted to intensify not only production but also its capital intensity: "The gentry [took] considerable initiative in intensifying and diversifying production," as Steven Eldred-Grigg notes, "draining, irrigation, tree planting, fencing, . . . mechanization and the very rapid development of raising sheep for mutton. . . . In every advance of the new mixed farming it was the gentry who showed the way . . . by [virtue] of their capital."[34] But here again, the outflow of capital after 1886 set limits on the possible.

Meanwhile the smallholder market shrank as estates economized by growing their own inputs. Smallholders were thus left with fixed debt burdens at a time of declining demand for their products. They could make up the difference between interest charges and their income from crops by working for the estates, but to do so threatened their status as independent producers by reducing them to the level of the swaggies they disliked and feared. Smallholders, like estate owners, tried shifting to mostly dairy and meat production. But smallholders also faced all the start-up costs of a new industry with even fewer resources than those available to estate owners.

A consideration of smallholders would be incomplete without reference to the many small villages containing the bulk of New Zealand's "urban" population as well as many smallholders. In 1886, 60 percent of all settlements with more than 100 inhabitants did not have more than 500 inhabitants, and a further 20 percent had no more than 1,000 people. By 1891 this pattern had intensified, despite the overall rise in the population, so that 75 percent of villages had populations between 100 and 500, and a further 10 percent had fewer than 1,000. None of these villages was self-sufficient or contained anything more than a rudimentary manufacturing and processing capacity. Rather, they depended on the prosperity of the surrounding agricultural community, because estates were relatively self-sufficient. Consequently, as John Martin argues, "small towns were extremely important in the Liberal thrust for closer settlement . . . Closer settlement meant more customers and greater demand for the services that these towns depended upon. . . . Their limited division of labour depended on close integration with the countryside."[35]

34. Eldred-Grigg, "Whatever Happened to the Gentry?" pp. 16–17.
35. Martin, "Development from Above," p. 93; quotation from ibid., p. 96.

The Crisis and Urban Labour and Manufacturing

The flight of capital combined with rising interest payments on the public debt forced an end to New Zealand's chronic balance of payments deficit. Capital inflows permitted merchandise imports to exceed merchandise exports, creating a balance of payments overhang of £44 million from 1840 to 1886. Even after borrowing slowed in the late 1870s, imports on average exceeded exports by approximately £1 million per annum between 1877 and 1887.[36] But capital outflows in the 1880s made it impossible for New Zealand to import beyond its means, causing a drastic contraction of imports. The decline in imports created opportunities for domestic capitals to manufacture import substitutes. Manufacturing employment increased two and a half times faster than population growth as the number of manufacturing jobs increased 43 percent from 1881 to 1886, and a further 16 percent to 1891. Within manufacturing, the number of jobs in industries without "natural" protection increased disproportionately. Employment in "naturally" protected industries, including construction, foods, and printing, rose only 24 percent, and their share of all manufacturing employment fell from 67 percent to 49 percent. Employment in industries facing world market competition, by contrast, accounted for the bulk of the increase in the 1880s, rising six times faster than naturally protected industrial employment. By the decade's end, New Zealand was a net exporter of certain specialized goods: gold dredges, wool presses, some agricultural implements, and even woolen textiles.[37]

Two unfavorable conditions make these employment increases all the more significant. The domestic market was not expanding rapidly, as immigrants avoided the depressed New Zealand economy. Over the decade of the 1880s, there were only 20,000 net new immigrants; the last half of the decade saw net out-migration.[38] Second, domestic manufacturers faced increased world market competition. Freight rates fell 50 percent 1875 to 1885, and a further 33 percent to 1895, while the prices of imported goods themselves fell. Together,

36. *New Zealand Official Yearbook,* 1895, broadsheet.

37. Sutch, *Colony or Nation?* p. 29; Simkin, *Instability of a Dependent Economy,* p. 63; C. Blyth, "Industrialization of New Zealand," *New Zealand Economic Papers,* vol. 8 (1974), p. 7; Armstrong, "Politics of Development," p. 295.

38. *New Zealand Official Yearbook* 1895, broadsheet. In contrast, for example, over 100,000 new migrants, 1872–1876, amounted to a quarter of the total population of the time.

these meant New Zealand manufacturers faced increasing competition in a small and stagnant market. Nevertheless consumer goods imports as a share of total imports fell from 54 percent of all 1880 imports to 32 percent of a smaller bundle of imports in 1890.[39] Perhaps tariff protection allowed local manufacturers to stay competitive? But Atkinson's tariff (1880–1884) was a low-revenue tariff, was eliminated by the Stout-Vogel government, and when reimposed by Atkinson in 1887–1890 was again a regressive revenue tariff.[40] As protection this was "too little, too late." Simkin notes: "The large fall in import prices [should] have made for a rise in the proportion of consumers' imports, not a fall. The prices of local manufactures must, therefore, have fallen more rapidly than those of imports."[41] Increased exploitation, not protection, appears to have provided manufacturers with the edge they needed to remain competitive and growing despite increased foreign competition. Wages fell in the 1880s. Much new manufacturing employment came from an increase in low-wage female workers; the ratio of female to male workers shot from 1 : 17 in 1881 to 1 : 5 in 1886.[42]

Increased exploitation and declining wages induced efforts to unionize which ran parallel to manufacturers' increasing protectionist sentiment, thus presumably increasing the pressure on manufacturers from overseas competition. By the mid-1880s, most urban crafts unionized under the 1878 Trades Union Act, but, just as in Australia, by the end of the 1880s a new unionism among unskilled and semi-skilled workers displaced the older benevolent society unionism organized under the 1878 Act. From 1888 to 1890, the number of unionized workers exploded from 3,000 to 30,000—primarily among mine, ship, dock and rail workers. With aid from the Australian Shearer's Union, shearers were partially organized in 1886.[43] The new unions naturally affiliated under the Maritime Council with their counterparts on the Australian continent. Growing tension between capital and labour matched developments across the

39. Simkin, *Instability of a Dependent Economy*, pp. 60–62.
40. Atkinson levied only a 20 percent ad valorem duty on clothing and shoes. See also Sutch, *Colony or Nation?* p. 30; Sinclair, "Significance of the Scare-crow Ministry," pp. 109–111.
41. Simkin, *Instability of a Dependent Economy*, p. 61.
42. Sutch, *The Quest for Security in New Zealand*, p. 66; Lloyd-Pritchard, *Economic History of New Zealand*, pp. 155, 179.
43. B. Brown, *Rise of New Zealand Labour* (Wellington: Price Milburn, 1962), pp. 1–2; J. Holt, "Political Origins of Compulsory Arbitration in New Zealand," *New Zealand Journal of History* 10 (October 1976), 99–100; J. Martin, "Whither the Rural Working Class in Nineteenth Century New Zealand?" *New Zealand Journal of History* 17 (April 1983), 40.

Tasman Sea, and, when the Maritime Council called for a general strike in 1890 (as described in Chapter 3), New Zealand's mining and maritime unions joined in.

Here the similarities end. Although New Zealand, like Australia, had a body of itinerant, fully proletarianized shearers, the proportion of local smallholders who supplemented farm income with seasonal work on estates was higher. Thus shearers' strength and sense of common interests was diluted because partially proletarianized smallholders were pitted against fully proletarianized itinerants.[44] Employers defeated the strikers more easily than in eastern Australia. New Zealand's higher unemployment rate created so many scabs that New Zealand actually "exported" scabs to the Australian continent in the 1890 strike. Only New Zealand railroad workers were more militant than their Australian counterparts; they joined the strike too. Railroad workers' participation led the Atkinson government to drop its neutral stance and intervene on behalf of employers, who otherwise would not have needed government intervention. As in Australia, this intervention politicized defeated labour unions. After the 1890 strike, five openly labor candidates were elected, but this political effort did not mature into a strong and separate party. "There was a wide disparity between various members of th[e Labor] group," notes Crowley, "and there was no conception of a Labor Party."[45] Not until after the 1913 general strike did a labor party emerge around a core of militant industrial unions, but worker militancy in 1890 did allow the forces in favor of reform and renewed borrowing to come to power in 1890–91.

RESOLVING THE CRISIS OF THE 1880S

We can now see why the political solution to New Zealand's crisis led to increased dependency and increased development, unlike Australia, where dependency decreased. In 1890 urban and rural labour, the petit bourgeoisie living in small towns, and the financial capitals most heavily involved in land speculation coalesced behind the Liberal Party. The Liberals advocated a program of industrial conciliation

44. Martin, "Development from Above," pp. 95–100, especially p. 98; Fairburn, "Local Community or Atomised Society?" pp. 149–153; D. Pearson, *Johnsonville: Continuity and Change in a New Zealand Township* (Auckland: Allen & Unwin, 1980); L. Toynbee, "Class and Social Structure in Nineteenth Century New Zealand," *New Zealand Journal of History* 13 (1979).
45. D. Crowley, "The New Zealand Labour Movement, 1894–1913" (M.A. dissertation, University of Otago, 1946), p. 9.

and closer settlement to link these disparate elements together against estate owners and their urban manufacturing and mercantile allies.[46]

THE LIBERALS AND LABOUR

As in 1890s Victoria, a "liberal" party straddling the political middle ground was able to attract considerable worker support and thus to reduce more radical labor movements to a disorganized rump.[47] Just as in Victoria, juridicized collective bargaining and regulation of working conditions were introduced to immobilize strategic transport unions while buying support from urban trades unions. 1891 saw creation of a Ministry of Labour and the beginning of a four year flood of labour legislation.[48] Like Australia, Conciliation was the most important and contentious part of this new state intervention into business. Rail workers' participation in the 1890 strike threatened perishable commodities like dairy and meat (exports of which had nearly doubled 1886–1894) produced by smaller farmers who supported the Liberals.[49] Consequently the bill introduced in 1892 and finally passed in 1894 included only railroad workers from among all government employees. W. P. Reeves, minister for labour, clearly set out the logic for their inclusion: "I think a great railway strike is perhaps one of the greatest industrial dangers which may threaten the people of New Zealand. . . . [It] would be the most damaging strike to the interests of the colony."[50] Unlike every other dispute

46. It would be interesting to compare New Zealand and South Australian politics in this time period, as they seem to have possessed remarkably similar social structures and policy outcomes.

47. Among others, see Brown, *Rise of New Zealand Labour*, p. 3 and *passim*; Crowley, "New Zealand Labour Movement"; C. Campbell, "The 'Working Class' and the Liberal Party in 1890," *New Zealand Journal of History* 9 (April 1975).

48. In 1891, the Truck Act, Coal Mines Act, and Factory Act (amended in 1894); in 1892, the Shops and Shop Assistants Act (amended in 1894), Contractors and Workmens Lien Act, Servants Registry Office Act; in 1894, Industrial Conciliation and Arbitration Act, amendment of Factory and Shops Acts. For legislation prior to 1890, see N. Woods, *Industrial Conciliation and Arbitration in New Zealand* (Wellington: Government Printer, 1963), pp. 319–320; see also Crowley, *New Zealand Labour Movement*, pp. 10–11.

49. Woods, *Industrial Conciliation and Arbitration*, p. 65; *New Zealand Official Yearbook* 1911, pp. 672–673.

50. *New Zealand Parliamentary Debates* (NZPD hereafter) vol. 77, p. 32, August 12, 1892. See also vol. 77, pp. 30–31, August 12, 1892; and vol. 78, pp. 165–175, September 16, 1892. For shipowners' views, see N. Moore, "Employers' Response to the Industrial Conciliation and Arbitration Bill, 1894" (M.A. essay, University of Auckland, 1973), p. 27.

covered by the Act, railway disputes had to go directly to compulsory arbitration, bypassing voluntary conciliation efforts.

Urban support for the bill came from small employers and employers of skilled and therefore craft labour; both employer groups voted by overwhelming margins against the larger employers in Parliament.[51] Large employers more were likely to have had estate owner participation in their ventures. Estate owners who had blocked the Bill in the upper house bowed to the Liberal Party's sizeable electoral margin in 1893.

But the very election that permitted the Bill to pass marked Reeves' political hightide. The election demonstrated smallholder and village voters' increased importance to the Liberals. Richard Seddon, linked to these groups, became prime minister when Ballance died in 1893, took over Reeves's Labour Portfolio in 1895, and "exiled" Reeves to London in 1896. Although Seddon afterward made occasional concessions—such as a small old-age-pension scheme in 1898—to retain workers' loyalty, the wave of reforms was over.[52]

Which urban groups, then, bore the costs of the renewed borrowing that funded the Liberals' land redistribution? Ultimately both manufacturers and labour paid part of the cost, though both prospered initially. Urban small employers enjoyed a decade of relative prosperity and complete labour peace after 1894, due largely to rural demand for consumer goods. This demand drove a 50 percent jump in manufacturing employment 1896–1901—four times the population increase. But these increases leveled off to a 15 percent increase, only half the rate of population increase in the decade 1901–11. The tariff created no new employment, for dairy and agricultural equipment entered free, negating domestic manufacturers' linkages to the expanding dairy export sector. Instead the share of manufacturing employment accounted for by industries with world market competition steadily declined from 51 percent in 1891 to 40 percent in 1921.[53] Once rural demand for consumer goods was saturated, New

51. Moore, *The Employers' Response*, pp. 24–26, appendices. See also R. Rudman, "Employer Organisations: Their Development and Role in Industrial Relations," in J. Howells, ed., *Labour and Industrial Relations in New Zealand* (Carleton, Victoria: Pitman, 1974). For estate owner opposition, see W. Rolleston's comments, NZPD 1892, vol. 78, p. 132.

52. See R. Shannon, "The Liberal Succession Crisis in New Zealand, 1893," HSANZ 8 (May 1958); J. Martin, *State Papers no. 2* (Palmerston North: Massey University Press, 1981), pp. 17–24; A. Metin, *Socialism without Doctrines* (Paris, 1901), pp. 251–256.

53. A. Maynard, "Strikes and the State" (M.A. diss., Auckland University, 1981) pp. 68–71; *Statistics of the Dominion of New Zealand; New Zealand Official Yearbook* 1911, pp. 98–99, 555–559; Blythe, "Industrialization of New Zealand," p. 7. Manufacturing employment stagnated and declined as a percentage of the total labor force after 1901.

Zealand manufacturing stagnated and manufacturers were unable to make a transition to production of capital goods. Manufacturing employment stagnated, and average machinery and plant values and horsepower employed per factory lagged behind Australian levels, especially after 1907. New Zealand's Conciliation Court passed a minimum wage soon after, but in real terms it was lower than 1890's wage level, and marginal employers were allowed to pay sub-minimum wages, which allowed small and inefficient firms to remain in the market.[54] Without pressure to invest, value added per employee fell 33 percent 1901–1911, not because wages were rising as a percentage of output, but because raw materials costs were. Though gross output rose 74 percent, food processing accounted for 54 percent of the increase.[55] Conciliation consequently created neither demand nor supply pressures accelerating domestic accumulation, as they had in Australia.

As in Australia, Conciliation pacified unions even as their numbers increased, for the court only granted preferential employment to unionists if unions acceded to court regulations mandating open entrance (to dilute militancy) and setting dues too low to sustain strike activity. The number of unionized workers rose from 10.7 percent of wage and salary earners to 18.7 percent from 1901 to 1911; lower than the proportion in Australia. In the meantime, increases in taxes and rents drove up the cost of living. Food prices rose 12 percent from 1899 to 1906.[56] Foreign and absentee landlords capitalized on rising urban employment to cream off wage rises through rent increases. The highest civil servant in the Labour Department wrote to Seddon in 1904: "The chief devourer of the wages of the worker and of the profits of the employer is excessive rent. . . . The tribute levied

---

54. *Statistics of the Dominion of New Zealand* 1909, vol. III, p. 427; 1915, vol. III, p. 66; 1918, vol. III, p. 87; OYBCWA (various dates); Crowley, "New Zealand Labour Movement," pp. 16, 117–120. New Zealand machinery and plant levels per factory were 79 percent the Australian level in 1911, horsepower per factory 96 percent. Maynard, however, in "Strikes and the State," sees a pattern of wage equality within specific industries.

55. *Statistics of the Dominion of New Zealand*, 1909, vol. II, p. 423; 1915, vol. III, p 66; 1918, vol. III, p. 87. Revised statistics presented in New Zealand Department of Statistics, *Industrial Production Statistics*, 1964/65 suggest a decline of only 20 percent in value added per worker 1901–1905. Wages rose after the 1905/6 census, perhaps from a combination of increased strike activity and the fixing of a minimum wage.

56. Crowley, "New Zealand Labour Movement," pp. 10–11, 21–22, 32–35, 46; Martin, "Whither the Rural Working Class?" p. 22; *New Zealand Official Yearbook* 1957, p. 1233, and various dates.

on the struggling colonists of New Zealand by this absentee [landlord-ism] would . . . stagger humanity."[57]

Workers had an out, though, for some could take up farming. But by 1906 all cheap farming land had been distributed; the Conciliation machinery was increasingly unable to handle disputes in what appeared a fair manner.[58] In the absence of both outlets, falling wages proved an intractable issue and 1907–08 saw a new wave of strikes as export prices fell. Workers openly split from the Liberal Party and formed a number of labor parties. Direct and political agitation culminated in the 1913 general strike, which, like the Maritime Strike in Australia a generation earlier, consolidated a labor party based in industrial unions.[59] But from 1901 to 1913, New Zealand labour and manufacturers marked time while Australia advanced.

The Liberals and Land Reform

Paralleling their labour reforms the Liberals began an ambitious program of state-sponsored subdivision with the Land and Income Assessment Act of 1891, which allowed the state to buy and redistribute land. The second step was the Advances to Settlers Act, which granted 5 percent mortgages to those buying land for farming. These two acts cemented the loyalty of the village petit bourgeoisie and of newly landed farmers, especially medium sized ones, to the Liberal Party. Between 1892 and 1909 the number of smallholders (holding less than 200 acres) increased 61 percent, and of medium holders (200–5,000 acres) 105 percent. Overall the number of holdings increased 71.6 percent (Table 24). The number of acres also doubled, with much of the increase coming from cultivated acres, signifying that land entered dairy and meat production rather than wool.

57. Archive of Business and Labour mss. no. (ABL) E97/7/1 1904, E. Treggar (Secretary for Labour) to R. Seddon (Prime Minister), May 31, 1904.
58. Campbell, "The 'Working Class' and the Liberal Party," p. 43, claims 44 percent of a random sample of selectors 1890–93 were "unskilled" workers. On conciliation, see Woods, *Industrial Conciliation and Arbitration*, pp. 53–56, 88–92; Crowley, "New Zealand Labour Movement," pp. 32–42.
59. Brown, *Rise of New Zealand Labour*, p. xii and *passim*. An Independent Political Labor League formed in 1905 and a Socialist Party formed in 1908. See also P. O'Farrell, "The 1908 Blackball Strike," *Political Science* 2 (March 1959); Maynard, "Strikes and the State"; Crowley, "New Zealand Labour Movement," pp. 55–58, 70–71; E. Fisher, "Review of the Political Labour Movement in New Zealand, 1898–1913" (M.A. dissertation, University of Victoria at Wellington, 1932).

CASES

Table 24. Changes in land distribution in New Zealand, 1892–1916

Year	1892	1901	1909	1916
Distribution of all Occupied Land by Size of Holding				
Holding size:				
<200 acres	9.1%	6.7%	6.7%	7.2%
200–5000 acres	37.3	33.9	42.1	48.1
>5000 acres	53.6	59.3	51.2	44.5
Total ('ooo ac.)	1939.7	3491.2	3820.4	4162.2
Distribution of Landowners by Size of Holding				
Holding size:				
<200 acres	74.1%	71.9%	69.5%	64.0%
200–5000 acres	24.4	26.8	29.1	34.5
>5000 acres	1.4	1.5	1.2	1.4
Total owners	43,777	62,786	75,152	77,229

SOURCES: *New Zealand Official Yearbook* 1892, p. 210, 1899, p. 321; *Census of New Zealand* 1901, p. lxi; *Statistics of the Dominion of New Zealand* 1909, vol. II, p. 394; 1918, vol. III, p. 25.

Getting the money to subdivide land and recapitalize the ailing Bank of New Zealand forced the Liberals to borrow abroad, abrogating explicit campaign promises to the contrary. The Advances to Settlers Act authorized the state to float up to £3 million in new loans to fund mortgages. Meantime the Liberal's electoral victory in 1890 proved insufficient to save the Bank of New Zealand and its subsidiary New Zealand Land and Mortgage from the 1893 crash. The Liberals borrowed £2.0 million to refloat the Bank, ramming legislation through in one night to save their favored Bank. The Bank's notes were made legal tender, and an Assets Realization Board was established to sell off as much of the Bank's £2.7 million of land holdings and the holdings of its subsidiaries as it could. In 1895 the Bank wrote off a further £900,000, requiring an additional infusion of £0.5 million from the state. At first slow, borrowing accelerated after the 1893 bank bailout and 1896 elections, when the center of gravity of the party shifted decisively from North Island urban groups (including labour) to newly created South and North Island farmers. London investors were willing to extend more credit to New Zealand because expanding meat and dairy exports raised New Zealand's total exports in the period 1888–93 34 percent over 1882–87 levels, producing a solid balance of payments surplus for the first time.[60]

The Liberals went to considerable lengths to conceal borrowing so as to minimize estate owner and lender fears of another crisis. Many noticed anyway: "Meantime the colony and its lands are being more and more delivered to the British moneylender (so far as loan capital is being employed [to settle farmers on the land])," editorialized AIBR. In London, W. James wrote that, "the Loan Policy which has been so skillfully hidden (and the hiding of this vast spending is regarded as one of Seddon's most astute acts) must soon come home to roost. . . ." Secret borrowing continued unabated into the 1900s, as T. A. Coghlan noted. "In spite of [New Zealand Prime Minister] Joseph Ward's perennial boasting of his independence of the London money market New Zealand is a perpetual if secret borrower here. The New Zealand High Commissioner's office is open to sell . . . debentures to any amount at any time."[61]

Land Reform, Speculators, and Estate Owners

The natural questions are: who paid the costs of renewed borrowing and what effects did it have on development? The traditional answer is that estate owners paid, through expropriation, albeit with some compensation. Indeed the Liberals couched their program in terms of an attack on estates and large landholders, by means of a "bursting up," or expropriating land tax, and *post hoc* the total number of estates shrank remarkably. But this reduction involved two separate processes. The first, total liquidation of speculator-held lands was a deliberate outcome of the Liberal's program. The second outcome, subdivision of functioning pastoral estates, came because of market and class struggle pressures, and not as a direct or intended consequence of the Liberal program.

Speculators and their creditors benefited to an extraordinary degree from Liberal borrowing and land purchase. Neither of the Liberal programs—Advances to Settlers nor Land and Income Assessment—immediately liquidated speculators' holdings. Rather, each round of advances and sales permitted successively larger rounds of

60. *New Zealand Official Yearbook* 1911, pp. 672–673.
61. First quotation, AIBR, November 20, 1899, p. 772. Second quotation, National Library of Australia mss. no. (NLA MS) 1540/1/1508, W.H. James (West Australian Agent General) to A. Deakin, August 17, 1906. Third quotation, NLA MS 1540/1/2335, T.A. Coghlan (NSW Agent General) to A. Deakin, March 25, 1909.

subdivision and sales, with incoming mortgage payments funding new mortgages. Although company (i.e. speculator) lands amounted to 30.6 percent of all holdings over 10,000 acres in 1892, they accounted for 36 percent of all state purchases 1892 to 1902, and 49 percent of all state purchases 1902 to 1910. Additionally in 1892–1902, 44 percent of all private purchases came from company-held lands. Company lands sold at twice the average rate of all privately-held land. The number of companies possessing land valued at over £50,000 dropped from fifteen in 1892 to only two in 1910, despite rising land values.[62] As a contemporary observer noted, liquidation dovetailed with efforts to save speculators' banks: "[bank] securities have risen steadily in value. The value of land increased by leaps and bounds from 1897, the unimproved value rising from £10 million to £20 million each year. This facilitated liquidation of the properties of the Assets Realization Board [of the bank of New Zealand] and assisted the banks generally in unloading their liquid assets." In contrast, an American visitor observed that "in the [subdivision] process the largeholder has not suffered . . . spoliation . . . The worst he can complain of is . . . a graduated land tax."[63] Estates by and large were not liquidated involuntarily by the Liberal program, nor did owners take advantage of the opportunity to sell off their land to small holders. Yet between 1890 and 1910 a significant portion of estate land was sold off or partitioned. The number of acres owned as estates of over 10,000 acres dropped 55 percent from 1892 to 1910.[64] This reduction is all the more remarkable for, as Eldred-Grigg argues, "throughout the depression their estates had not been a burden to [owners], but on the contrary were providing large profits. It seems unlikely that at the beginning of a curve of upward growth men long accustomed to making profits in the depression would abandon their investments simply because the price they could get was increasing."[65] Why then did subdivision occur? Three forces pushed estate owners toward subdivision. Two partially related to, but were not actually part of the Liberal program, and the last derived from market forces. The first force was increasing discontent on the part of the rural

62. J. Gould, "Twilight of the Estates," AEHR 10 (March 1970), pp. 4–9. Gould, pp. 3–7, thinks that by 1910 it was likely that all company-held lands had been sold off; see also Ward, "New Zealand Gentry, 1890–1910," p. 172.

63. H. D. Bedford, quoted in Sutch, *Colony or Nation?* p. 33. Second quotation, Irvine and Alpers, *Progress of New Zealand in the Century*, p. 335.

64. Gould, "Twilight of the Estates," pp. 6, 9–10.

65. Eldred-Grigg, "Whatever Happened to the Gentry?" p. 20. In the area Eldred-Grigg studied, the number of estates over 5,000 acres dropped from forty-five to two in this period; p. 19.

proletariat. The years 1892–93 and 1896 saw "spates of fire raising" and of "poaching on estates"—forms of resistance well known to the displaced Irish and English peasants who formed the bulk of the rural landless—in the area Eldred-Grigg studied. Despite widespread, albeit small scale, land ownership, nearly half the rural population— shepherds, labourers, shearers, domestics—possessed no land at all, and thus were a group ready for outrages. The scale of outrages forced the gentry and large farmers to get up a protective society, while politicians worried about the specter of English- or Irish-style land wars.[66] The real Irish land wars provoked a sympathetic response among New Zealand's Irish, who organized many Land League branches to raise money for Irish Nationalist Davitt. These branches also turned to "strik[ing] terror into the hearts of squatters."[67] Liberal pronouncements about the evils of largeholding probably fueled discontent as much as their labour control policies (regulating swaggie movement and employment after 1900) dampened it.[68] In response to outrages, estate owners tried to lower the salience of their holdings by selling off small parcels of land, and settling land upon their children and relatives. Both tactics related to the second— economic—pressure.

The second pressure—falling prices for wool and fixed interest burdens—motivated a switch to intensive forms of cultivation. But this switch was hampered by the size of existing estates, which were oriented to wool production. Divesting to relatives created medium-sized family farms more workable for mutton farming. Divestment also reduced the need for seasonal and hired labour—precisely the type most associated with incendiarism. The average number of hired pastoral hands fell 65 percent, 1891 to 1911.[69] Finally, and here the Liberal hand shows clearly, the new progressive land tax encouraged even a fictitious subdivision to avoid the tax's higher reaches. But as Professors Gould's and Ward's figures show, such taxes were no deterrent either to acquiring or maintaining estates, for the number of

66. Eldred-Grigg, "Whatever Happened to the Gentry?" pp. 4–5, 17–19; Fairburn, "Local Community or Atomised Society?" pp. 149–153; NZPD 1888, vol. 72, p. 252; D. Hamer, "Sir Robert Stout and the Labour Question," in Chapman and Sinclair, *Studies of a Small Democracy*, p. 89 and *passim*; M. Fairburn, "The Rural Myth and the New Urban Frontier: An Approach to New Zealand Social History 1870–1940," *New Zealand Journal of History* 9 (April 1975), 12. Fairburn characterizes most early settlement efforts as "economically irrational," concluding that social control was the primary concern.
67. *Otago Daily Times*, April 18, 1881, quoted in R. Davis, *Irish Issues in New Zealand Politics, 1868–1922* (Dunedin: University of Otago Press, 1974), pp. 136–141.
68. J. Martin, *State Papers no. 2* (Palmerston North: Massey University Press, 1981), p. 24.
69. Martin, "Whither the Rural Working Class?" p. 34.

individuals owing estates valued over £50,000 increased 28 percent from 1892 to 1910.[70]

In short, estate owners neither paid taxes nor lost their property for borrowing and subdivision. Rather, pressure from below pushed estate owners into passive acquiescence in Liberal "redistributive" policies, which dampened the fire of discontent among the landless. Estate owners could not afford to block Liberal settlement plans, nor, because the costs of redistribution did not fall on them, had they any motivation to contest Liberal policy.

Three groups paid most of the cost of redistribution and debt: the Maori, urban labour, and family farmers. Much of the land the Liberals made available for settlement that did not come from speculators came from the Maori, who lost more than a third of their remaining holdings in this period.[71] Separation of the Maori from their land led to a number of millenarian, political, and self-help movements, such as those led by Rua Kenana and Te Whiti, the Young Maori Party, and the self-rule parliaments at Kotahitanga and Kauhanganui.

As noted above, urban labour's real wages eroded after the 1890s. Customs continued to provide the biggest piece of government revenues, but without any mitigating protective effects. From 1901 to 1914, alcohol taxes' share of customs revenue rose from 32 percent to 43.5 percent; with other regressive taxes on consumption goods, they provided around 70 percent of customs revenue.[72]

Family farmers bore most of the costs of redistribution. They bore not only the direct costs of the 5 percent mortgage for their state advances, but also the labour costs involved in capitalizing their enterprises. Both David Bedggood and Harriet Friedmann argue forcefully that the latter costs were considerable.[73] Second, not all family farmers started off equal, or stayed family farmers. The mid-

---

70. Ward, "The New Zealand Gentry, 1890–1910," p. 172; Gould, "Twilight of the Estates," *passim.* Rising land values must, however, have accounted for part of this increase.

71. Condliffe, *New Zealand in the Making,* pp. 78–79; Bedggood, *Rich and Poor in New Zealand,* p. 13, and *passim.*

72. Lloyd-Pritchard, *Economic History of New Zealand,* p. 212.

73. Bedggood, *Rich and Poor in New Zealand,* pp. 54–55. H. Friedmann, "World Market, State, and Family Farming: Social Bases of Household Production in the Age of Wage Labor," *Comparative Studies in Society and History* 20 (1978), 545–586; and Friedmann, "State Policy and World Commerce: The Case of Wheat 1815 to the Present," in P. McGowan and C. Kegley, eds., *Foreign Policy and the Modern World System* (Beverly Hills, Cal.: Sage, 1983); I. Weston, "Farm Overhead Charges in New Zealand," *Economic Record* 8 (May 1932). The best estimate for the 1900s is Weston's: that 45 percent of farm income in the early 1930s went to mortgages, insurance, transportation, and commissions.

dle segment of holdings grew fastest, indicating a division into well-to-do and marginal farms (see Table 24). Each price decline on world markets threw many of the newer and more inefficient farmers back into the ranks of the landless or partially landless from which they had advanced. Significantly, the number of sharemilkers, who rented cows and land in exchange for one third of production, increased steadily after 1901, when price competition emerged among dairy producers world wide.[74]

POLITICAL CONSEQUENCES OF RENEWED BORROWING

A political phenomenon provides the best indicator of the changes in farmers' feelings, as successful farmers grew increasingly distant from the Liberal Party. The Liberals had chosen first to pass the costs of debt on to their urban working class allies. Later, in a replay of the politics of the 1880s, the Liberals increasingly alienated their mass base in the countryside. Just as workers opted out of the Liberal alliance to protest the debt burden they felt, so did farmers. Established farmers began to resent the taxes they paid for new roads and facilities that served new farmers drawn from among the rural proletariat and semi-proletariat. With most speculator-held land sold off, the cost of providing land to these labouring groups was much higher than for their employer predecessors, and foreign debt in the 1900s grew faster than in the 1890s. Land taxes increased after 1900 absolutely and as a proportion of all taxes.[75] Though the absolute amounts were small compared to the customs, the obvious link between rising taxes and the cost of settling new farmers alarmed established farmers.

Meanwhile changing patterns of rural class relations caused the interests of the previously antagonistic pastoral and dairy and agricultural owners to converge. From 1896 to 1906, small proprietors in dairy and agriculture had been in conflict with big pastoral employers. But after 1906, employers in all rural sectors found themselves facing similar labour situations, as dairying became increasingly proletarianized and graziers shifted to family scale meat production.[76]

74. B. Bellringer, "Conservatism and the Farmers" (M.A. dissertation, University of Auckland, 1958), p. 13.
75. Lloyd-Pritchard, *Economic History of New Zealand*, p. 213.
76. Martin, "Whither the Rural Working Class?" pp. 29, 32–34. Since total rural employment was increasing, and since many workers must have attempted to start farms or worked on "shares," it is unlikely that a coherent rural labour movement could have emerged in this period.

Table 25. Ratio of wage earners to employers in three rural sectors, and employees as a percentage of each sector's labour force, New Zealand, 1891–1911

	Pastoral		Agriculture		Dairy	
Year	Ratio	%	Ratio	%	Ratio	%
1891	6.79	73	1.89	23	—	—
1896	6.54	73	1.83	27	—	—
1901	4.22	62	1.78	29	0.69	12
1906	3.66	55	1.57	31	0.60	13
1911	2.35	44	2.30	34	1.07	19

SOURCE: Calculated from Martin, "Whither the Rural Working Class?" pp. 32–34.

(See Table 25.) Rural employers regrouped under William Massey's Reform Party, which called for retrenchment, decreased customs on imported dairy equipment, and other means for shifting the debt burden.[77] These common rural interests built the foundation for Reform Party political dominance from 1912 until the Depression. Unlike Australia's Country Party, which depended on proportional voting to elect representatives, New Zealand's Reform Party was able to generate absolute majorities out of a large and united group of rural landed and employing interests. And in New Zealand, unlike Australia, a strong and effective Farmers Union formed in 1900, before the first New Zealand Employers Federation formed.

ECONOMIC CONSEQUENCES OF RENEWED BORROWING

Liberal borrowing from FY 1891/92 to FY 1912/13 increased New Zealand's overseas debt from £37.6 million to £87.5 million, 50 percent faster than Australia's rate of overseas borrowing. (See Table 26.) By 1914 only 17 percent of debt was locally held, compared to Australia's 31 percent; public debt service continued to claim 4.6 percent of GDP.[78] This new debt allowed the Liberals to embark on a positive-

77. Bellringer, "Conservatism and the Farmers," pp. 13–15; W. Gardner, "Rise of W. F. Massey, 1891–1912," *Political Science* 13 (March 1961), and Gardner, "W. F. Massey in Power, 1912–1925," *Political Science* 13:2 (September 1961), *passim*. Among "land owners," only sharemilkers and other partially landed farmers remained loyal to the Liberals, for their future land ownership depended on continued Liberal overseas borrowing.

78. *Statistics of the Dominion of New Zealand* 1909, 1915; *New Zealand Official Yearbook* 1895, broadsheet, 1914, p. 848; OYBCWA no. 4, p. 852; AIBR, November 20, 1893, p. 100.

Table 26. Growth of New Zealand public debt, 1895–1914

Year (FY)	Total debt (£ millions)	Per capita debt (£)	Debt service (£ '000s)	Debt service per capita
1895/6	42.3	60.1	1,684	2.27
1900/1	48.6	62.8	1,746	2.14
1905/6	59.7	67.0	2,087	2.24
1910/1	77.7	77.0	2,458	2.32
1913/4	91.7	84.1	2,888	2.53

SOURCE: *Statistics of the Dominion of New Zealand* 1909, 1915

sum political program whose major economic consequence was agricultural development: land use became more intensive as speculator-held land was turned to intensive dairy and meat agriculture.[79] But it is important to note that this borrowed money was mostly used to finance land acquisition, and was not invested in "development" per se. The growth made possible by new debt was largely confined to rural areas, for the Liberals' tariff policies removed any scope for the New Zealand internal bourgeoisie in manufacturing, such as it was, to become a national bourgeoisie as in Australia. There was new "manufacturing" investment in meat packing and dairy processing plants. Unlike in Argentina, most of these were locally owned, but unlike in Australia no metal-working or raw steel industry emerged.[80] Without increasing demand from an enlarged market for labour consumption goods, or politically created links to the expanding agricultural market, development in manufacturing had to wait until debt service in the crisis of the 1930s made importing virtually impossible. Thus Senghaas is only partially correct in arguing that New Zealand "developed" in this period, for a debt-financed solution to the problem of agricultural land ownership, although it made agricultural development possible, did little to help and perhaps hindered manufacturing development.

While New Zealand's meat and dairy exports commanded reasonable prices in the London market, servicing the expanded debt was

79. Investors responded to the opportunities created by increased borrowing; the implicit annual rate of real public and private accumulation accelerated from 2.58 percent to 5.69 percent per annum, 1890–1898; Dowie, "Studies in New Zealand Investment," p. 137.

80. *Statistics of the Dominion of New Zealand* 1915, vol. III, p. 66, 83. Meat processing plants were 1.5 percent of all factories, but employed 7.3 percent of all factory labour, used 16.9 percent of all factory horsepower, owned 10 percent of all factory machinery and plant investment, and produced 23 percent of all factory output by value. Value of output per unit labour was three times the manufacturing average.

not a problem. But when prices dropped and incoming loans no longer covered outgoing service, New Zealand again found itself in difficulties. World War I provided a guaranteed market at wartime prices for New Zealand's agriculture and so temporarily eased the problem, but after the war the debt problem reemerged in full bloom. By FY 1931/32 foreign debt stood at £163.5 million, debt service at £6 million.[81] Unlike the 1880s, the crisis of the 1930s in New Zealand required active outside intervention by the metropolitan state and its financial institutions. The Niemeyer Commission of 1931 sponsored by the Bank of England arranged for the orderly transfer of 6 percent of New Zealand's GNP per annum through the 1930s. In 1987 total foreign public debt stood at NZ $21.7 billion, or 36 percent of GDP.[82] Although Niemeyer is long dead, and the modern IMF has not intervened, the Labour Party is presently engaged in a far-reaching restructuring of the economy to make existing export industries profitable without subsidies, to create a primary government budget surplus, and to free the market for redistribution of labour and capital within New Zealand without state interference. The Labour party hopes thus to reduce the debt burden while still enabling the creation and capitalization of new export industries. In other words, New Zealand has been running in place since 1900.

81. United Nations, *Public Debt of Member Nations* (New York: United Nation, 1948), p. 100.
82. Reserve Bank of New Zealand *Bulletin*, 49 (December 1986), 555; ibid., 49 (July 1986), 331; R. Douglas, *Budget 1988, Part II: Annex and Tables* (Wellington: GPO, 1988), pp. 11-14, 29.

CHAPTER SIX

Argentina

Where Australia and New Zealand's political and economic trajectories are too often seen as similar, those of Argentina and the Antipodes are too often seen as dissimilar. Argentina's failure to continue developing in the mid-twentieth century and its apparently monolithic landed class both seem to differentiate it from the Antipodes. In this chapter I argue that Argentine politics have an organic similarity to Antipodean politics. First, late-nineteenth century Argentina resembles New Zealand in that intra-elite struggles over debt dominated politics. While Argentina experienced three distinct export booms—wool, wheat, and beef—fights over speed of borrowing and its consequent costs pitted speculators against established wool growers, then producers of wheat against producers of wool and mutton, and finally integrated producers of wheat and beef against producers of wool, beef, and flax. These fights were not just over taxes but also over the rate of inflation, a "hidden" tax. Conflict between those who easily made the transition to the new exports and those who required more foreign investment to do so lay beneath this struggle of "commodities," for the former were loath to subsidize the latter, and the state was too weak to enforce any discipline on producers. Second, nineteenth-century Argentina was not doomed to underdevelopment, as so many assume. The social structures causing underdevelopment—labour surpluses, landlord sterilization of surplus as rent, and displacement competition—did not begin to emerge in Buenos Aires and the Littoral provinces until after 1914. Instead, as in the Antipodes, labour shortages and large numbers of owner-operators fostered a highly developed rural economy. Argentina's crucial differences with the Antipodes revolved around the absence in Argentina of a strong imperial or central state that could control land ownership and maintain a stable currency. Because Argentine land-

CASES

owners could acquire land cheaply and could inflate away their debts, they avoided the foreclosure visited upon Australian largeholders. Landholders thus survived into the twentieth century and transformed themselves from owner-operators into rentier landlords. By diverting surplus from investment to consumption, from profit to rent, they encouraged at least stagnation if not underdevelopment. As this last difference grew out of Argentina's colonial history, it is useful to begin by looking at the separation of the Platine provinces from Spain in 1810.

EARLY HISTORY: WEAK STATE, DIVIDED POLITY

Unlike the Antipodes, what came to be called Argentina did not start as an entrepot that expanded into its interior. The Spanish established the interior towns *cum* provinces of Argentina as way-stations for Andean silver exports and as suppliers of agricultural and petty crafts to the mines.[1] Although these towns were the most dynamic part of the imperial economy, as the Spanish Empire disintegrated they increasingly lapsed into autarky. Meanwhile Buenos Aires, formerly a backwater port subordinate to Montevideo, came into its own, increasing its control of the limited foreign trade of the entire Platine region. It became a classic triangular entrepot, selling hides, jerky and tallow to the United Kingdom and to the slave economies of Brazil and Cuba, buying manufactures from Britain. Downriver transport to either Buenos Aires or Montevideo cost three pence per hide, while overland transport per hide cost fifteen pence for fifty miles. Purchase, slaughter, and tanning costs ran to nine pence, and a hide fetched about thirty pence in Buenos Aires, so organized export production much more than 50 miles inland was unprofitable. This limited export activity, and there were only 327 landowner-producers in Buenos Aires province in 1800, although gauchos occasionally brought hides in from the interior.[2]

Thus Argentina had two contending economic poles, the autarkic interior and trading Buenos Aires. These poles meant that early Ar-

1. See, inter alia, A. Ferrer, *The Argentine Economy* (Berkeley: University of California Press, 1967), chap. 3; M. Burgin, *Economic Aspects of Argentine Federalism* (Cambridge: Harvard University Press, 1946), pp. 114–116.
2. H. Ferns, *Britain and Argentina* (Oxford: Clarendon Press, 1960), pp. 56, 81–82, 113; Burgin, *Economic Aspects of Argentine Federalism*, pp. 117–118; A. Zimmerman, "Land Policy in Argentina," *Hispanic American Historical Review* 25 (February 1945), 5.

gentine politics revolved around the question of what area "Argentina" should include, and what constitution it should have.[3] At one end were producers and landowners in the interior provinces, who desired a loose federation, giving them enough autonomy to protect indigenous industries and a *pro rata* distribution of customs revenues originating in Buenos Aires. Paraguay represented the most extreme version of this position. After participating in the early constitutional conventions, it successfully broke away from the political control of the Viceroyalty of Buenos Aires and established itself as an independent state. At the other end were Buenos Aires merchants, who desired a "unitary" government in which their control of both foreign affairs and trade, especially including the customs, would allow them to extract resources from the interior to benefit their own accumulation. In between were Buenos Aires province graziers. Merchants dominated their exports of jerked beef and hides through a system of commercial credit called *habilitaciones*.[4] This group desired federalism, but solely to prevent merchants from nationalizing the customs and dominating them. Their federalism did not extend to a desire to share the customs with the interior provinces; they preferred to use the customs revenues everyone paid to subsidize their own expansion.

At first the merchant Unitarians seemed likely to triumph. From 1816 to 1824, constitutions and the state became increasingly centralized. Within the Buenos Aires area graziers and merchants had combined to form a stable government; Governor Martín Rodríguez represented the graziers' interests and Foreign Minister Bernardino Rivadavia represented the interests of the merchants. The cotton textile boom in Britain created a secondary boom in Buenos Aires, because leather bound together the looms making those textiles. On one estate for which data are available, the average price per head of cattle sold tripled between 1810 and 1819, while the number of head sold increased 60 percent; from 1822 to 1827, exports rose from 60,000 to 350,000 head.[5] Second only to the cotton-exporting American south, the Plata was the favorite child of British overseas investors. On the basis of this demand, Rivadavia tried to emulate Alexander Hamilton, consolidating the support of the for-

---

3. The argument that follows is taken from Burgin, *Economic Aspects of Argentine Federalism*.

4. Ferns, *Britain and Argentina*, p. 81.

5. Burgin, *Economic Aspects of Argentine Federalism*, p. 30; J. Scobie, *Argentina: A City and a Nation* (New York: Oxford University Press, 1971), p. 64; see also Ferrer, *Argentine Economy*, pp. 46–47.

eign and domestic "creditor interest" through public loans, enlisting formal British support through the Anglo-Argentine Treaty of 1825, and centralizing political control by promulgating the unitary constitution of 1826 and reforming the fisc. Rivadavia contracted two loans, first converting Buenos Aires's extant short term overseas debt into £1.5 million of bonds at four to six percent interest, and then borrowing £1 million for harbor and other improvements.[6] Rivadavia's downfall came from three things he did to back the loans. He increased taxes, levying a *"contribución directa"* of 0.08 percent on commercial activity, 0.06 percent on manufacturers, 0.02 percent on grazing, and 0.01 percent on farming. To establish collateral for the loans, he passed a law of emphyteusis which transferred ownership of all land to the state, and required rents to be paid to the central government.[7] Paralleling these attempts to centralize the fisc, Rivadavia tried to conquer the fertile but politically disorganized Banda Oriental (Uruguay), and to remove Montevideo as a competitor. But the interior provinces refused to support Buenos Aires with the *contribución directa*, and Buenos Aires graziers squatted rather than pay rent to the state.[8] A series of civil wars and betrayals left General Manuel Rosas in control, representing Buenos Aires graziers, without resolving the underlying tensions.

From 1829 to 1851, Rosas consolidated a loose federal regime retaining customs revenue for Buenos Aires pastoralists but giving the provinces autonomy and protectionist internal tariffs.[9] He defaulted on Rivadavia's loans, which angered the British but did not prevent a slow expansion of exports.[10] Rosas' military activities supplied graziers' two key needs, land and labour. Gauchos traditionally roamed freely over the plain, killing the cattle they found and trading their hides for the few manufactures they needed. Graziers needed a way to secure both cattle and workers. To prevent the "leakage" of labor to the frontier, Rosas made anyone not contracted to an em-

6. Ferns, *Britain and Argentina*, pp. 100–101, 103.

7. Burgin, *Economic Aspects of Argentine Federalism*, pp. 47, 49; Ferns, *Britain and Argentina*, pp. 104, 132–133; Zimmerman, "Land Policy of Argentina," p. 11.

8. Burgin, *Economic Aspects of Argentine Federalism*, pp. 48–50. See also H. Ferns, "Britain's Informal Empire in Argentina, 1806–1914," *Past and Present* no. 4 (November 1953), pp. 67–69.

9. See J. Lynch, *Argentine Dictator: Juan Manuel de Rosas, 1829–1853* (Oxford: Clarendon, 1981), for a general survey of the period.

10. Burgin, *Economic Aspects of Argentine Federalism*, pp. 73–75, 237–248; Ferns, *Britain and Argentina*, pp. 212, 220–224. Despite the voluntary nature of Rosas's default, it should be noted that several American states also defaulted in the next few years, suggesting that general economic conditions would have forced Argentine default anyway; debt service would have amounted to 60 percent of state revenues.

ployer liable for five years military service.[11] The army then pushed gauchos and Indians away from the frontier, opening up land. With Rosas' connivance between 1832 and 1850, Buenos Aires landowners used Rivadavia's law of emphyteusis to appropriate over 35 million acres at prices rarely over 4.5 pence per acre. Rosas also inaugurated a policy of spending land rather than the state's cash revenue, granting over 4 million acres to soldiers who promptly resold them to speculators.[12] Disregard by *estancieros* of state control of the land was paralleled by contemporaneous Australian graziers' squatting. But *estancieros* legally acquired land on the cheap, in contrast to Australian graziers who had to acquiesce when the imperial state's reassertion of control over land through the leasing system legitimized squatting. In Argentina, the state simply gave away its residual control over land. Thus Argentine landowners acquired land much earlier and more cheaply than either Australian or New Zealand graziers. The rise of the wool economy and the subsequent fall of Rosas did nothing to change this.

RISE OF THE WOOL ECONOMY AND POLITICAL "UNIFICATION"

As in Australia, increasing overseas demand for wool after wool textile production was mechanized caused conflict as some producers desired to change from coerced to free labour, get access to foreign loans, and improve transportation systems. Argentina experienced political centralization, not subdivision as in Australia. Demand for wool drove a rapid expansion of wool production in Buenos Aires. From 1810 to 1850, the number of sheep grew from 250,000 to 5 million, 80 percent of them in Buenos Aires province, and wool went

11. R. Slatta, "Rural Criminality and Social Conflict in Nineteenth Century Buenos Aires Province," *Hispanic American Historical Review* 26 (February 1946), 452–456; Ferns, "Britain's Informal empire in Argentina," pp. 65–66. Rosas merely enforced the system of coerced labour then in place. Although slavery was formally abolished in 1813, an 1815 law declared that all non–property owners had to have their employment certified every three months at the risk of being drafted for five years. The closest parallel to the gauchos is probably Canada's *metí* (French-Indian) *voyageurs*, who gathered pelts on an erratic and uncontrolled basis for export.

12. Zimmerman, "Land Policy of Argentina," pp. 11, 14, and *passim*. 4.5 pence was about one tenth of a gold peso. The upset price in NSW when land sales commenced was more than twice as high. Zimmerman, p. 12, quotes Carcano as saying, "The militia kept the government in power and the soil kept the militia." F. McLynn, "Economic Trends and Policies in Argentina during the Mitré Presidency," *Jarhbuch fur Geschichte von Staat, Wirtschaft und Gessellschaft Latinamerikas* 19 (1982), 261, claims that 235 men acquired 17.6 million acres in Buenos Aires province in those years.

from nil to 17.5 percent of export value.[13] Meanwhile it became increasingly profitable for the littoral provinces of Santa Fe, Corrientes, and Entre Rios, and the interior province of Córdoba to increase exports of jerky, hides, and wool. But more export production by Buenos Aires and the littoral required more and better labour, capital, and railroads, which Rosas' policy of confrontation with Britain made impossible. Opposition to Rosas was particularly intense in the littoral provinces, for while Buenos Aires could and did finance its own rail system, it could not provide one for all of the littoral provinces. Littoral producers desired unmediated access to international markets, but did not want to wait for Buenos Aires to provide them with railroads. If Rosario, a small but good harbor in Santa Fe upriver from Buenos Aires, were opened to foreign trade, and a railway built from Córdoba to Rosario, Córdoban producers would save about 150 miles of overland transport and approximately 20 percent of transport costs, while Rosario would capture the benefits of being an entrepot. Entre Rios Governor Justo Jose de Urquiza, who owned 500,000 sheep, led the revolt against Rosas, and became president of the interior Confederation, believed that a Rosario-Córdoba railway was "indispensible to Confederation political and economic wellbeing."[14] But the littoral provinces lacked enough revenue to build their own Córdoba-Rosario railway. Foreign investors wanted access to Buenos Aires customs revenue instead of the land grants the Confederation offered. Buenos Aires' monopoly on customs thus blocked the transport essential to provincial growth.[15]

Especially within Buenos Aires province, there was dissatisfaction with Rosas' labour "policy" of conscription and limited immigration. In rural Buenos Aires, capricious enforcement of passport laws drove men past the frontier, depriving graziers of workers. The passport

13. Scobie, *Argentina*, p. 83; R. Cortés Conde, *First Stages of Modernization in Spanish America* (New York: Harper and Row, 1974), p. 123; C. Lewis, *British Railways in Argentina, 1857–1914* (London: Athlone Press, 1983), p. 28. See D.C.M. Platt, *Latin America and British Trade, 1806–1914* (London: Adam and Charles Black, 1972), for a general survey of changing trade patterns. See L. Randall, *A Comparative Economic History of Latin America* (Ann Arbor, Mi.: University Microfilms, 1977), p. 207, for comparative price series on agricultural exports. At this point most Argentine wool went to the United States, not Britain; after the U.S. raised the tariff on wool, Belgium moved to first place.

14. Quotation from P. Goodwin, "The Central Argentine Railway and the Economic Development of Argentina, 1854–1881," *Hispanic American Historical Review* 57 (November 1977), 615. See Burgin, *Economic Aspects of Argentine Federalism*, p. 118; McLynn, "Economic Trends and Policies," p. 264.

15. See also Ferrer, *Argentine Economy*, p. 53, and chap. 7 *passim*, for a discussion of this conflict.

laws and coercion were steadily relaxed after the 1852 "revolution," and immigrants provided a steady source of workers unfamiliar with the gaucho-style subsistence alternatives to wage labour. The immediate cause of the revolt against Rosas was his threat to go to war with Brazil and Paraguay in 1851, which would have frightened away foreign capital and soaked up workers. Most of Rosas' closest supporters abandoned him in favor of Urquiza.[16]

Creating the Conditions for Foreign Investment

Rosas' departure did not resolve differences between littoral and Buenos Aires producers on the key issues of investment and railroads, nor did it create a state capable of resolving or accommodating those tensions. Both areas fought to define the nature of the Argentine state and the terms on which Argentina entered world wool markets during the next decade; the littoral and interior provinces created the Republic of Argentina while Buenos Aires stood aloof.[17] The battles of Cepeda and Pavón set the terms for reunion, preserving considerable internal autonomy for Buenos Aires province while assuring Urquiza and the littoral of financial concessions. A fractured state resulted, with Buenos Aires province continuing to function as a state within a state while the central state represented and ruled over the rest of the country.[18] Beneath this fracture lay an economic reality

16. Burgin, *Economic Aspects of Argentine Federalism*, pp. 27–29, 266–268; Slatta, "Rural Criminality and Social Conflict," pp. 456–460; H. Ferns, *Argentina* (London: Benn, 1969), p. 92. Graziers also began fencing in the 1840s to lower the need for labour; C. Taylor, *Rural Life in Argentina* (Baton Rouge: Louisiana State University Press, 1948), p. 143. For a good general survey of the transition period from Rosas to Republic, see J. C. Brown, *Socio-economic History of Argentina, 1776–1860* (London: Cambridge University Press, 1979).

17. Both the Republic and Buenos Aires tried to buy British support, the former by granting steamship and railway concessions, the latter by resuming payments on the long-defaulted loan of 1824. The British government recognized the Republic in 1856. Despite British recognition, investors preferred to wait for Republican control of Buenos Aires' revenues; Ferns, *Britain and Argentina*, pp. 316–317. How the Argentine state was constituted in mid-century is a largely unstudied question. For the beginnings of an analysis, see F. Murphy, "State Formation in Argentina and the War of the Triple Alliance" (M.A. thesis, New School for Social Research, 1988).

18. Ferns, *Britain and Argentina*, p. 314, argues that Buenos Aires during the 1850s was about to begin autonomous growth, and that compromise with the Republic destroyed this chance. He points to the locally financed Ferrocarrile del Oeste (railway) as evidence of the ability to expand without foreign loans. See R. Scalabrini Ortiz, *Historia de los Ferrocarriles Argentinos* (Buenos Aires: Reconquista, 1940), for the *locus classicus* of arguments that self-finance was possible. Whatever the possibilities for autonomous growth, this ability to finance at least small-scale rail construction was what divided Buenos Aires merchants and perhaps graziers from the Republic.

that set the tone for future conflicts. The littoral and interior needed Buenos Aires revenue to prosper, but Buenos Aires was not so dependent. With the Provincial government supplying 30 percent of the capital, Buenos Aires investors in 1857 began constructing their own railway, the Oeste, into the heart of the sheep belt outside the port. Under Bartolomeo Mitré and his supporters, Buenos Aires agreed to subsidize railways for the interior, making possible a compromise with Urquiza. But without a strong state, this compromise was always in doubt.

Mitré's accession to the presidency thus cleared away the obstacles to foreign debt–financed expansion of the wool economy. As in New Zealand, the political prerequisite to the first big wave of borrowing was fiscal centralization. Mitré centralized the fisc, eliminating the provinces' internal tariffs by promising them subsidies and trying to stabilize the currency. These reforms were only partially successful, for the provinces, especially Buenos Aires, continued to issue money. Mitré also set the conditions under which railroads would be built. Unlike the self-financed Oeste, or the land grants proposed for the Central Railroad, Mitré encouraged private firms to build railroads with government profit guarantees on concessionaires' capital investment. Railroads were obliged to maximize their profit, but should they fall short of 7 percent, the state would make up the difference. Rail equipment was to be imported duty-free. Though the central state rarely owned railroads outright as in Australasia, it actively invested in them, controlling approximately 44 percent of the capital invested up to 1880.[19] To finance guarantee obligations and undertake other improvements, the National Government issued gold notes overseas. This first wave of borrowing lasted about twelve years, until the crisis of 1875. (See Table 27.) During this wave the British invested about £22.6 million in Argentina, with 56.2 percent placed in Government loans, 31.8 percent in railways and trams, 6.4 percent in banks, and 2.3 percent in factories producing Liebig's meat extract.[20] Because of its guarantees and its silent participation in railways, the

19. Ferns, *Britain and Argentina*, pp. 325–326; H. Peters, *Foreign Debt of the Argentine Republic* (Baltimore: Johns Hopkins University Press, 1934), pp. 25–26. See J. Williams, *Argentine Trade under Inconvertible Paper Money, 1880–1900* (New York: Greenwood Press, 1969), p. 87, for an extensive description of the guarantee system. See C. Lewis, "British Railway Companies and the Argentine Government," in D. C. M. Platt, ed., *Business Imperialism* (Oxford: Oxford University Press, 1977), pp. 412, 416, on Argentine holdings (which declined to 26 percent by 1890 and 14 percent by 1909).

20. I. Stone, "British Direct and Portfolio Investment in Latin America before 1914," *Journal of Economic History* 37 (September 1977), 706. Ferns, *Britain and Argentina*, p. 327, gives a value of £23.1 million.

Table 27. British holdings in Argentina by type, 1865–1913

Year	Public* (£ mil)	Private Portfolio (£ mil)	DFI (£ mil)	Total (£ mil)	Railroad length, kilometers
1865	2.2	—	0.5	2.7	246
1875	16.5	—	6.1	22.6	1,956
1885	26.7	—	19.3	46.0	4,502
1895	90.6	3.4	97.0	190.9	14,116
1905	101.0	2.2	150.4	253.6	19,794
1913	184.6	37.0	258.7	479.8	32,491

*Includes national, provincial, municipal, and cédula issues.

DFI = Direct Foreign Investment, primarily in railways. Great Britain accounted for approximately 90 percent of foreign investment in Argentina before 1900; 80 percent afterwards.

Source: Stone, "British Direct and Portfolio Investment," p. 706.

state was actually responsible for servicing roughly 80 percent of foreign investment, a level exceeding Antipodean state obligations.

Conflicts over the Cost and Level of Borrowing

The conflicts that emerged in Argentina during the first wave of borrowing replicated those in New Zealand, and set the pattern for later conflicts. Three things motivated conflicts among the Argentine elite: differing transportation needs for different products; differing timing of the need to get transport and improve herds; and differing needs for immigrant labour.[21] Like New Zealand estate owners, established Buenos Aires wool exporters wanted less borrowing, lower taxes, and mild inflation after borrowing had created the basic transportation infrastructure they needed. Their interests were expressed most vehemently by the *Autonomista* wing of the Liberal Party. Interior land speculators and potential producers wanted more borrowing, higher taxes, and currency stability to encourage expansion of the transportation network. Their interests were most often represented by the *Urquicista* Federalists. The second stage of conflict, after the wave of borrowing between 1880 and 1889, replicated this fight. Again, established export producers of wool and mutton wanted

21. See F. McLynn, "The Argentine Presidential Election of 1868," *Journal of Latin American Studies* 11 (November 1979); and McLynn "Political Instability in Córdoba Province during the Eighteen-sixties," *Ibero-Amerikanische Archiv* N.F. Jg. 6 (1980), for an analysis of these political struggles that unfortunately sees them as factional fights without making an effort to relate them to differences among producers.

lower taxes and rapid inflation. Wheat producers, who needed a much denser rail network, and cattlemen, who needed to improve the quality of their beef to enter food markets in the UK, opposed them. Because of Argentina's weak federalism, this largely turned into fights over inflation, not taxation.[22]

Until 1880, the wool-producing area of Argentina was the inner ring of the Buenos Aires pampas, about 75 to 100 miles from the port.[23] Wool required much less transport infrastructure than grains or meat, for its value in relation to its weight and bulk made it possible to transport it profitably on wagons or oxcart from 20 to 80 miles.[24] Until 1879, this was also roughly the outer limit of railroads and secure production in Buenos Aires province. From 1862 to 1874, the Mitré-Sarmiento regimes, brokering relations between Buenos Aires and the Interior through the *Nacionalista* wing of the Liberal Party, encouraged just enough foreign investment to provide railways for Buenos Aires province while placating the more important interior provinces. For example, the Buenos Aires–sponsored Oeste and the Southern, which opened up the wool pampas to the southwest and southeast, respectively, of Buenos Aires, expanded rapidly over profitable routes; the nationally-sponsored Central from Rosario to Córdoba put out extensive stretches of unprofitable rail through the littoral provinces. Buenos Aires grew rich as wool exports rose from 21 to 37 million pounds between 1850 and 1861, and then, stimulated by enlarged access to transport, jumped to 90 million pounds in 1864, 137 million pounds in 1870, and 179 million pounds in 1875, when they constituted 53 percent of export earnings (see table 28).[25]

22. These conflicts continued into the twentieth century, this time as the fight between cattle breeders and fatteners P. Smith describes in *Politics and Beef in Argentina: Patterns of Conflict* (New York: Columbia University Press, 1969). For another sectoral/geographical analysis of Argentine politics, see J. Tulchin, "Relations Between Labor and Capital in Rural Argentina, 1880–1914," in D. C. M. Platt and G. di Tella, eds., *Political Economy of Argentina* (London: MacMillan, 1986), and Tulchin, "El Credito Agrario en la Argentina, 1910–1929," *Desarrollo Económico* no. 71 (October 1978).

23. S. Hanson, *Argentine Meat and the British Market* (Stanford: Stanford University Press, 1938), p. 111.

24. J. Scobie, *Revolution on the Pampas: A Social History of Argentine Wheat, 1860–1910* (Austin: University of Texas Press, 1964), pp. 11–12.

25. On the Central Argentine Railway in general, see Goodwin, "Central Argentine Railway and the Economic Development of Argentina"; Scobie, *Argentina*, p. 119; Ferns, *Britain and Argentina*, p. 351. On wool, see H. Sabato, "The Wool Trade and Commercial Networks in Buenos Aires, 1840s-1880s," *Journal of Latin American Studies* 15 (May 1983) 51–52; Scobie, *Revolution on the Pampas*, p. 42; McLynn, "Economic Trends and Policies," p. 266; C. Diaz-Alejandro, *Essays on the Economic History of the Argentine Republic* (New Haven: Yale University Press, 1970), p. 5. McLynn, "Argentine Presidential Election of 1868," argues that Sarmiento deviated from the Mitré line. This

Table 28. Composition of Argentine exports, 1829–1904 (as percentage of export value)

	1829	1850	1875–79	1880–84	1890–94	1900–04
Wool	0.6	7.6	52.9	58.1	38.3	26.5
Mutton	—	—	—	—	2.5	3.8
Hides/skins	67.6	64.8	38.1	31.6	25.9	14.1
Jerked beef	6.3	7.9	8.2	5.1	4.8	1.1
Grains*	—	—	0.5	5.2	27.4	48.3
Beef**	—	—	—	—	0.5	4.4
Other***	1.3	10.5	—	—	0.6	1.8

*Wheat, corn, linseed.
**Chilled, frozen, canned.
***Tallow before 1880, then primarily *quebracho* products.
Sources: Cortés Conde, *First Stages of Modernization*, p. 123; Diaz-Alejandro, *Essays on the Economic History of the Argentine Republic*, p. 5. Lewis, *British Railways in Argentina*, has significantly different figures for the 1850–1870 period.

Meanwhile interior and littoral land owners wanted to cash in on wool, to bring new land into production of wheat, and to switch to production of beef from hides and jerky. Events in Santa Fe illustrate the primary motives for speculation and switching. Santa Fe had set up a large number of agricultural colonies in order to liquidate apparently valueless public lands. By 1872, forty-four colonies on 100,000 acres in Santa Fe were producing one quarter of Argentina's wheat, causing land values to skyrocket. Driven by internal demand as much as external, wheat lands expanded to 2.5 million acres by 1895. From one of the poorest provinces, Santa Fe rapidly became one of the richest, remaining the geographical center of the cereals belt through World War I.[26] To a lesser extent, Santa Fe's neighbors also participated in the shift to wheat; between them, Córdoba and Entre Rios grew more wheat than lusher Buenos Aires by the 1880s. Interior

---

is plausible regarding their policies towards the Paraguayan War, for the war prevented Mitré from fully making good his promises of federal financial support for the interior. Sarmiento's anti-war policy implied continued accommodation with the interior, whose electoral support he won.

26. The best single source is E. Gallo, *La Pampa Gringa: La Colonizacíon Agrícola en Santa Fe, 1870–1895* (Buenos Aires: Editorial Sudamerica, 1986). See also Republica Argentina, Comisión Directiva del Censo, *Segundo Censo Nacional* (Buenos Aires, 1898), vol. 3, pp. 36, 165 (hereafter Second Census); Scobie, *Revolution on the Pampas*, pp. 38, 42; Ferns, *Britain and Argentina*, p. 424; Diaz-Alejandro, *Essays on the Economic History of the Argentine Republic*, p. 37; R. Whitbeck, *Economic Geography of South America* (New York: McGraw Hill, 1926), p. 227; E. Gallo, *Farmers in Revolt* (London: Athlone Press, 1976), p. 5. Land values in the interior, while absolutely lower than in Buenos Aires, appreciated faster.

landowners observed the enormous profit and capital gains on land to be made by simply selling land to immigrant wheat farmers; then, by renting it out to them at its new capitalized value; and finally, when demand in Britain and technology combined to make meat exports possible, by the even greater profits in integrating wheat and cattle production. But making the transition from extensive harvesting of hides to each of these new commodities required considerable public and private investment.

Wheat needed a much more extensive network of rails than wool or mutton. The outer limit of profitable overland wheat transshipment to a railroad was fifteen to twenty miles, and the outer limit of profitable transportation to a port was between 125 and 175 miles.[27] Wheat in Santa Fe benefitted early from the Central Railway's Rosario-Córdoba line. But future expansion of wheat production, and valorization of speculative land purchases, required construction of a denser rail network. The later introduction of beef cattle reinforced this desire, since they could not be driven over extensive distances without losing significant amounts of weight. On an individual scale, cattle raisers needed capital to improve herds and estates. Liebig's extraction process for beef broth provided the first alternative to hides and jerked beef after a plant was set up in 1865. But where the scrawny native cattle raised for hides and jerked beef were adequate for Liebig's purposes, breaking into other English meat markets meant that ranchers had to find capital to raise crossbred animals and provide them with water and fences. The problem was how to get or attract the capital needed for this transformation.

The logical source of revenue—land sale receipts—was unavailable, for the interior provinces had begun a vast sell-off of public lands at cheap prices just as interior producers tried shifting production.[28] Though this partly helped interior producers by giving them land cheap, it also hampered their efforts. First, it meant that no ready source of provincial revenue was available for investment in social overhead, especially railways. At the same time, war with Paraguay and internal rebellions against the centralizing Mitré regime prevented Mitré from fully making good his promise of subsidies. The interior got little, aside from the irreducible political minimum, a

27. Hanson, *Argentine Meat in the British Market*, p. 119.
28. McLynn, "Economic Trends and Policies," pp. 261–266. Entre Rios and Córdoba had alienated all their land by 1885.

subsidy to the Central Railroad.[29] Without revenue, the interior required foreign investment to provide railroads, which Buenos Aires had not. Second, Buenos Aires graziers began buying land in the interior provinces to pasture their flocks, which, while destroying the old antagonism between provinces *qua* provinces, raised barriers to entry for inland producers.[30] The interior's greater need for stable currency and state-led investment triggered conflicts over taxes and inflation as the first wave of foreign investment petered out. In contrast with New Zealand, Buenos Aires producers may be regarded as "cautious" borrowers to the interior's "bold."

Taxes. Unlike New Zealand, where cautious borrowers dominated politics after the first borrowing wave, in Argentina, bold borrowers dominated. Nicholas Avellaneda's accession to the presidency in 1874 put a bold borrower in command just as Argentina's first fiscal crisis emerged. In 1874, declining prices for both wool and hide drove down customs revenues, forcing the government to abandon gold payments on its external obligations. Although the London investment house Baring Brothers tided the government over with a short term loan, foreign investment slowed down after 1874.[31] This left Avellaneda with only two methods to subsidize interior development—retrenchment to free revenue for investment or increased taxes on Buenos Aires wool exporters. After cutting public spending and employment one third, he raised the wool export tax from 4 percent to 6 percent in 1877, while lowering the export tax for Liebig's extract, which came from interior cattle. Tariffs on wheat, flour, wine and sugar protected interior growers. As Buenos Aires wool producers exported far more than interior producers, these taxes would have fallen disproportionately on them. Avellaneda also passed legislation encouraging smallholding settlement with free grants of 250 acres, in an unsuccessful effort to create a market for land. For their part, Buenos Aires graziers resisted right from the start interior efforts to expand at their expense. The 1874 economic

29. F. Murphy, "Wool, War, and the World Market: Argentina in the 1860s" (New School for Social Research, 1987), p. 15.

30. Gallo, *Farmers in Revolt*, pp. 14–15. See also Gallo, *Agricultural Expansion and Industrial Development in Argentina, 1880–1930* (Buenos Aires: Instituto Torcuato de Tella, 1970). The paper peso price of land remained relatively stable, enabling wool exporters to use their gold export receipts to envelop land.

31. Ferns, *Britain and Argentina*, pp. 379–381; Peters, *Foreign Debt of the Argentine Republic*, p. 32; see also Randall, *Comparative Economic History of Latin America*, pp. 89–96.

downturn prompted an unsuccessful revolt by Mitré against Avellaneda's election. Buenos Aires wool interests and their allies then resorted to the harassment of British investors in order to slow foreign investment. The late 1870s thus saw increasing opposition to and depredations of foreign capital invested in banks and railways. The London and River Plate Bank was legally relieved of its gold supply at one point; the Southern Railway Company was the object of calls for expropriation.[32] But Buenos Aires wool producers had an even greater weapon for controlling interior borrowers: inflation.

Differential Effects of Inflation. The intense debates over hard versus soft money in the 1860s illuminate this conflict at the same time that contemporary analyses tend to obscure it. Argentina had both paper and gold currency. Gold pesos (G$) exchanged at a fixed rate with convertible European currencies (5 G$ = 1 £); paper pesos (P$) exchanged at a fluctuating rate for gold pesos depending on the rate of inflation or deflation. Most analyses correctly argue that exporters deliberately caused inflation because it acted as an "export bonus."[33] Exporters paid most of their production costs in paper pesos, but received gold for their products. Land, wages and other inputs tended to have "sticky" paper prices, that is, their cost did not rise as fast as inflation, and exporters generally were debtors in paper currency. Inflation thus reduced their real debt burden, while allowing them to engage in arbitrage with their workers, buying ever-larger sums of the paper pesos used for wages with their gold-denominated export receipts. But the error many analyses make is that they assimilate all landowning and producing classes with exporters to explain the origins of inflation; in fact, inflation *hurt* certain landowners and producers, provoking political fights over currency.

Inflation penalized producers of grain and beef because until the late 1880s and late 1890s, respectively, they largely sold most of their production in domestic markets, receiving paper currency. Mutton

32. B. Garcia-Holgado, *De Mitré A Roca: Politica, Sociedad y Economia 1860–1904* (Buenos Aires, Editorial el Coloquia, n.d.), p. 43; D. Guy, "Carlos Pellegrini and the Politics of Early Argentine Industrialization," *Journal of Latin American Studies* 11 (May 1979), 127 and *passim*; Scobie, *Argentina*, p. 121; P. Snow, *Argentine Radicalism* (Iowa City: University of Iowa Press, 1965), pp. 4–5; D. Rock, *Argentina, 1516–1982* (Berkeley: University of California Press, 1985), p. 131; Ferns, *Britain and Argentina,* pp. 380–386.

33. See Williams, *Argentine Trade under Inconvertible Paper Money,* pp. 174, 200; and A. Ford, *The Gold Standard, 1880–1914: Britain and Argentina* (Oxford: Clarendon Press, 1962), p. 91, for classic accounts. McLynn, "Economic Policy and Trends," p. 272, notes that sheep raisers were hurt by war-enforced deflations in the late 1860s. Ferns, *Britain and Argentina,* p. 440, also makes the "export bonus" argument for inflation.

and wool producers were the most vertically integrated producers, frequently controlling even their own freezing works.[34] They primarily used local labour, and they were located relatively closer to ports, and so used the rails relatively less than interior producers. For them, inflation was an export bonus. All but their transport costs could be paid in paper, and so rose less than the paper value of their gold receipts. But this was not true for beef and wheat producers. Inflation made it harder for them to import capital goods and to buy land. They used substantial amounts of imported labor and had higher transport costs, for their products were both bulky and distant from ports of exit. The rails passed on the costs of inflation by pegging their rates to the gold premium, and in turn bought labour peace with gold-linked wages.[35] Wheat, financially more significant than beef from 1870 to 1900, required substantial numbers of migrant Italian harvesters (*golondrinas*). They had to be paid gold-linked wages, as they only migrated because of the huge wage differential between Argentina and home; both home wages and transoceanic fares were in convertible currency.[36] Far from an "export bonus," wheat-beef producers probably paid an "import penalty."

Inflation also made it more difficult for the central state to finance the railroads that wheat and beef producers as a group needed. As in New Zealand, the central state only captured control of land revenues after the provinces had alienated the bulk of land, leaving customs as the main source of revenue. But the government collected customs in paper pesos, while paying its overseas obligations in gold. Inflation thus created a fiscal "price scissors" for the state, as it needed more and more paper pesos to buy the gold pesos it used for debt service. In turn, this made subsidized extensions of the railroads into the interior less likely. Finally, inflation and fiscal crisis made foreigners unwilling to invest money in Argentina. Though Avellaneda managed to stumble out of his crisis, the unraveling of Argentine finances during the 1880s demonstrates these processes in full flower.

Stumbling Out of the Crisis. Unable to attract foreign capital, Avellaneda sponsored a series of anti-Indian campaigns by General Julio Roca in 1878–79 to expand the amount of land available to interior producers in southern Buenos Aires and northwest Santa Fe. With

34. R. Gravil, *The Anglo-Argentine Connection, 1900–1939* (Boulder Colo.: Westview Press, 1985), pp. 72–76; J. Crossley and C. Greenhill, "River Plate Beef Trade," in Platt, *Business Imperialism*, p. 291.

35. Lewis, "British Railway Companies and the Argentine Government," p. 409.

36. Scobie, *Revolution on the Pampas*, pp. 60–61.

Avellaneda's blessing, Roca granted huge tracts of newly conquered land to provincial graziers and *arrivistes*. These grants effectively doubled the land area open to grazing or cultivation before 1900, adding 25 million arable acres that later constituted the heart of the wheat and beef cattle area.[37] New landowners—potential wheat ranchers and cattlemen—saw Roca as the logical successor to Avellaneda, whose term ran out in 1880. Buenos Aires wool producers put up Governor Tejador, Mitré's protégé, as their choice. The Mitristas felt that Roca had overly favored interior provincials in his land distributions, even those in the newly secured southern Buenos Aires province. Roca had spent six years organizing allies in the interior into the Partido Autonomista Nacional, and his regular soldiers triumphed over the hastily organized Buenos Aires militia. He sealed his triumph by having the central state absorb Buenos Aires province's foreign debt.[38]

REESTABLISHING THE PRECONDITIONS FOR FOREIGN INVESTMENT

With Roca's presidency, a new wave of borrowing began as declining world market prices—35 percent in 1880–82—caused the interests of both sets of producers to converge.[39] By the late 1870s, wool producers again needed to borrow to intensify wool production so as to compete with Australia, and to begin mutton production. Expanded production and decreasing internal transport costs—the first railroads—had helped to offset falling wool prices, and maintained Argentina as a credible threat to Australia's dominance of wool markets. But falling prices motivated wool growers to seek higher-value-added products, mostly by producing mutton in addition to wool. Wool production tapered off through the 1880s as mutton production increased.[40] In the interior, falling wool prices stole the fruits of victory from those contemplating switching to wool. Instead, follow-

37. Scobie, *Revolution on the Pampas*, pp. 117–118. Nominally, investors bought bonds to finance the campaign; the bonds were then redeemed for land at a real cost of about two pence per acre. Whitbeck, *Economic Geography of South America*, p. 244. Bahía Blanca in southern Buenos Aires became a major wheat export port in the 1900s. For comparison, France had 11 million cultivated acres in 1892.

38. Gallo, *Farmers in Revolt*, pp. 24–25; Snow, *Argentine Radicalism*, p. 5; Ferns, *Britain and Argentina*, pp. 388–392; Williams, *Argentine Trade under Inconvertible Paper Money*, pp. 34–37; Randall, *Economic History of Latin America*, vol. II, p. 99.

39. Randall, *Economic History of Latin America*, vol. II, p. 99.

40. Goodwin, "Central Argentine Railway," pp. 618, 622; Ferns, *Britain and Argentina*, pp. 393, 407; Sabato, "Wool Trade and Commercial Networks in Buenos Aires," pp. 51–52.

ing the example set in Santa Fe, they intensified their efforts to induce wheat-growing colonies; their transition to beef production would not really get underway until the late 1880s. As late as 1887, 48 percent of meat exports were still salted beef.[41] Both sets of producers thus desired more foreign investment at the same time, for, as Randall notes: "Adoption of fencing . . . depended on the proximity of the railroads: only where cheap transport was available would the cost of the improved product that fencing made possible be compensated for by a sufficient increase in net return."[42] Because the Banco de la Provincia de Buenos Aires remained closed from 1881 to 1883 after its battle with the Banco Nacional, Buenos Aires borrowers had an additional incentive to borrow abroad.

Bolstered by this convergence of wheat and wool interests behind renewed borrowing, Roca moved decisively to establish currency convertibility, restore public credit and renew railroad investment. Roca and his Finance Minister Romero pegged paper money to gold, eliminated provincial currencies, and forced a conversion to gold-backed money by 1883. To control emission of unbacked paper money, only the Banco Nacional and four other semipublic banks were permitted to issue notes. By 1883, paper freely exchanged for gold at par. No new "paper" issues occurred until December 1886, and the gold premium remained stable. Fully convertible pesos assured foreign railway investors of stable and repatriable receipts, and bondholders of regular coupon redemption, spurring investment in Argentine public notes and guaranteed railroads at roughly three times the rate of the 1860s and 1870s.[43] Foreigners invested as much in 1883–84, after convertibility was established, as they had in 1865–73. During Roca's term, foreigners invested £16 million in public issues, £8 million in railroads and/or private ventures. (See Table 29.) Roca doubled Argentina's railroad system to nearly 5,000 miles, allowing a rapid expansion of wheat farming; between 1880 and 1885, cereals' share of exports jumped from 0.9 percent to 11.9 percemt, even as total exports grew 35 percent.[44]

41. Scobie, *Argentina*, p. 120; J. Fogarty, "Staples, Super-Staples, and the Limits of Staple Theory: Argentina, Australia, and Canada Compared," in D. C. M. Platt and G. di Tella, eds., *Argentina, Australia and Canada: Studies in Comparative Development, 1870–1965* (New York: St. Martin's Press, 1985), p. 26.
42. Randall, *Economic History of Latin America*, vol. II, p. 100.
43. Williams, *Argentine Trade under Inconvertible Paper Money*, p. 45.
44. R. Cortés-Conde, "Trends of Real Wages in Argentina, 1880–1930," Centre for Latin American Studies Working Paper no. 26 (Cambridge University, 1976), p. 11; Peters, *Foreign Debt of the Argentine Republic*, p. 35; I. Stone, "British investment in Argentina," *Journal of Economic History*, 32 (1972), 546; Randall, *Economic History of Latin*

Table 29. Foreign investment in Argentina under Roca, 1881–1886 (millions of G$ except column 5)

Year	(1) New debt (flow)	(2) Service	(3) Balance of payments on trade	(4) Net inflow 1-(2-3)	(5) Service as % exports
1881	14.9	12.0	2.2	4.3	21%
1882	25.3	15.7	−0.9	8.7	26
1883	47.4	19.5	−20.2	7.8	33
1884	39.7	27.6	−26.0	−13.9	41
1885	38.7	22.6	−8.3	7.8	27
1886	67.6	26.8	−25.6	15.2	39

SOURCES: Williams, *Argentine Trade under Inconvertible Paper Money,* pp. 45–47, 93–94, 100–101, 104; Ford, *The Gold Standard,* p. 195.

Buenos Aires producers of wool and mutton preferred cash in hand to finance breeding for mutton rather than wool, water tanks and fences, and freezing works. Rather than borrowing publicly for railroads, they sought foreign capital by issuing state-backed paper peso–denominated mortgage bonds called *cédula.* One of the national or provincial mortgage banks would give the landowner *cédula* of face value up to half the value of the land the owner mortgaged to the bank. The owner sold the *cédula* on the open market to realize their value, preferably in gold or another convertible currency. The proceeds of this sale were invested in fencing (imports of wire quadrupled 1880–86 vs. 1875–80), improved pasturage, new land, and the like.[45] The state banks paid a fixed amount of interest in paper pesos on the *cédula,* so the buyer of the *cédula* essentially was buying a paper denominated bond; *cédula* interest rates thus were significantly higher than other bonds in order to attract foreign investors.[46] A landowner could offer the mortgagee bank either convertible currency or *cédula* to retire the mortgage. The value of the stream of paper pesos a *cédula* created determined its market "value" so a given *cédula*'s value depreciated with the paper peso. With inflation, exporters could eventually buy back devalued *cédula* on the open market, repay the issuing bank, and reap huge capital gains. The Banco Hipotecario de la Provincia de Buenos Aires first issued *cédula* in 1872; before 1875 very few *cédula* were issued, and even fewer found their way

---

America, vol. II, p. 100. Roca also tripled the Department of Agriculture's budget; Randall, p. 103.

45. Randall, *Economic History of Latin America,* vol. II, p. 100.
46. Williams, *Argentine Trade under Inconvertible Paper Money,* pp. 75, 79.

Table 30. Cédula issues and debt service, Argentina, 1872–1890

Year	Nominal cédula sales (P$ '000s)	Cédula foreign sales (G$ '000s)	Debt service on foreign sales (G$ '000s)
1872 to 1886	$ 49,745	na	na
1887	94,679	$54,138	$ 5,492
1888	93,618	46,621	9,498
1889	153,894	55,885	10,981
1890	59,987	13,975	12,716

SOURCE: Williams, *Argentine Trade under Inconvertible Paper Money*, pp. 84–86.

overseas. 1886 saw formation of the Banco Hipotecario Nacional, inaugurating *cédula*'s entry into the formal London bond market with a virtual explosion of issues (see Table 30).[47] Between 1875 and 1886, P$ 76.5 million *cédula* were issued. The first issues had relatively high par values—90 and 84–but later issues, primarily originating from interior provincial banks, started at 81. From 1887 to the Baring Crash, the Banco Nacional issued P$ 81.7 million *cédula*; provincial banks, led by Buenos Aires, issued another P$ 230–270 million.[48]

This surge in investment culminated in a mini-crisis late in 1884, partly as a consequence of the earlier battle between the Banco Nacional and Banco de la Provincia de Buenos Aires. 1884 Argentina ran its first overall balance of payments deficit since the 1874–76 crisis. While borrowing still exceeded service, exports dropped because of faltering British demand and poor weather. The demand for gold to finance the import overhang forced the weakened Banco de la Provincia de Buenos Aires to suspend free conversion; seven months later, the Banco Nacional had to do so as well. Despite Roca's pledge to restore convertibility within two years, paper pesos were not convertible until 1899. Carlos Pellegrini, Finance Minister under Avellaneda, was sent on an emergency patch-up mission to London. As buyers distrusted Argentina's ability to service its loans, he had to

47. Ferns, *Britain and Argentina*, pp. 370–371; Williams, *Argentine Trade under Inconvertible Paper Money*, pp. 84–85; C. Jones, "British Investors and London Press Coverage of Argentine Affairs, 1870–1890," Centre for Latin American Studies Working Paper no. 2 (Cambridge University, 1976), p. 14.

48. Peters, *Foreign Debt of the Argentine Republic*, p. 45; Williams, *Argentine Trade under Inconvertible Paper Money*, pp. 81–84. Another G$ 20 million and 5 million were issued by the Banco Nacional and provincial banks, respectively. Being gold-denominated, they were not subject to inflationary depreciation, and so will be excluded from this discussion.

give bankers a first mortgage on Argentine customs receipts to float a
G\$ 42 million loan.[49] Pellegrini's success in 1886 restored the condi-
tions for continued borrowing. At this point, however, Roca passed
on the presidency to his son-in-law, Juárez Celman.

The Undoing of Convertibility

Juárez Celman's efforts to continue Roca's work came undone in
two ways. First, his efforts to make good on Roca's pledge to restore
convertibility actually led to rapid depreciation. Second, his efforts to
secure foreign capital at all costs were incompatible with short-term
solvency. To keep Roca's promise of convertibility and thus to continue foreign investment, Celman promulgated the Law of the Guaranteed Banks in 1887.[50] Any bank could issue paper notes if it arranged for a gold reserve to back those notes. The Banco Nacional
gave these banks treasury notes paying 4.5 percent interest, which the
banks sold abroad to get gold. This gold was to be deposited in the
Banco Nacional to provide a specie backing for the Guaranteed
Banks' paper emissions, which could not exceed their gold deposit. In
principle this ought to have led to a perfectly stable paper currency;
in practice the value of paper notes rapidly depreciated. Under Roca,
the limited number of note-issuing banks were tightly supervised by a
national government committed to convertibility and with a sufficiently powerful president to enforce discipline. Under the considerably weaker Celman, banks were essentially self-regulating, for no one
checked up on their note issues. Celman's law restored Buenos Aires'
ability to print money, as each province formed its own bank under
the new law, and the landowners on the boards of those banks issued
paper to suit their own needs without reference to either their bank's
reserves or debtors' creditworthiness. Most banks issued paper pesos
without reference to their specie deposits at the Banco Nacional; only
40 percent of the gold purchased with the treasury notes was actually
delivered to the Banco anyway.[51] The premium on gold—the number of extra paper pesos needed to purchase G\$ 100—rose from 35 in

49. Peters, *Foreign Debt of the Argentine Republic*, pp. 38–39, 40–41; Ferns, *Britain and Argentina*, pp. 402–403. The loan equalled about £8.3 million.
50. Williams, *Argentine Trade under Inconvertible Paper Money* chap. 5, is the best treatment of this. See also J. Hodge, "Carlos Pellegrini and the Financial Crisis of 1890," *Hispanic American Historical Review* 50 (August 1970), *passim*. These banks functioned like the "Free Banks" of the American Jacksonian Era.
51. Randall, *Economic History of Latin America*, vol. II, p. 111.

1887 to 91 in 1889, before jumping to an average of 151 in 1890.[52] The premium's rise was one third higher than actual paper emissions, indicating rapid erosion of confidence in convertibility. Internally, a prisoner's dilemma situation forced the producers controlling each bank to print money so that they could reap maximum benefits before everyone else's lack of discipline caused a crash.

Second, Juárez Celman represented the interests of the least-capitalized and most speculation-minded of the littoral and interior landlords. Their prosperity depended on a massive increase in borrowing. If a decision were made to halt borrowing or investment on "economic" grounds, they would be unable to reap speculative gains either by selling to new entrepreneurs or by shifting their own production profiles. Celman aimed to maximize the benefits from foreign capital for his clientele before the state became insolvent.[53] And that is precisely what happened. Building at three times Roca's rate of expansion, Celman nearly doubled the rail net, pushing track into areas ahead of demand.[54] (See Table 31.)

Inflation, overborrowing and rail subsidies combined for the third time to bankrupt the national government, and once more Buenos Aires banks led the way to unconvertibility.[55] As before, inflation destroyed the central government's ability to collect enough revenue to meet its gold obligations; the state used more and more of its customs revenue to buy less and less of the gold it needed to remit abroad. From 1885 to 1889, real service payments doubled, but the state needed roughly quadruple the number of paper pesos it had needed in 1885, for P$ 191 bought only G$ 100. Revenues, however, had barely doubled in paper terms, and only 3 percent of revenues

52. Williams, *Argentine Trade under Inconvertible Paper Money*, p. 111. The amount of paper money in circulation went from P$ 94 million in 1887 to P$ 245 million in 1890; Hodge, "Carlos Pellegrini and the Financial Crisis of 1890," p. 500.

53. T. Duncan, "La Politica Fiscal Durante el Gobierno de Juárez Celman, 1886–1890. Un Audaz Estrategia Financiera Internacional," *Desarrollo Económico* 23 (April 1983), argues that Celman deliberately courted national bankruptcy, believing that the debtor should get maximum benefit of loans. This is plausible, but it is equally plausible that Celman realized that with Argentina's weak federal and fiscal structure, bankruptcy was inevitable, and thus that as much capital should be brought over as possible before things collapsed.

54. Ford, *The Gold Standard, 1880–1914*, p. 195; A. Ford, "British Investment in Argentina and Long Swings, 1808–1941," *Journal of Economic History* 31 (September 1971), 660.

55. Hodge, "Carlos Pellegrini and the Financial Crisis of 1890," p. 502. Buenos Aires' *cédula* bank alone defaulted £5 million in 1891; Williams, *Argentine Trade under Inconvertible Paper Money*, p. 93.

Table 31. Foreign investment in Argentina under Juárez Celman
(millions of G$ except column 5)

Year	(1) New debt (flow)	(2) Service	(3) Balance of payments on trade	(4) Net flow**	(5) Service as % of exports
1887	153.5	37.3	−32.9	83.3	44
1888	242.8	49.5	−28.3	167.0	50
1889	153.6	59.8	−74.4	19.4	66
1890	45.4	60.2	−41.4	−56.3	60
1891	8.2	31.6*	−36.0	12.7	31

* = service decreased in 1891 because of default.
**Net flow = New debt less service less BOP on trade.
SOURCES: Williams, *Argentine Trade under Inconvertible Paper Money*, pp. 45–47, 93–94, 100–101, 104; Ford, *The Gold Standard*, p. 195.

were in gold. By 1890, the national government had a deficit of P$ 36 million.[56] As the gold premium rose, foreigners cut back lending, making it impossible for the state to roll over old loans. As the cost of buying gold increased, so did the state's gold obligations. From 1886 to 1889, unprofitable railroad extensions raised guarantee payments tenfold, from G$ 384,000 to G$ 3,738,000. In 1890 they would have hit G$ 4.5 million had the state not defaulted. Despite increases in the area cultivated (22 percent in 1888–90 alone) the rails' rate of profit fell from 5.05 percent to 2.63 percent, increasing the gap between their actual rate of return and the state-guaranteed rate.[57] The national government also owed G$ 4 million per year on the gold notes backing the Guaranteed Banks, but lacked the gold that sale of these notes had raised. All told, the central government was responsible for nearly £100 million of *cédula*, national and provincial debt.[58] (See Table 32.) Unlike 1874, Baring Brothers was unable to bail out Argentina, and the customs had already been mortgaged. In July 1890 "Argentina"—the Banco de la Provincia de Buenos Aires—defaulted; in November 1890 Baring Brothers, holding roughly £1.5 million in unsalable Argentine notes, went into receivership.

56. Peters, *Foreign Debt of the Argentine Republic*, p. 35. Williams, *Argentine Trade under Inconvertible Paper Money*, p. 118. The deficit equalled about £3 million.

57. Williams, *Argentine Trade under Inconvertible Paper Money*, pp. 91, 94; Ferns, *Britain and Argentina*, p. 444; Hodge, "Carlos Pellegrini and the Financial Crisis of 1890," p. 511; Cortés-Conde, *First Stages of Modernization in Spanish America*, p. 130. In the event, default lowered payments to G$ 2.9 million.

58. Hodge, "Carlos Pellegrini and the Financial Crisis of 1890," pp. 504, 512.

Table 32. Argentina's public debt and debt service in the late 1880s

Year	New debt (national, provincial, municipal) (G$ mil.)	Service including RR guarantees (G$ mil.)	Net inflow (G$ mil.)	Gold premium
1886	41.6	19.9	21.8	39
1887	46.5	22.3	24.2	35
1888	91.8	25.1	66.7	48
1889	30.8	30.5	0.3	91
1890	0	28.2*	−28.2	151

*Decline occurred from default.
SOURCE: Williams, *Argentine Trade under Inconvertible Paper Money*, p. 100.

RESOLVING THE CRISIS OF 1890

Argentine producers had an option that made internal political resolution of the crisis relatively easy, compared to Australia and New Zealand: a managed default. The difficulty of public defaults left Australian capitals to try to put the cost of debt service on each other. In contrast, Argentine producers united to pass the cost onto foreign lenders by decreasing service without actually repudiating public loans. What then took time was renewing foreign lenders' confidence in Argentine state finance. Following an abortive coup by the Unión Cívica, representing middle class elements in Buenos Aires hurt by inflation, Roca replaced Juárez Celman—who was threatening repudiation—with his agent Carlos Pellegrini. Repudiation would have been a disaster. Land values had fallen 50 percent from 1889 to 1890, trapping much speculative capital, and producers of wheat and beef in the littoral and southern Buenos Aires province had barely begun to breed cattle for meat, not hides (see Table 33 and 34).[59] Pellegrini himself was "utterly opposed to debt repudiation."[60] Once more, representatives of the littoral wheat-beef complex needed to put things aright, to assure the investment they needed to finish their transition.

First Pellegrini and then Roca's ex-Finance Minister, Romero embarked on a program comprised of bridging loans and another round

59. D. Rock, *Argentina, 1516–1987* (Berkeley: University of California Press, 1987), p. 159.
60. Quotation from Gravil, *Anglo-Argentine Connection*, p. 24. See also Hodge, "Carlos Pellegrini and the Financial Crisis of 1890," p. 504. On the Unión Cívica Radical, see Snow, *Argentine Radicalism*, and D. Rock, *Politics in Argentina, 1890–1930* (Cambridge: Cambridge University Press, 1975).

Table 33. Geographic distribution of Argentine production, 1895 and 1908

	Percentage of total in 1895			Percentage of total in 1908		
	Sheep (head)	Wheat (acres)	Cattle (head)	Sheep (head)	Wheat (acres)	Cattle (head)
Buenos Aires	70.8%	17.9%	38.9%	61.5%	40.1%	35.6%
Santa Fe	2.7	50.3	14.0	1.4	24.1	11.7
Entre Rios	8.3	14.2	11.6	10.4	5.0	10.8
Córdoba	3.5	14.3	9.5	3.0	26.0	9.1
Corrientes	1.9	—	14.5	4.7	—	14.7
Subtotal littoral	16.4	78.8	49.6	19.5	55.1	46.3
Rest of Argentina	12.8	3.2	11.5	18.1	4.8	21.8
Total	100.0	100.0	100.0	100.0	100.0	100.0

of currency and fiscal reform. This program was implemented in two stages, first in 1890–91, then in 1893. In 1891, Pellegrini pledged to withdraw P$ 45 million from circulation so as to obtain a £12–15 million bridging loan from a consortium centering on the Rothschild's bank and backed by the Bank of England. Rothschilds felt that Argentine exports would eventually catch up with the costs of debt; the Bank of England had a pressing desire to keep Baring Brothers (and thus all of British haute finance) afloat by allowing it to liquidate unsold Argentine holdings. The £15 million allowed Argentina to

Table 34. Ratio of crossbred to native animals by region in Argentina, 1895–1908 (the larger the number, the more complete the transition)

	Sheep		Cattle	
	1895	1908	1895	1908
Buenos Aires	5.0	43.5	1.0	9.8
Santa Fe	1.3	1.9	0.2	0.7
Entre Rios	2.3	6.3	0.2	1.4
Córdoba	0.5	6.7	0.1	0.2
Corrientes	2.2	0.9	0.02	1.0

SOURCES: Second Census, pp. 165, 190–191, 200, 224; Argentine Republic, Comisión del Censo Agropecuario, *Agricultural and Pastoral Census of the Nation,* Buenos Aires 1909, vol. I, pp. 134–139, vol. II, pp. 1–30.

service its debt, thus keeping its notes marketable.[61] Coupons from the bridging loan were to be accepted in lieu of both import and export customs duties.

Pellegrini retrenched, cancelling a P$ 100 million *cédula* sale scheduled by Celman and substituting a largely unsuccessful P$ 100 million forced loan. More important, he radically changed the tax system, making customs, including export taxes, 100 percent payable in gold. He imposed direct taxes on capital, obliging joint stock companies to yield 7 percent of their revenues, banks 10 percent. These taxes largely fell on foreign firms, which were more likely to be incorporated. The working class was hit by major increases in alcohol and tobacco taxes.[62] To control inflation, Pellegrini liquidated the Banco Nacional and forced banks to publicize their (typically inaccurate) records. A 2 percent tax on deposits in non-guarantee banks also served to redirect funds to the guaranteed ones, in hopes this would firm up the ratio of specie to paper.

Who Paid?

Pellegrini reduced Argentina's real debt service from £14 million (G$ 70 million) to about £3.5 million (G$ 17.5 million), in a managed default that avoided permanently closing Europe's banks to Argentina. The bridging loan accounted for much of this reduction. Pellegrini's actions confirmed the possibility of continued investment, averting both repudiation and hyper-inflation. Producers of wheat and beef could then make common cause with older landlords against the more radical of their erstwhile allies in the Unión Cívica Radical. The problem then became one of shifting as much of the burden as possible onto the foreigners until the market restored land and export values.

The *Arreglo Romero* (Romero's deal) of July 1893 confirmed that Argentina's foreign public creditors would bear the brunt of Argentina's difficulties. Baring Brothers was freed of its obligation to pay

61. Hodge, "Carlos Pellegrini and the Financial Crisis of 1890," pp. 507–508.
62. Hodge, "Carlos Pellegrini and the Financial Crisis of 1890," pp. 508, 511–513; Ferns, *Britain and Argentina*, pp. 456–457, 462; Guy, "Carlos Pellegrini and the Politics of Early Argentine Industrialization," *passim*. As with the forced loan, gold payment for customs took some time to enforce. The incidence of taxes on capital may not have fallen as heavily on foreigners as it might appear, however, for many Argentine firms incorporated themselves in London for legal reasons; see D. Guy, "La Industria Argentina, 1870–1940: Legislacion Comercial, Mercado de Acciones y Capitalizacion Extranjera," *Desarrollo Económico* 22 (February 1982).

the Argentines for the unsold notes it held, but the Argentines got a five-year reduction of interest payments to a level approximating 30 percent of contracted values and a moratorium on amortization payments until 1901. Such interest as was paid went directly to the Bank of England for redistribution to British shareholders. In 1896 all railroad guarantees were converted into G$ 50 million face value of 4 percent bonds, immediately halving guarantee payments. The central government resumed provincial bonds, exchanging them for its own notes at significant discounts, and, occasionally, without payment of defaulted interest. Finally in 1899 the paper peso was permanently fixed at 0.44 gold pesos (i.e., P$ 2.27 to G$ 1).[63]

That Argentina had greater power with its creditors than the Antipodean colonies did arose from its sovereignty and from creditor disunity. No Governor General could dismiss an Argentine government the Bank of England found unfavorable, as happened in New South Wales in 1931. Despite British preeminence, other European nations held at least one-fifth of Argentine debt. Unlike the Antipodes, whose London issues typically were monopolized by one banking house, Argentina typically floated its loans through consortia. Argentina thus could play off creditor governments and direct creditors against one another. In negotiations, Argentina dealt with railroad firms individually, rather than through their "Railway Committee."[64] Fear of a domestic financial collapse pushed British lenders of last resort to support Argentina directly in hopes of supporting Barings indirectly. But, as Charles Jones observes, Argentine leverage only allowed it to push lenders into various forms of refinance, not into sending new capital.[65]

Private creditors, lacking even the limited leverage that public creditors had, lost more. Henry Ferns sums it up: "The money invested in *cédulas* was substantially lost."[66] No *Crédit Foncier* schemes were proposed to rescue the capital investors had sunk into Argentine mort-

63. Ferns, *Britain and Argentina*, p. 473, 476, 479; Hodge, "Carlos Pellegrini and the Financial Crisis of 1890," p. 511.

64. A. Ford, "British Investment in Argentine Economic Development," in D. Rock, ed., *Argentina in the 20th Century* (London: Duckworth, 1975), p. 16; C. Jones, "European Bankers and Argentina 1880–1890," Centre for Latin American Studies Working Paper no. 3 (Cambridge University, n.d.), p. 1; Lewis, "British Railway Companies and the Argentine Government," pp. 401–402.

65. Jones, "European Bankers and Argentina," pp. 10–12.

66. Ferns, *Britain and Argentina*, p. 425; the loss was not necessarily experienced by the original purchaser of the *cédula*, who may have resold it in the market before inflation picked up.

gages via *cédula*. The falling price/falling profit dynamics of the 1880s led to the engrossment and foreclosure of Australian graziers, but in contrast Buenos Aires graziers were able to use inflation to void the claims of commercial capital and the land companies. Argentine land-owners continued to control both production and profits while foreign capital bore the cost of the profit crunch. Some of the foreign-owned banks that invested in land were liquidated.[67] Thus in Argentina there was no internal crisis of private capital corresponding to that in the Antipodes. Rather there was an external crisis with thousands of foreign *cédula* holders holding devalued claims. In 1900 some P\$ 150 million of cédula were quoted as low as 9 percent of face value.[68]

What about workers? Unlike the Antipodes, where virtually all classes were squeezed to meet public debt service, Argentine workers bore a relatively smaller part of the cost because it was Argentina's foreign creditors who largely lost. Clearly the workers' tax burden increased, as direct taxes on alcohol and tobacco that garnered 3 percent of revenues in 1891 contributed 17 percent by 1908, even while export taxes were steadily reduced.[69] But regarding real wage trends there is some controversy. The traditional argument claims that inflation led to falling real wages, implying that workers paid a considerable burden. But in a revisionist account, Cortés Conde argues that real wages rose from 1885 to 1913; a slight reverse in 1893–96 merely slowed immigration.[70] It was probably urban middle-class groups, consumers of significant amounts of imported goods whose prices were linked to gold, that felt increased inflation as declining real wages. The Unión Cívica revolt of July 1890, and the later free-trade orientation of urban political parties and labour groups, suggest that this is correct. Wage workers, who consumed domestically-produced goods with stable paper prices, probably did well in the labour-short economy. In contrast to southeast Australia's unemployment during this period, there was a "constant demand for workers," according to James Scobie.[71]

67. Ferns, *Britain and Argentina*, p. 481; Gallo, *La Pampa Gringa*, pp. 174–177, 238–241.

68. Williams, *Argentine Trade under Inconvertible Paper Money*, p. 122.

69. A. Martinez and M. Lewandowski, *The Argentine in the Twentieth Century* (Boston: Maynard Small, 1913), pp. 306–307.

70. Williams, *Argentine Trade*, is the *locus classicus* of the traditional view; Cortés Conde, "Trends of Real Wages in Argentina, 1880–1910."

71. Scobie, *Argentina*, p. 132.

POLITICAL, DEVELOPMENT, AND DEPENDENCY CONSEQUENCES

Politically, resolution of the Baring crisis only confirmed the predominant power of landowners; unlike Australia and New Zealand, foreign creditors were unable to promote any subaltern groups to counter the power of local producers. Although the crisis exacerbated conflicts among Argentine producers, in the long term it created the prerequisite conditions for a more complete unity. First, the temporary reduction of service payments and consequently of export taxes permitted wheat-beef producers finally to catch up with wool-mutton producers. As a typical history revealingly notes: "Agricultural development during Pellegrini's presidency was the most favorable since that of Avellaneda."[72] By 1900 no farm within 175 miles of Buenos Aires was more than ten miles from a railroad station.[73] Cattle producers largely completed the transition to production of high quality beef. Second, the interests of all producers grew together as interior stockraisers began supplying animals to Buenos Aires fatteners, and Buenos Aires producers integrated stockraising and cereals production. "The real development of agriculture in the province of Buenos Ayres dates only from 1895. Until then it was considered merely as a country especially adapted for stockraising," wrote two local businessmen in 1913. "It was believed agriculture was out of the question."[74] By 1908 the differences in capitalization and quality imperfectly observed in Tables 33 and 34 had partially disappeared, though regions remained committed to different products.[75] Landowners' unity permitted them to remain firmly in control of politics, using the tried and true methods of voting fraud, exclusion of non-citizens, and intimidation to control elections. The Unión Cívica Radical stagnated after 1891; the new Socialist Party, representing the urban free professions and the petit bourgeoisie, stayed small. Although the 1890s and 1900s saw many increasingly violent general strikes, the army put these down. With the salient exception of Santa Fe, few rural strikes occurred, nor were there many New Zealand style "outrages."[76] Unlike Australian shearers, fully proletarianized workers such as the *golon-*

72. Garcia-Holgado, *De Mitré a Roca*, p. 166. My translation.
73. Hanson, *Argentine Meat and the British Market*, p. 119; Gallo, *La Pampa Gringa*, pp. 233–236.
74. Martinez and Lewandowski, *The Argentine in the Twentieth Century* p. 142.
75. See Tulchin, "El Credito Agrario en la Argentina, 1910–1926," for a good statement of continuing economic differences; see Smith, *Politics and Beef in Argentina*, for an analysis of conflicts between cattle breeders and fatteners; its very title discloses the end of the old pattern of conflict.
76. See Gallo, *La Pampa Gringa*, chap. 9, and Gallo, *Farmers in Revolt, passim*.

drinas had no stake in agitation in Argentina, for they desired only to accumulate enough to buy land at home. Unlike New Zealand's semi-proletarianized agricultural workforce, Argentine tenant farmers had less opportunity and reason to organize, for they were a class of petit entrepreneurs. While most tenants remained tenants, many succeeded in becoming true owners. "First year a harvester, second sharecropper, third contractor, fourth capitalist." This popular phrase reflected the reality that between 1880 and 1914, the absolute number of small owners increased 60 percent. This process of social mobility combined with ethnic, religious, and occupational divisions among tenants to damp down class conflict in much the same way New Zealand's land redistribution had done.[77]

Development Consequences

Argentina experienced an extraordinary economic boom as beef and wheat exports flourished; average exports roughly doubled 1890–94 to 1900–04 and tripled to 1910–14. This boom drew people and capital. Immigration roughly doubled the population from 1895 to 1914; by 1914, 75 percent of Buenos Aires residents were foreign-born.[78] Foreigners invested increasing amounts of capital directly in railroads and food processing for export. But the boom assured neither long-term development nor less dependency.

The survival of landowners as a coherent class had ambiguous consequences for development, but did not insure underdevelopment. Argentine landowners responded to changing prices and market opportunities by steadily increasing the valued added to their products, not by attempting to depress wages.[79] Exporters of hides and wool in the 1880s, in the 1890s they exported frozen, live and canned meat exports (mostly mutton), and then changed to higher quality frozen meats and chilled beef by World War I. (See Table 35.) Landowners constructed elaborate production systems rotating wheat, alfalfa and beef cattle on their land. Tenants grew wheat for three to five years, planted alfalfa in their last year, and then moved on to a different piece of land. Cattle then fed on the alfalfa for five years. By 1914, 16 millions acres were under wheat; yoked to wheat, alfalfa acreage expanded from two million acres in 1895 to 19 million acres by 1914.

77. J. Fogarty, "The Comparative Method and the 19th Century Regions of Recent Settlement," *Historical Studies Australia and New Zealand* 19 (1981), 417; Gallo, *La Pampa Gringa*, pp. 88–105, chap. 7.
78. Scobie, *Revolution on the Pampas*, pp. 27–29.
79. See Gallo, *Agricultural Expansion and Industrial Development*, for a general survey.

Table 35. Meat as a percentage of total
value exported from Argentina,
1887–1907

	1887	1897	1907
Jerked beef	48	22	4
Live cattle	28	43	7
Frozen beef	nil	1	51
Other*	4	4	16
Live sheep	1	13	1
Frozen mutton	19	17	20

*Beef extracts, meat flour, canned meat.
SOURCE: Crossley and Greenhill, "River
Plate Beef Trade," p. 294.

This integrated production—the *cultivos combinados*—maximized yields of each product and used the land much more intensively than monocultural production, for alfalfa increased the stock-carrying capacity of the land by a factor of six. Although they subcontracted wheat production to tenants, landowners made significant investments in this process of intensification. For example, from 1888 to 1912, the number of windmill-driven water wells increased from 237 to 69,598. Breeding for fatter, beefier shorthorn cattle raised the proportion of crossbreeds in Buenos Aires province to 90 percent.[80] Table 35 above illustrates nicely the change in the quality of beef exports. By 1914, chilled and frozen beef exports were second only to grain exports in value. The contrast between Uruguayan and Argentine beef production reveals the extent to which Argentina managed to become a low-cost, high-efficiency producer of beef for world markets. Despite its locational advantage, in 1913 Uruguay still processed 72 percent of its cattle for hides, jerked beef, or beef extract—all low-quality products, approximately the same percentage as in Argentina at the time of the Baring Crisis. Meanwhile Argentine beef was delivered to Buenos Aires docks at 60 percent of the cost of equivalent quality U.S. beef to Chicago railheads. Argentine beef dominated upscale markets in Britain, while Antipodean meat was shunted to working-class neighborhoods.[81] In the southern part of Buenos Aires

80. Whitbeck, *Economic Geography of South America*, pp. 231–232; J. Fogarty, "Staples, Super-Staples, and the Limits of Staples Theory," in Platt and di Tella, *Argentina, Australia, and Canada* (New York: St. Martin's Press, 1985), p. 26–27; Taylor, *Rural Life in Argentina*, p. 143.

81. Whitbeck, *Economic Geography of South America*, pp. 231, 287; D. Denoon, *Settler Capitalism* (Oxford: Oxford University Press, 1983), pp. 107–112; Gravil, *Anglo-Argentine Connection*, pp. 62, 67. Uruguay also lagged behind in the switch from sheep for

province large landlord-run monocultural wheat farms using wage labour were highly capital-intensive operations.[82] With respect to their own holdings, then, landowners behaved like capitalist producers and not like rentier landlords.

Nonetheless, most analyses point to precisely this system as causing or continuing underdevelopment in Argentina, arguing that landowners' use of tenant farmers blocked development by preventing intensification of agriculture and depriving manufacturers of a market large enough to permit industrial development. The first clearly is mistaken on both empirical and theoretical grounds. The immigrant Italians who became tenants came to Argentina precisely because intensification occurred; in neighboring Uruguay the persistence of *extensive* stockraising meant a relative absence of tenants and agriculture. Second, tenants in and of themselves should not automatically block mechanization of agriculture; quite the contrary. English agriculture was heavily tenanted after the eighteenth century, and nonetheless became and remains highly developed, producing extremely high yields through "industrial" agriculture. In the early 1900s in Australia at least one-fifth of wheat growers were sharecroppers; in the non-south United States, one-quarter of all farmers were full tenants.[83] One might argue that a quantitative difference turned into a qualitative difference, as about two-thirds of Argentine farmers were tenants. Two factors, though, suggest that tenancy in and of itself as an economic phenomenon was not a decisively regressive step for Argentine agriculture.

First, the alternative to tenancy was *not* more "capitalist" forms of agriculture. Generalizing from North America (and, by extension Australia), Harriet Friedmann argues that family farms were better suited to absorbing the fluctuations and secular decline in wheat prices that occurred until 1896 than were capitalist forms of wheat farming only using wage labor and constrained by the need to show a

---

wool, to sheep for both meat and wool, as well as in the conversion of pastoral to agricultural land. Argentina supplied 95 percent of Britain's imported chilled beef after 1912, and a consistent 30–40 percent of its frozen beef after 1900.

82. J. Tulchin, "Relations between Labor and Capital in Rural Argentina 1880–1914," in Platt and di Tella, *Political Economy of Argentina*, p. 25 and *passim*.

83. For Australia, see *Official Yearbook of New South Wales* (OYBNSW) 1909/1910, p. 198; for the United States, calculated from U.S. Department of Commerce, Bureau of the Census, *Historical Statistics of the United States*, series K1–16. 1890 saw the lowest levels of tenancy in the non-south United States, when 21.5 percent of all farmers were full tenants. The southern United States had consistently higher levels of tenancy, rising from 36.3 percent in 1880 to 49.6 percent in 1910.

profit.[84] In this period, she notes, family farmers displaced capitalist forms of production everywhere that the state did not make extraordinary efforts to protect capitalist agriculture. The choice for Argentine agriculture was thus not between tenant agriculture and capitalist agriculture, but between family farmers who owned their land and family farmers who did not. Indeed, in some sense Argentine tenancy was a more capitalist form of agriculture than subsidized family farming in Australia, because the Argentine system permitted a market-driven reallocation of land, labor and machines, in contrast to the relatively immobile Australian system.[85] Argentine agriculture was as productive as Australian. Argentine wheat production in 1900 yielded 12.7 bushels per acre, surpassing the Australian yield of 8.6 bushels per acre and roughly double Uruguayan yields; in 1910 Australian and Argentine yields were roughly equal.[86]

Second, Argentine wheat farmers and cattlemen did not resort to low-wage, labor-intensive production methods, despite the presence of a surplus labor pool in the deep interior. Internal migrants by and large worked as cowboys, while Argentine tenants and landowners alike preferred *golondrinas* for harvest labor.[87] As migrants, *golondrinas* were politically more docile and thus more desirable than the technically enfranchised peons. But *golondrinas* represented a high-cost solution to the problem of harvest labor. They received £40 to £50 for their four months work, which approximated Australian wage rates, and was about six times the peons' wage rate. The expense of using *golondrinas* made harvesting amount to 60 percent of production costs for wheat farmers. Tenants responded to the high cost of

84. H. Friedmann, "World Market, State and Family Farming: Social Bases of Household Production in the Age of Wage Labor," *Comparative Studies in Society and History* 20 (1978).

85. For perceptive comments, see J. Fogarty, "Comparative Method and the Nineteenth Century Regions of Recent Settlement," p. 417. Here it is important to note that Antipodean family farmers who "owned their land" were in effect generally "tenants" of the banks holding their mortgages. Tulchin, "Relations between Labor and Capital in Rural Argentina," also suggests that capitalist bonanza farming on virgin land was more prevalent in Argentina, especially in southern Buenos Aires and La Pampa, than in the Antipodes.

86. Australian farmers typically faced harsher climactic conditions, however. Argentine data from Scobie, *Revolution on the Pampas*, p. 87; and Rock, *Argentina, 1516–1987*, p. 164. Australian data calculated from B. Mitchell, *International Historical Statistics for the Americas and Australasia* (New York: Columbia University Press, 1983), pp. 223–226. For comparison, U.S. yields in 1900 were 13.9 bushels per acre, in 1910 14.4 bu/acre; Canadian yields averaged 13.2 bu/acre in 1901 and 14.9 bu/acre in 1911. United States Department of Commerce, Bureau of the Census, *Historical Statistics*, series K445–485; M. Urquhart and K. Buckley, *Historical Statistics of Canada* (Toronto: Cambridge University Press, 1965), p. 351.

87. Gallo, *La Pampa Gringa*, pp. 275–277.

harvest labor by substituting machine for human labor. Though acreage and the number of machines expanded rapidly, the number of *golondrinas* stayed fairly constant at 100,000 from 1890 to 1911.[88] Just as with smallholders in Australia, the vast area cultivated and the high cost of harvest labor forced Argentine tenants to mechanize. "In view of the scarcity of labor," writes Scobie, "[manual] techniques and equipment would scarcely have enabled Argentina to become an important producer of wheat. Mechanization was the answer."[89] By 1914, £20 million worth of agricultural machinery, including 18,000 reapers, was in use; but half as many Australian farmers used virtually the same amount.[90] Why did this disparity exist?

It was not a function of the methods of *estanciero* and tenant production. It was, rather, the political more than the economic consequences of the continued power of large landowners that limited agricultural and industrial development in Argentina. Tenants' political weakness reduced their ability to invest. As in Australia, "the substantial mechanization of Argentine agriculture," noted Scobie, was "ultimately amortized from the limited profits and savings of the colonists and tenant farmers."[91] But Argentine tenants were systematically drained by the owners of credit, land and transport, limiting their ability to invest in more machinery. Both Australian smallholders and Argentine tenants faced rapacious grain merchants, monopolistic shippers, and flint-hearted creditors. But Australian smallholders were able to temper the exactions of these intermediaries through political action that was facilitated by ties with neighbors and possession of the franchise. Argentine tenants had no ties to specific areas, were frequently moved, and as first-generation immigrants

88. Gallo, *La Pampa Gringa*, pp. 225–229; Scobie, *Revolution on the Pampas*, pp. 60–61, 81; Randall, *Economic History of Argentina in the Twentieth Century*, p. 90; Taylor, *Argentine Rural Life*, p. 145; Denoon, *Settler Capitalism*, p. 97; (Australian) Commonwealth Bureau of Census and Statistics, *Production Bulletin*, no. 9, p. 34. *Golondrinas'* transatlantic fares approximated two weeks' wages. Only when World War I forcibly interrupted the trans-Atlantic flow of Italians did Argentine landowners mobilize low-wage interior labor for the harvest. Roughly 24 percent of the population was engaged in agriculture in Argentina and Australia.

89. Scobie, *Revolution on the Pampas*, p. 82. Ferrer, *The Argentine Economy*, p. 121, echoes this: "High output per person in agriculture enabled Argentina to feed its large population and generate a sizable export surplus while employing only a minor portion of its labor force."

90. Scobie, *Revolution on the Pampas*, pp. 60–61, 81; Randall, *Economic History of Argentina*, pp. 90–91; Commonwealth Bureau of Census and Statistics, *Production Bulletin*, no. 9, p. 34; Gallo, *La Pampa Gringa*, pp. 229–233; McLean, *Victorian Rural Outputs Inputs and Mechanization*, p. 167.

91. Scobie, *Revolution on the Pampas*, p. 82. See Friedmann, "World Market, State, and Family Farming" for an explanation of how those limited savings were created.

generally lacked the franchise. Both Argentine tenants and small-holders had little success with direct action. Smallholder revolts in 1893 in Santa Fe province were historically too early to garner support from tenants or urban workers; a tenant strike in 1912 dissipated in the face of promises to reform lease conditions and grain marketing. So tenants were unable to challenge parasitic intermediaries successfully. Four foreign firms dominated both agricultural credit and grain marketing. Their agents, usually the owner of the local tavern or general store, bought ungraded wheat and arranged short-term credit at interest rates running from 30 to 50 percent.[92] To the exactions of intermediaries were added higher rents after 1900. Even in Santa Fe, the province in which conditions most favored smallholders, rent seems to have more than doubled between 1895 and 1914, while tenure periods halved.[93] All of these factors reduced tenants' ability to invest, and to the extent that landowners consumed rents, rather than productively invested them, they tended to retard further development in agriculture. The landowners' own credit system shows that it was politics that mattered more than economics, for they borrowed exclusively from the Banco Nacional, which directly or indirectly controlled over 70 percent of rural credit in 1914, rather than from the more rapacious open credit market.[94] The owner-run beef ranch, integrated with tenant grain production, thus contained elements of the surplus-sterilizing landlord so typical of underdevelopment.

Did the survival of large landholders also have economic effects that limited urban-industrial development? Dieter Senghaas, for example, would argue that industrial development depends on linkages arising from the flatter distribution of income associated with small landowners, and thus that in Australia farmers provided a major "middle-class" market reserved by the tariff for manufacturers.[95] Supply-side forces—high wages in manufacturing—also drove industrial development in Australia. The farmer market made higher lev-

92. On Argentina, see Scobie, *Revolution on the Pampas*, pp. 81, 89, 140–141 and chap. 6 in general; Gravil, *The Anglo-Argentine Connection*, p. 42 and chap. 2; and C. Solberg, "Land Tenure and Land Settlement: Policy and Patterns in the Canadian Prairies and the Argentine Pampas," in Platt and di Tella, *Argentina, Australia and Canada*. On Australia see E. Dunsdorfs, *Australian Wheat-growing Industry* (Melbourne: Melbourne University Press, 1956); and B. Graham, *Formation of the Australian Country Parties* (Canberra: Australian National University Press, 1966). See Tulchin, "El Credito Agrario en la Argentina," for an excellent analysis of credit that unfortunately falls outside our time period. Argentine farmers did physically attack lenders and grain merchants, although without any coordination or organization; see Gallo, *Farmers in Revolt*.
93. Gallo, *La Pampa Gringa*, pp. 104–105.
94. Rock, *Politics in Argentina*, pp. 27–28.
95. Senghaas, *European Experience*, pp. 146–151.

els of domestic manufacturing investment profitable, while labor strength and judicially set high wages forced manufacturers to intensify production to remain profitable. Australian manufacturers thus made considerable investments in capital goods for production and in the production of capital goods for agriculture. By 1913 Australian manufacturers had roughly twice as much installed horsepower per worker as Argentine, employed, proportionate to population, a third more industrial workers than did Argentine, and had only slightly less capital invested in machinery and plant alone as Argentine manufacturers had invested in machinery, plant *and* land.

Senghaas's argument is at best only partially true for Argentina. Clearly, mobile tenants would be unwilling to invest in housing and immovable capital goods for production, like wells. This decreased consumption narrowed the market available to urban manufacturers and so made industrial development more difficult. But the rapid growth of Argentine urban and rural population still provoked a wide industrialization in consumer goods production, as output and the number of factories doubled and the number of workers more than doubled between 1895 and 1914. Overall, Argentina and Australia both had roughly the same proportion of agricultural to industrial workers. But Argentina's expansion took place almost entirely in artisanal shops; the average number of workers per Argentine factory was two-fifths the Australian average by 1914, largely because the Australian average had grown while the Argentine stayed flat.[96] Here it again appears that the political, not the economic, consequences of continued large landholding constrained industrial development by eliminating supply-side pressures. Urban workers, despite organizing by Anarchists, yearly trades union conferences after 1900, and several violent general strikes, were unable to force up wages to Australian levels. As in Australia, the military broke up strikes; unlike Australia, immigrant workers and many of their employers lacked the franchise and so had no recourse to political action. Consequently Argentine

96. See for example the discussion of agriculture-led industrial growth in Santa Fe in E. Gallo, *La Pampa Gringa*, pp. 246–251. Data calculated from various *Official Yearbooks of the Commonwealth of Australia*, E. Tornquist, *Desarrollo Económico* (Buenos Aires, 1920), pp. 31–36; C. Taylor, *Argentine Rural Life*, p. 121; and E. Gallo, *Agricultural Expansion and Industrial Development in Argentina, 1880–1930* (Buenos Aires: Instituto Torcuato, 1970), pp. 7–11. By 1914 over 40 percent of Australian factories employed more than 100 workers, with an average of 21.5 workers per factory. In Argentina the average was 8.4 workers per factory; only meat packing plants, which averaged over 2000 employees each, showed any degree of concentration. Roughly the same proportion of the population engaged in agriculture in both countries: 23.7 percent in Argentina, 24 percent in Australia.

manufacturers had neither the incentive to substitute capital for labor, nor the opportunity to ally with their workers against landowners. What weakened linkages between agriculture and industry was not an absence of demand so much as the absence of a protected market for local producers of capital goods for agriculture. Landowners' political survival enabled them to shift part of the burden of debt service onto the urban middle and working classes through imposts and tariffs. This, plus fear of a repetition of the 1887–97 inflation, caused the political leadership of the middle and working classes to oppose new or increased tariffs adamantly when they came to power.[97] Without tariffs, there was no way to link manufacturing growth to agricultural prosperity. Agricultural demand for capital goods inevitably led to imports, not to local production as in Australia. Indeed, Australian manufacturers exported agricultural machinery to Argentina in this period.[98]

Despite all these obstacles to development, Argentina had, and attained considerably more development than its Latin American neighbors. Diaz-Alejandro estimates Argentine per capita GDP (in 1970 U.S. dollars) at $780 in 1901, (compared to Brazilian per capita GDP at $190), rising to $1030 in 1913 ($230) and $1200 in 1928 ($340).[99] The ratio of factory to artisanal production in Argentina was consistently higher than the rest of Latin America through 1960,

97. See C. Solberg, "The Tariff and Politics in Argentina, 1916–1919," *Hispanic American Historical Review* 53 (1973); R. Munck, "Cycles of Class Struggle and the Making of the Working Class in Argentina, 1890–1920," *Journal of Latin American Studies* 19 (1987); R. Thompson, "Limitations of Ideology in the Early Argentina Labour Movement: Anarchism in the Trade Unions, 1890–1920," *Journal of Latin American Studies* 16 (May 1984); Rock, *Politics in Argentina*, on strikes and political attitudes toward the tariff.

98. Gallo, *Agricultural Expansion and Industrial Development in Argentina, 1880–1930*, p. 13, notes the utter absence of coal and iron in Argentina, and claims that Australia's deepening of development was considerably eased by the presence of both in large quantities when World War I cut off iron imports. This is, at best, a weak argument, as Argentina had access to American steel until 1917. Local production of iron is not necessarily a benefit; in the Australian case, indeed, the backward linkages by and large were felt in Britain. The benefit derived by Australia from a local iron industry was that industry's use of its tariff-derived monopoly position to concentrate profit for investment in large scale projects. But a state iron authority in Argentina could have achieved the same thing by acting as a monopsonistic purchaser of foreign iron and reselling as a monopolist to the domestic market. This would have permitted the state to capture a major part of the monopoly profits accruing to foreign iron suppliers, especially under the conditions of surplus capacity existing in the inter-war years, and probably would have improved the balance of payments. On Australian exports to Argentina, see *Official Yearbook of the Commonwealth of Australia*, 1910.

99. C. Diaz-Alejandro, "Argentina, Australia and Brazil before 1929," in Platt and di Tella, *Argentina, Australia and Canada*, pp. 98–99.

even aside from food processing.[100] The 1930s, when Argentina
lowered tariffs on British manufactures, and the Perón era, with its
influx of *descamisados* from the labour-surplus interior, was the period
when stagnation turned towards underdevelopment.[101]

Dependency Consequences

Although landowners avoided foreclosure by foreign capital, and
triumphed politically, the resolution of the 1890s crisis did not decrease Argentine dependency. The ease with which both railroad
guarantees and public claims had been voided concealed significant
weaknesses. First, there was no reclamation of control over productive circuits as occurred in Australia. Uncertainty whether the 1899
fixation of paper pesos at G\$ 0.44 would hold meant that owner-
exporters preferred to reinvest in their own highly profitable operations rather than in railroads, repatriation of the public debt, or even
meat packing.[102] Without new investment, Argentine firms retained
control of only one-fourth of meat packing, mostly of those producing export mutton or meat for domestic consumption. As they had
done with creditors in the 1880s and 1890s, Argentine producers
preferred to play American and British meat packers off against one
another, happily extracting higher prices from the competition.[103]
Why repatriate public debt when the real cost of borrowing was dropping, and foreign capital and workers could be made to carry the
cost? The vast expansion of rural production created so much European confidence in Argentine credit that interest rates on public issues steadily dropped while they sold at par.[104]

Second, in the absence of Argentine restrictions or competition,
foreign capital expanded its domination of railroads, credit and export processing. Argentina had sold off locally-owned railroads dur-

100. F. Weaver, *Class, State and Industrial Structure* (Westport, Conn.: Greenwood
Press, 1969), pp. 98, 145.

101. But see T. Halperin Donghi, "Argentine Export Economy: Intimations of Mor-
tality, 1894–1930," in Platt and di Tella, *Political Economy of Argentina*, for a contrary
view.

102. Martinez and Lewandowski, *The Argentine in the Twentieth Century*, p. 94. In 1907
the Ley Mitré permanently ended railroad guarantees while formally limiting their
profits. See Lewis, "British Railway Companies and the Argentine Government," for a
discussion.

103. Gravil, *Anglo-Argentine Connection*, pp. 70, 72, 76. Shares of the meat packing
market in 1910 were: United States, 41.2 percent; Britain, 33.9 percent; Argentina,
24.9 percent.

104. Peters, *Foreign Debt of the Argentine Republic*, p. 48.

ing the 1890 crisis, liquidating capital at fire sale prices to pay current expenses. By 1913, foreign investment in railroads generated about £11.2 million in repatriable surplus, almost seven times the outflow in 1890. Transportation's share of the economy grew from 4.8 percent of GDP in 1900 to 8.3 percent in 1913.[105] Four big grain marketers dominated the supply of credit to farmers and thus drained surplus out of the rural economy. Argentine capital thus lost control of several dynamic sectors in the economy. Total foreign investment in Argentina tripled to £650 million in 1900–13. Service on this pool required £31.2 million, which, though only 75 percent as heavy in proportion to the pool of investment in 1913 as the £12 million debt service of 1890 had been, represented a 25 percent increase relative to GDP.[106] So while landowners were able to fend off foreign capital in their own sphere and remain dynamic, they were unable or unwilling to expand that activity to other spheres, especially grain production.

On the whole then, the particular class coalition emerging out of the crisis of 1890 failed to pursue policies to decrease Argentine dependency. Unlike Australia, where by 1914 domestically controlled investment had significantly displaced foreign investment, in 1914 foreign holdings in Argentina were approximately equal to domestic holdings. At best, Argentine control of investment had stayed constant as a consequence of owner-exporter control of politics. Argentine exporters remained an interior bourgeoisie under no compulsion to limit foreign investment as Australia's interior manufacturing bourgeoisie did. The 1930s saw a confirmation of Argentina's subordinate status and debt in the Roca-Runciman pact. Where Argentina reduced tariffs in exchange for an assured market for beef in England, Australia increased them and deepened its industrial development.[107] Perón's attempt during World War II, however inept, to duplicate certain aspects of the "Australian package" by linking wages and protection thus came two generations too late. Though Perón could use World War II to reclaim ownership for Argentina of Brit-

105. Calculated from A. Ford, "British Investment in Argentine Economic Development," in Rock, *Argentina in the Twentieth Century*, p. 33; Stone, "British Direct and Portfolio Investment in Latin America"; Ferrer, *Argentine Economy*, p. 92; Martinez and Lewandowski, *The Argentine in the Twentieth Century*, p. 94; Randall, *An Economic History of Argentina*, p. 2.
106. Calculated from Ford, *The Gold Standard*, pp. 88–89; Randall, *An Economic History of Argentina*, p. 2.
107. See Gravil, *Anglo-Argentine Connection*, for a survey of this period.

ish-held railroads, he had neither favorable terms of trade nor expanding international markets to drive industrial accumulation. In Perón's time, the window of opportunity that had permitted an interior bourgeoisie to develop into a national bourgeoisie in Australia had closed in Argentina.[108]

108. Carlos Waisman's perceptive *Reversal of Development in Argentina* (Princeton: Princeton University Press, 1987), came to my attention after this book went to press. It advances more compelling reasons for underdevelopment in the Perónist and post-Perónist period.

CHAPTER SEVEN

South Korea

> *Korean*: Who won the Vietnam War? Tell me—who won the war in Vietnam?
>
> *Western Reporter*: I believe it was the Provisional Revolutionary Government . . .
>
> *Korean*: You're *wrong*! You Americans are sometimes very naive! All the PRG got was a countryside full of bomb craters and a capital in political and economic ruin. The *real* victor of the Vietnam War was Park Chung Hee.
>
> M. Fleming, "The Post-Vietnam Militarization of ROK Society"

The astounding economic successes of South Korea and the other Asian newly industrializing countries (NICs)—Taiwan, Singapore, Hong Kong—"disprove" Dependency theory for many critics. For neoclassical analysts, success was simply a matter of policies that "got the prices right." For those looking at state institutions, success came from the power to enforce and the choice of correct developmental policies.[1] Both analyses beg the question. The neoclassical analysts confront a straw-man version of Dependency theory with an example of development, while ignoring the considerable role the state played in the NICs' success; it is unreasonable to claim that market forces alone caused NIC development. Those who look only at state institutions attack a more textured but still incomplete version of Dependency theory, typified by Cardoso and Faletto's third situation of dependency—dependency on multinational corporations—and then use development in the absence of MNCs to argue that dependency was also absent. But this begs the question of why these policies worked.

---

1. For representative articles, see B. Balassa, *The NICs in the World Economy* (New York: Pergamon Press, 1981), for the neoclassicals; for institutionalists, see S. Haggard's review article "The Newly Industrializing Countries in the International System," *World Politics* 38 (January 1986); see also citations in Chapter 1.

South Korean's success actually tends to confirm both lines of Dependency theory, by providing a case in which the relevant variables are, to a certain extent, reversed from the usual. Thus this chapter will examine South Korea by focusing both on the absence of underdevelopment, and on the sources of investment capital, the origins of domestic accumulation, and the absence balance of payments crises during industrialization. While South Korea has been able to avoid underdevelopment, this has come at the price of Australian-style dependency on borrowed foreign capital. Each of South Korea's development crises *cum* advances required renewed foreign borrowing as a precondition for continued investment and accumulation.[2]

WHY NO UNDERDEVELOPMENT IN SOUTH KOREA?

Dependency theory's external forces line predicts that capitalist penetration of pre-capitalist societies will produce underdevelopment. Displacement of indigenous people from traditional occupations leads to overcrowding on the land and low wages; these social structures remove both the incentive to invest in labour-saving devices and a market wide enough to make those investments profitable. Diversion of surplus into rent makes it difficult to mobilize capital for investment. Dieter Senghaas would add that low-productivity agriculture and low wages prevent linkages from emerging between export activity and domestic markets, thus depriving domestic producers of growth stimuli. For theorists of this line, the prescriptive policy is redistribution of land and thus of income in the agricultural sector. Redistribution, they argue, solves both the supply and demand constraints on development by eliminating the drain of rent on producer incomes and making more surplus available for productive investment. Employers also have to match the imputed wages workers could make on the land; both inside and outside agriculture, increased wages then stimulate substitution of machines for human labour. Finally, a more prosperous agriculture would create a larger potential market for domestic manufactures. In part, events in Korea, as well as Taiwan, uphold the descriptive but not necessarily the prescriptive parts of this analysis, for land reform in and of itself cannot stimulate development. Confirming the external forces line's insights,

2. I chose to examine South Korea, rather than Taiwan, because the processes are clearer in South Korea than in Taiwan. Taiwan is not an exception that proves the rule—or disproves it, for that matter—but in Taiwan the disjuncture between state and society is so great as to make the "internal forces" line's insights almost useless.

Japanese colonization did create an attenuated form of under-development, which post-colonial land reforms prevented from running its full course.

Japanese colonization of Korea had two phases, each of which mitigated underdevelopment. In the first phase, from annexation in 1910 until 1931, Japan remade Korea as an agricultural complement to its own industry. A complete land survey established private property in land and gave Japanese control of nearly half of Korea's paddy land while consolidating Korean landlords' support for Japanese rule. Korean landlords collaborated with Japanese administrative organs and land companies in forcing Korean peasants to maximize rice production for export to Japan. By 1939 roughly half of Korean rice was shipped to Japan. In 1933, the Japanese tried unsuccessfully to promote production of cotton and wool.[3] But peasant resistance to the Japanese policy of buying below the cost of production limited the introduction of these two non-subsistence crops. Soon after, war gave industrial production a higher priority than production of fibers and the project was dropped.

In theory, Japan's introduction of what was more or less an export monoculture in rice ought to have had the same underdeveloping effects as the introduction of sugar, coffee, or cocoa elsewhere in the world. And indeed, as external-forces Dependency theory predicts, Japanese colonization produced overcrowding on the land, unequal distribution of productivity and incomes, penury, and productivity increases in the export sector only.[4] Three factors mitigated these tendencies, however. Because the Japanese made rice the mono-cultural export, and were unable to impose production of wool and cotton, the typical peripheral division of production into commercialized export agriculture and marginalized subsistence production did not occur. Instead, South Korea inherited an agricultural system organized around production of a subsistence crop rather than one biased towards producing non-subsistence crops with a limited do-

3. See Choy Bong Youn, *Korea: A History* (Tokyo: Chas. E. Tuttle, 1971), pp. 155–156, 160; Choi Hochin, *Economic History of Korea* (Seoul: Samsung Printing, 1971); A. Grajdanzev, *Modern Korea* (New York: Institute of Pacific Relations, 1944), pp. 92–102, 226, and *passim*; P. Kuznets, *Economic Growth and Structure in the Republic of Korea* (New Haven: Yale University Press, 1979), p. 14. For parallel processes in Taiwan, see S. Ho, *The Economic Development of Taiwan 1860–1970* (New Haven: Yale University Press, 1978); and T. Gold, *State and Society in the Taiwan Miracle* (Armonk, N.Y.: M. E. Sharpe, 1986), chap. 3. For a comparative overview, see B. Cumings, "Origins and Development of the Northeast Asian Political Economy: Industrial Sectors, Product Cycles, and Political Consequences," in Frederic C. Deyo, ed., *The Political Economy of the New Asian Industrialism* (Ithaca: Cornell University Press, 1987).
4. Grajdanzev, *Modern Korea*, pp. 85–87, 108, 112–114, 117–118.

mestic market. Second, rice, an extremely labour-intensive crop in Asia, was not suited to plantation-style production with a marginal and parttime labour force. The production unit remained the tenant peasant family on a small plots, encouraging productivity increases.

The second phase of Japanese colonization, from 1931 to 1945, also lessened tendencies towards creation of the pool of unemployed typical of underdevelopment. Japan's further expansion into Asia created an outlet for the considerable numbers of Korean peasants who were displaced from the land. By 1938, approximately 10 percent of Korea's population had left Korea for Japan proper, Manchukuo, or Russia.[5] In this period Korea also benefited from "development by invitation" as Japan prepared for war. Desiring autonomy from and control over the untrustworthy *zaibatsu* (industrial combines closely tied to their controlling banks), the army began to industrialize the Korean peninsula and Manchukuo. New industry absorbed 100,000 otherwise landless peasants. Still, industrialization was less important than the choice of rice over a non-subsistence crop for the later absence of underdevelopment.

Industrialization also gave Korea an enduring foundation for modern industry, more by way of demonstration than of enduring physical assets. Total industrial production roughly doubled from 1920 to 1930, and again from 1930 to 1939, with the output of modern industry rivaling household production. While retaining about 88 percent of shares, the Japanese permitted Korean capital to participate in these industrial ventures, thus creating a nascent bourgeoisie.[6] Though war destroyed virtually all Korean industrial facilities, Japanese industrialization of Korea had a profound effect on institutions that complemented the effects of rice farming. The example of state-run, specifically military-run industrial development, with strict control over private enterprise, provided a positive model of lasting value. The Imperial Army's industrialization of Korea and Manchukuo set the political pattern for the industrialization of both Koreas.[7] Overall then, Japanese colonization created less underdevelopment than did European colonization elsewhere.

5. Grajdanzev, *Modern Korea*, p. 81.
6. Choy Bong Youn, *Korea*, p. 163; Grajdanzev, *Modern Korea*, pp. 148–151, 172. Choy, p. 166, explains Japanese willingness to permit Korean participation by quoting Finance Minister Takahashi: "If there were no Korean enterprises the big Japanese capitalists would face masses of hostile Korean workers."
7. See Cumings, "Origins and Development of the Northeast Asian Political Economy," p. 56; P. Evans, "Class, State and Dependence in East Asia: Lessons for Latin Americanists," p. 214; and C. Johnson, "Political Institutions and Economic Performance: The Government-business Relationship in Japan, South Korea and Taiwan," p.

After decolonization, politically-motivated land reforms blocked the underdeveloping effects that world markets usually exert.[8] Two successful land reforms established the preconditions for industrial growth in South Korea by eliminating landlords. The first, carried out by the U.S. military government in 1948, sold about 700,000 acres formerly owned by the Japanese to almost as many tenants at the low cost of three times the land's average yearly production. The second, which the Rhee government completed by 1958, set a three-hectare ceiling on all holdings. Both created a highly egalitarian pattern of land distribution in which more than two-thirds of families owned land capable of providing subsistence.[9] Land reform eliminated the second structural feature of underdevelopment, diversion of surplus into rent and its sterilization through investment in more land. Instead, land reform created opportunities to divert surplus to a developmentalist state for investment in industry.

SOUTH KOREAN EFFORTS AT DEVELOPMENT THROUGH ISI

As with Argentina, the absence of underdevelopment at a particular time is no guarantee that development will continue. Should productivity remain stagnant, gains elsewhere in the world can again exert displacement pressures on the stagnant economy, while population increases may exacerbate land pressures and lower wages. Thus we must turn to a second, more interesting question: How did South Korea turn its opportunity for development into forward movement? For Senghaas, land reform itself was almost sufficient; others say Korea did nothing more than "get the prices right," acclaiming the

---

153; all in Deyo, *Political Economy*. Taiwan also experienced "development by invitation." Here, however, learning by example was more limited as the Taiwanese elite was largely destroyed after the so-called "February 28th (1947) Incident." The Kuomintang (KMT), however, had evolved its own image of state-led industrialization under Sun Yat Sen, expressed through the "three people's principles."

8. In Taiwan, the process of rice farming and land reform, plus destruction of Taiwanese landlords in the February 28th incident, parallels events in South Korea. Hong Kong and Singapore had no "land" to reform. Although their peripheries are clearly underdeveloped, political control of population movement prevents the labour surplus there from depressing wages in the entrepot.

9. Choy Bong Youn, *Korea: A History*, pp. 342–345, 352; D. Cole and P. Lyman, *Korean Development: The Interplay of Politics and Economics* (Cambridge: Harvard University Press, 1971), p. 21; E. Lee, "Egalitarian Peasant Farming and Rural Development: The Case of South Korea," *World Development* 7 (April/May 1979) 494. The gini coefficient for land distribution was 0.38 in 1965.

four Asian NICs as exemplars of *laissez-faire* capitalism.[10] But most analysts point to a wide range of institutional and policy efforts to account for success, saying an autonomous, *dirigiste* state crafted increasingly competitive export industries, and so avoided the balance of payments crises that typically halted Latin American industrialization. In Latin America, import substitution industrialization (ISI) created the conditions for its own failure for three reasons. First, domestically-oriented consumer goods industries used imported intermediate goods but did not generate the foreign exchange needed to buy those goods. Second, import of intermediate goods and the inefficiencies associated with small and protected markets meant that consumer goods industries could not mobilize enough capital to make the transition to capital goods production. At the same time, though, diversion of investment funds from agriculture to industry decreased a country's ability to continue exporting and so further exacerbated the imbalance of payments. Finally, penetration by multinational corporations (MNCs) brought with it economies of scale, but also profit repatriation that also contributed to imbalance of payments. South Korea's successful avoidance of a balance-of-payments crisis through export-oriented industrialization thus suggests that dependency is a matter of policy choices alone to those who deprecate Dependency theory. An export-oriented strategy balances payments and so permits further industrialization. But in focusing solely on export-oriented industrialization as a strategy to avoid imbalance of payments, they overlook four more fundamental issues: How did South Korea create and mobilize surplus for investment? How did South Korea avoid an oversupply of labour that might halt development? What was the true role of exports in development? And what sources other than exports helped balance payments? The following sections thus concentrate not just on institutional and policy factors relating to balance of payments and export-oriented industrialization, but also on the effects of policy on surplus mobilization, labour absorption, and the artificial widening of the domestic market. Korean policies successfully avoided underdevelopment, Cardoso and Faletto's dependency of the third (MNC) kind, and the narrow domestic market that impeded Latin American industrialization. But mobilization of investment funds for development, and the policy of using exports to expand the domestic market, have created debt dependency for Korea.

10. Senghaas, *The European Experience*, pp. 170–177.

Rhee's Round of ISI, 1954–1960

South Korea's first experiment in import substitution industrialization (ISI), under Rhee, paralleled the problems and processes of Latin American ISI efforts, except to the crucial absence of MNCs. As with Latin American ISI, South Korean ISI was "protected and nurtured behind a wall of tariffs, overvalued exchange rates and other obstacles to foreign entry," as Bruce Cumings put it. Protection levels were greater than Mexico's, for example.[11] Unlike the Latin American experience, Korea's consumer goods ISI did not end abruptly with a balance of payments crisis, because U.S. aid equaled 80 percent of capital formation 1953–1962, or 80 percent of imports. By the late 1950s, South Korea produced many of its basic consumer needs, though, given low income levels, these industries were not particularly sophisticated. But as foreign aid declined towards the end of Rhee's regime, so did investment, both relative to GNP and absolutely.[12] South Korea then experienced declining economic growth rates and overcapacity, rather than the typical and more superficial consequence of Latin American style ISI, a payments crisis. After 1957, the last postwar reconstruction year, GNP growth decelerated from 7.6 percent per annum to 1.1 percent in 1960, the lowest increase since 1945. (See Table 36.) The Rhee regime failed to mobilize domestic savings for investment, so domestically controlled investment averaged less than 2 percent of GNP.[13] Private investment activity revolved around arbitrage, speculation, and political access to import licenses and foreign exchange, rather than production.[14] Decreasing growth, rising unemployment, and the impending end to U.S. aid fueled the student movement that toppled the increasingly corrupt Rhee government in 1960. The military under Park Chung Hee in turn displaced the new civilian government in 1961, when urban

11. Quotation from Cumings, "Origins and Development of the Northeast Asian Political Economy," p. 68; see also Cole and Lyman, *Korean Development*, p. 187. On protection levels, see A. Amsden, "The State and Taiwan's Economic Development," chap. 3, in P. Evans, D. Rueschmeyer, and T. Skocpol, eds., *Bringing the State Back In* (New York: Cambridge University Press, 1985), pp. 88–89.

12. E. Mason et al., *Economic and Social Modernization of the Republic of Korea* (Cambridge: Harvard University Press, 1980), p. 85; Bank of Korea, *National Income in Korea* (Seoul, 1982), pp. 214–223. South Korea exported only $1 of goods for every $4 it imported in this period.

13. Bank of Korea, *National Income in Korea*, pp. 358–359; Kuznets, *Economic Growth and Structure*, pp. 78, 152, reports that overcapacity was especially acute in food processing, a key ISI industry, by the early 1960s.

14. Kim Kyoung-Dong, "Political Factors in the Formation of the Entrepreneurial Elite in South Korea," *Asian Survey* 16 (May 1976), 467–469.

Table 36. South Korean investment under Rhee, 1954–1962

Year	GNP (annual compound % growth rate)	GDCF* index (1954 = 100- Won 255 billion)	Percentage of GDCF from foreign sources
1954	5.1	100	14.5
1955	4.5	102	25.6
1956	−1.4	76	17.9
1957	7.6	147	12.2
1958	5.5	124	3.9
1959	3.8	90	4.4
1960	1.1	93	9.4
1961	5.6	116	0.5
1962**	2.2	116	20.2

*GDCF = Gross domestic capital formation.
**First full year of Park Chung Hee regime; start of Five Year Plan.
SOURCE: Bank of Korea, *National Income of Korea*, pp. 146–147, 174–177, 358–359.

unemployment hit 28 percent.[15] Here, clearly, South Korea was at a critical juncture. Absent growth in employment, a rising population would create the unemployed surplus population associated with underdevelopment. Absent some effort at domestically controlled accumulation and production, the economy would remain dependent on imported goods and foreign capital to function.

EXPORT-ORIENTED INDUSTRIALIZATION, 1963–1972

The Park regime, forewarned of declining U.S. aid, and prodded by officials of the U.S. Agency for International Development (AID), eventually turned to export-oriented industrialization (EOI) to balance payments and, perhaps deliberately to cope with its deeper problems. But the regime's success rested not merely on an EOI strategy to avoid an imbalance of payments. Unlike Rhee, the Park regime made a variety of institutional initiatives to extract and mobilize surplus for investment, to use EOI to prevent a surplus population problem from emerging, and to use EOI to enlarge the domestic market artificially. Though EOI succeeded as a development strategy, by absorbing excess workers and enlarging the market, it did not end dependency. EOI depended on foreign loans to subsidize investment in export

15. Choy Bong Youn, *Korea*, p. 325; Kim Nak Kwan, "Is Korea's Export Promotion Scheme Consistent with her Industrialization?" *Asian Economies* no. 1, (June 1972), pp. 34–35; Kuznets, *Economic Growth and Structure*, p. 111.

industry, and on aid and geopolitical factors to avoid an imbalance of payments.

Primitive Socialist Accumulation

Investible surplus for the new export promotion scheme came from two sources: increased foreign investment and debt, and increased exploitation of the peasantry. Evgenii Preobrazhenskii had argued in the 1920s that the only way for a state-directed program of industrialization to get started was to use its control of the commanding heights of industry to squeeze surplus from the peasantry. By altering the terms of trade between manufactured and agricultural goods in industry's favor, the state could channel surplus from agriculture to industry in a process Preobrazhenskii called "primitive socialist accumulation."[16] While there is no evidence that South Korean planners consciously followed Preobrazhenskii, their situation and policies closely resembled that of the Soviet Union in the 1920s.[17] South Korean planners consciously distorted agricultural markets and internal terms of trade to finance industrialization. As with the Soviet

16. Preobrazhenskii argued that to make a transition from an underdeveloped, largely agricultural, economy to a highly developed industrial economy, the Soviet Union had to concentrate and invest large amounts of surplus in industry. Given its existing economy, only agriculture initially could provide this surplus; industry on its own could not generate sufficient surplus for self-sustained growth. Two lines emerged from Preobrazhenskii's thinking. One, laid out by Nikolai Bukharin, explicitly rejected confiscation of grain by taxes or by outright violence (like Preobrazhenskii's own position); the other, Stalin's, was less hesitant. Bukharin, like Dieter Senghaas and W. A. Lewis, argued for industrial investment driven by demand from agriculture. Peasant prosperity, encouraged by the state, would accelerate accumulation in the consumer goods industries, in turn leading to demand for investment in the heavy industries. Accumulation in the consumer goods industries and peasant savings would provide sufficient surplus for heavy industrialization. As this book went to press, Chih-Ming Ka and Mark Selden's excellent article "Original Accumulation, Equity and Late Industrialization: the Cases of Socialist China and Capitalist Taiwan," *World Development* 14 (October 1986), was brought to my attention. This article makes a more developed case for primitive accumulation.

17. L. Jones and I. Sakong, *Government, Business, and Entrepreneurship in Economic Development: The Korean Case* (Cambridge: Harvard University Press, 1980), p. 141, note that, "an ostensibly private enterprise economy has utilized the intervention mechanism of public ownership to an extent which parallels that of many countries advocating a socialist pattern of society." The KMT's contacts with the Soviet Union during the 1920s and 1930s, and its earlier and more successful policy of squeezing agriculture, suggest a more conscious and conscientious emulation, however; see Amsden, "Taiwan's Economic History: A Case of Etatisme and a Challenge to Dependency Theory," *Modern China* 5 (July, 1979), *passim*.

Union, the growth of industry eventually diminished the need to derive investment funds from agriculture.[18]

The Grain Management Law of 1950 gave the government complete control of procurement and marketing of grains, and it used U.S. grain (received as aid under PL-480) to lower the market price of the grain it bought.[19] State sales of cheap U.S. PL-480 grain depressed the ratio of prices that farmers received to prices farmers paid from 113.6 : 100 to 94.3 : 100 between 1963 and 1968. Consequently, rural income fell sharply, relative to urban income. By 1968, the average rural worker received only 27 percent of the average urban worker's income; relative to urban households, rural household income dropped 10 percent from 1963 to 1968. Farmers suffered absolute declines in real income after 1964, and did not recover 1964 levels until 1970.[20] The beneficiaries of this policy were State enterprises supplying farmers, especially those producing fertilizer. The state also kept rice prices down through a 1965 program called "Food for Work." One hundred thousand metric tons of PL-480 grain were distributed to thousands of peasants for subsistence while they bench-terraced and irrigated thousands of new acres. This program expanded acreage 15 percent, while soaking up surplus rural population by generating 45 million man-days of work.[21]

Downward pressure on rural prices and income increased the supply of cheap urban labour two ways. First, cheap grain held down the cost of subsistence for urban workers. The share of personal consumption income going to food declined from an average of 57.0 percent in 1960-62 to 47.6 percent in 1970-72.[22] Second, declining

18. See M. Ellman, "Did Agricultural Surpluses Fund Investment in the Soviet Union's First Five Year Plan?" *Economic Journal* 85 (December 1975).

19. Lee, "Egalitarian Peasant Farming and Rural Development," pp. 495–495; Kuznets, *Economic Growth and Structure*, pp. 135–136; Kim Dong Hi, "Small Farmer Economy and Development Policy with Special Reference to Korea," *Asian Economies* no. 19, (December 1976), p. 6. Though the government typically bought only 10 percent of total output, it was the premier purchaser, as only 30–50 percent of the total crop was marketed.

20. P. Hasan, *Korea: Problems and Issues in a Rapidly Growing Economy* (Baltimore: Johns Hopkins University Press, 1976), p. 52; D. Rao, "Economic Growth and Equity in the Republic of Korea," *World Development* 6 (March 1979), p. 387; Cole and Lyman, *Korean Development*, pp. 147–151. The state also centralized control over lending to farmers. Rao cautions that income statistics may understate the actual gap, for rural data includes inflation-driven nominal inventory gains that bias them upward.

21. Cole and Lyman, *Korean Development*, pp. 91, 145–146.

22. Bank of Korea, *National Income of Korea*, pp. 195–196; Kuznets, *Economic Growth and Structure*, p. 60. In 1953/55, 62.7 percent of income went to food; now roughly 40 percent does.

rural income forced marginal farmers, the young, and the "extra" children—especially the women—of farm families to migrate to the cities. Over four million people migrated between 1963 and 1970. Despite rapid population growth, the rural population held steady, while Seoul alone absorbed some three million migrants.[23] Massive migration and cheap food created a pool of low wage labour for industry. Paul Kuznets provides data that allow us to judge the importance of cheap rice. Productivity in the South Korean plywood industry was only 43 percent of Japanese levels, while wages were 33 percent of Japanese wages in 1967. Since Korean real wage costs worked out to 75 percent of the Japanese level, South Korean producers were competitive, and gained plywood export market shares at Japan's expense.[24]

Foreign Lending and Investment

The other major source of investment capital was foreign loans and, on a very limited scale, direct foreign investment (DFI). Japan bought normalized relations in 1965 for $ 500 million in aid and yen purchases. Normalization opened Korea to Japanese investment, and over the next seven years the Japanese loaned an additional $581.3 million, largely as commercial credit. U.S. sources lent $1.2 billion by 1972. Although the absolute amounts invested were small compared to U.S. and Japanese investment worldwide, foreign capital provided approximately 40 percent of total South Korean investment from 1966 to 1972.[25]

The government initially regulated DFI through the 1962 Foreign Investment Encouragement Law. Its limitations on profit remittance and expatriate employment were liberalized in 1966 when relations with Japan were normalized. The new Foreign Capital Inducement

23. Ki-Do Woo, "Labor Force, Wage Level, and Economic Growth in Korea," *Asian Economies* no. 2 (September 1972), pp. 30–35. From 1962 to 1977, 7.5 million people migrated from the countryside to the city. Phyllis Kim, "Saemaul Agriculture: Korean Farmers Prop Up Export Oriented Economy," *AMPO Japan Asia Quarterly* 12 (1980), 4–5; Lee, "Egalitarian Peasant Farming and Rural Development," p. 510. Lee's sources claim there were nine million rural-to-urban migrants between 1959 and 1975. See Kim Chang Soo, "Marginalization, Development, and the Korean Workers' Movement," *AMPO Japan Asia Quarterly* 9 (1977), 22, for statistics on Seoul.

24. Kuznets, *Economic Growth and Structure*, p. 162.

25. Cole and Lyman, *Korean Development*, p. 111; J. Sano, "Foreign Capital in South Korean Development," *Asian Economies* no. 23 (December 1977), p. 44; Bank of Korea, *National Income in Korea*, pp. 178–179; Cha Byung Kwon, "Import Substitution and Industrialization: The Korean Case," *Asian Economies* no. 3 (December 1972), p. 9. See also Kuznets, *Economic Growth and Structure*, ch. 7.

Law removed the old 20 percent limit on profit repatriation, encouraged portfolio investment by permitting repatriation no matter what level of equity a foreign investor held, and removed employment restrictions.[26]

Institutional Changes

Institutionally the South Korean government retained control over domestic and foreign investment through a series of reforms and policy bureaus. The most important institutions were the Economic Planning Board (EPB), which managed the EOI strategy, and a variety of state banks that controlled the direction of investment. Headed by the Deputy Prime Minister to prevent bureaucratic inertia, the EPB was responsible for economic planning, for vetting and supervising foreign investment, for directing research and development efforts, and for controlling the provision of foreign exchange and credit to key sectors and specific firms.[27] The EPB thus centralized many functions dispersed across a number of bureaucracies in other countries, giving the South Korean government extraordinary control over the economy.

The EPB's first task was to discipline the financial group called *chaebol*. The new military government wanted them to become the Korean equivalent of the Japanese *zaibatsu*, in which a variety of industrial ventures closely linked to a bank or source of capital acted cooperatively against other combines while exploiting dependent subcontractors. Under threat of prosecution they were turned from arbitrage to productive investments.[28] The EPB channeled investment funds to these firms through a vast series of export subsidies and

26. P. Drysdale, *Direct Foreign Investment in Asia and the Pacific* (Canberra: Australian National University Press, 1972), pp. 245–246. Well over half of DFI in this period came from Japanese firms, which, unlike U.S. firms, were willing to accept these conditions. See Sano, "Foreign Capital and Investment in South Korean Development"; Park Tong Sup, "Japanese Capital and Korea's Economy," *Asian Economies* no. 6 (September 1973), pp. 41–44; Ozawa Terutomo, *Multinationalism, Japanese Style* (Princeton: Princeton University Press 1979).
27. Cole and Lyman, *Korean Development*, pp. 86–87, 102, 195. The state funded 50 percent of scientific research in Korea. F. Bunge, *Korea: A Country Study* (Washington, D.C.: American University, 1982), p. 118. There is no study of the EPB corresponding to C. Johnson's study of the Japanese Ministry, *MITI and the Japanese Miracle* (Stanford: Stanford University Press, 1982), but one is sorely needed. See Haggard and Cheng, "State and Foreign Capital in the East Asian NICs"; and Johnson, "Political Institutions and Economic Performance"; both in Deyo, *Political Economy*, for general observations on the EPB.
28. Kim Kyoung-Dong, "Political Factors in the Formation of the Entrepreneurial Elite in South Korea" is the best study; see also Choy Bong Youn, *Korea*, pp. 332–335.

incentives. The EPB also used its control over foreign borrowing to channel foreign exchange selectively to industries it wished to promote, while the Ministry for Commerce and Industry controlled imports through a system of licenses. Both linked any given firm's access to imported raw materials and intermediates to its success in exporting.[29] The Bank of Korea and Korea Development Bank were given control over credit allocation through their ability to guarantee foreign loans, and, eventually, through a reform of interest rates that channelled savings away from the informal market towards official banks.[30] Parallel to this, a highly autonomous and politically insulated Office of National Taxation was created in 1966.

The EPB and banks used a vast array of export and investment subsidies to channel funds to firms for investment in targeted industries. Export profits were tax-exempt; foreign exchange for import of intermediate inputs was provided at 84 percent of the market rate; low (at times negative) interest loans were made available; electricity rates were cut 20 percent. Preferential loans amounted to 2032 billion Won, 1963–1971; 79.4 percent of these loans were made in the 1968–71 period. Kuznets estimates that subsidies were 18 percent of export value. Subsidies made export activity profitable, while the incentive system made them a necessity if firms wanted to import intermediate goods used in production for domestic consumption. Thus encouraged, exports per capita increased 46 percent from 1965 to 1970. To accelerate development, subsidies to the chemical and metals industries were the highest, at 136 percent and 230 percent of the average, respectively.[31]

29. Kuznets, *Economic Growth and Structure*, pp. 157–159; Kim Nak Kwan, "Is Korea's Export Promotion Scheme Consistent?" p. 45.

30. Cole and Lyman, *Korean Development*, pp. 176–179, 181–194; R. Luedde-Neurath, "Export Orientation in South Korea: How Helpful is Dependency Thinking to its Analysis?" *IDS Bulletin* 12 (December 1980), 49; C. Hamilton, *Capitalist Industrialization in Korea* (Boulder, Colo.: Westview 1986), pp. 48–49; Park Yung Chul, "Foreign Debt, Balance of Payments, and Growth Prospects: The Case of the Republic of Korea, 1965–1988," *World Development* 14 (1986), 1027. Y. Ro, D. Adams, and L. Hushak, "Income Instability and Consumption-savings in South Korean Farm Households, 1965–1970," *World Development* 9 (February 1979), 189, report that income instability, especially for farmers, led individuals to perceive income gains as transitory and thus induced high saving rates.

31. Kim Nak Kwan, "Is Korea's Export Promotion Scheme Consistent?" pp. 40–41; Cha Byung Kwon, "Subsidy Implicit in the Preferential Loans of Financial Institutions," *Asian Economies* no. 9 (June 1974), pp. 26–27, 38; Kuznets, *Economic Growth and Structure*, p. 74; IBRD, *World Tables* (Baltimore: Johns Hopkins University Press, 1985), p. 101. Inflation often ran at 7 percent per month, while loans were let at 6 percent. Kim Nak Kwan, p. 42 estimates that subsidies equalled 21–34 percent of export values between 1966 and 1970; Hasan, *Korea*, puts subsidies in the 15 percent range. Cha

Development and Dependency Consequences of ISI/EOI, 1962–1972

In growth terms, the Park government's export promotion scheme was a great success. From 1961 to 1965, gross, domestic capital formation averaged 12.5 percent annual increases annually; from 1965 to 1970, 30.4 percent. GNP grew twice as fast from 1965 to 1970 as in the five preceding years. Manufacturing increased from 14.5 percent to 20.8 percent of GNP between 1963 and 1972, even as GNP itself increased 9.1 percent per annum. Absolutely, manufacturing value-added quadrupled in constant terms between 1966 and 1973, a growth rate of 21.7 percent per annum. This increase clearly was export-driven, with the share of export-related employment in manufacturing increasing from 5.8 percent in 1960 to 25.9 percent in 1970, the share of manufactures in exports going from 12.5 percent to 76 percent, and the share of manufacturing value-added going to exports rising from 4.2 percent in 1962 to 38.5 percent in 1968.[32]

EOI clearly prevented unemployment and underdevelopment from emerging after land reform by absorbing a disproportionate share of new workers. Export industries or those linked to them created 50 percent of new employment from 1963 to 1969, even though exports' share of GNP was only 15.7 percent, and at a time when unofficial estimates put unemployment at 15 percent.[33] Avoiding underdevelopment, however, did not guarantee development, for both agriculture and small industry remained undeveloped while large scale industry developed at their expense.

Government pricing policies limited agricultural development. Low prices not only removed the incentive to invest but also caused cultivated acreage to decline 10 percent from 1969 to 1970 even as grain imports grew. Mechanization remained low—0.6 horsepower per hectare—with proportionally only one-seventh as many power tillers as in Taiwan and only one-hundredth as many as in Japan by 1972.

Byung Kwon, studying interest rate subsidies only, calculated the value of subsidies at between 2.32 percent (1965) and 3.82 percent (1971) of all value added in manufacturing.

32. Bank of Korea, *National Income of Korea*, pp. 154–157, 259–260, 358, 362. Calculated in 1970 U.S. dollars, value added per worker went from $823 in 1960 to $1245 in 1970. L. Westphal, "Republic of Korea's Experience with Export-led Industrial Development," *World Development* 6 (March 1978), 360, 370; Koh Sung Jae, "Role of Small Scale Industry in Korean Economic Growth," *Asian Economies* no. 2 (June 1972), p. 9.

33. Kuznets, *Economic Growth and Structure*, p. 161; Hamilton, *Capitalist Industrialization*, p. 42. Shirley Kuo, *The Taiwan Economy in Transition* (Boulder, Colo.: Westview Press, 1983), pp. 61–63, observes a similar phenomenon in Taiwan, where labour-intense export industries in the 1960s created 65–70 percent of new employment.

As Kuznets comments, reform without access to credit and fertilizer was useless for agricultural development.[34]

The same result obtained in light industry. Although value-added per worker increased, the ratio of labour to capital in manufacturing actually increased 16 percent between 1960 and 1973, because export industries were highly labour-intensive small and medium-sized firms. These firms generated 53.1 percent of exports but only 22.3 percent of total manufacturing output.[35] But exports did not stimulate development among small firms because, as a Korean economist has noted, there was a "virtual absence of efforts to increase labour productivity and lower the cost structure through the introduction of labour saving and labour complementary devices and production methods. Most of these industries [were] geared to profit maximization not through their own improvements [but by] sizable export subsidies irrespective of efficiency criteria."[36] Exports were by and large simple and unsophisticated products; wigs, textiles, and clothing together accounted for 47 percent of manufactured exports.

Where development did occur was among the *chaebol*, and here Chalmers Johnson, and Stephan Haggard and Tun-jen Cheng correctly assess the importance of state policy. By limiting MNC DFI to 2.7 percent of GDCF during 1965–73 and shutting out imports, the state allowed parastatal firms and the *chaebol* to dominate a closed market, while its EOI policy enlarged that market by expanding the number of small domestic export firms that the *chaebol* serviced. Those domestic firms were the most active exporters. Although exports were relatively unprofitable, and only generated one dollar of net foreign exchange for every two dollars of overseas sales, expanding overseas sales drove more profitable domestic expansion. The *chaebol* supplied small firms with producer goods, then assembled and

34. It should be noted that any mechanization was a great advance over previous conditions, contributing to a decline in the number of hours of labour per hectare cultivated. Kim Dong Hi, "Small Farmer Economy and Development Policy," p. 7; Hasan, *Korea*, p. 240; Lee, "Egalitarian Peasant Farming and Rural Development," pp. 495–496; Kuznets, *Economic Growth and Structure*, pp. 47–48, 138.

35. Westphal, "Republic of Korea's Experience with Export-led Industrial Development," p. 370; Koh Sung Jae, "Role of Small Scale Industry," pp. 5–7 and 8–10, suggests that workshops with fewer than five employees, which are not enumerated in manufacturing censuses, accounted for one-third of manufacturing employment in the 1960s; Kim Nak Kwan, "Is Korea's Export Promotion Scheme Consistent?" p. 47; Kuznets, *Economic Growth and Structure*, pp. 161–163. Small firms were later especially predominant in the "bonded" trade of the Export Zones.

36. Kim Nak Kwan, "Is Korea's Export Promotion Scheme Consistent?" p. 39, quotation from p. 46; see the similar conclusion in Park Yung Chul, "Foreign Debt, Balance of Payments, and Growth Prospects," p. 1024. Note, however, that subsidies went disproportionately to *chaebol* rather than to small firms.

exported some components that small firms produced. Under state pressure, the *chaebol* steadily expanded their hold over overseas marketing of small firms' goods, and reinvested their monopoly profits in production of increasingly sophisticated goods. Although average factory size remained one-third the U.S. level, from 1963 to 1972 employment in factories with more than 200 employees went from 34 percent to 55 percent of all workers, and these factories' share of value added rose from 47 percent to 72 percent of all value added in South Korean manufacturing. State guardianship of *chaebol* markets ensured a steady increase in articulation of the economy, as measured by input-output tables.[37] Light industry, the main exporter, depended less and less on imported inputs; but the newly created heavy industry in turn remained highly dependent on imported goods. Exports thus served as the engine for stead upstream expansion by the *chaebol*. The *chaebol* monopoly position in the economy allowed them to accumulate on the backs of small firms and consumers.[38] State policy thus accelerated domestically-controlled accumulation. EOI without protected markets for the *chaebol* would have led to increased imports; protection without EOI, as in Latin America, would have led to early saturation of domestic markets.

The importance of state action is especially clear in the emergence of the machine tool industry.[39] Though machinery is a critical upstream industry for metals and other manufacturing, economies of scale dictate high levels of specialization in their manufacture. The size of the final market thus critically determines this industry's devel-

37. On factory size, see Kuznets, *Economic Growth and Structure*, pp. 153, 158–159, 165. With subsidies, the profit rate on exports averaged 2.22 percent, on domestic sales 9.49 percent. Kuznets, p. 154, says "the pattern of tax-tariff-subsidy is consistent with a pattern of import substitution that has emphasized replacement of manufactured materials." On state control of imports, see R. Luedde-Neurath, "Import Controls and Export Oriented Development: A Reexamination of the South Korean case, 1962–1982," Institute for Development Studies, Sussex, mimeo, 1983; see also Hasan, *Korea*, p. 42; *Far Eastern Economic Review*, February 26, 1987, pp. 47–48. On input-output, see Hamilton, *Capitalist Industrialization in Korea*, ch. 3 and 4; Song Byung Nah, "Production Structure of the Korean Economy: International and Historical Comparisons," *Econometrica* 45 (January 1977), 147–162, for an exploration of South Korea's input-output structure.

38. On import dependency, see Cole and Lyman, *Korean Development*, pp. 160–162. Eventually the state had to step in and impose price controls to limit monopoly pricing of consumer goods because of *chaebol* gouging. Kuznets, *Economic Growth and Structure*.

39. For a parallel process in Taiwan, see A. Amsden, "The Division of Labor is Limited by the Type of Market: The Case of the Taiwanese Machine Tool Industry," *World Development* 5 (March 1977); and Amsden, "The Division of Labor is Limited by the *Rate of Growth* of the Market: The Taiwan Machine Tool Industry Revisited," Harvard University Graduate School of Business Administration, mimeo, 1983.

opment. Even with state guardianship, this industry only had a growth rate one-third the average manufacturing rate.[40]

Dependency and the Boom

What then of dependency? The state's careful exclusion of DFI not only created a space for *chaebol* expansion, it also preserved the state's political autonomy by avoiding an economic structure akin to Latin America's. Unlike Latin America, where external interests were internalized by an interior bourgeoisie linked to MNC accumulation, state control over investment and trade meant Korea's bourgeoisie became dependent on the state as financer of both investment and the exports that drove growth.[41] Only in electronics did a "classic" (i.e., Latin American) situation of dependency on MNCs emerge. By 1972, 73 percent of electronics exports were components incorporated in MNC production downstream, and 55 percent of exports were produced by MNC wholly owned subsidiaries using Korean labor. The "economic viability of the Korean electronics firms," wrote Kun Mo Chung, was "controlled by foreign electronics firms, which not only dominate the supply end of part and components but also, in many cases, distribution of Korea produced electronic goods in the overseas market."[42] But because this industry represents the extreme case, it demonstrates the degree to which the Korean state insulated most industries from MNC control.

The state also used its political position within U.S. global hegemony to avoid a classic balance-of-payments crisis during this first phase of export oriented industrialization. The first Five-Year Plan, 1962–1966, created exactly the same payments problems as in typical Latin American ISI even though Korean consumer goods markets started with less foreign penetration than had those of Latin America. From 1961 to 1965, the payments deficit on merchandise trade steadily widened as infrastructure investment designed to promote exports caused increased imports of oil, cement, and consumer goods. The

40. Kuznets, *Economic Growth and Structure*, pp. 150–155.

41. Evans, especially, as well as Haggard, Cheng, and Johnson, (all in Deyo, *Political Economy*), correctly assess the importance of shutting out MNCs in this process. See J. Zysman, *Governments, Markets, Growth* (Ithaca: Cornell University Press, 1985), for general considerations on the role financial systems play in state control of the economy.

42. Kun Mo Chung, "Commercial Transfer of Foreign Technology to the Electronics Industry in Korea," *Asian Economies* no. 13 (June 1975), pp. 7–8; see also Hasan, *Korea*, pp. 177–186. In 1969, electronics accounted for 6.7 percent of Korean exports; because of its high import content, the electronics sector had a negative balance of payments.

gap between exports and imports increased by 31.1 percent in constant terms, from 1962 to 1966. Aid covered the deficit, accounting for 30.8 percent of imports in 1962–66.[43] As aid tapered off after 1966, the Park regime used its relationship with the U.S. state to earn foreign exchange by mobilizing, literally, some of the excess labour flowing out of rural areas. At the beginning of the second Five-Year Plan, the U.S. needed and was willing to pay for mercenary troops and construction workers for the Vietnam War. Paid several hundred times their normal salary, these soldiers generated $927 million from 1967 to 1969, an amount roughly equal to 20 percent of exports or of all government investment during those years. Paralleling this export of labour to war, some 144,000 other Koreans worked overseas between 1963 and 1976, remitting at least $1,139 million.[44] Korean construction firms used their accumulated experience from Vietnam War contracts to compete successfully for the first wave of development projects from the Organization of Petroleum Exporting Countries (OPEC). Because the largest portion of export labour foreign exchange came from Korean mercenaries, the epigraph at the head of this chapter is accurate in labeling Park Chung Hee the victor of the Vietnam War: soldiers made up for the payments imbalance that traditionally subverted ISI efforts.

But the absence of an overt balance-of-payments crisis and dependency on MNCs only obscures the way Korea's mounting debt created the kind of dependency associated with export-led development in the 1880s. Like the 1880s exporters, South Korea borrowed heavily to finance export expansion. Thus what brought the South Korean economy to crisis in the early 1970s was not a payments crisis but a debt crisis. Foreign debt financed growth in the 1960s at both a national and a firm level, with the state on lending what it borrowed abroad. Disbursed foreign debt went from $309 million in 1965 to $2.4 billion in 1971, and service from $20 million to $400 millon. The cost of that debt now drove return on equity among the *chaebol* from 6

43. Hasan, *Korea*, p. 216; Cha Byung Kwon, "Import Substitution and Industrialization," pp. 6, 20–21; Kim Nak Kwan, "Is Korea's Export Promotion Scheme Consistent?" pp. 34–35; Bank of Korea, *National Income of Korea*, pp. 214–215, 218–219.
44. G. McT. Kahin, *Intervention* (New York: Knopf, 1986), pp. 335–336. *AMPO Japan Asia Quarterly* 8 (1976), 54. Some sources claim that ROK mercenaries in Vietnam themselves remitted $1.7 billion, which is more than the total given by AMPO. Kuznets, *Economic Growth and Structure*, p. 71, argues that exports to Vietnam were not responsible for the export boom. But this misses the point, for the link is not between the export boom and the absolute amount of exports to Vietnam, but whether the additional "exports" represented by soldiers' pay prevented an imbalance of payments. See also Cole and Lyman, *Korean Development*, pp. 134–135.

Table 37. South Korea's long-term and medium-term foreign debt, 1964–1972

Year	Debt* ($ mil)	Service ($ mil)	Service as % of exports	Foreign share of GDCF
1964	$83.6	$8.6	—	48.1%
1965	119.5	7.5	1.9%	42.2
1966	309.2	18.1	2.8	39.0
1967	562.4	46.2	5.0	40.2
1968	1049.2	75.3	6.0	43.1
1969	1567.8	125.1	8.3	36.9
1970	1886.9	289.4	10.8	35.4
1971	2427.5	328.1	11.0	44.0
1972	2873.5	399.0	7.6	26.7

* = Disbursed outstanding debt.
GDCF = gross domestic capital formation.
SOURCES: Bank of Korea, *National Income of Korea*, pp. 286–287; Kim Nak Kwan, "Is South Korea's Export Promotion Scheme Consistent?" p. 45; IBRD, *World Tables*, 1985, pp. 102–103; Hasan, *Korea*, p. 225.

percent in 1969 to 4.4 percent in 1971, preventing mobilization of surplus for investment in upstream industries. (See Tables 37 and 38.) Real investment *fell* 6.5 percent from 1969 to 1972.[45] Rather than a payments crisis making it impossible for firms to move upstream to capital goods production, as in Latin America, high levels of debt made it impossible for them to mobilize enough capital for investment upstream. With half the population on the land, the 1960s squeezing of agriculture made it difficult to open domestic markets as a source of further expansion.[46] Indeed, politically this crisis manifested itself through the emergence of Kim Dae Jung's New Democratic Party as the champion of small business and peasants.[47] In 1971 the NDP narrowly lost what was widely seen as a rigged election.

What had happened? As in Australia and the other dominions, the South Korean state had borrowed to create state-run infrastructure for export industry and to pay for direct export subsidies. The ultimate beneficiaries of export activity thus were *chaebol* (who received the bulk of the subsidies) and overseas consumers. But subsidized exports implied a transfer of value overseas, so neither the state nor

45. The most concise study is Park Yung Chul, "Foreign Debt, Balance of Payments and Growth Prospects." See also Hasan, *Korea*, pp. 209, 225, 250; J. Frieden, "Third World Indebted Industrialization: International Finance and State Capitalism in Mexico, Brazil, Algeria, and South Korea," *International Organization* 35 (Summer 1981), p. 425.
46. Ki-Do Woo, "Labor Force, Wage Level, and Economic Growth in Korea," p. 41.
47. Cole and Lyman, *Korean Development*, pp. 235–237.

Table 38. Debt burden in Korean manufacturing, 1967–1971

	1967	1968	1969	1970	1971
Interest as % of net sales	5.4	5.9	7.8	9.2	9.9
Net profit as % of liability and equity	6.8	5.3	3.7	2.5	1.0
Debt to equity ratio	151.2	201.3	270.0	328.4	394.2

SOURCES: Cha Byung Kwon, "ISI and Industrialization," p. 36, for 1967 data; Hasan, *Korea*, p. 250, for 1968–1971 data.

the *chaebol* generated sufficient value to service debt merely through their limited profits from exports. Just as the Dominion states could not make their debtors bear the full cost of borrowing without precipitating an economic collapse, export industry could not repay the South Korean state. Instead, light industry lost value to the protected, oligopolistic *chaebol* when it bought inputs from them; its modernization was thus inhibited. The South Korean state in 1971 thus was caught in the same bind as the Australian states in the 1890s—the existing system of production could not carry the dual burden of debt service and subsidy at its current level of productivity. If the state forced the *chaebol* to pay the full cost of debt, or if the *chaebol* raised either export prices or prices of producer goods to small exporters in order to pay interest, export revenues would drop, because Korean exports were highly price-sensitive.[48] The result would be a balance of payments crisis and an end to growth as imports of crucial intermediate goods fell. As in the Antipodes, the only answer to this economic dilemma was intensification of production. Just as Australian pastoralists' creditors used a politically mediated change from extensive grazing to intensive dairy and wheat farming to recover their sunk investments, a change from light to heavy industrial activity and exports would generate more value added. At existing levels of debt, South Korean firms could not make the necessary investments to finance intensification; as debt service increased relative to exports, the South Korean state was increasingly unable to borrow to fund investment either. In this contradiction between desire and ability lies South Korean dependency. The essential component for renewed economic growth and accumulation was external to the South Korean system. Several contingent factors made the crisis worse. Devaluation had worsened the Won cost of debt service for individual firms; the

48. See Kwack Sung Yeung, "Economic Development of the Republic of Korea," chap. 3, in L. Lau, ed., *Models of Development: A Comparative Study of Economic Growth in South Korea and Taiwan* (San Francisco: Institute for Contemporary Studies, 1986), p. 118, on price sensitivity.

U.S. government was winding down both PL-480 aid and the Vietnam War, both of which threatened the balance of payments; and the Nixon textile tariff shock also undercut the viability of continuing with light exports.[49]

RENEWED BORROWING AND INTENSIFICATION OF PRODUCTION

South Korea made significant political and institutional changes in 1971–72 to continue both industrial development and growth through a process of intensification.[50] Renewed foreign borrowing underpinned this intensification of production, reinforcing the existing pattern of debt dependency. After bailing out troubled firms, the state supported intensification by shifting from direct labour exports to labour exports mediated through export processing zones, starting the *Saemaul Undong* (New Village) agricultural movement; and militarizing society via the 1972 declaration of martial law and the *Yushin* Constitution (which, not incidentally, also removed the NDP as a political threat). Institutionally, control over planning shifted from the EPB, which had opposed deepening and borrowing, to a tight group centered in the Ministry of Commerce and Industry (MCI). In 1973 they published the "Heavy and Chemical Industry Development Plan" (HCIDP), which targeted shipbuilding, steel, chemicals, cement, fertilizer, electronics, and machinery for development.[51]

Export Processing Zones and Intensification

The first quid pro quo for the continued foreign finance South Korea needed, suggest Haggard and Cheng, was creation of the Masan Free Export Zone (FEZ) in 1970.[52] The Masan FEZ was "more of

49. Haggard and Cheng, "State and Foreign Capital in the East Asian NICs," pp. 123–124, focus on these events and military concerns as the key variables, but had sufficient capital been available, increased textile tariffs ought not have mattered so much.

50. See Cumings, "Origins and Development of the Northeast Asian Political Economy"; Cumings and others see in these changes a parallel to the rise of "bureaucratic authoritarianism" in Latin America. See G. O'Donnell, *Modernization and Bureaucratic Authoritarianism in Latin America* (Berkeley: University of California Press, 1973), for the original argument. The parallel rise of the authoritarian ideology *Jungche* in North Korea is also worth note.

51. Haggard and Cheng, "State and Foreign Capital in the East Asian NICs," p. 123; Park Yung Chul, "Foreign Debt, Balance of Payments and Growth Prospects," pp. 1029–1030.

52. Haggard and Cheng, "State and Foreign Capital in the East Asian NICs," p. 113. Taiwan had already opened an FEZ at Kaoshiung in 1965. On Japanese desires to shift light industry overseas, see Ozawa Terutomo, *Multinationalism, Japanese Style*, chap. 3.

the same" in that it again mobilized the vast outflow of rural labour to earn foreign exchange. Instead of sending labour abroad, the FEZs provided a captive and disciplined workforce for foreign capital's use. Japan's desire for cheap labour coupled with its unwillingness to import ex-colonial guestworkers along the European pattern encouraged creation of FEZs where Japanese capital could marry cheap—typically female—labour. Japanese firms in highly competitive sectors quickly established production in the Masan FEZ; there, wages stood at one-fifth of the minimum in Japan, forced overtime was the norm, and there were no pollution laws. The Masan FEZ employed 25,000 manufacturing workers and exported $110 million worth of goods by 1974. Other FEZs modeled on Masan were established. By 1975 foreign firms invested $700 million in the FEZs, representing 17 percent of investment in manufacturing, generating 40 percent of manufacturing exports by 1974.[53] 1971 thus marked a turning point in the trend of South Korea's payments balance. Before 1971, the payments deficit was actually larger than absolute merchandise exports; after 1971, exports were an increasingly larger multiple of the payments deficit.

South Korea benefited in three ways from the FEZs. First, their increased employment continued the pattern of labour absorption through increased exports, simultaneously avoiding underdevelopment while increasing the domestic market. Second, even though the increased foreign exchange earnings the FEZs generated were limited to the value added in the zones, that foreign exchange enabled the state to renew borrowing on the basis of increased export revenues. Finally, as Haggard and Cheng argue, the FEZs isolated foreign capital by limiting their access to the local economy. While many criticize FEZs for precisely this reason, in this case segregation continued to preserve and enlarge the domestic market for the *chaebol*. The free enterprise zones thus reinforced Park Chung Hee's policy of excluding MNCs even as direct foreign investment increased.

Agriculture and Intensification

Agriculture presented both opportunity and danger to the Park regime in the early 1970s. The loss of American PL-480 aid threatened cheap wages, so the regime needed to find ways of increasing

---

53. Study Group on Japan-Korea Relations, "Masan Free Export Zone," *AMPO Japan Asia Quarterly* 6 (1974), 101–102; and ibid., 8 (1976), 58–69; Frieden, "Third World Indebted Industrialization," p. 426. By 1978, $940 million had been invested, so the biggest inflow was 1970–1975.

rural productivity. The subsidized industries of the first wave of ISI faced overcapacity, but continued agricultural stagnation blocked expansion of their domestic markets. Funds used to subsidize this first generation of industry were needed for the next. Agriculture's stagnation and low mechanization (compared to Taiwan) meant opportunities for more and deeper ISI, but these had to be done without driving up rice prices and thus urban wages. The regime used the *Saemaul Undong*, or New Village Movement, to exploit this opportunity and peasants simultaneously. The *Saemaul* program promised increased rural incomes and consumption, through a rapid improvement of roads, housing, and other social infrastructure, and by substituting hybrid rice (and fruits and vegetables) for traditional rices. All of these increased farmer's consumption of goods either in oversupply, or targeted for expansion under the HCIDP—ceramics, fertilizer, cement. For example, the government-controlled National Agricultural Cooperative Federation forced peasants to switch to higher yielding but less profitable forms of rice requiring increased inputs of fertilizer and pesticides. Under this stimulus, the consumption of pesticides increased 331 percent in the two years between 1974 and 1976, versus only a 10 percent increase during the entire decade preceding 1974; consumption of fertilizer increased 319 percent from 1970 to 1976.[54] These increases formed the basis for increased output and profitability in the chemical industry.

Profitable fertilizer production and cheap rice for the cities was built into the government-set terms of trade between fertilizer and rice. The Agricultural Co-ops had a monopoly on fertilizer sales, buying fertilizer at between Won 62,000 and Won 92,000 per ton, and selling it to farmers at Won 122,000 per ton.[55] The world market price for fertilizer in the late 1970s was about Won 55,000 per ton. Peasants bought fertilizer on credit, by mortgaging their future rice at the prior year's rice price or by borrowing privately at 3–5 percent

54. Kim, "Saemaul Agriculture," pp. 56–58, 62–64; Lee, "Egalitarian Peasant Farming and Rural Development," p. 497. Cultivated acreage decreased during the *Saemaul* period; Hasan, *Korea*, p. 240. By 1976 half of rice acreage was the new "Tong-il" strain. As with Green Revolution rice elsewhere, local consumers disliked this bad tasting rice, so its price fell relative to traditional rice. The government thus was able to continue its policy of low food costs for urban workers, while increasing its purchase price for marketed rice.

55. Kim Chang Soo, "Marginalization, Development, and the Korean Workers' Movement," p. 25; H. Sunoo, "Economic Development and Foreign Control in South Korean Development," *Journal of Contemporary Asia* 8 (1978), 323–324. This process paralleled Taiwan's earlier and more successful experience; see Amsden, "Taiwan's Economic History."

interest per month. Kim estimates that fertilizer firms gained $1,690 million between 1975 and 1978 this way, which they used to subsidize exports.[56] Peasants also became increasingly indebted. From 1975 to 1985, average farm household debt jumped from $185 to $2,300.[57]

Most of the *Saemaul* movement's improvements came from farmers themselves. Of the $567 million officially invested in *Saemaul* projects between 1971 and 1974, 22 percent came from government spending and 78 percent came from "volunteer" labour amounting to 215 million man-hours of work.[58] Rural income and consumption thus increased because farmers were working longer hours and increasing their debt. Predictably, farmers left for the city in even larger numbers to avoid this burden and to find non-farm sources of income. Although the farm population had held steady in absolute terms from 1962 to 1969, by 1976 it had decreased by 15 percent, and the number of farm households fell 5 percent. Much of the decrease came from smaller, marginal farms under 0.5 hectare.[59] Equally predictable, mostly women left, so the 1970s saw the rise of two complementary female labour pools. The first staffed the Free Export Zones, the second, large-scale *kisaeng* prostitution for growing hordes of male Japanese tourists. Increased domestic demand for a variety of heavy industrial import substitution goods thus rested on coerced consumption. Farmers had to put in extra hours for the *Saemaul* Movement; they required fertilizer to grow the improved variety of rice foisted upon them; they depended ever more on non-farm income to survive. Increased pressure on farmers created the conditions for increased foreign exchange earnings by creating an easily exploitable pool of female labour.

Yushin and Intensification

Apart from its role in suppressing Kim Dae Jung's political challenge, the imposition of martial law and the new *Yushin* constitution of 1972 created the industrial counterpart to the rural *Saemaul* movement. *Yushin*'s militarization of production held down wages while raising productivity, to generate the higher profits needed for debt

56. Kim, "Saemaul Agriculture," pp. 5, 11; in terms of 1975 U.S. dollars. See also Sunoo, "Economic Development and Foreign Control in South Korean Development," p. 323.
57. *New York Times*, April 7, 1987, p. 7.
58. Hasan, *Korea*, pp. 159–164.
59. Kim Chang Soo, "Marginalization, Development, and the Korean Workers' Movement," p. 24; Kim Dong Hi, "Small Farmer Economy and Development Policy," p. 8.

service and new investment. *Yushin* quashed the nascent labour movement crystallizing around the suicide of labour activist Chon Taeil in
1970, preempting worker activity with state imposed unions or simple
repression. Strikes were outlawed, union leaders beaten and fired,
and soldiers guarded the more important production sites. Though
1976 and 1979 saw protests and (illegal) strikes, and union membership grew from 537,000 in 1974 to roughly 1,200,000 in 1980, unions
remained firmly under state control.[60] Under *Yushin*, total labour
costs as a percentage of production costs fell by 1975 to 84 percent of
the 1971 level, and had recovered only to 93 percent by 1979. Productivity increases far outstripped increases in real wages, while the average work week, already one of Asia's highest, rose.[61]

The battle between wages and inflation, and continuing increases in
productivity, led to rapid growth of underemployment in the "services" sector. By 1982, 46.1 percent of the workforce was in services,
twice as many as in manufacturing, and the share of services in the
economy was higher than in the U.S., indicating that underdevelopment remains a potential problem. Although the average cost of living for a five-person family in Seoul was Won 85,000 per month, 60
percent of workers earned less than Won 30,000 per month, and 78.8
percent less than Won 45,000. In part this reflected a two-tiered
employment system, for workers in the *chaebol*'s subcontractors got
between 69 percent to 76 percent of the *chaebol* wage.[62]

Renewed Borrowing and Intensification

With domestic workers and farmers working harder than ever to
fund ongoing debt service, Korean attempts to capitalize a wide range
of heavy industries in the mid-1970s continued to rely on foreign
loans. Foreign sources provided 45 percent of capital investment in
targeted industries. Though, predictably, only 15 percent of this
came as DFI, the need for capital motivated liberalization of rules

60. See F. Deyo, "State and Labor: Modes of Exclusion in East Asian Development,"
in Deyo, *Political Economy*, pp. 188–189; and *Far Eastern Economic Review*, April 3, 1986.

61. Park Young Ki, "Labor and the Business Environment in Korea," *Asian Economies*
no. 35, December 1979, pp. 32–33; Deyo, "State and Labor," p. 197; T. Scitovsky,
"Economic Development in Taiwan and South Korea, 1965–1981," in Lau, *Models of
Development*, p. 180. The average work week increased from 54 hours in 1970 to 60
hours in 1980. It now hovers around 57 hours; *Far Eastern Economic Review*, August 27,
1987, p. 17.

62. Koo Hagen, "Political Economy of Income Distribution in South Korea: The
Impact of State Industrialization Policies," *World Development* 12 (October 1984), 1030–
1032; Kim Chang Soo, "Marginalization, Development, and the Korean Workers'
Movement," pp. 28–30.

governing DFI.[63] This borrowing permitted Korean expansion into heavy industry but also constrained its ability to expand the domestic orientation and control of production. Between 1970 and 1975, debt increased 140 percent as the government borrowed $3.7 billion.[64] From 1975 to 1979, debt expanded even more rapidly—263 percent on a higher base—as various shipbuilding, steel, chemical, and transport projects were launched, and as the rush of DFI into the FEZs tapered off.[65] Borrowing allowed high rates of growth and capitalization of Korean capital goods industry. By the end of the decade, Hyundai owned the world's largest corporate shipyard at Ulsan, and the largest machinery plant at Changwon. Heavy industrial exports doubled between 1970 and 1980 to 42 percent of all exports, as exports increased 650 percent. Thirty-three thousand cars were exported, and the Pohang complex was producing 5.5 million tons of steel a year. More important, the capital stock per worker roughly quadrupled from 1968 to 1980.[66]

To ensure that South Korea captured the maximum amount of foreign exchange from its exports, the state also stepped up efforts to take control of export sales. "General Trading Companies" (GTC) were created in 1975 to help the Korea Overseas Trade Association, set up in the 1960s, displace the Japanese trading companies and the U.S. retail firms then dominating distribution of Korean exports. Being a GTC brought access to state-guaranteed letters of credit, foreign exchange, and lower import duties, but to become a GTC a firm had to sell $ 10 million of goods to ten markets through ten branch organizations.[67]

63. Haggard and Cheng, "State and Foreign Capital in the East Asian NICs," p. 124. Overall, DFI rose from 3.7 percent of net foreign investment 1967–1971 to 7.9 percent 1972–1976, because of investment in the FEZs and South Korea's hunger for investment. S. Haggard and Chung-il Moon, "The South Korean State in the International Economy," in J. Ruggie, ed., *Antinomies of Interdependence* (New York: Columbia University Press, 1983), p. 151.

64. Frieden, "Third World Indebted Industrialization," p. 426.

65. IBRD, *World Debt Tables 1986/87* (Baltimore: Johns Hopkins University Press, 1986), pp. 226–229.

66. Frieden, "Third World Indebted Industrialization," p. 426; Kwack Sung Yeung, "Economic Development in South Korea," in Lau, *Models of Development*, p. 119; IBRD, *World Tables* (1985), pp. 102–103; Park Yung Chul, "Foreign Debt, Balance of Payments and Growth Prospects," p. 1037.

67. Haggard and Chung-il Moon, "South Korean State in the International System," p. 167. These conditions were made progressively more rigorous, with additions to the number of markets, branches, and geographic dispersal. In 1974 the four largest *sogo shosha* controlled 40 percent of Korea's foreign trade; H. Sunoo, "Economic Development and Foreign Control in South Korean Development," p. 323; *AMPO Japan-Asian Quarterly* 8 (1976), 9.

THE CRISIS OF THE 1980S

Just as "Vietnam" exports eased the first phase of EOI, masking the imbalance of payments, increased "heavy" exports made the HCIDP appear successful in the 1970s. Outstanding debt as a percentage of exports actually fell, though debt increased between 1974 and 1978.[68] But both debt and debt service as a percentage of GDP increased after 1979, when growth slowed in the oil-shocked core. (See Table 39.) Collapse of the highly leveraged Yulsan group, political protests culminating in the Kwangju uprising, Park Chung Hee's assassination in October 1979, and a 5.2 percent decline in GNP in 1980 signalled the start of a new period of political and economic crisis reminiscent of the 1970–72 period.[69] After 1980, the core became increasingly unwilling to accept South Korean exports or to supply new loans (although certainly more willing for South Korea than for Brazil or Argentina). Five years later, the *Far Eastern Economic Review* was still writing of "an economy littered with failed industrial schemes, particularly in the area of heavy industry."[70] Overcapacity in the industries the HCIDP had targeted in the 1970s recreated the 1970–72 crisis at a higher level. Once more, the state had to choose between subsidizing continued expansion or paying back debt. The state lacked the resources to continue financing industries whose profitability depended on subsidy, but overcapacity and low productivity in those industries prevented them from becoming profitable in their own right. Government intervention after Chun Doo Hwan's 1980 coup thus concentrated on forcing mergers to rationalize production and decrease intra-industry competition, and on restricting credit. *Chaebol* were ordered to hold debt at the 1983 level through 1984–85, while the government earmarked 35 percent of new credit for small and medium-sized firms. Just as in the 1970–72 crisis, control over DFI was loosened in 1980 to attract alternative sources of capital.[71]

---

68. IBRD, *World Debt Tables 1984/85*, p. 133.

69. *Far Eastern Economic Review*, October 26, 1985, p. 106. Yulsan's collapse is thought in part to have been engineered by Park because of its ties to Kim Dae Jung and the NDP. Park's death was not the sole cause for crisis, for the other Dragons also experienced economic difficulty at this time. See "Export-led Slowdown," *Far Eastern Economic Review*, September 26, 1985.

70. *Far Eastern Economic Review*, September 26, 1985, p. 106.

71. Haggard and Cheng, "State and Foreign Capital," point to increased royalty payments for the technologies used in the new heavy industries as a source of difficulty, which I would not dispute. Debt service, however, was far larger than royalty payments. Of 999 industrial subsectors defined by the South Korean government, the number open to foreign investment rose from 44 percent in 1980 to 66 percent in 1984 (in

Table 39. South Korea's debt and debt service, 1974–1985

	Debt^ ($ mil)	Debt* as % of GNP	Debt service* ($ mil)	Debt service* as % of exports	Debt service* as % of GNP
1974	4724	23.3	549.8	10.3	2.9
1976	7250	23.7	910.3	9.6	3.2
1978	11,731	22.5	1818.8	10.6	3.6
1979	14,293	21.2	2561.7	13.1	4.0
1980	16,680	25.8	2708.4	12.0	4.4
1981	19,508	27.2	3398.6	12.4	5.5
1982	21,499	28.3	3716.2	13.1	5.2
1983	23,071	28.6	3743.4	12.3	5.0
1980	29,774	26.9	2769.7	12.3	4.6
1981	33,369	28.3	3495.2	12.8	5.3
1982	37,767	29.7	3844.5	13.6	5.5
1983	40,933	29.6	4147.3	13.6	5.5
1984	43,248	30.3	4671.3	13.9	5.7
1985	47,996	35.8	5030.1	15.2	6.1
1986	43,000 (est.)				
1987	40,000 (est.)				

1974–83 series does not include short term debt.
1980–85 series includes short term debt.
^ = All debt (public, publicly guaranteed, and private).
* = Public and publicly guaranteed debt or debt service only.
SOURCES: IBRD, *World Debt Tables* 1984/85 ed., pp. 132–134; IBRD, *World Debt Tables* 1986/87 ed., pp. 226–229; 1986–87 estimates, *Far Eastern Economic Review,* June 25, 1987, p. 86.

Nevertheless, by 1984 the 30 top *chaebol*, accounting for 75 percent of output and 29.2 percent of value-added in the entire economy in 1983, owed $10.5 billion to nominally domestic creditors (the five privately owned banks and state banks—who in turn owed money to foreigners) and $19.2 billion to foreign creditors. Their debt-to-equity ratio was 4.5 : 1, considerably higher than the Korean manufacturing average of 3.6 : 1.[72] In a counterpoint to Yulsan's 1979 collapse, Kukje, the sixth-largest *chaebol*, disintegrated in February 1985 with a

---

manufacturing, from 69 percent to 89 percent). In October 1985, 102 more areas were opened to foreign investment; by 1988 government plans call for 90 percent of subsectors to be open. *Far Eastern Economic Review*, December 12, 1985, pp. 74–75; "Foreign Investment Nagged by Cross Interests," *Business Korea*, July 1985.

72. *Far Eastern Economic Review*, December 12, 1985, p. 71; Koo Hagen, "Political Economy of Income Distribution in South Korea," p. 1037. For comparison: West German firms had peak debt-equity ratios of 4.1 : 1 in 1981–82, Japanese firms 3.3 : 1 in 1974–79. These traditionally are highly leveraged economies. The U.S., Britain, and Canada all normally fluctuate in the range of 1 : 1 or even lower; *Economist*, June 21, 1986, p. 108. The top ten *chaebol* generated 50 percent of South Korean exports; *New York Times Magazine*, December 14, 1986, p. 112.

debt-to-equity ratio of 9.1 : 1.[73] To fund this debt, the *chaebol* had to increase either domestic or overseas sales. The government crackdown on unions led to falling real wages, constraining the domestic market for heavy industrial goods, particularly autos and consumer durables.[74] Aside from the exigencies of neo-protectionism, *chaebol* could not produce internationally competitive goods without access to the technology that the MNCs control. This dilemma increasingly eroded the state's ability to control MNC access to the domestic market and control over domestic firms. The automobile and semiconductor/electronics industries typify the dilemmas and possibilities Korean heavy and light industry faces.

From Debt Dependency to DFI Dependency?

The government promoted a domestic auto industry by legislation mandating 100 percent domestically-produced content in 1974, and followed through by encouraging Hyundai, Daewoo (previously called Saehan), and Kia to enter the market.[75] By the early 1980s, the industry could produce over 300,000 cars, but was running at only 30 percent of capacity.[76] The government tried to rationalize the industry by forcing a merger of Hyundai Motor and Daewoo Motor, but GM, holding 50 percent of Daewoo Motor stock, vetoed this. Domestic sales have increased since 1981, but Daewoo Motor alone, when planned expansion comes on-line in 1988, will produce roughly double what South Korea absorbed in 1984.[77] In this classically fordist industry, workers cannot afford their own products, for wages are roughly U.S. $2.50–3.00 per hour.[78] With so much capacity, profitability depends on exports, and exports on low wages, since low productivity relative to U.S. and Japanese producers is balanced only by low wages. Therefore in 1986 when management and labour at

73. *Far Eastern Economic Review*, September 26, 1985, p. 100; December 12, 1985, p. 71.

74. Park Yung Chul, "Foreign Debt, Balance of Payments, and Growth Prospects," Table A8; *Far Eastern Economic Review*, August 27, 1987, pp. 16–17.

75. For general studies of the auto industry see R. Cole, ed., *The American and Japanese Auto Industries* (Ann Arbor: Center for Japanese Studies, University of Michigan, 1984); K. Okada, *Motor Vehicle Industry in Asia* (Singapore: Singapore University Press, 1983).

76. T. Tsuchiya, "Structural Crisis in the Economy," *AMPO Japan Asia Quarterly* 13 (1981), 28–29; *Wall Street Journal*, November 16, 1984, p. 1; *Economist*, March 6, 1982, p. 79. Similar levels of overcapacity existed in the electronics industry.

77. *Far Eastern Economic Review*, February 27, 1981, p. 57; *Wall Street Journal*, November 16, 1984, p. 1.

78. *Economist*, May 24, 1986; *New York Times Magazine*, December 14, 1986, p. 34. This is roughly double to triple the manufacturing average, however; *Economist*, August 15, 1987, p. 51.

Daewoo Motor seemed to be evolving a fordist pact on their own, the state stepped in, voiding a strike settlement favorable to workers and jailing union leaders. In the more recent rounds of strikes, however, the state has urged the auto companies to raise wages, so as to maintain the labour peace and production necessary to service debt.[79]

So far, the export-led strategy in autos has been successful, in the sense that Hyundai, Daewoo, and Kia Motors are all exporting much of their output to the North American market. Hyundai Motor seems likely to become the fourth-largest exporter, after Toyota, Nissan, and Honda.[80] But in this most successful of Korean heavy export industry, Cardoso and Faletto's third, MNC, form of dependency is emerging. Kia and Daewoo rely heavily on Ford/Mazda and General Motors technology respectively, Hyundai less so on Mitsubishi. Korean access to the U.S. market also depends on the MNC connection. Now that U.S. monetary policy has devalued the dollar relative to the yen below the ¥160/$ point at which Nomura Associates believes Korean auto manufacturers can be price-competitive with Japanese manufacturers, Korean firms have earned a place in the global strategy of U.S. auto firms.[81] (See Table 40 below.) Led by GM, U.S. firms are deliberately importing from Korean and other NIC auto firms the cheap small cars they no longer can produce profitably. With these cheap cars, they hope to erode Japanese firms' share of the low end of the market, while controlling the upper end with their newly automated plants. The Japanese majors thus will be cramped in what U.S. manufacturers hope is a shrinking middle.[82] Most notably for GM, a diversity of suppliers ensures that U.S. firms retain control over Korean production and market access.

The same pattern is visible in electronics, continuing the pattern set

79. *Far Eastern Economic Review*, April 3, 1986, pp. 46–47; September 3, 1987, p. 47.

80. Hyundai Motor planned to export 75 percent of the 610,000 cars it produced, Daewoo Motor about 100,000, and Kia Motors about 80,000 in 1987. Hyundai also is constructing a plant in Quebec to produce about 100,000 cars; but as currently envisaged it will be unable to take advantage of the U.S.-Canadian Auto Pact. *New York Post*, May 5, 1987. *Wall Street Journal*, September 17, 1986, December 4, 1986, February 5, 1987.

81. *Economist*, May 24, 1986; *Far Eastern Economic Review*, May 19, 1987, pp. 136–138.

82. Mitsubishi imports the Hyundai "Excel" as the "Precis"; Chrysler in turn imports Mitsubishi's "Mirage" as the "Colt." Ford also imports the "Tracer" from Mexico. In November 1986, Japanese auto exports had fallen 15.1 percent from the prior year's sales. In mid-1987, *Automotive News* was predicting that Japanese firms would fall short of their import "quota" in the U.S. market, and in early 1988 Nissan announced plans to cut back export production. Japanese firms, led by Honda, have responded by expanding production in the U.S.; see *San Francisco Chronicle*, December 27, 1986; *New York Times*, April 7, 1987; *Far Eastern Economic Review*, April 3, 1984; *Economist*, May 24, 1986; ibid., February 29, 1988, pp. 54–55; *Wall Street Journal*, November 16, 1984.

CASES

Table 40. U.S. links to Korean and minor Japanese auto firms, mid-1980s

GM	Suzuki (Japan) 6 % equity. Joint production: 200,000 cars. "Scamp" sold as Chevrolet "Sprint."	Isuzu (Japan) 40 % equity. "I-mark" sold as Chevrolet "Spec- trum."	Daewoo (South Korea) 50 % equity. Import sold as Pontiac "LeMans."
Ford	Mazda (Japan) 24 % equity. Joint production 240,000 cars.	Kia (South Korea) 10 % equity by Ford; 8 % equity by Mazda; 2 % equity C. Itoh. Import sold as Ford "Festiva."	Ford (Mexico) Import sold as Ford "Tracer."
Chrysler	Mitsubishi (Japan) 20 % equity. "Mirage," "Rampage," "Ram 50," & "Conquest" sold via Dodge.		Hyundai (South Korea) 15 % equity by Mitsubishi. "Excel" sold as Mitsubishi "Precis."

Equity held by U.S. firm except as indicated; joint production in U.S. except as indicated.

SOURCES: *Economist,* May 24, 1986; *Business Week; Wall Street Journal,* March 8, 1988.

in the early 1970s. In semiconductors, government policies gave Korean firms enough of a start that they could consider licensing and co-production agreements with U.S. firms. U.S. firms for their part were willing to concede the highly competitive and very low profit manufacture of technologically simple memory chips to the Koreans. For U.S. firms, it was worth trading technology for licensing fees because U.S. firms were unable to compete with Japanese firms in those markets anyway. License fees were better than losing the low end entirely. Korean firms accepted these opportunities with alacrity. Korean firms thus are already using state-of-the-art technology to produce 256 kilo-byte memory chips, DRAMs and they plan one-megabyte chips; in 1987 Korean firms exported $800 million worth of IBM personal computer clones. The recent U.S.-Japan semiconductor agreement has also created a market opening for South Korean firms. But the same pattern of joint ventures, licensing and marketing control found with autos also is found in the electronics industry. South Korean producers are restricted to highly competitive markets for goods with low profit margins, such as the glutted PC-clone market. New products, high-value added steps and production of complex components have been retained in the U.S. and Japan. Meanwhile, Korean producers have been whipsawed as the price of dollar-denominated goods and the value of the dollar have fallen,

264

while the Yen price of imported components (roughly half of product value) has risen.[83]

Overall, as U.S. firms try to squeeze Japanese producers between low-end Korean imports and high-end U.S. products, U.S. MNCs (with 42 percent of manufacturing DFI) have displaced Japanese firms (37 percent) as the largest source of DFI in South Korean manufacturing. Afraid to create Korean competitors, 50 percent of new Japanese DFI in Korea is now in services, and Japanese firms are notoriously strict about licensing technology to Korean firms.[84] This process in a global context is good for South Korea. GM's choice of Daewoo meant its withdrawal from the Philippines and standstills at projects in Thailand and Taiwan.[85] South Korea need not worry that its heavy-goods markets in the core will be swamped by a horde of low-wage copycats in the Pacific Rim, South Asia, or West Africa. The Asian NICs' disproportionate share of LDC exports of manufactures is unlikely to slip much.[86] The same preferential treatment that South Korea's position in U.S. global security concerns accorded it during its first efforts at ISI, bolstered by its potential middleman position between the U.S. and the People's Republic of China, should also continue to benefit South Korea in the coming years. But none of this is enough to assure South Korea of a steady progress into the core, despite President Roh's ambition to enter the OECD by 1993. Although Taiwan's status as a political pariah makes South Korea the most likely candidate for elevation into the various directorates of "World Capitalism, Inc."—IMF, BIS, Group of 20, OECD, etc.—debt and South Korea's internal economic structure make this advance uncertain.

Debt and Internal Impediments to Autonomy

The central tension for South Korea in the coming years will be among wages, profits, and debt repatriation—precisely the tensions

83. *Far Eastern Economic Review*, July 21, 1983, p. 65; ibid., December 12, 1985, p. 70; ibid., July 9, 1987, pp. 54–55; ibid., September 17, 1987, pp. 61–62; *Electronic Business*, May 15, 1985, p. 48; *Wall Street Journal*, September 7, 1984, p. 30; July 17, 1985, p. 35.
84. T. Shorrock, "U.S. Steel's Pohang Strategy," *AMPO Japan Asia Quarterly* 17 (1985), 3–4; *Economist*, May 21, 1988, survey, pp. 18–19.
85. *Economist*, September 21, 1985, pp. 70–71.
86. W. Cline, "Can the East Asian Model of Development be Generalized?" *World Development* 10 (February 1982), 81–90, provides an interesting mathematical exercise showing the difficulty the core would have absorbing exports if all the LDCs behaved like the Gang of Four.

Australia faced ninety years ago. The problem will be to maintain sufficiently high productivity growth that enough surplus will be available for both debt service and reinvestment, while returning enough surplus as wages that the domestic market becomes an increasing source of growth.

South Korea lacks the internal distribution of income that in Japan was the basis for sustained domestic growth. Japan's internal market—absolutely, and relatively on account of the distribution of income—was considerably larger than South Korea's now is. The Japanese Sohyo Union's "Spring-Wage Offensives" of the 1960s and early 1970s won real wage rises far in excess of what state-managed South Korean unions are capable. In the 1960s and early 1970s, Japan exported barely one-third as much, as a proportion of GNP, as South Korea now does.[87]

But in South Korea, the necessities of repaying debt while staying competitive dictate continued low wages, and thus a narrower domestic market, even if continued reliance on exports to maintain capacity utilization prevents complete collapse of that market. While South Korean real wages rose 40 percent between 1980 and 1986, they are still lower than those in industrial Latin America, where producers of autos and consumer durables are constantly troubled by saturated markets; South Korean real wages have lagged considerably behind productivity, which doubled.[88] In each crisis, wage rises have always taken second place to investment, and the share of indirect taxes in revenue has risen from 53.5 percent in 1965 to 63.3 percent in 1980.[89] Finally, while the evidence is contradictory, income inequality seems to be rising.[90] All these indicate it will be difficult to expand the

---

87. IBRD, *World Tables* 1985.

88. Park Young Ki, "Labor and the Business Environment in Korea," pp. 32–33; Deyo, "State and Labor," p. 197; *Economist*, August 15, 1987, p. 52.

89. Koo, "Political Economy of Income Distribution in South Korea," p. 1034; Deyo, "State and Labor," pp. 185, 188. The share of income paid by the worst-paid as taxes has also increased.

90. There is considerable debate on equality and inequality in South Korea. All agree that inequality is lower than in most other LDCs. But poor survey techniques make the data used for inter-temporal comparisons unreliable; see Kuznets, *Economic Growth and Structure*, pp. 94–99. Some of this data suggests that inequality has been increasing; while the gini coefficient stood at 34.4 in 1965, by 1982 it had reached 40; see Koo, "Political Economy of Income Distribution in South Korea," p. 1034. For other reflections on inequality in South Korea and its role in development, see Evans, "State, Class, and Dependence in East Asia," pp. 217–220, and Deyo, "State and Labor," pp. 196–199; I. Adelman and S. Robinson, *Income Distribution Policy in Developing Countries: Korea* (Oxford: Oxford University Press, 1978); Rao, "Economic Growth and Equity in the Republic of Korea"; Lee, "Egalitarian Peasant Farming and Rural Development," especially p. 499.

domestic market to the point where domestic sales generate enough capital to sustain growth.

Debt in the meantime continues to claim a significant share of GDP, decreasing the resources available for investment. So far, aided by the "three blessings" of low oil prices, decreasing interest rates, and a high Yen, South Korea has been able to use its post-1986 balance of payments surplus to reduce its total debt by about 25 percent. Although national savings have increased from 21 percent to 36 percent of GNP, investment's share has fallen from 33 percent to 29 percent; because it is the surplus savings that are diverted to debt repatriation. This has two implications. First, South Korea cannot count on dis-saving to stimulate increased domestic consumption that could tide the economy over any unforeseen foreign recessions, exchange rate jitters and protectionists impulses. Second, interest costs for the largest firms are running at twice their net profits, and continue to reduce their investments. This explains why the less-burdened small and medium firms have seen their share of manufacturing value added increase from 28 percent in 1980 to 40 percent in 1988. But these are the firms most likely to suffer if wages rise, for their productivity is low and their machinery is aging. One study of small Korean electronics and textile firms found they were half as productive as comparably-sized Japanese firms.[91]

So the tension between debt service and the desire, or need, to expand internal markets will surely rule South Korea's future for the next decade. Though it is presumptuous to predict anything—given the wave of strikes and political surprises from 1987 to 1988—there seems no easy escape from dependency for South Korea. Labour strife will undoubtedly continue as a generation of committed urban-industrial workers takes over from a generation of peasant-workers.[92]

91. *Economist*, February 20, 1988, p. 22; ibid., May 21, 1988, survey p. 16; *Far Eastern Economic Review*, February 26, 1987, p. 48; ibid., June 25, 1987, p. 86; ibid., August 27, 1987, p. 17; ibid., September 3, 1987, p. 99; ibid., September 17, 1987, p. 62. The rising Yen has also undermined efforts to repatriate debt, for significant portions of Korean debt is Yen denominated. The Korea Export Bank saw its total overseas debt rise because of the changing Dollar-Yen ratio; *Far Eastern Economic Review*, April 9, 1987, pp. 121–122. Textile firms, typical of small industry, produce 15 percent of manufacturing value-added with 30 percent of manufacturing labour.

92. Only 7 percent of workers are unionized in South Korea vs. an average of 14 percent in Taiwan, Singapore and Hong Kong; *Far Eastern Economic Review*, April 3, 1986, p. 44. But they are concentrated in large urban industrial facilities conducive to organization, and have a tradition of organization from "below." See Deyo, "State and Labor"; and Cho Soon Kyoung, "Labor Process and Capital Mobility: Limits to the New International Division of Labor," *Politics and Society*, 14 (1985), 185–222, for prescient considerations on labor control in South Korea; see C. Sabel, *Work and Politics* (Cambridge: Cambridge University Press, 1985), chap. 3, for a discussion of "peasant workers."

Both the state and industry will have strong incentives to compromise on wages, not just to increase internal markets but also to buy labour peace and so continue exporting and servicing debt. This could take the form of an American-style fordist pact linking wages to productivity, or, more likely, a Japanese-style pact linking bonuses to productivity and "quality." But a host of low-wage competitors elsewhere are poised to move into Korean export markets if rising wages are not offset by increased productivity. How then will South Korea finance the increased productivity? The answer seems to involve choosing between two different sorts of dependency. Either South Korea can renew borrowing to finance investment and to maintain debt service, thus perpetuating its current form of dependency, or it can invite the MNCs in, with their high-productivity technology and labour management, and so transform its situation to one resembling Cardoso and Faletto's third dependency situation, in which either the state or the *chaebol* begin to behave like interior bourgeoisies. Clearly, political autonomy in this latter situation will still be high, given the existing institutional capacity and the ideological proclivities of any likely South Korean regime. But Australia's interior bourgeoisie was not overly fond of foreign capital either. Production, productivity and capitalization all should continue to grow, for after all, South Korea controls half the investment occurring in South Korea, and aggressive state policy and rising wages will continue to drive development. But this too was the situation in Australia this century. This is not the worst situation to be in, certainly better than that of Mali, or for that matter Malaysia. But it is not a situation in which the policy choices include an alternative to dependency.

CHAPTER EIGHT

Conclusion

> By "export of capital" I mean the export of value which is intended
> to breed surplus value abroad.
>
> Rudolph Hilferding, *Finance Capital*

Chapter 1's disaggregation of the "external forces" and "internal
forces" lines of Dependency theory showed that they have different
political implications. Changes in dependency are linked to the outcomes of conflicts among capitalist groups; changes in development
or underdevelopment, to conflicts between labour and capital. Chapter 2 argued that debt dependency in the Dominions involved surplus
transfers invidious to possibilities for domestic control of accumulation. This led to intense conflicts among different capitalist groups
during the crises of the 1890s as each tried to shift or escape the cost
of debt.

THE POLITICS OF DEPENDENCY

In Australia a fairly cohesive group of manufacturing capitalists,
concerned about domestic accumulation, forged temporary alliances
with other groups to oppose foreign rentiers and capitalists in a two-
stage process. Domestic manufacturers' on-again, off-again alliances
with labour and segments of domestic financial capital proved dur-
able enough to block a Federal constitution favoring foreign interests,
and to keep foreign capital and its allies essentially out of political
power during the Commonwealth's infancy. Part of foreign capital's
weakness came from its destruction of major segments of the domestic exporting class—pastoralists—who were its natural allies. Al-

though manufacturers failed to eliminate foreign claims to surplus or to attain complete political dominance, they significantly reduced the foreign presence in Australia through a number of positive policies increasing domestic control over accumulation. Much of the new economic growth in federated Australia created domestically controlled accumulation circuits, without incurring new claims by foreign capital via either public or private debt. The rate of growth of public debt was much lower than in either New Zealand or Argentina, and was slower than the increase in GDP, which more than doubled 1897 to 1913.[1] Although some domestic accumulation was driven by external markets (overseas sales of agricultural goods) the tariff and the Australian Industries Protection Act largely preserved upstream demand from agriculture for domestic producers. Foreign capital's share of the economy and the benefits it gained from export subsidies decreased, thus decreasing Australia's dependency.

In Argentina, exporters were divided over the level and costs of foreign investment, but found a common interest in passing the costs of debt on to foreign investors. Inflation voided foreigners' private claims on exporters through *cédula*, while making public debt unserviceable. Although foreign capitals, backed by the Bank of England, reestablished gold-denominated claims (there was no formal default), the payment schedule of the *Arreglo Romero* favored Argentine landowners and their state, and consequently received round criticism from English bondholders. Foreign investors, Baring Brothers, and their stockholders, and their creditors bore the brunt of the devalorization of the *cédula* and the suspension of payments. Nevertheless, an easy early victory proved costly in the long term. The success of Argentine landowners in besting foreign creditors facilitated their partial transformation from owner-operators receiving profit to landlords receiving rent. Meanwhile, the easy victory of the landowners encouraged them to permit renewed borrowing and investment. More and more Argentine-created surplus was sterilized through investment in land; meanwhile foreign capital expanded its control of both transport and grain production. Private rail ownership, despite termination of state subsidies, permitted foreign capital to control an important share of the economy. Public debt did not expand dramatically, but private foreign investment did. In the absence of positive steps to create new circuits of domestically controlled accumulation,

---

1. Reliable GDP estimates are from N. Butlin, *Australian Domestic Product*, (Cambridge: Cambridge University Press, 1962), pp. 10–11; GDP increased 217 percent 1900/01–1913/14.

Table 41. Changes in foreign investment, 1900–1914

	Australia	Argentina	New Zealand
Percentage increase in:			
Public debt	15 %	93 %	189 %
Private debt	Decrease	105 %	?
(DFI and portfolio)	(var. est.)	(+ FR, U.S. = 131%)	(constant)

NOTES: Because GNP/GDP data for Argentina and New Zealand are unreliable, changes in foreign investment are presented relative to the prior stock of investment, rather than to GNP/GDP. In all three countries, GNP/GDP expanded after 1900. There was an outflow of private investment from Australia 1900–12, but the amount is disputed. Change in Argentine public and private debt is estimated, as the best data (Stone) shows the change only from 1905 to 1913, and does not consider French and U.S. holdings. They raise the increase in private debt to approximately 131 percent. Rosenberg suggests that private investment in New Zealand did not change in this period but little data are available.

SOURCES: Butlin, *Australian Domestic Product*; NZOYB; OYBCWA; Peters, *Foreign Debt of the Argentine Republic*; Stone, "British Direct and Portfolio Investment in Latin America"; Rosenberg, "Capital Imports and Growth."

foreign investment kept pace or perhaps exceeded domestic accumulation. Foreign capital's share of fixed capital actually increased, reflecting domestic capital's rural orientation, and blocking further expansion of domestic capital into industrial circuits. GDP seems barely to have outraced the increase in foreign investment.[2] Argentina up to 1914 thus continued at about the same or at a slightly increased level of dependency as before the 1890 crisis, but the nature of that dependency already was beginning to shift towards Cardoso and Faletto's third situation of dependency, on multinational corporations, here expressed through foreign direct investment in single-purpose firms dominating food processing and transport.

In New Zealand, while there was potential for opposition to foreign financial capital among the functioning estates and their subaltern allies in manufacturing, this opposition faltered. Despite their export orientation, estate owners opposed a bailout of foreign investments in speculative land holdings because this would have hindered their own accumulation. Estate owners successfully resisted attempts to preserve foreign investments in the 1880s; the Bank of New Zealand crashed as a result. But the position of the estate owners' eroded in the 1890s. Their subaltern manufacturing allies never gained strength, for es-

2. A. Ferrer, *The Argentine Economy* (Berkeley: University of California Press, 1967), p. 229. L. Randall, *Economic History of Argentina* (New York: Columbia University Press, 1968), p. 2, suggests Argentine GDP roughly doubled in constant terms, 1900–14; British investment alone roughly doubled in those years, to which must be added the increasing French, U.S., and German stakes.

tate owners saw no need to create a high-price domestic manufacturing capacity when imports were cheaper. The estate owners' position weakened when their labour force got restive and when the price of wool fell in world markets. To make a successful transition to the new markets in meat, while containing their labour force, estate owners had to acquiesce in the renewed borrowing that tightened English bondholders' grasp on the fisc. Foreign public debt tripled under the Liberals; although no good estimates for GDP exist, it clearly did not grow faster than foreign debt. However, unlike Argentina, state ownership of railways meant that foreign private investment was channelled into meat processing alone, and so was limited.

The different fates of the Argentine and the Antipodean private creditors had profound political and economical consequences. In Australia, the initial advantage of commercial lenders in dominating the pastoral sector turned into a disadvantage, for in the depressed 1890s merchants and land companies found themselves saddled with millions of pounds of illiquid and low profit property. This illiquidity led land companies and speculators to search for a political solution that would revalorize their holdings. The only compromise that was acceptable—because it was a political solution—involved the subdivision and sale of those properties to smallholding farmers. Anglo-Australian creditors foreclosed on Australian largeholders. Largeholders as a class ceased to exist, and individual largeholders found themselves forced to merge with other rural interests, including the newly created smallholders, to express their interests politically. In this alliance, smallholders increasingly held the upper hand.

New Zealand speculators were also stuck with unproductive land. They depended almost entirely on smallholders for political support in order to liquidate their investments in land. Although New Zealand's largeholders survived, in a mutated form, they confronted an entrenched group of smallholders after the 1890s. Still, unlike Australia, largeholders' descendants dominated rural politics.

Argentine landowners, in contrast, were not foreclosed, for cédula prevented this, nor did they suffer an extended drain on the surplus their enterprises returned to them; default obviated the necessity. Even more than their New Zealand counterparts, estancieros remained fairly profitable and on their own managed a transition to new products and production methods capable of returning higher profits than hides or wool. Where Antipodean creditors' defense of their economic interests created groups of smallholders, Argentinean defeat of their creditors meant that smallholders numbers remained low in proportion to estancieros. Although "natural" world market forces

Table 42. Dependency and the relative strength of capitals

	Australia	Argentina	New Zealand
Domestic manufacturers	strong	weak	weak
Domestic primary producers	weak	strong	medium
Foreign capital	medium	medium	strong
Dependency	decrease	constant	increase

caused Argentine farming to be organized, like Antipodean, on a family basis, Argentine family farmers remained politically weak tenants and subcontractors.

The different outcomes in Australia, Argentina, and New Zealand suggest that not only the relative distribution of power between foreign and domestic capital but also the distribution of power within domestic capital determines the effects of efforts to reduce dependency. (See Table 42.) Interior bourgeoisies confronted with a choice between being slowly reduced to comprador status or striving to become national bourgeoisies do not appear to respond uniformly to this pressure. Manufacturers, or capitals oriented to domestic markets such as early agricultural producers, were more likely to seek to enlarge the domestic market. Those with international markets were indifferent to the size of the domestic market, but not to their own survival. They confronted foreign capital, but do not seem to have been motivated to create domestically-centered accumulation projects. Thus Argentine exporters were content to shift debt service back onto foreign capital without trying to enlarge domestic accumulation circuits, and New Zealand estate owners acquiesced in renewed borrowing as long as it was clear they would not bear the burden.

However, this study does not provide enough information to determine whether the decisive variable affecting an interior bourgeoisie's decision to confront foreign capital is market orientation (domestic vs. overseas) or what is being produced—primary products vs. manufacturing. (See Table 42.) The South Korean case suggests that it is market orientation that matters most, but more investigation is warranted. South Korea also suggests that the size of the market available to interior bourgeoisies is critical. By linking a protected domestic sector to a dynamic export sector, Korea successfully created and enlarged domestic accumulation circuits. Clearly, Victorian manufacturers would have had a harder time becoming a "national" bourgeoisie if Australian federation had not given them a larger internal market. But Argentina was just as large a market as Australia, indicating that political and strategic factors can remedy disadvantages or can ruin advantages of size.

For labour, dependency changed only the parameters of the negotiating strategy it used with capital, not the strategy or situation itself. Labour, when it successfully organized, confronted foreign capitalists much as it did domestic capitalists, except that labour had a greater incentive to ask foreigners for higher wages because they were less likely invest in the future. Conflict with foreign capitals as employers then depended on their willingness to pay those wages. Since they typically had the resources to pay, there often was less conflict between foreign capitalists and labour than there was between labour and domestic capitalists. With foreign rentiers, however, labour had greater conflicts, because they typically paid the taxes used to finance this debt. Whether this led to an alliance between domestic capitalists and labour against foreign rentiers or capitalists depended on other factors. Pre-federation NSW Labor did ally with foreign capital, gaining the franchise and some legal protection for organizing activity in the 1890s. In turn, this political strength permitted post-Federation Australian labour to ally more willingly with manufacturers than Argentine labour had been willing to do. With access to the political arena, it made sense for Australian labor to try winning economic concessions through political action. But it also reflects the harder time Australian labour had in the 1890s; unemployment, emigration and declining wages were much greater than in 1890s Argentina, where workers experienced significant upward mobility. Battered, Australian labour more willingly compromised with manufacturers over tariff protection, especially since foreign rentiers seemed to blame for government retrenchment and depression. Argentine workers had less reason to compromise with manufacturers, and their experience with increased customs and excises turned them away from tariffs. Similarly, the fact that NSW labour willingly allied with free-trade foreign rentiers against local manufacturers during the 1890s shows that a protectionist "nationalist" alliance was not a given in Australia.

Abstractly, it should make no difference in principle to labour whether the investment underlying jobs and wages is foreign-owned or domestic. Rather, distribution of the benefits of investment is what should concern labour. This suggests that where "nationalist" alliances of labour and domestic business emerge other factors are at work; for example, perhaps Catholic Irish workers against Protestant English rentiers in Australia. Certainly the unwillingness of the Argentine immigrants constituting the bulk of urban working and entrepreneurial classes to naturalize themselves prevented both an anti-British alliance and, through political exclusion, an anti-landowner alliance. By the 1930s, however, immigrants' children were citizens, and urban working and entrepreneurial classes did ally under Perón against foreign capital.

Here the South Korean experience is ambiguous, since the state has so carefully insulated labour from direct contact with foreign capital except in export processing zones. We can perhaps look to Singapore for an indirect insight confirming labour's willingness to confront foreign capital. Unlike South Korea, Singapore is thoroughly penetrated by foreign capital, which provided nearly 70 percent of manufacturing employment by 1978. Alone among the East Asian "Gang of Four," Singapore's government aggressively pursued policies pushing up wages, acting in some sense as a master union for all Singaporean workers.[3] Without a group of domestic businesses clearly willing to raise wages, South Korean workers are unlikely to join a "nationalist" alliance against foreign banks. As virtually all firms are involved in the export trade, the kind of domestic business-labour alliance Australia saw in the early 1900s would be hard to forge in Korea.

THE POLITICS OF DEVELOPMENT

Unsurprisingly, "development" issues—bread and butter gains—are more salient in conflicts between labour and capital than among capitalists themselves. Workers pursued no conscious strategy in favor of "development," for what they wanted was a bigger slice of the pie. Nonetheless, the more successful those struggles, the greater the pie and the development, because capitalists responded by increasing productivity. As the external sources theorists argue, labour pressures and strength are one manifest cause of development, if not the only one. Development thus occurred according to the relative strength of labour versus capital. The increased exploitation that accompanies development makes distribution issues more salient for labour than for domestic capitals, for workers react to increased mechanization by trying to capture part of the obvious increases in productivity. Thus

3. On DFI, Stephan Haggard and Tun-jen Cheng, "State and Capital in the East Asian NICs," in Frederic C. Deyo, ed., *The Political Economy of the New Asian Industrialism* (Ithaca: Cornell University Press, 1987), p. 99. Government behavior is not surprising, given the origins of the Peoples Action Party in the labour movement; see F. Deyo, *Dependent Development and Industrial Order* (New York: Praeger, 1980).

NSW and New Zealand coal mines, where mechanization proceeded fastest, saw bitter strikes despite conciliation, because the fairness of the original bargain seemed to have come undone.

For domestic capitals, however, development per se was not necessarily a desideratum. Rather, they desired accumulation, which could be accomplished only by increasing the amount of surplus available for investment. Increases in surplus production could be attained either by increasing the productivity of labour or by depressing wages. If valorization does not depend on workers' consumption (or even sometimes where it does), individual capitalists may still seek to increase profits and accumulation by pushing down wages, even if this makes domestic markets smaller. This logic underlay the strategies of Australian mine-owners, Australian and New Zealand farmers, and Argentine beef exporters, none of whom had any concern to increase the development of their nations. A similar logic likely motivates Korean businesses, since export markets are as large as domestic markets for most firms. Productivity increases were only motivated by the state, in the past, and today, by fear of other low wage LDCs. The key role of the South Korean state in forcing development upon manufacturers parallels the Australian Liberal Party's efforts to induce greater mechanization. The key question here is whether anything in society is acting to protect capitalists' general interests from the consequences of their particular desires.

Australia, where labour was strongest, experienced development across virtually all sectors. (See Table 43.) This development accelerated because manufacturers' political leadership combined with labour to institutionalize the unions which had emerged in the 1880s, in exchange for protection of manufacturing accumulation circuits. Unions, conciliation, and the minimum wage forced manufacturers and especially domestic exporters of minerals, wool, and agricultural products to mechanize their production to the fullest extent. Meanwhile, protection gave manufacturers a guaranteed link to other sec-

Table 43. Development and the relative strength of capital and labour

	Australia	New Zealand	Argentina
Domestic manufacturer	strong	weak	weak
Urban labour	strong	medium	weak
Development increase	large	medium	small
Landowners	weak	medium	strong
Farmers	strong	strong	weak
Rural labour	strong	medium (?)	weak
Development increase	large	large	medium

tors so that they could profitably invest in their own mechanization. A protected domestic market induced investment in iron and steel production.

New Zealand, where labour strength was lower than Australia but greater than Argentina, had middling levels of development. Although unions were institutionalized in 1894 by the Conciliation Act, real wage levels actually fell, in contrast to Australia's experience. The fall in real wages removed both the incentive to mechanize manufacturing and a market that would have supported that mechanization. There was no political push for mechanization. Manufacturing stagnated until the revival of industrial unionism combined with externally imposed protection in World War I and the Depression. Nevertheless agriculture was rapidly and fully mechanized. Small farmers were willing and were forced by world markets to invest considerable amounts of their labour in improvements to land, stock, and implements in order that they might retain control of their mortgaged land. Just as labour unionized, small farmers organized cooperatives, marketing associations, and a political party to confront both their landlord (the state) and world market forces. Similarly, increased mechanization enabled family farmers to do without the rootless and dangerous hired labour that had troubled the 1890s.

Argentina, where labour was weak in both rural and urban areas, saw the least development. Unlike New Zealand, high turnover and migration made old-fashioned resistance among the rural proletariat difficult. Landholders were able to impose sharecropping and unstable land tenures on tenant farmers. Landowners' indifference permitted foreign grain marketers to fatten at the expense of farmers. Although mechanization of agriculture occurred, unstable tenure dissuaded tenant farmers and credit conditions prevented them from making improvements to the same degree as in the Antipodes. Still, Argentine agriculture was more developed than other Latin American agricultures. Only in stock breeding, where landowners were direct entrepreneurs controlling their own credit, did Argentina surpass its competitors. As in New Zealand, powerful rural interests blocked efforts to foster manufacturing. In Buenos Aires, landlords and their middle class allies used the state to repress both manufacturers and workers. The industrial unions in meat packing plants, that, like Australian shearers and miners, might have acted as a vanguard for the entire labour movement, were smashed; so were several general strikes. Manufacturers retained their original citizenship, and so lost access to the political arena that so well served Australian manufacturers' interests. Employment and production expanded but productivity stayed flat; and free trade, perpetuated through the Depression by treaty with Britain, discouraged any expansion upstream.

The discussion above does not address a key connection between dependency and development. Although the politics and effects of dependency and underdevelopment differ, changes in productivity affect both. Development and economic autonomy have synergistic effects. Increases in productivity (and the rate of surplus value) permit an acceleration in accumulation. If this increase occurs in domestically controlled sectors, then their more rapid accumulation will enable them to outpace foreign investment, increasing autonomy. Increased autonomy means more surplus is potentially available for investment in increased productivity. Precisely this "magic circle" phenomenon underlay Australia's increased autonomy before World War II. Domestically controlled growth created a larger pool of surplus capable of paying for both debt service and new investment. So far, South Korean success has rested on a parallel process, for the state has reserved the fastest growing sectors for domestic capital, encouraging investment in increased productivity and higher value added processes. Although the Heavy and Chemical Industry Development Plan (HCIDP) may have created overcapacity and perpetuated dependency in the short run, the shift to these higher-value-added processes from the wigs and the toys of the 1960s is better for South Korea in the long run. Whether or not South Korea can continue to move upstream, however, remains an open question.

DEPENDENCY, DEVELOPMENT, AND POLITICS

The three different paths followed by Australia, New Zealand, and Argentina also suggest significant points about politics in dependency and development. First, the crucial variable in the evolution of rural development and the later politics of dependency was not the strength of *labour* versus landholders so much as it was the strength of *creditors* versus landholders. Australian labour was more organized and mobilized than either New Zealand or Argentine labour because it faced industrial-style working conditions and was committed to staying and fighting. Still, the export sector—shipping, finance, graziers—handily defeated the strikes of 1890–92. It is hard to imagine Australian labour on its own confronting and containing graziers politically. More likely a New Zealand or Argentine-style solution would have defused or repressed rural tensions. What increased Australian labour's strength relative to graziers was that the creditors had foreclosed upon the graziers, and then Labor's two alliances, with public debt holders and then with manufacturers against foreign capital. Labour's experience in New Zealand and Argentina tends to confirm the importance of these elements for where largeholders were not displaced by creditors, the largeholders by and large remained in place. What may differentiate Australian Labor Party from the others is the skill and discipline it showed in political struggles after Federation.

Second, both national sovereignty and the specific ways in which foreign creditor–domestic landowner relations were structured were important in determining how conflicts between foreign creditors and domestic debtors played out. Argentine landowners insulated themselves by contracting mortgages via banks they controlled and by issuing paper-denominated debt. But equally important was the inability of foreign bondholders to forge any electoral alliances in a political system in which force was a trump card to be played not just against labour but also against other capitalists. Foreign capital was thus both politically and economically weak. In Australia, creditors had immediate control over graziers' sterling-denominated mortgages, and the political system permitted alliances with subaltern groups. Consequently graziers could be and were foreclosed upon. Alignments between specific sets of foreign creditors and labour also worked to graziers' disadvantage.

Third, although foreign creditor–domestic debtor relations are important, there seems to be little in the way of an organizational or technical determinism that would enable prediction of who will ultimately win these conflicts. One could argue, for example, that the different trajectories of Australia/New Zealand and of Argentina are contained in the technical requirements of wool and dairy as compared with beef. Wool requires minimal processing before export, and such processing could be done with relatively little capital investment. Dairy production was best done by small production units— family farmers—and, again, processing could be done cooperatively and on a small scale. In contrast, beef production required expensive centralized processing and refrigeration works. Thus, while foreign capital could not dominate Antipodean production by controlling one key position in the production chain, foreign meat packers could dominate Argentine beef production. Perhaps, then, it could be argued that dependency was ordained in the kind of commodities in which local producers chose to specialize; but this is disproved by the Queensland experience. There, in a state dominated by export interests, foreign capital, and industrial labour, beef and mutton production did not require centralized packing. Plants were decentralized, and often locally owned.[4] The centralization of the Argentine meat trade therefore had as much to do with internal politics—the ability to centralize production safely in the face of a more docile labour movement and Buenos Aires' drive to dominate the interior—as with specific technologies. Ezequiel Gallo's detailed study of Santa Fe province similarly shows that the decline of cereal milling and shipping in Rosario followed closely upon Buenos Aires' efforts to link Rosario with its railroad network.[5] These three considerations all indicate that there are no given outcomes from the various shocks external actors and markets unleash on similar societies; politics plays the largest part in what happens.

A COUNTER-EXAMPLE: THE UNITED STATES

One final counter-example will perhaps best illustrate the dependency-creating effects of dominion public debt as well as the importance of politics. The U.S. in its origins and for much of its early history, resembles the Dominions, and can be thought of as a Dominion that managed to become autonomous.[6] Like the Dominions, U.S. export production was initially done with coerced labour—slaves in the south and indentured servants everywhere.[7] The American south specialized in tobacco and cotton for export to Britain. Much of the early development of these monocultures—slave purchase, land clearing, transport—was funded by British capital. Like Argentina under Juárez Celman, southern planters mortgaged their property to banks which in turn sold abroad public notes the state governments had given them. Why then did the U.S. avoid dependency?

No doubt a number of contingent factors contributed to U.S. autonomy, among them that proximity to Europe meant larger immigrant flows and thus a larger absolute market for domestic capitals,

4. S. Hanson, *Argentine Meat and the British Market* (Stanford: Stanford University Press, 1938), pp. 55–61.
5. E. Gallo, *La Pampa Gringa* (Buenos Aires: Editorial Sudamerica, 1986), pp. 248–251.
6. For a more complete account, see chap. 8, Herman Schwartz, "Foreign Debt and Dependent Development in the Dominions" (Ph.D. dissertation, Cornell University, 1986).
7. Booming external demand in the 1820s and 1830s led to an American political crisis over the type of labour used in export industry like the Dominion crises in the 1840–50s, but the peculiarities of U.S. federalism led to an imperfect resolution in the 1830s—the "Missouri Compromise." This temporizing measure led to even greater conflict later.

and that the United States also had the advantages of attempting industrialization earlier than the other Dominions.[8] But, aside from the Revolution, three political choices and struggles in the four decades 1820–60 prevented the emergence of a structure of dependency typical of the Dominions, and thus prevented surplus transfers on the scale of the Dominions. We can ignore Revolution as a factor because independence in Latin America did not directly lead to development and autonomy.

The first significant political choice arose when the destruction of the Second Bank of the United States in the Jacksonian period early removed federal guarantees to foreign capital and thus created disincentives to foreign investment in public securities. These disincentives grew after Mississippi and other southern states defaulted or went into arrears in the late 1830s and early 1840s. But even before the defaults, the structure of U.S. federalism made such borrowing less pernicious than in the Dominions because state governments could tax only their own residents to pay for subsidized infrastructure investment.[9] Where Argentine federalism permitted and predisposed producers and provinces to shift borrowing costs onto other provinces and groups, U.S. federalism and the compromises over slavery and tariffs prevented federal revenues from subsidizing investment after the National road was completed. Indeed, Jackson retired the federal government's debt, even as state borrowing increased. Later proposals to distribute the central government's budget surplus or have it assume state debts tended to favor non-borrowing states, a shift of resources from dependent states to autonomous ones.[10] So northeastern manufacturers did not subsidize cotton producers. Unable to shift the burden, cotton producers, like Argentine producers, chose default when service became impossible in the late 1830s.

Second, just as in the Antipodes, falling cotton prices meant that as cotton export production became less profitable, millions of dollars were locked up in slaves and land. But because of federalism, the abolition movement, and the Civil War, no "bail-out" of slave owners was possible. As with Australian graziers, the falling prices–falling profits problem destroyed export producers, albeit in a different

8. America at the time of the Revolution had a population of 4 million, a figure not attained by Australia until after Federation.
9. See G. Callendar, "The Early Transportation and Banking Enterprises of the States in Relation to the Growth of Corporation," *Quarterly Journal of Economics* 17 (November 1902), for a concise survey of states' investment activity.
10. See data in *Census of the U.S.*, 1880, vol. 7, "Valuation, Taxation and Public Indebtedness," pp. 524–526, 528–530.

fashion. Falling profits motivated the search for new slave lands that in turn provoked the Civil War. Before the Civil War some groups proposed a solution analogous to the *Crédit Foncier* schemes of the Antipodes, arguing that the central government should buy out southern slave owners. But investment in cotton production was destroyed by Emancipation, rather than being extracted in a tax financed bail-out.

Finally, the use of land grants, rather than borrowing or profit guarantees, to encourage rail construction allowed capitalization of railroads without the creation of extensive foreign debt and future claims to surplus. Although the federal government gave up the potential gains to be made from land sales, it also never contracted massive overseas public debt to finance railroads. The railroads in turn were responsible for making sure that they captured enough of the value of the land they opened up to make themselves profitable enough to pay dividends on foreign-owned stock. In a similar fashion homesteading allowed creation and capitalization of a major domestically controlled export industry without recourse to overseas borrowing to bail out prior producers.

These three factors reduced the weight of foreign capital in the American economy and prevented surplus transfers on a Dominion scale. (See Table 44.) Local financial resources were sufficiently large to handle demand. While foreign capitals did invest huge sums in the U.S., their overall share of activity was small. Net foreign investment never rose above 1.5 percent of GNP or 6.0 percent of Gross Domestic Saving (GDS) in the period 1860–1890.[11] On average, Net Foreign Investment was only 0.8 percent of GNP and 3.2 percent of Gross Domestic Capital Formation (GDCF). The result was a qualitative and quantitative reduction in foreign claims to surplus and therefore to surplus transfer. Only about 0.5 percent of U.S. GNP went abroad in debt service, compared to the Dominions' transfers, larger by tenfold. In the end, rather than foreign capital draining and crowding out domestic capitals, the reverse occurred. As Edelstein aptly remarks: "The average realized, risk adjusted returns to U.S. railway securities [for British investors] were better than those on UK railway securities. . . . The point is that U.S. farming, mining, and manufacturing probably offered even better returns but local investors got there first."[12]

11. M. Edelstein, *Overseas Investment in the Age of High Imperialism* (New York: Columbia University Press, 1982), pp. 233–234, 243.
12. Edelstein, *Overseas Investment in the Age of High Imperialism*, p. 238.

Table 44. Relative foreign share of capital formation, Australia, Canada, and United States, 1860–1900

| | Net foreign investment (flow) 1860–1900 as percentage of: | | |
	GDCF	GDS	GNP
Australia	34.0	51.5	5.2
Canada	42.5	73.0	6.2
United States	3.2	3.4	0.8

SOURCES: Butlin, *Australian Domestic Product*, pp. 6–7, 20–21, 30, 416; Edelstein, *Overseas Investment in the Age of High Imperialism*, p. 234.

IMPLICATIONS FOR DEPENDENCY THEORY

The winds of economic nationalism are blowing strong in Latin America. . . . The recent burst of nationalism is in fact a reaction to long term and increasingly intolerable dependence on foreigners. The development strategy of [Import Substitution Industrialization] . . . has not only failed to achieve [its] aims but has in fact aggravated the situation and nature of "dependencia."
Osvaldo Sunkel, "Big Business and 'Dependencia'"

Recasting of Dependency theory into my two "lines" has two major theoretical implications. One concerns its status as a method, the other concerns its current conceptualization of the world.

Dependency Theory as Method

Splitting Dependency theory into two linked problematics, one concerned with the quality of investment and the process of productivity increases (development) and the other with the quantity of investment and control of the economy (dependency), reaffirms Dependency theory's utility while forcing reconsideration of the classic categories it uses to understand the world. An examination of "staples" theory affirms the continued utility of a Dependency theory split into questions of development and dependency. Staples theorists assert that the technological imperatives of specific export commodities

283

shape the economy, polity, and society of the exporter.[13] It is thus a crude version of world systems theory, in so far as it asserts that the international division of labour shapes internal politics and political structures. We have already shown above that different commodities cannot be held responsible for the different outcomes among our three nineteenth-century cases. But even when the export staple is constant, the rise of the wool economy in Australia, New Zealand, and Argentina had paradoxical political effects from the point of view of staples theory. Wool induced decentralization in Australia, as NSW relinquished control over Queensland and Victoria to their respective entrepot cities. In Argentina it required centralization under entrepot Buenos Aires (but only after ten years of fighting). In New Zealand, wool caused centralization of several entrepots under a government dominated by no single entrepot. While wool later created parallel political and economic crises in these same three places, the specific outcomes of these crises were very much determined by relations among different capitals and between capital and labour. Only in the most general sense does staples theory, and by extension world systems theory, provide any guide here; a reconstructed Dependency theory focusing on relationships between different classes and class fractions more accurately highlights the nature and likely course of those crises.

But reconstruction also suggests changing Dependency theory's classic categories. Dependency theorists' pervasive conflation of the concepts "underdevelopment" and "dependency" leads them to a one-dimensional view of the world split into core and periphery. The Wallerstein/world systems refinement of this dichotomy through the addition of the semi-periphery merely segments this one-dimensional view of the world. It continues to assume that dependency and under-development can be aggregated into one phenomenon (and thus one measure), and used to assign countries and regions to their place in the global hierarchy. But the residual, ragbag collection of countries that world systems analysts place in the semi-periphery only high-lights the tension between Dependency theory's two lines.[14] Are Bra-

13. See H. Innes, *Problems of Staple Production in Canada* (Toronto: Ryerson, 1933); M. Watkins, "A Staple Theory of Economic Growth," *Canadian Journal of Economics and Political Science* 29 (1963); G. O'Donnell, "Comparative Historical Formations of the State Apparatus and Social-economic Change in the Third World," *International Social Science Quarterly* 32 (Autumn 1980).

14. P. Evans, *Dependent Development* (Princeton: Princeton University Press, 1979), p. 291, notes "the absence of a well-defined, theoretically grounded means of designating the members of the 'semi-periphery'" and suggests as "a simpler, interim measure . . . sheer [economic] scale."

zil and Canada, or Iran and East Germany, really fundamentally alike as "semi-peripheries"?

Dependency writers' categorization problem arises from confusion of dependency and underdevelopment as variables, which creates a bipolar view of the world. Most of Dependency theory's categorization efforts have been attempts to cut up this one dimensional continuum into more and more categories. But this does not change the underlying problem, for it only serves to expand the original one-dimensional continuum. If, however, dependency and development are separated as variables, we have, not a varying number of ungrounded categories cut out of a one-dimensional continuum, but four grounded categories.[15]

Two variables create a two-by-two matrix (see Figure 3) on which we can place different countries, although only simple and interim measures are presently available. As a measure of the level of dependency, I would suggest the ratio of real foreign claims to surplus, to the total usable surplus generated in a given country. To an extent this measure is approximated by total foreign interest and profits as a percentage of gross domestic investment. Either measure ought to reflect the degree to which a country's accumulation may be hindered by transfers abroad. Development is similarly amenable to measurement, although the data are more difficult to extract—as productivity in a given economy (the average magnitude of value added per worker in all sectors), adjusted by a measure of the degree of disarticulation (perhaps using input-output data). Such a measure would avoid the pitfalls inhering to arbitrary distinctions between manufactured and agricultural goods, terms of trade between those goods, and invalid measures such as GNP.[16]

Dominion-like countries would be those with high levels of development and high levels of dependency; dependency here being an unhappy concatenation of debt and DFI-induced dependency. Core areas are developed and autonomous, that is, net creditors. The pe-

15. Two, with core and periphery; three with semi-periphery; three and a half, following Evans, *Dependent Development*, p. 290, who calls dependent developers "one subset of the [semi-peripheral] countries." Many variations can be found, for example, in the Sage *Annuals of the World System* (Beverly Hills, Calif.). Our four categories exclude two others that do not participate in the world economy: pre-capitalist formations (if any are still left) not yet incorporated into the world economy, and former peripheral countries that have been pushed out of the world economy by contraction of its perimeter. Here I am thinking of regions like the Sahel, or Uganda, which have been left to their own devices in the aftermath of de-colonization.

16. For example, a high GNP per capita may reflect high levels of rent, rather than equaling high levels of productivity, as the example of the oil exporters shows.

Figure 3. Social formation typologies

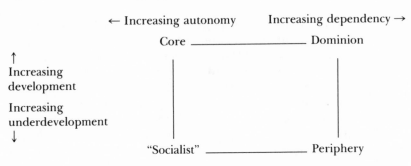

riphery is dependent and underdeveloped. The "socialist" countries
would be those from which foreign capital was expelled—hence their
autonomy—as a consequence of the social disruptions caused by
capitalist penetration—hence their underdevelopment. Naturally, no
real country corresponds purely to any of the "corners" of the matrix.
Neither dependency and nor underdevelopment is an absolute situation, and, both, despite the qualitative difference in social relations,
can vary in intensity. But heuristically, they enable us to understand
the consequences of different strategies for reducing dependency,
underdevelopment, or both. Clearly, South Korea has made great
strides in development, but remains dependent. Far from becoming
like Japan, it will more likely resemble Australia if it continues to
develop. Other countries, such as Tanzania and Albania, have sacri-
ficed rapid development for autonomy. The new categories also allow
differentiation among the countries called by the IBRD "industrial
market economies," which most dependency writers generally lump
into the core. What are the consequences of increased foreign debt
for countries like Denmark, whose foreign public debt in 1970 was
12.6 percent of GDP, in 1988 40 percent? or for those like Ireland,
where U.S. DFI grew 25.5 percent per annum from 1977 to 1982?[17]
Far from becoming "semi-peripheral," Denmark continues to be highly developed; but, like South Korea although from a different direction, it is becoming more and more "Australian." Ireland, lacking all
but the lightest industry but possessing an efficient, if subsidized,
agriculture, rather resembles New Zealand.[18] Disaggregation, then,

17. United States Department of Commerce, *Survey of Current Business*, esp. August
1986; *Economist* October 8, 1988, p. 72.
18. There is shipbuilding in Belfast (Eire *irredenta*), but it would disappear without
constant subvention from London. The Common Market's agricultural policy presently
seems to subsidize Ireland's efforts to attract foreign investment.

permits more precise analysis of the whole middle range of countries that different subsections of Dependency theory have found difficult to deal with.

Dependency Theory as Ideology

Many northern social scientists argue that Dependency theory is not a social science paradigm but in fact a thinly disguised ideology.[19] Paradoxically, while Dependency theory is cloaked in marxist terminology it often is used or articulated by the bourgeoisie in dependent countries in defense of their particular interests.[20] (Cardoso's first work studied the Brazilian bourgeoisie to see if, how, and why it differed from its Northern counterparts.) Distinguishing between dependency and development explains this paradox. Dependency theory does in fact contain a strong element of ideology, revolving around the internal forces line's concern with dependency as a conflict between and among foreign and local capitalists. It rationalizes the failure of various domestic bourgeoisies to accumulate while offering them a rallying point for political struggles against both internal and external class fractions that benefit from surplus transfers. As Tulio Halperin-Donghi tells us:

> [Andre Gunder] Frank's [Dependency Theory] writings were not only attractive to th[e] left-leaning public. . . . He also had something to offer those who looked at Latin America's predicament from a perspective less concerned with immediate revolutionary prospects. . . . These observers found it difficult to accept the explanations that described Latin America as a latecomer into the industrial world that, would, in due time, repeat the process of . . . Europe and the U.S.[21]

The ideological elements of Dependency theory thus surface when internal bourgeoisies attempt to put an end to surplus transfers. They

19. For the most entertaining among many critics, see R. Packenham, "Plus ça change . . . ," *Latin American Research Review* 17:2 (1982). See also the special issue on dependency theory in *International Organization* 32 (Winter 1978), and B. Warren, *Imperialism: Pioneer of Capitalism* (London: Verso, 1980), chap. 7. I tend to agree with Warren regarding the nature of Dependency theory. See also R. Chilcote, *Theories of Development and Underdevelopment* (Boulder Colo.: Westview Press, 1984), who, while apparently disagreeing about disaggregation, concurs on the nationalist sentiment within Dependency theory.

20. The best study here is J. Kahl, *Modernization, Exploitation, and Dependency in Latin America* (New Brunswick, N.J.: Transaction Books, 1976).

21. T. Halperin-Donghi, "Dependency Theory and Latin American Historiography," *Latin American Research Review* 17 (1982), 118.

must do so partly by political means, because economic arrangements tend to perpetuate surplus transfers through positive feedback structures. The internal bourgeoisie therefore needs its own political allies to outweigh the power of foreign capitals and their allies, and this generally means seeking out allies from the so-called (in Latin America) "popular" classes. To rally these groups, the internal bourgeoisie needs a radical ideology, but one which nevertheless will continue to safeguard its essential interests. Dependency theory admirably fits these contours. Employing marxist language, it can rally the masses by articulating their interests in a way that makes sense, because the masses are in fact exploited, and moreover doubly exploited by foreigners as capitalists and rentiers. Yet because the problematic of Dependency theory's internal line is domestic accumulation, and precisely because it focuses attention on the exploitation of the nation by foreigners, rather than on the exploitation of all workers by all capitalists, it simultaneously protects the interests of those national and internal bourgeoisies who articulate Dependency arguments. Dependency theory allows local capitalists to articulate claims about exploitation of workers and the nation that do not challenge their own hegemony.

The deracinated forms of Dependency theory that crop up in Australia, New Zealand, and Canada focus to a much larger degree on the question of "buying back the farm" or national control than on questions of exploitation and inequality than do the Latin variants.[22] In these countries, underdevelopment and its concomitant inequality are absent; when theorists complain about dependency's effects on labour, they usually worry about increased unemployment, not starvation. These "white-flour" versions of Dependency theory reflect the compression of domestic capital between a fairly mobilized labour force on the one hand and foreign capital on the other. Domestic capital needs a defense, but not one that will unduly aggravate an already politicized and powerful labour movement. Typically, the Australian Labor Party now finds itself coming to the rescue of Australian business, much as it did in the 1900s, and out of the same concern that the links of business to foreign capital will reduce wages and employment in the long run. The New Zealand Labour Party is similarly restructuring New Zealand's economy in the 1980s.

But as a rallying cry, Dependency theory can only be plausible if

22. See, inter alia, W. Sutch, *Colony or Nation?* (Sydney: Sydney University Press, 1966); E. L. Wheelwright, *Australia, a Client State—Sold Off!* (Sydney, 1983); and, of course, K. Levitt, *Silent Surrender* (New York: Liveright, 1970).

transfers really occur. Ideology must point to real events to if it is to move individuals to support political positions through elective affinities. I trust that the case studies convince the reader of the heuristic utility of focusing on conflicts over surplus transfers in the analysis of dependent social formations, where transfers hinder the ability of the interior bourgeoisies to accumulate. As for social reality, there is no better way to end this book than by recalling the ending to Brian Fitzpatrick's *British Empire in Australia*. Marxist Fitzpatrick, like Liberal Coghlan, always gave pride of place to labour in his writing, but, like Coghlan, he was concerned about another set of Australians too: "The reservoir of Australian labour and industry has never failed to provide a stream tributary to the broad river of English wealth."[23]

23. B. Fitzpatrick, *British Empire in Australia* (Melbourne: Macmillan, 1969), p. 348. Note that he says "English," not "British."

Index

Agriculture
  in Dependency theory, 10–14, 235
  mechanization, 227
  as motor for industry, 183, 193, 230
Amin, Samir, 11, 13, 17
Anti-socialist Party (Aust.), 106, 138,
    140, 156, 158. *See also* Free Trade
    Party
Argentina
  agriculture, 224–226
  banks, 202, 208, 211–216, 219, 221
  beef, 197, 204, 206, 208, 210, 211,
    217, 219, 222–224, 228, 232
  cleavages, 195–196, 201, 203, 222
  compared to Australia, 195–196, 202,
    217, 220–222, 226–227, 229–230,
    269–278
  compared to New Zealand, 195, 203,
    207, 209, 211, 223, 269–278
  federalism, 196–197
  foreign capital, 197, 200, 217, 219
  foreign debt, 3, 202, 209, 211, 213,
    216, 219, 232
  graziers, 196, 199, 203, 212, 221–223,
    232, 270, 272
  inflation, 195, 204, 207, 208, 215
  interior, 197, 203, 205
  labour, 34, 201, 221, 227, 229, 274–
    279
  land sales, 39, 199, 206
  manufacturing, 229, 230
  mutton, 203, 206, 209–210, 222–223,
    231
  speculators, 203, 217
  taxes, 221
  transition, 206, 211, 222

transport, 196, 200, 203, 204, 206,
    211, 222
wheat, 204–207, 209–211, 217, 219,
    222–223, 225–226
wool, 199–202, 204, 207, 210–211,
    222–223, 285
See also Railroads, *entries for individual
    provinces*
Arreglo Romero, 219
Arrighi, Giovanni, 28
Atkinson, Harry, 170, 176, 180–181
Australia, 19, 269–279
  Broken Hill Pty., 71, 85
  development, 145, 153–156
  domestic financial capital, 58–59, 85,
    89–90, 111, 134
  early history, 57
  1893 Bank Crash, 84–85
  foreign capital, 40, 56, 84, 60, 65, 67–
    68, 72–74, 80–91, 94, 103, 117,
    137, 150, 269–271
  foreign debt, 3, 60, 61, 71, 87–91,
    115–120, 160–161
  "Fusion," 138–143, 153
  graziers, 57, 60, 64, 66–67, 71, 89, 91,
    111, 123, 134, 197, 271
  Labor parties, 69, 72, 77, 83, 159
  labour unions, 34, 66, 67
  Land Acts, 38, 60
  manufacturing, 59
  pastoral finance cos., 64–65, 85, 87
  revenue, 61, 64, 74–75, 78, 89–92,
    94–95, 98
  wool, 57–58, 61, 63–65, 70–71, 85,
    115–116, 123, 129, 135, 146, 285
  See also Federation, Internal bour-

Cornell Studies in Political Economy

EDITED BY PETER J. KATZENSTEIN

Library of Congress Cataloguing-in-Publication Data

Schwartz, Herman M., 1958–
  In the dominions of debt.

  (Cornell studies in political economy)
  Includes index.
    1. Debts, External—Developing countries—History—
19th century—Case studies. 2. Debts, External—
Developing countries—History—20th century—Case
studies. 3. Developing countries—Dependency on
foreign countries—History—19th century—Case studies.
4. Developing countries—Dependency on Foreign countries—
History—20th century—Case studies. 5. Australia—
Economic conditions. 6. New Zealand—Economic conditions.
7. Argentina—Economic conditions. 8. Korea (South)—
Economic conditions—1960–   . I. Title. II. Series.
HJ8899.S38 1989   336.3'435'091724   88-43289
ISBN 0-8014-2270-1 (alk. paper)